D1315922

DATE DUE

HIGHSMITH #45230

Printed
in USA

RESPONSIBLE
DRIVING

American Automobile Association
Heathrow, Florida

GLENCOE

Macmillan/McGraw–Hill

Lake Forest, Illinois   Columbus, Ohio   Mission Hills, California   Peoria, Illinois

OESTERLE LIBRARY, NCC
NAPERVILLE, IL 60566

REVIEWERS

Robert Freeman, Past President
AMERICAN DRIVER TRAFFIC SAFETY EDUCATION
ASSOCIATION (ADTSEA)

Ray Kracik, Past President
ILLINOIS DRIVER EDUCATION ASSOCIATION

Del Freeman, Specialist for School and
Traffic Safety
OREGON DEPARTMENT OF EDUCATION

Phillip Fugawa, President
NEW HAMPSHIRE DRIVER TEACHER'S EDUCATION
ASSOCIATION

Peggy Fujawa, Past President, Region I
New Hampshire Driver Education Teacher's
Association
PROFILE JR./SR. HIGH SCHOOL
NEW HAMPSHIRE

Dale E. Roe, Past President
VIRGINIA DRIVER EDUCATION TEACHER'S
ASSOCIATION

Lou Autry, Director, Driver Education
REGION 10 EDUCATION SERVICE CENTER
TEXAS

F. Michael Williard, President, North
Carolina Driver Traffic Safety Education
Association
WEST FORSYTH HIGH SCHOOL
NORTH CAROLINA

John Harvey, Past President
AMERICAN DRIVER TRAFFIC SAFETY EDUCATION
ASSOCIATION (ADTSEA)

Hayden Dawson, Chair, Department of Driver
Education
ELK GROVE HIGH SCHOOL
CALIFORNIA

Editorial Development in Cooperation with Curriculum Concepts,
a Division of Dialogue Systems, Inc.
Design and Production: Curriculum Concepts

Copyright © 1993 by the American Automobile Association. All rights reserved. Originally
copyrighted © 1987, 1980, 1975, 1970, 1965, 1961, 1955, 1948, 1947, by the American
Automobile Association under the title *Sportsmanlike Driving*. Except as permitted under
the United States Copyright Act, no part of this publication may be reproduced or distributed in any form or by any means, or stored in a database retrieval system, without prior
permission of the publisher.

Send all inquiries to:
GLENCOE DIVISION
Macmillan/McGraw-Hill
936 Eastwind Drive
Westerville, OH 43081

ISBN: 0-02-635945-6 (Student's Edition)
ISBN: 0-02-635946-4 (Student's Edition; soft)

Printed in the United States of America

1 2 3 4 5 6 7 8 9–VH –99 98 97 96 95 94 93 92

C
629,283
G 48 r
1993
pt. 1

COORDINATING AUTHOR

DR. FRANCIS C. KENEL
STAFF DIRECTOR OF TRAFFIC SAFETY (RETIRED)
AMERICAN AUTOMOBILE ASSOCIATION
HEATHROW, FL

CONSULTING AUTHORS

DR. JAMES AARON
DRIVER PERFORMANCE CONSULTANT
PALM HARBOR, FL

DR. JOHN W. PALMER
ASSOCIATE PROFESSOR
ST. CLOUD STATE UNIVERSITY
ST. CLOUD, MN

DR. MAURICE E. DENNIS
COORDINATOR AND PROFESSOR
TEXAS A&M UNIVERSITY
COLLEGE STATION, TX

AAA STAFF AUTHORS

DR. THOMAS H. CULPEPPER
MANAGING DIRECTOR
TRAFFIC SAFETY AND ENGINEERING DEPARTMENT
AMERICAN AUTOMOBILE ASSOCIATION
HEATHROW, FL

CHARLES A. BUTLER
MANAGER, DRIVER SAFETY SERVICES
AMERICAN AUTOMOBILE ASSOCIATION
HEATHROW, FL

ρREFACE

Well, this is it. You're going to learn to drive, and you're probably in a big hurry to get behind the wheel. However, driving is something that you cannot rush into. There is a lot of essential driving information that you need to know first. It's important that you understand that risk is always present for the driver, but good drivers learn more effectively to manage risk. Good drivers reduce risk by managing visibility, time, and space and the available traction. We want you to be a good driver.

We've spent many years working on safe driving strategies and attitudes and at the same time working with young people like you who can't wait to drive. *Responsible Driving* has been written with you in mind. We want you to know the rules and the facts about driving, but we also want you to know why they are important. This book tells you the *What* and *How* about driving, and it always tells you the *Why*.

The American Automobile Association, which you probably know as AAA or Triple A, is part of the team that has helped put *Responsible Driving* together. AAA is an organization that has the greatest resources in the world on driving. We have used these resources in *Responsible Driving* to help you understand what driving is all about.

As you begin *Responsible Driving*, you'll see that the first unit is titled "Starting With You." It begins that way because we care about you, AAA cares about you, and we want you to care about yourself and those with whom you will share the roadway. You're at the beginning of a very big moment in your life—the day you get your driver's license. We're happy to have the opportunity to help you learn how to use it safely and responsibly.

DR. FRANCIS C. KENEL
DR. JAMES AARON
DR. JOHN W. PALMER
DR. MAURICE E. DENNIS
DR. THOMAS H. CULPEPPER
CHARLES A. BUTLER

CONTENTS

LESSON ONE

Determining Personal Need When Considering Buying a Car 282
    FYI ● CULTURAL CROSSROADS: Sylvia Oneice Lowe 282

LESSON TWO

Factors That Are Involved in Selecting a Car 284
    TIPS FOR NEW DRIVERS: Used-Car Checks 286

LESSON THREE

How to Obtain Financing for a New or Used Car 288
    THE MATH CONNECTION: Loan Interest 288

LESSON FOUR

Choosing and Purchasing Automobile Insurance 290
    ADVICE FROM THE EXPERTS: Chuck Hurley, *Senior Vice President,* 294
        Communications, Insurance Institute for Highway Safety

CHAPTER REVIEW

    Key Points/Projects 295
    BUILDING MAP SKILLS: Understanding Map Symbols 296
    Chapter Test and Driver's Log 297

LESSON ONE

Checking Your Car Before and After You Start the Engine 300
    TIPS FOR NEW DRIVERS: Having Your Car Serviced or Repaired 301

LESSON TWO

Becoming Familiar with the Engine and Power Train 303
    FYI ● CULTURAL CROSSROADS: Janet Guthrie 303

LESSON THREE

Understanding and Maintaining Car Systems. 306
    THE SCIENCE CONNECTION: Carbon Monoxide 307

LESSON FOUR

Suspension, Steering, Brakes, and Tires 312
    ADVICE FROM THE EXPERTS: Jack Herr, *Senior Service Specialist,* 316
        Approved Auto Repair, AAA

CHAPTER REVIEW

    Key Points/Projects 317
    BUILDING SCIENCE SKILLS: Graphing Braking Distances 318
    Chapter Test and Driver's Log 319

SPECIAL CONTENTS

CULTURAL CROSSROADS

Tips for New Drivers

CURRICULUM CONNECTIONS

THE ➤ **Curriculum CONNECTION**

BUILDING MAP SKILLS

BUILDING CURRICULUM SKILLS

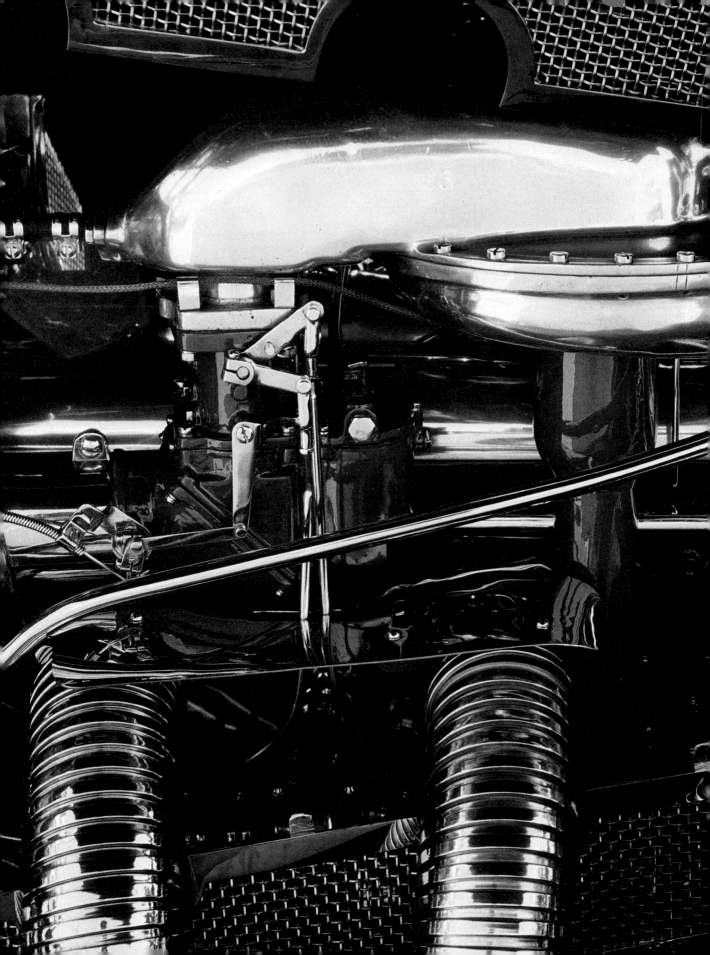

UNIT

STARTING WITH YOU

Driving begins with you. You must ask how *you* will deal with the risk of driving, how *you* will handle the responsibility of driving, and how *you* will respond to social pressures that may affect your driving. This unit will help you consider these questions, questions that only you can answer.

UNIT CONTENTS

ASSESSING AND MANAGING RISK

Whenever you walk or ride on our nation's streets and roadways, you become part of the highway transportation system. It
is important to learn how to use the system safely
and responsibly.

CHAPTER 1 OBJECTIVES

The Highway Transportation System and Risk Management

1. Name the three parts of the highway transportation system.
2. Explain how, and by whom, the highway transportation system is regulated.
3. Describe five ways you can reduce driving risk within the highway transportation system.

Understanding and Applying the SIPDE Process

4. Define and explain the steps of the SIPDE process, including the approximate time/distance needed to *search, identify, predict, decide,* and *execute.* Describe how the SIPDE process can be applied while driving.

Understanding and Using the Smith System

5. Explain the importance of the Smith System, including *Aim high and look ahead, Keep your eyes moving, Get the big picture, Make sure others see you,* and *Leave yourself a way out.*

The Value of Taking a Driver Education Course

6. Describe the advantages to be gained from a driver education course, regarding knowledge; ability to manage time, space, and visibility; and the awareness of limiting factors.

The Highway Transportation System and Risk Management

FYI

Some American Indian peoples used a *travois* to transport goods. A travois consisted of two poles tied together in the shape of a V with a net lashed between them. The point of the V was harnessed to a dog or horse, and the pole ends dragged on the ground.

A vast network of highways, streets, and roads crisscrosses the United States. Each day, millions of drivers travel these roadways.

As you prepare to join the other drivers on our nation's roads, remember that your goal is not just to learn to drive. It is to learn to drive safely and responsibly.

What Is the Highway Transportation System?

Cars and trucks, streets and highways, drivers, cyclists and pedestrians—these are all part of the highway transportation system, or the HTS. The main goal of this complex system is to enable people and goods to move from place to place as safely and efficiently as possible.

Highway Concept and Design

Early American roads were built along the routes of existing trails and were constructed with little or no planning. Nowadays an army of engineers is needed just to plan today's more complex highways.

Engineers must plan the route of the highway, the construction of bridges along the route, exit and entrance ramps, where traffic signs are going to be located and what they will say, and anything else pertaining to the highway. Even the curves must be planned carefully to make sure they are banked, or tilted, properly.

How many different kinds of motor vehicles can you think of? More than 190 million registered vehicles travel within the HTS, ranging from large vehicles, such as tractor-trailers and buses, to small vehicles, such as motorcycles and mopeds. There are vehicles of every imaginable description, from flashy new luxury cars to beat-up old pickup trucks.

Motor vehicles in the HTS differ in more than just appearance and age, however. They also vary in how they handle. A heavy truck, for instance, does not accelerate, steer, or brake the same way that a lightweight sports car does. How well an owner cares for his or her vehicle also affects performance.

Motor vehicles vary, too, in safety features and in their ability to protect drivers and passengers in case of a *collision*, or crash. For example, drivers of solidly built cars equipped with air bags are far less vulnerable to injury than are motorcyclists or the drivers of most subcompact cars.

Roadways

Nearly 4 million miles of roadways link the counties, cities, and towns of the United States. These roadways range from multilane superhighways to twisting country roads to car-choked city streets.

Some roadways are smooth and well maintained, while others are peppered with cracks, bumps, and potholes. Driving the great assortment of roads found in the HTS is a challenge, especially at night and in poor weather.

People

The people who use the highway transportation system include more than 160 million drivers, passengers, cyclists, and pedestrians—in other words, just about everyone! Most of these people act responsibly when using the roads, whether driving, riding, or walking.

Some people, however, behave in an unsafe or irresponsible manner. They drive recklessly, cross streets without looking, and weave their bikes through heavy traffic. Such people pose a serious danger to other roadway users. This is just a sample of the behaviors that drivers must anticipate and learn to cope with.

How Is the HTS Regulated?

Federal, state, and local governments work together to regulate the highway transportation system. For example, federal law established a maximum speed limit of 55 miles per hour in 1974. This law has since been revised to allow speeds of 65 mph in certain areas if the individual states decide to do so. However, enforcing this and other traffic laws is the job of state and local police.

Federal and State Requirements

To set uniform standards for various aspects of vehicle and driver safety, the federal government passed two other important laws:

The National Traffic and Motor Vehicle Safety Act requires car makers to build certain safety features, such as safety belts and shatterproof windows, into their motor vehicles. This law also requires manufacturers to correct vehicle defects discovered after car models are sold.

The National Highway Safety Act established specific guidelines for state motor vehicle safety programs. Each state must follow these guidelines. They govern such matters as vehicle registration and inspection, driver licensing, traffic laws and traffic courts, and highway construction and maintenance.

SAFETY TIPS

It takes $7\frac{1}{2}$ to 8 seconds for a tractor-trailer to stop and about 4 seconds for a car to stop when traveling 50 mph. If a truck is following your car too closely, either change lanes or allow the truck to pass you.

The way highways in the HTS are numbered can tell you something about the road on which you're traveling. A sign like this, for example, means that you're on the Interstate Highway System. But if you know your numbers, such signs can give you additional information.

If the number on a sign is odd, it means that the road goes north and south. An even-numbered sign means that the road goes east and west.

The numbers on the interstate go from 5 to 95. The greater the even number, the farther north you are. The greater the odd number, the farther east you are.

Imagine that you're on Interstate 90. That's an even number and close to 95, so you are traveling in the northern part of the United States.

The National Highway Safety Act allows each state to set its own *statutes*, or laws, that concern highway safety. Many of these statutes are of special interest to teenage drivers. In eight states, for example, teens under a certain age—usually 17 or 18—are not allowed to drive at night. In other states, teenagers must be enrolled in high school before they can get their driver's licenses.

Cities and towns, too, pass driving regulations that must be obeyed within their limits. In all cities except for New York City, drivers may turn right at red lights except where expressly prohibited.

How Can You Reduce Risk Within the HTS?

Driving involves *risk*—the chance of injury to yourself or others and the chance of damage to vehicles and property. The first important step toward responsible driving is realizing that this risk is *real*—probably much more real than you think.

◆ In any given year, the likelihood of your being involved in a collision is about 1 in 5. Your chances of suffering an injury that is serious enough to disable you are about 1 in 83.

◆ In a typical year, some 40 percent of all teenage deaths occur through motor vehicle crash injuries.

◆ Eighty-five percent of traffic deaths occur in the first collision in which the car's occupants are involved.

◆ Forty-nine percent of vehicle occupant deaths involve one car.

No matter how confident you may feel when you get behind the wheel of a car, or how well you've mastered the basics of driving, the risk of being involved in a collision is always present. There are, however, actions you can take to maximize your control over driving situations and to minimize the risk.

Risk is always present. The chances that you will be in a collision within the year are 1 in 5. ▶

◀

Most drivers overestimate their ability to manage risk and underestimate actual risk.

◀

Poor weather can be a contributing factor in the degree of risk that drivers face.

Understanding and Reducing Risk

Many factors contribute to the degree of risk when you drive. Some are obvious, such as bad weather or poor roads. Others, such as the condition of your car, may be less obvious, but they are just as important to consider.

Driving responsibly means assessing the risk and doing all you can to reduce or control it. Here are five ways to do that:

Keep your car in top condition. Are your brakes working properly? Are your tires properly inflated and your windows clean? The better the condition of your car, the more control you have when you're driving.

Anticipate the actions of others. Wise drivers drive defensively. They identify cues to behavior that help them predict how other roadway users will act or react. Because drivers and pedestrians often act without thinking or communicating, you must learn to search for clues.

In daylight hours, you can see the low beams of an oncoming car from 4,700 feet away, or a little less than a mile. You can see an oncoming car without headlights only from 2,500 feet away, or about half a mile.

WHAT WOULD YOU DO?

What factors are contributing to risk? What steps could you take to reduce risk?

Take steps to protect yourself and others. Wearing safety belts can save you and your passengers from death or serious injury. Turning on your low-beam headlights at all times, even during daylight hours, reduces risk by increasing the ability of others to see you.

Drive only when you're in sound physical and mental condition. Are you feeling alert and clear-headed? Are you concentrating on your driving—or thinking about tomorrow night's date? To drive safely, you need to be 100 percent behind the wheel.

Make a conscious effort to develop your driving skills. Working to improve your driving habits and abilities will help to protect you and your passengers.

Managing Visibility, Time and Space

As you learn to drive, you'll learn numerous guidelines to help you make sound driving decisions. One basic principle underlies virtually all of these guidelines: the wise management of visibility, time, and space.

Visibility refers to what you can see from behind the wheel and how well you see it, and to the ability of others—pedestrians and other drivers—to see you. When you're driving, reduced visibility means increased risk. On the other hand, when you take steps to increase visibility, you decrease risk.

Time and *space* come into constant play when you're driving. *Time* can refer to the ability to judge your speed and the speed of other vehicles. It can also refer to how long it will take your car or another vehicle to stop.

Space refers to distance. Wise drivers keep a margin of space between their cars and other vehicles when they drive. This allows them room to maneuver in dangerous situations.

You will read about visibility, time, and space throughout this book, because all three are crucial elements in safe and responsible driving. In fact, managing the various factors related to visibility, time, and space is the key to reducing risk when you drive.

CHECKPOINT

1. What are the three parts of the highway transportation system?
2. Who regulates the highway transportation system? Give examples.
3. What are some ways you can reduce driving risk?

Understanding and Applying the SIPDE Process

Driving is challenging because you need to do many tasks at once. You have to control the car, watch the roadway and off-road areas, read signs, and be alert for the sudden actions of other drivers.

Because you have so much to keep track of when you're driving, it is helpful to use an organized system to gather and process information. An organized system will help you make sound decisions and reduce driving risk.

What Is SIPDE?

One easy-to-use system for dealing with the challenge of driving is known as the SIPDE process—short for *search, identify, predict, decide,* and *execute*. SIPDE is a five-step process. You use it to:

1. *Search* the roadway and the off-road areas 20 to 30 seconds ahead for information that can help you plan a path of travel. (Twenty to 30 seconds equals about $1\frac{1}{2}$ to 2 blocks at 25 to 30 mph in the city and about $\frac{1}{2}$ mile at 50 to 65 mph on the highway.)

2. *Identify* objects or conditions within 12 to 15 seconds ahead that could interfere with your planned path of travel.

3. *Predict* what actions or changes in conditions on or near the roadway could increase the level of risk.

4. *Decide* what action or actions to take at least 4 to 5 seconds ahead to control or reduce risk.

5. *Execute* your decision.

ENERGY TIPS

Use the SIPDE process to help you judge when to reduce speed or increase following distance, and thereby avoid unnecessary stops. Each time you stop and then accelerate again, you burn extra fuel.

◀
The SIPDE process can help you to manage risk in many different situations.

Use your rearview and side mirrors to help you search all around your car. ▶

Let's see how you can use the SIPDE process to manage visibility, time, and space.

Search

When you *search,* you try to gather as much information as possible about what is happening on or near the roadway.

Use a systematic search pattern to gather information. First scan the road 20 to 30 seconds ahead, then look to the sides. Then glance in your rearview and side mirrors to check for traffic behind you. Next, check the sides of the road again. Then again survey the road ahead for on-going or oncoming traffic.

Identify

To *identify* information important to you as a driver, you need to do more than simply look. You have to think about what you're looking for.

Your aim is to identify as early as possible any objects or conditions that could become a threat to your path of travel.

Much as a detective investigates a crime scene seeking important clues, a driver needs to investigate the road-way and identify possible problems as far in advance as possible—at least 12 to 15 seconds ahead.

Suppose you're driving on a narrow two-way street in a residential neighborhood. There are cars parked along the road, vehicles behind you, cars coming toward you in the other lane, and people on the sidewalk. Along your side of the road, you *identify* a young girl on a bicycle. As you get nearer, you can see she's wobbling and having trouble steering the bicycle.

Predict

As you scan the roadway and note the position of vehicles, pedestrians,

"Better to be safe than sorry" is a maxim with special relevance for drivers. Never assume that a driver, cyclist, or pedestrian sees you and will not enter your path of travel. When appropriate, tap your horn or flash your lights. Always be prepared to steer or brake to avoid a collision.

and objects, you can make *predictions* about what might happen and prepare for it.

In the situation with the young girl on the bike, you might *predict* the possibility of her veering into your path or falling off her bike in front of your car.

Decide

Once you've identified a potentially threatening object or condition and predicted what might happen, you can *decide* how best to minimize the risk of a collision.

Keep in mind that most situations allow you a choice of actions. As with any decision, you need to weigh the possibilities. What are the likely consequences of the actions you're considering? Which actions will be most effective in minimizing risk to yourself and others? The purpose of using the SIPDE process is to give yourself

Tips for New Drivers

Identifying Information

Here are some objects and conditions to identify as you drive.
- vehicles, pedestrians, or objects that are in your path or could enter your path
- vehicles, pedestrians, or objects close to the back or sides of your car
- vehicles, objects, or roadway features that limit your visibility and may conceal objects or conditions
- signs, signals, and roadway markings
- roadway surface conditions

as much time as possible to make a wise decision.

What will you decide to do as you get closer to the girl on the bike?

You could steer closer to oncoming cars while passing her. You could tap your horn lightly to warn the girl that you are behind her. You could

◄

The bicyclists and parked cars present potentially threatening conditions to the driver.

reduce your speed. You decide to combine all three actions in order to minimize risk.

Execute

The final step in the SIPDE process is to *execute* the decision you've made. In most instances, executing a decision simply means making a routine maneuver. Occasionally, however, you may have to take some kind of emergency action.

Here are the steps you would execute to avoid colliding with the girl on the bicycle. First, slow down and prepare to stop if necessary. Next, wait for a break in the oncoming traffic. Then lightly tap your horn. Honking loudly might frighten the girl into losing control of her bike. Finally, cautiously pass the bicyclist, allowing her as much space as possible. By waiting for a break in the traffic flow before steering around the girl, you'll minimize the risk of colliding with an oncoming car.

WHAT WOULD YOU DO?

Using the SIPDE process, explain how you would manage risk in this situation.

Applying the SIPDE Process

The SIPDE process fosters safe driving by enabling you to manage visibility, time, and space. While it is important to understand what the process is, it is far more important to practice applying it.

When you're behind the wheel, simply knowing what the letters SIPDE stand for won't help you to drive safely. What *will* help you is making the principles of this process an automatic part of your own thinking—and driving.

For example, you can minimize risk by using the SIPDE process to identify threatening objects or conditions as far in advance as possible. The sooner you realize that you may be faced with a threatening situation, the sooner you can take evasive action to reduce the risk.

Similarly, you can keep threatening objects or conditions apart by using the SIPDE process to help you separate one from another. For instance, suppose you're driving along a two-lane road. Up ahead, you see a bus approaching. You also see a group of boys walking along your side of the road. Rather than pass both the boys and the bus at the same time, adjust your speed so that you can pass each one separately. By separating them in this way, you've simplified the situation and reduced the risk of a collision.

4. What are the steps of the SIPDE process?

THREE

Understanding and Using the Smith System

Like the SIPDE process, the Smith System is a series of principles designed to help you to drive safely and defensively.

What Is the Smith System?

The Smith System consists of five driving guidelines. Understanding and using these guidelines is far more important than memorizing their exact wording.

Aim High and Look Ahead, Not Down

Look well ahead of your car as you drive. Do not look down at the road directly in front of you. As a general rule, try to look about 20 to 30 seconds ahead. Remember that 20 to 30 seconds ahead means about $1\frac{1}{2}$ to 2 blocks at 25 to 30 mph in the city and about $\frac{1}{2}$ mile at 50 to 65 mph on the highway. Note that aiming high and looking ahead is similar to the first step, search, in SIPDE.

Keep Your Eyes Moving

Roadway and off-road conditions are always changing. Search the scene constantly. Stay alert for changes on the roadway or potentially dangerous conditions that might require you to adjust the speed or position of your car.

SAFETY TIPS

Driving on a long stretch of straight highway can be monotonous, but don't let your attention waver. Continue to scan the roadway. Unexpected developments—a car getting a flat tire, for example, or a pedestrian running across the roadway—may occur at any time.

◀
Spot possible dangers early by aiming high and looking well ahead, not down.

Driving with your low-beam headlights on insures that others will be able to see you. ▶

?

WHAT WOULD YOU DO?

How would you use the Smith System in this situation?

Get the Big Picture

Search the whole scene, not just a part of it. As you approach an intersection, for example, you need to search for vehicles and pedestrians moving in all directions, for traffic-control devices, and for anything that might block your vision or otherwise increase risk.

Make Sure Others See You

Communicate with others, drivers as well as pedestrians. Always drive with your low-beam headlights on. Drive where others can see you, signal your intention to turn, and tap the brake pedal so that your brake lights warn following drivers that you're slowing or stopping.

Leave Yourself a Way Out or a Margin of Safety

Always leave yourself a path of escape—a way to avoid a collision. Position your car so that you keep a margin of space around it. In the previous example of the girl riding the bicycle, for example, leaving yourself a way out meant waiting for a break in the oncoming traffic before steering around her.

CHECKPOINT

5. What are the guidelines of the Smith System?

The Value of Taking a Driver Education Course

Whether you're cruising along a sunny country road or stuck in a snarl of city traffic, the responsibility for operating your car safely is yours. Driver education will help you meet that responsibility.

What Can You Gain from a Driver Education Course?

A driver education course will help you become an alert and knowledgeable driver capable of dealing with a wide range of driving situations.

Knowledge

Through driver education, you will gain:

◆ an understanding of the ways in which your personality, emotions, and maturity affect your driving
◆ an understanding of how to maneuver and control your car so as to minimize risk in different driving environments and under various road conditions
◆ an insight into the ways in which alcohol and drugs impair driving, and knowledge of the penalties for their use
◆ a knowledge of traffic laws and administrative laws, rules of the road, and signs and signals
◆ a foundation of consumer information, such as guidelines for buying, insuring, and maintaining a car and tips for trip planning
◆ an understanding of the parts of a car and of how a car works

◆ a knowledge of what to do in case of emergency

▲
Driver education will help you learn to become a responsible driver.

Ability to Manage Visibility, Time, and Space

Driver education will increase your awareness of the roadway and its surroundings. You'll learn how to manage visibility, time, and space. You'll learn to maximize your own safety as well as that of your passengers, other drivers, and pedestrians.

Driver education will help you to evaluate and respond to the constantly changing driving environment. You will learn how to manage and minimize risk by thinking ahead and by preparing for threatening situations that may develop.

Dr. Francis C. Kenel, Staff
Director of Safety (Retired), AAA

Dr. Francis C. Kenel

Risk means the chance of injury, damage, or loss. The purpose of this book is to help you develop the knowledge, skills, and habits that can enable you to manage risk.

The most important ability of good drivers is positioning the vehicle so that their ability to see and the ability of others to see them is maximized. When a vehicle is positioned properly, adjusting speed becomes easier. Equally important is using safety belts and restricting driving if you are not in top physical condition.

?
WHAT WOULD YOU DO?

What threatening conditions do you see? How do you think you should handle them?

Awareness of Limiting Factors

To become a safe and responsible driver, you need more than driving skill. You also need to understand that there are factors that can seriously interfere with your ability to drive, such as:

♦ the feeling that there is little or no risk involved in driving and that if a collision occurs, it's "the other person's fault"
♦ your emotional state
♦ the effects of an illness or injury— or the side effects of the medicine you may be taking for it
♦ the effects of alcohol and drugs

The knowledge you gain through driver education and the experience you acquire behind the wheel will develop your driving skills and decision-making abilities. How you use these skills and abilities, however, is up to you. Only you can decide to be a *responsible* driver.

MEN WORKING

CHECKPOINT

6. How can a driver education course be of value to you?

CHAPTER 1 REVIEW

KEY POINTS

LESSON ONE

1. Motor vehicles, roadways, and people make up the highway transportation system. The main goal of this system is to enable people and goods to move from place to place as safely and as efficiently as possible.

2. Federal, state, and local governments work together to regulate the highway transportation system. For example, state and local police enforce traffic laws passed by federal, state, and local governments.

3. Five ways you can reduce driving risk within the highway transportation system are: keep your car in top condition, anticipate the actions of others, take steps to protect yourself and others, drive only when you're in sound physical and mental condition, and make a conscious effort to develop your driving skills.

LESSON TWO

4. SIPDE is short for *search, identify, predict, decide,* and *execute.* Using **SIPDE,** drivers search the roadway and off-road areas 20 to 30 seconds ahead for information that can help them select a planned path of travel; identify objects or conditions 12 to 15 seconds ahead that could interfere

with their planned path of travel; predict what actions or changes in conditions on or near the roadway could increase the level of risk; decide at least 4 to 5 seconds ahead what action or actions to take to control or reduce risk; and then execute their decision.

LESSON THREE

5. The Smith System is a series of principles designed to help you drive safely and defensively. Aim high and look ahead so you can better search the roadway. Keep your eyes moving because conditions are always changing. Getting the big picture requires scanning the whole scene. Make sure others see you so you can communicate better with others on the roadway. Leave yourself a way out. Leave yourself a path of escape in order to avoid a collision.

LESSON FOUR

6. Through a driver education course you can gain a knowledge of cars and driving; develop your ability to manage visibility, time, and space and make sound driving decisions; and become aware of factors that can seriously interfere with driving ability.

PROJECTS

1. Obtain a copy of your state driver's manual. Read the table of contents, then take some time to skim through the book. What topics are emphasized? What charts and illustrations does the book include? Does the manual include sample test questions?

2. While riding as a passenger in a car, identify objects on or near the road ahead, and think about what actions you might take to minimize driving risk. Also, try predicting what other drivers will do. Compare your predictions with what actually happens. How often are you correct?

BUILDING MAP SKILLS

Using the Map Scale

People drive to get from one place to another. But they don't always know how to get there or how far they will have to drive. One way to make sure of your destination and the distance you'll need to travel is to use a road map.

Suppose you want to drive from San Jacinto, California, to Indio. You're going to travel north on highway 79 to Route 10 and then southwest to Indio. Now you know how you're going to drive there, but how can you figure out about how many miles you'll be traveling?

Look at the map scale to help you figure out the distance. The numbers along the top show the distance in miles. The scale shows you that 1 inch on the map is equal to about 25 actual miles.

You can use a ruler or a piece of string to estimate your traveling distance. Just find out how many inches long your route on the map is, and then multiply by 25.

Try It Yourself

1. About what distance is it between San Jacinto and Indio along highways 79 and 10?

2. If you travel at an average speed of 50 miles an hour, how long will it take to get from San Jacinto to Indio?

3. Driving at the same average speed, how long will it take you to get from Perris to La Jolla?

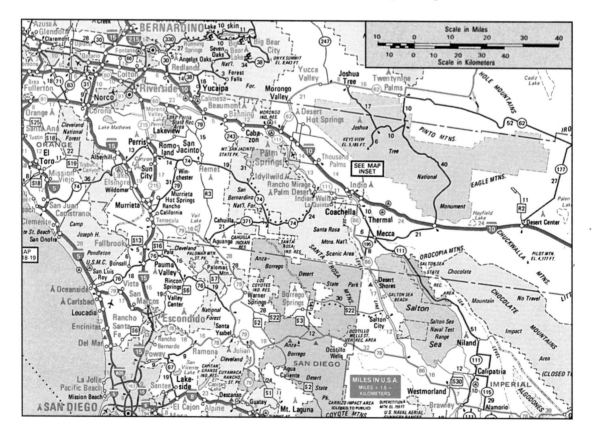

CHAPTER 1 REVIEW

CHAPTER TEST

Write the letter of the answer that best completes each sentence.

1. The highway transportation system is made up of
   a. motor vehicles, people, and buildings.
   b. roadways, people, and motor vehicles.
   c. cars, trains, and airplanes.
2. Scanning the road 20 to 30 seconds ahead is equal to looking
   a. about a ½ mile ahead at 25 to 30 mph in the city.
   b. about ½ mile ahead at 50 to 65 mph on the highway.
   c. about a ½ block ahead at 25 to 30 mph in the city.
3. Always driving with your headlights on
   a. increases your ability to be seen.
   b. increases engine efficiency.
   c. allows you to pass in a no-passing zone.
4. When you gather information about the roadway and surroundings, you
   a. execute.
   b. predict.
   c. search.
5. Under the National Traffic and Motor Vehicle Safety Act, car makers must
   a. provide for vehicle registration.
   b. build safety features into their cars.
   c. offer a choice of models to customers.
6. Risk in driving
   a. does not pertain to good drivers.
   b. depends on the confidence of the driver.
   c. is always present.
7. The Smith System is
   a. a three step process.

b. regulated by the National Motor Vehicle Safety Act.
   c. a series of principles designed to help you drive safely.
8. Driver education can provide you with
   a. a knowledge of the rules of the road.
   b. discounts on car purchases.
   c. automobile insurance.
9. The highway transportation system is regulated by
   a. the National Highway Safety Act.
   b. the FBI.
   c. federal, state, and local governments.
10. *Visibility* refers to your ability to
    a. see and be seen.
    b. judge the speed of your car.
    c. drive without wearing eyeglasses.

Write the word or phrase that best completes each sentence.

SIPDE   highway transportation system
    motor vehicles   designers
    Smith System   visibility

11. The goal of the _____ is to enable people and goods to move safely and efficiently.

12. Cars, trucks, and buses are examples of _____ .

13. When you drive, reduced _____ means increased risk.

14. "Make sure others see you" is a basic principle of the _____ .

15. _____ is a system designed to help you gather information in an organized way.

DRIVER'S LOG

In this chapter, you have learned about ways to manage risk while driving. Write three paragraphs that give your personal view on the following:
◆ How would you evaluate the possibility of your

being involved in a collision? Explain.
◆ What kinds of situations do you feel hold the greatest risk for you as a driver?
◆ What steps will you take to manage the risks that you consider the most serious?

KNOWING YOURSELF

Whenever you get behind the wheel of a vehicle, you must be certain that you are both physically and emotionally fit to drive. It is important to recognize and control physical and emotional factors that might impair the driving task.

CHAPTER 2 OBJECTIVES

Emotions Affect Your Driving Ability

1. Describe three effects your emotions can have on your driving.
2. Describe at least six ways to control the effects your emotions may have on your driving.

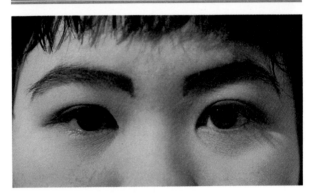

How Vision Affects Your Ability to Drive

3. Explain why good vision is critical.
4. Explain how to compensate for such vision problems as poor depth perception, color blindness, and night blindness.

Temporary Physical Conditions that Affect Your Ability to Drive

5. Describe how fatigue affects driving ability and how to fight fatigue.
6. Explain the ways that short-term illnesses and injuries may affect driving.

Long-Term Physical Factors that Affect Driving Ability

7. Describe the ways that hearing loss affects driving ability.
8. Identify several ways that drivers can compensate for physical disabilities.
9. Describe how aging and chronic illnesses can affect driving ability.

Emotions Affect Your Driving Ability

Responsibility. Maturity. Self-control. No doubt you've heard these words spoken many times over the years by parents, teachers, and other adults.

As a new driver, those same words will again take on important meaning for you. When you're behind the wheel, it's not just driving skill that matters. It's your ability to think clearly and make sound, responsible driving decisions.

How Do Emotions Affect Your Driving?

Throughout your life you experience a range of strong feelings, both positive and negative: joy, sadness, anger, fear. Such feelings are part of what it means to be alive.

However, strong emotions can affect the way you see and think and distract you from driving. Lost in thoughts and daydreams, whether happy or sad, you may pay less attention to what is going on around you. You may miss important road and traffic information, causing you to make unsafe driving decisions.

When you experience a strong negative emotion, you may feel the need to do something forceful. If you're driving, you may have an impulse to act out your emotion by driving recklessly—a very dangerous and irresponsible attitude to take.

Inattention

Strong feelings have the power to focus all your attention on one thing. You may become obsessed with an idea or a person. If you've just won a tough game, maybe you review the big play in your mind again and again. If you're in love, maybe you can't stop thinking about your boyfriend or girlfriend.

Whatever the cause of the emotion, it can interfere with your driving by taking your attention away from the road. You may be so preoccupied that you drive dangerously—speeding or taking other risks—without even realizing what you're doing.

Lack of Concentration

Sometimes you can't seem to concentrate on anything. You may feel anxious about a date or excited about

SAFETY TIPS

Don't let conversation with passengers distract you while driving. If you have a serious or emotional matter to discuss with a companion, do so after you've parked the car.

Strong emotions can have an effect on your driving. They can interfere with your ability to manage risk. ▼

getting an A on a test. Your mind may be spinning with ideas or fantasies.

This is not a good state of mind to be in when you're driving. If you can't concentrate, you should let someone else drive or else wait until you're better able to focus on the driving task.

Ability to Process Information

Safe driving is a full-time job for your mind as well as for your body. You not only have to see and hear the signs and signals of the roadway, you also have to use good judgment based on the information you gather. The decisions you make can mean the difference between safe driving and dangerous driving.

If your mind is in the grip of a strong emotion, your ability to process information about the roadway may be diminished. It may seem as if you're in a kind of twilight zone where the things you see and hear on the road don't connect with your ability to reason and make sound judgments. Some people call this "being in a daze," "spacing out," or "tuning out." Whatever it's called, such a state of mind seriously decreases your ability to manage risk.

How Can You Control Your Emotions?

Though sometimes it may not seem possible, you *can* learn to control your emotions when you have to. You can also take steps to avoid or minimize problems relating to your emotional state. Often, just by admitting to yourself that you're upset or angry, you can calm yourself down.

▲
Don't let your emotions get the better of you. Instead, learn ways to control your emotions.

Maintain a Mature Attitude

You exhibit a mature attitude when you show respect for order and safety and take responsibility for your actions. You should assume a mature attitude as soon as you enter your car, and put aside strong emotions while you drive. Be courteous even if you happen to feel angry. In other words, put your emotions on "hold" and concentrate on driving safely.

Identify Troublesome Situations

Identify situations that may upset or annoy you, and deal with them in a mature way. When a situation is likely to bother you—bad weather or an unexpected traffic jam, for example—take a few deep breaths, say to yourself "I won't let this get to me," and focus your attention on driving.

Anticipate traffic situations that irritate you, and prepare yourself. You know, for example, that traffic is

ENERGY TIPS

Idling in heavy traffic wastes fuel. Find a route to your destination that is not heavily traveled.

?

WHAT WOULD YOU DO?

You're already late. How would you deal with your emotions and with getting to your destination in this situation?

heavy at rush hour. If you must drive then, you have a choice to make. You can grit your teeth and snarl at the traffic. Or you can tell yourself "I know traffic is going to be slow now, but this won't last forever. I'm not going to let it bother me." Then you can drive safely and patiently.

Plan Ahead

Advance planning can reduce stress and avoid problems. Will your planned route take you near a stadium at the same time that sports fans are crowding the roadways? Perhaps you can leave home earlier. Will you be traveling on a highway that is partially closed for repair? Try to find an alternate route.

Always allow enough time to get where you are going—extra time if you know you'll be traveling in heavy traffic or bad weather.

Expect Mistakes from Others

Rather than let yourself get irritated by every instance of bad driving you encounter, accept the fact that everyone makes mistakes at one time or another. Drivers may be distracted, inexperienced, or even intoxicated. Never assume that other drivers will drive safely or obey all rules.

Don't Drive When Upset

If anger or other strong emotions have you "in a state" when you're about to get into your car, think twice before driving. Better to wait until your feelings settle down and you're better able to concentrate. Something as simple as taking a walk may be enough to clear your mind so that you can drive safely.

Don't Drive When Depressed

Feelings of grief, hopelessness, or intense anxiety may last for several days or more. Such emotions may make it dangerous to drive. Stay off the road until these feelings subside.

Train Yourself Always to Use Correct Procedures

Get into the habit of using safe driving procedures. Your goal should be to make such procedures automatic, no matter what your emotional state may be.

CHECKPOINT

1. How can strong emotions affect your driving?
2. How can you control your emotions when you drive?

How Vision Affects Your Ability to Drive

Your sense of sight is the most important of the senses that affect your ability to drive. In fact, 90 percent of the decisions you make while driving are based on information you gather with your eyes. If you're having trouble seeing, your ability to drive safely is in serious jeopardy.

Why Is Good Vision Critical to Driving Ability?

Being able to see well means more than simply having "20/20 vision." It means being able to see straight ahead and to the sides and being able to perceive depth as well as color.

If your ability to see clearly is impaired, you will have difficulty adjusting your car's speed and position to minimize risk. You will not be able to scan the roadway far enough ahead to spot a threatening condition early. You will also have trouble identifying signs, signals, and roadway markngs.

To check your ability to see clearly, you should be tested for *visual acuity* (clear vision) by a health care professional or by your local department of motor vehicles. The visual acuity test measures how well you can see and whether or not you need to wear glasses or contact lenses to improve your vision.

Field of Vision

When you are standing still and looking straight ahead, you can see what is directly ahead and also what

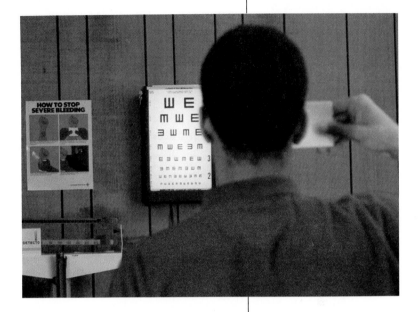

is at an angle to your right and left. This is your *field of vision*.

Your vision is clearest in a narrow beam directly in front of you, your *area of central vision*. Vision at angles to your right and left is called *peripheral vision*. This vision enables you to notice objects and movement to your sides. When you are in forward motion as you drive, your field of vision narrows. You need to move your eyes from side to side to detect any potentially dangerous conditions.

How Can You Compensate for Vision Problems?

If you have a problem with depth perception, distance perception, night blindness, or color blindness, you can learn to compensate when you drive.

▲
Have your vision tested regularly. Good vision is crucial to risk management.

If you are driving with your high beams on, don't blind drivers coming toward you. Switch to low beams when oncoming traffic is within 500 feet.

Poor Depth Perception

Depth perception gives a three-dimensional perspective to objects. It helps you judge the relative distance between two objects. Any time you look at an object far away from you, you are using depth perception. When you estimate the distance between yourself and the object, you're using distance judgment.

Depth perception and distance judgment work together. They are especially important when you drive because they help you control your following distance and adjust your position in traffic. If you generally have trouble judging distances, you'll have even more difficulty when you're in a moving car.

To compensate for poor depth perception, increase your following distance. You can also compare the speeds of the cars coming toward you.

Color Blindness

The most commonly used colors in traffic are red, green, and yellow. If you have normal color vision, you won't have a problem recognizing these colors when you see them. Some people, however, are *color blind*. These people are unable to tell the difference between red and green or between blue and yellow.

Color-blind people can drive safely. They can tell the meaning of signs and signals by their shape and position, or by reading the words printed on them.

Night Blindness

Even if you have 20/20 vision, you don't see as well at night as you do during the day. At night your visual acuity, field of vision, depth perception, and color vision are all reduced. For some people, seeing at night is even more difficult.

If seeing at night poses a particular problem for you, you may have a condition known as night blindness. Have your eyes checked, and avoid driving at night.

One of the biggest problems in night driving is glare caused by the sudden brightness of the headlights

THE SCIENCE CONNECTION

A person who can read 3/8-inch-high letters clearly from a distance of 20 feet, without glasses or contact lenses, is considered to have normal visual acuity. This is called 20/20 vision because at 20 feet, that's what most people with normal vision can see. People with 20/40 vision can see at 20 feet what people with normal vision can see at 40 feet. A person with 20/40 vision sees less accurately or clearly than someone with 20/20 vision.

Eyeglasses or contact lenses improve eyesight, but they do not necessarily improve it to 20/20 vision. Some people's vision cannot be made better than 20/70 with glasses or contact lenses. Some states grant these people restricted driving licenses, allowing them to drive only under certain conditions, such as during daylight hours.

Tips for New Drivers

Driving at Night

When you drive at night, you need to compensate for reduced visibility. Here are some steps to take:

- Drive more slowly than you would during the day. Adjust your speed to the range of your headlights. Increase your following distance to 3 seconds or more.
- Keep your eyes moving. Don't stare at brightly lighted areas. Keep your attention on the street-level activities around you and in the direction in which you're heading.
- Make sure your windshield and headlights are clean.
- Use your headlights wisely. Use your high beams when possible, such as on long stretches of empty highway. Switch to low beams for city driving and when following vehicles or meeting oncoming vehicles.
- Avoid driving near your usual bedtime. Your level of alertness is low at this time.

of oncoming vehicles. Whether you look directly at the approaching beams or not, the pupils of your eyes narrow to adjust to the brightness. Your eyes then take a moment to readjust to the darkness of night. During this time you may be temporarily blinded.

Here are some ways to deal with the danger of glare.

◆ Don't look directly at the headlights of an oncoming car. Instead, look beyond them and direct your attention to the right edge of the roadway, keeping the approaching car in your peripheral vision.

◆ Reduce your speed if you are momentarily blinded by glare.

◆ Keep alert to possible glare situations that may arise, as on curved or hilly roadways. When you anticipate such a situation, turn your eyes away from it, keeping it in your peripheral vision.

CHECKPOINT

3. Why is good vision important?
4. What can you do to compensate for poor depth perception? For night blindness?

WHAT WOULD YOU DO?

You are driving at night and are having trouble seeing the road. How could you ensure the safety of yourself and your passengers?

Temporary Physical Conditions that Affect Your Ability to Drive

Everyone experiences a "down time" during the day. For most people, this period occurs sometime between 1 and 5 P.M. During a "down time" period, which usually lasts from 15 to 20 minutes, people are at very high risk for falling asleep unless they are involved in a challenging activity.

At times, you'll have to decide whether or not you feel physically well enough to drive—or whether it's safe to ride with another driver. Conditions such as fatigue, a cold, the flu, or an injury may be temporary, but these conditions can affect your ability to make good decisions while driving.

You've already read about two important factors affecting a driver's ability to operate a car: emotional state and vision. Various other physical factors can limit or impair driving ability.

In some instances, you can compensate for a limiting physical condition. Other times, however, your wisest course of action is not to drive at all.

How Does Fatigue Affect Your Driving Ability?

Nearly everyone experiences fatigue at times. You probably know how it feels. You're tired and not very alert. You don't feel mentally sharp. Maybe you're cranky, rude, or overly sensitive. You may feel so "out of it" that you doze off without meaning to. Imagine how dangerous such a state of weariness can be when you're driving a car!

Fatigue affects your whole body and mind. Your senses are impaired or slowed down. You may drift into a state called *highway hypnosis*, and could nod off. If you're trying to drive, you may not see moving objects very clearly. You could ignore

Fighting Fatigue

Fatigue is usually temporary and easily overcome. The best way to overcome fatigue is to stop doing whatever you're doing and get some rest.

Before You Drive
- Get plenty of rest.
- Avoid heavy, fatty foods.
- Don't drink alcoholic beverages.

While You Drive
- Make sure there is a good flow of fresh air in the car. If your car is overheated or poorly ventilated, you may become sleepy.
- Wear sunglasses to cope with glare from sun and snow.
- Take turns driving with someone else.
- Turn on the radio. Sing, whistle, or talk to yourself.
- Stop regularly, get out of the car, and walk, jog, or do other light exercise for a few minutes.

critical information—signs, lights, sounds—or not recognize it at all. You may misjudge speed and distance or be tempted to take unnecessary risks. You may even fall asleep at the wheel.

When you feel fatigued, you're clearly in no condition to begin a long drive. If you're already on the road and find yourself getting sleepy, you're better off pulling over than trying to continue driving. Although it's usually not a good idea to sleep in your car at the side of the road, here are some tips if you have no choice but to stop and rest.

◆ At night, stop at a lighted roadside rest area. If you can't find such an area, make sure you are as far off the highway as possible.

◆ Roll down a window just enough so that fresh air comes into the car but not enough that someone might be able to enter the car from outside.

◆ Turn off the engine to avoid carbon monoxide poisoning. Lock all the doors.

◆ Leave your parking lights on, but turn off all other electrical equipment.

◆ Before you begin to drive again, get out of the car and make sure you are fully awake.

How Do Short-Term Illnesses or Injuries Affect Your Driving?

A temporary illness, such as a cold, flu, or allergy, can make it risky for you to drive. So can an injury, such as a broken bone or a pinched nerve. The discomfort or pain you experience can distract your attention from the road and lessen your ability to manage visibility, time, and space.

If you can't avoid driving when you're ill, at least try to minimize the amount of driving you do. Allow extra time to get where you're going. Drive more slowly than you normally would, and keep your attention focused on driving, not on how you feel.

Be especially careful about driving if you're taking any medication. Always read the information that appears on medicine containers. Some labels specifically warn against driving. Indeed, some medications for common illnesses can cause drowsiness, nausea, headache, or dizziness —conditions that are extremely dangerous for the driver of a car.

CHECKPOINT

5. How can fatigue affect your driving? How can you fight fatigue?
6. What effect can temporary illness or injury have on your driving?

WHAT WOULD YOU DO?

Describe your driving strategy for the next few hours until you reach your destination.

Long-Term Physical Factors that Affect Driving Ability

Some people face long-term or permanent physical challenges. Science and medicine, along with advances in technology, have greatly improved the driving potential of individuals.

How Does Hearing Loss Affect Driving Ability?

Your sense of hearing is an important guide to conditions on the roadway and within your own car. The sound of a siren, horn, or train signal warns you of possible danger. You may hear the sound of a vehicle in your blind spot before you actually see the vehicle. Sounds from your own car may alert you to engine, muffler, or tire trouble.

Drivers with a hearing loss may be able to compensate by wearing hearing aids. They can rely more on their vision, frequently scanning the roadway, and making good use of the rearview and side-view mirrors.

How Can Challenges Caused by Physical Disabilities Be Met?

A few years ago, it would have been virtually impossible for a person with cerebral palsy or a spinal cord injury to drive. Such challenges, called physical disabilities, often created

SAFETY TIPS

All vehicles emit carbon monoxide gas. It can make you physically ill or even kill you. Have your car's exhaust system checked regularly. Avoid driving a car that has an exhaust leak or a broken tailpipe. Such defects allow harmful exhaust gases to be trapped beneath the car, even when the car is moving. These gases may leak up into the car's interior.

Special devices enable many people to drive who would otherwise be unable to do so. ▶

obstacles that were impossible to overcome. With the development of modern science and technology, however, such disabilities are no longer permanent barriers. Although the severity of a person's physical disability still impacts on driving ability, new types of equipment such as joy stick driving systems, voice-activated controls, and modified vehicles, can greatly increase his or her driving potential.

For example, many people who do not have full use of their legs are able to drive with the aid of such special devices as hand-operated brakes and accelerators. Those without arms can utilize special rings that are attached to the steering wheel, dashboard controls, door locks, radio controls, and so forth. Artificial limbs, called prosthetic devices, enable these drivers to grasp the rings and operate the car.

Special vans are made for people who use wheelchairs. These vans are equipped with wheelchair lifts that can be operated from inside or outside the vehicle, as well as with extra space that permits the driver to smoothly transfer from a wheelchair to special power seats.

Drivers who have no ability to turn their heads or shoulders can use extra large rear-view mirrors to extend their vision over a wider area.

Anyone with a physical disability who wants to drive a car, and is able to show that he or she can do so safely, can get a license. Usually, such individuals are required to undergo a comprehensive medical assessment that determines their potential to drive. Special centers, called driver evaluation facilities, are designed specifically for this purpose.

How Do Aging and Chronic Illnesses Affect Driving Ability?

Aging and chronic illnesses are other long-term physical factors that can affect a person's ability to drive.

Aging

As a young person, your reaction time is likely to be faster and your sense of sight keener than that of an older person. Older people, however, can call on their driving experience to help them reduce risk and anticipate threatening conditions. They can also compensate for possible age-related limitations by reducing driving speed and by avoiding roadways that have heavy traffic.

As you encounter older drivers and pedestrians, be respectful of their age and experience. Slow down and

▲ *Older drivers can call on their experience to help them manage risk.*

Be especially careful when you see elderly pedestrians. Persons 75 years of age and older have the highest pedestrian death rates.

Marquita Dudley, Driver Safety Coordinator, Traffic Safety and Engineering Department

Marquita Dudley

It takes four to seven years of experience before the average driver's crash probability starts to decline. Driving a car is complex and dangerous. You must learn to minimize risk.
- Be patient and exercise self-control.
- Be attentive. Don't let things or others interfere with your ability to concentrate.
- Make an effort to control your emotions, and avoid driving if you are upset or depressed.
- Don't drive if you are fatigued.
- Take full responsibility for your actions behind the wheel.

WHAT WOULD YOU DO?

What would you tell this woman about driving?

be patient. Someone will do the same for you one day.

Chronic Illnesses

A chronic illness is one that lasts over a long period of time or one that recurs often.

Some chronic illnesses such as epilepsy, arthritis, diabetes, and asthma can be treated and controlled by medication. However, the medication itself can result in side effects such as drowsiness, dizziness, headache, and nausea that interfere with safe driving. To obtain a driver's license, people with chronic illnesses must furnish proof that the illnesses are under control and that the medication they're taking won't cause side effects that impair driving ability.

CHECKPOINT

7. How can impaired hearing affect your ability to drive?
8. How can physically disabled drivers compensate?
9. What effect do aging and chronic illnesses have on driving ability?

CHAPTER 2 REVIEW

KEY POINTS

LESSON ONE

1. Emotions such as joy, sadness, anger, and fear can cause you to be inattentive, interfere with your ability to concentrate, and hinder your ability to process information while driving.

2. You can make an effort to control your emotions by maintaining a mature attitude and identifying situations that may cause you to become upset. You can also plan ahead to avoid traffic problems, expect mistakes from other drivers, avoid driving if you are upset or depressed, and train yourself to use correct procedures.

LESSON TWO

3. You must have good vision in order to adjust your car's speed and position to minimize risk. Good vision also enables you to identify signs, signals, and roadway markings.

4. To compensate for poor depth perception, practice judging the distance between two objects; for color blindness, learn the meaning of signs and signals by shape and position; for night blindness, drive slower than you would in the day.

LESSON THREE

5. Fatigue impairs your senses. It could cause you to nod off or fall asleep while driving, ignore critical information, and misjudge speed and distance. You can fight fatigue by getting plenty of rest, avoiding alcoholic beverages and heavy foods, opening the windows to get fresh air, wearing sunglasses to cope with glare, stopping the car and moving around, and taking turns driving with someone else.

6. Short-term illness or injury can cause pain or discomfort, which can distract your attention from the road and lessen your ability to manage visibility, time, and space.

LESSON FOUR

7. Hearing loss may prevent you from being aware of sounds that warn you of possible danger, such as the sounds of sirens or horns and can prevent you from being aware of problems within your own car.

8. People without full use of their legs can drive with the aid of devices such as hand-operated brakes and accelerators. With the aid of prosthetic devices, those without arms can drive using special rings and dashboard controls. People who cannot turn their heads or shoulders can use extra-large mirrors; those who use wheelchairs can use specially equipped vehicles.

9. Aging can affect a driver's reaction time and eyesight. Some medications for chronic illnesses may have side effects that interfere with safe driving.

PROJECTS

1. Emotional factors play an important part in the way people drive. What are some ways that people could be reminded to maintain a mature attitude and to be courteous and patient while driving?

2. While you are a passenger, close your eyes. Use your other senses to gather information. Can you identify the sounds you hear? Can you tell whether the car is speeding up, slowing down, or making a turn?

BUILDING CRITICAL THINKING SKILLS

Kitty O'Neil

Kitty O'Neil is five feet three inches tall and weighs only ninety-eight pounds, but her accomplishments are giant-sized. She has held the women's world land speed driving record of 512 mph and went on to become the second-fastest human with a speed of 618 miles per hour. Of course, both of these records were accomplished in specially designed cars driven at test sites and not on highways.

Ms. O'Neil has also set records as a champion drag boat racer and water skier, and is a former American Athletic Union national diving champion. She uses the skills that enabled her to set these records in her work as a movie stunt woman. Among other things, she has jumped off six-story buildings, pretended to be drowning, and has been set on fire.

Why does Kitty O'Neil do these things? As she says, one reason is to prove that physically challenged people "can do anything." Kitty O'Neil has been deaf since she was four months old. Kitty believes that she owes her will to succeed to her mother, a woman of Cherokee descent who died when Kitty was 21 years old. She taught Kitty how to talk and play the cello and the piano, and rewarded Kitty whenever she perfected a new skill. Kitty says that she would like to show others that her mother's encouragement and support "has paid off beyond anyone's hopes."

What Do You Think Now?

Does the story of Kitty O'Neil change or confirm your opinion of the capabilities of physically challenged people? Explain your answer.

CHAPTER 2 REVIEW

CHAPTER TEST

Write the letter of the answer that best completes each sentence.

1. Strong emotions can
   a. affect your night vision.
   b. help you drive safely.
   c. interfere with your driving judgment.

2. If you are severely fatigued, you should
   a. avoid driving.
   b. drive with your high beams on.
   c. drive quickly to your destination.

3. A physical factor that may affect driving ability is
   a. the effects of medication.
   b. the color of your eyes.
   c. a feeling of sadness.

4. A person who cannot see well at angles to the left and right has difficulty with
   a. night vision.
   b. depth perception.
   c. peripheral vision.

5. One way to deal with glare from the headlights of oncoming cars is to
   a. look right at the car's headlights.
   b. look at the right edge of the road.
   c. increase speed to get past the car quickly.

6. As a driver, it is your responsibility to drive
   a. your friends to school.
   b. only when you are able to concentrate.
   c. no matter how you're feeling.

7. Drivers who are unable to turn their heads or shoulders can use
   a. revolving seats.
   b. extra-large rearview mirrors.
   c. a thickly padded seat cushion.

8. To control your emotions in traffic, it's wise to
   a. yell at other drivers.
   b. daydream about pleasant events.
   c. expect others to make mistakes.

9. If you train yourself always to use correct procedures, you will
   a. reduce risk no matter how you may feel.
   b. never have a collision.
   c. be able to drive without paying attention.

10. Most of the information you gather about traffic situations comes from
    a. other drivers.
    b. your vision.
    c. your sense of hearing.

Choose the phrase that best completes each sentence.

> field of vision   wheelchair lifts
> mature attitude   lack of concentration
> depth perception   sense of hearing

11. Your ____ helps you judge the distance between cars.

12. Having a ____ means respecting safety and taking responsibility for your actions.

13. Your ____ includes what you can see both directly in front of you and at an angle to the sides.

14. Strong emotions can lead to a ____ when you drive.

15. Modified vehicles for the physically disabled may include ____ .

DRIVER'S LOG

In this chapter, you have learned about how emotional and physical factors can affect the driving task. Write at least two paragraphs giving your ideas on the following questions.

◆ What "sets you off" emotionally?
◆ How will you control these situations and emotions?

CHAPTER ◆ 3

HANDLING SOCIAL PRESSURES

As a driver, you will be responsible for your safety as well as that of your passengers and other roadway users. It is important to learn how to base your decisions on good judgment and not on a desire to "go along" with the crowd.

CHAPTER 3 OBJECTIVES

Alcohol's Effect on You, Your Health, and Your Future

1. Describe how alcohol can affect you.
2. Name some of your responsibilities regarding drinking.
3. Explain how to identify a problem drinker.

Alcohol and Its Effects on Driving

4. Explain how alcohol affects your driving ability.
5. Name the laws about and penalties for driving while intoxicated.

How Other Drugs Affect Driving Ability

6. Describe other kinds of drugs that affect your driving ability.

Distractions Can Increase Driving Risk

7. Describe how distractions can hinder your driving ability.

You are at an exciting, yet confusing, time in your life. Sometimes people treat you as an adult, other times as a child. Learning to cope with this partial independence is a natural stage of growing up. It is the time when you are very vulnerable to *peer pressure,* or the influence of friends who are in your age group.

Peer pressure can influence the way you dress, your taste in music, and even the way you walk and talk. This is usually harmless.

However, peer pressure can also influence you in ways that can damage you and your future; one of the ways is if that pressure causes you to experiment with drinking alcohol. Understanding how alcohol has the potential to destroy your hopes, dreams, and ambitions can help you to resist destructive peer pressure.

How Can Alcohol Affect You?

Alcohol is a powerful drug—it can change the way you act, the way you think, and the way you feel. Many teens experiment with alcohol to overcome feelings of shyness, inhibition, unhappiness, or because it makes them feel like part of the group. However, alcohol is a dangerous drug. You can begin drinking to be part of the "in" crowd, but you can become a problem drinker, addicted to alcohol, and all alone.

Alcohol addiction can creep up slowly and take complete control of

your life. School, friends, family, plans for the future become meaningless to the problem drinker. In the end, problem drinkers don't need alcohol to make them feel good— they need it just to feel "normal."

Many teens feel secure. "That won't happen to me," they say. "I'll be able to control my drinking." However, people can't know beforehand if they will be able to control their drinking or if alcohol will control them. The only way to be sure that you will not become a problem drinker is not to pick up that first drink. Two things are certain: choosing not to drink guarantees that you will *not* become addicted to alcohol; choosing to drink guarantees that there is a chance you *will* become addicted to alcohol.

What Are Your Responsibilities Regarding Drinking?

Whether or not you choose to drink, you have certain responsibilities to yourself and to your friends who drink.

◆ What is your responsibility to a friend who has been drinking? If you are with someone who has been drinking, don't let that person drive. You can help by taking the car keys, driving yourself, calling your parents for a ride, calling a taxi, or making other arrangements.

◆ What is your responsibility if you serve alcohol to someone? If you host

You are not alone. If you or someone you know has a drinking problem you can contact:

**Alcoholics Anonymous
P.O. Box 459
Grand Central Station
New York, NY 10163**

**Alateen
P.O. Box 862
Midtown Station
New York, NY 10018**

a party and serve liquor, you are legally responsible for the actions of your guests if they drive while they are intoxicated. If an intoxicated guest is injured or dies in a collision, or if the guest injures or kills someone else, you could be sued or sent to jail.

◆ What can you do if you or someone you know is a problem drinker or is afraid he or she may be at risk of becoming one? There are support groups to help problem drinkers and their relatives, friends, and loved ones. These groups promise to keep any information confidential. Two such groups are Alcoholics Anonymous, or AA, and Alateen.

Alcoholics Anonymous is listed in your local phone book. AA is an organization for people who feel that they might have a problem with alcohol or know that they have a problem and need help. Alateen is a support group for young people who have an alcoholic parent, sibling, or friend.

What Are the Symptoms of a Problem Drinker?

Before you can offer help to a problem drinker or know if you need that help yourself, you must be able to recognize the signs of problem drinking. Look for changes in a person's behavior or life situation such as loss of initiative, frequent lateness and absences from school, loss of friends, and trouble with the law. In addition, a person with a drinking problem often drinks alone, becomes secretive, has trouble sleeping, drinks more than was originally planned, and suffers from memory loss or blackouts.

Other symptoms can be seen in the serious health problems that can afflict the problem drinker or alcoholic. Alcohol abuse can result in liver failure, heart disease, inflammation of the pancreas, cancer, brain damage, convulsions, and malnutrition.

Alcoholism is a disease. Its consequences are devastating, and include loss of self-esteem, loss of friends and family, and even loss of life. The best defense against this disease is to say "No" when you are offered that first drink.

CHECKPOINT

1. What can be the consequences of alcohol use?
2. What are your responsibilities to yourself and to your friends who drink?
3. How would you recognize the signs of a problem drinker and what might you do to help that person?

WHAT WOULD YOU DO?

You and a friend are offered a drink. You say, "No," but your friend wants to try one. What will you say to your friend?

Alcohol and Its Effects on Driving

When you are behind the wheel of a car, all of your senses must be on red alert. You must be able to react quickly to potentially threatening conditions and then make split-second decisions. Being a good driver takes skill and judgment. No matter how good a driver you are, however, alcohol *will* decrease your skill and damage your judgment.

EFFECTS OF ALCOHOL

Amount of beverage	Concentration of alcohol in bloodstream	Typical effects
1 cocktail (1½ oz. whiskey) 1 glass (5½ oz.) wine 1 bottle (12 oz.) beer	0.03%	Slight changes in feeling.
2 cocktails 2 glasses (11 oz.) wine 2 bottles beer	0.06%	Feeling of warmth, mental relaxation, slight decrease of fine skills, less concern with minor irritations and restraints.
3 cocktails 3 glasses (16½ oz.) wine 3 bottles beer	0.09%	Buoyancy, exaggerated emotion and behavior, talkative, noisy, or morose.
4 cocktails 4 glasses (22 oz.) wine 4 bottles beer	0.12%	Impairment of fine coordination, clumsiness, slight to moderate unsteadiness in standing or walking.
5 cocktails 5 glasses (27½ oz.) wine 5 bottles beer	0.15%	Intoxication—unmistakable abnormality of bodily functions and mental faculties.

How Does Alcohol Affect Driving Ability?

Even one drink might be enough to impair your ability to drive safely. From the moment alcohol enters your bloodstream, you begin to lose your ability to think clearly. Even a small amount of alcohol causes changes in your coordination. It should not come as a surprise that at least half of all highway deaths are alcohol-related. This is just one of the frightening facts about driving and alcohol.

Facts About Alcohol and Driving

These facts tell you why drinking and driving is a recipe for disaster.

◆ More than 3,000 teenagers are killed each year in the United States in alcohol-related car crashes. Nearly half of those killed had *not* been drinking, but were victims of someone who had.
◆ Six out of every 10 highway deaths of people from 16 to 20 years old are alcohol-related.
◆ In fatal crashes involving only one car, two-thirds of the drivers are legally intoxicated.

In spite of these terrible statistics, alcohol is the most widely used and abused drug in the world. Yes, it is a drug, and it is deadly.

Even one drink of alcohol causes changes in the body. That is because alcohol is not digested, as food is.

THE ➤
SOCIAL STUDIES CONNECTION

Candy Lightner has said, "If you care enough, you can accomplish anything." On May 3, 1980, her daughter, 13-year old Cari Lightner, was struck and killed by a car driven by a drunk driver. From that tragedy arose an organization, Mothers Against Drunk Driving (MADD), that is estimated to have saved over 5,000 lives that might otherwise have been lost. Candy Lightner founded MADD. In the years since Cari's death, Ms. Lightner and MADD have labored to convince the public that drunk driving is a criminal act. She calls drunk driving "the only socially accepted form of homicide."

MADD has convinced Congress to standardize the drinking laws so that it is illegal in all states to sell alcoholic drinks to anyone under the age of 21. Today, there are more than 360 chapters of MADD, and the 50 states have passed more than 400 laws dealing with drunk driving.

Rather, it is absorbed into the bloodstream through the walls of the stomach and small intestine. Once in the bloodstream, the alcohol displaces oxygen and is quickly carried to all parts of the body. Alcohol has the greatest effect on the brain because the brain requires huge quantities of blood. A drinker's mental and physical abilities become diminished.

Myths and Facts About Alcohol

Alcohol is one of the most misunderstood and widely-used drugs. The truth about alcohol is the best weapon against it.

There are plenty of myths about alcohol. Let's look at the facts.

MYTH: Wine and beer are not the same as hard liquor.
FACT: Not true! Sure, there's more alcohol in an ounce of liquor than in an ounce of beer. However, a 12-ounce bottle of beer or a 12-ounce wine cooler has more alcohol than a one-ounce shot of 80 proof liquor.

MYTH: You can't get drunk on a full stomach.

FACT: A full stomach just means that alcohol is absorbed into the bloodstream a little more slowly. *All* of that alcohol will still get into the bloodstream and travel to the brain and other parts of your body.

MYTH: Drinking and driving is fun.
FACT: Drinking and driving is the single largest health risk for people under 30 and the number-one killer of teenagers.

MYTH: You must drink because friends want you to even though you are the driver.
FACT: Real friends wouldn't want you to hurt yourself or others. Tell them the facts about alcohol.

MYTH: Black coffee, a cold shower, lots of exercise, or all three together can quickly sober up a drinker.
FACT: No way! The body can't burn up much more than $\frac{1}{2}$ ounce of alcohol in an hour. Nothing can speed up the process. So if someone has two glasses of wine, it will take about three to four hours before the wine is out of his or her body.

MYTH: Alcohol makes you feel better when you're down in the dumps.

FACT: Not really. Alcohol is a depressant, or "downer." It can make you feel worse than you did to begin with.

MYTH: Even if you've been drinking, you have to drive to get places.
FACT: You have choices. A nondrinking friend can do the driving. Or you can call a cab, call home, or take the bus and pick up the car tomorrow.

The Physical Effects of Alcohol

After you've had one to three drinks, your chances of getting into a car crash are about seven times greater than they would be if you were sober. Why is that?

The answer is that alcohol slows down the part of the brain that controls muscle movement and reflexes.

Reaction time After two or more drinks, a driver becomes physically slower and less alert.

Coordination Movement gets sloppy and uncoordinated. Drivers who have been drinking cannot make split-second decisions. They have trouble steering and may step on the brakes too late or miss them entirely.

Depth and distance perception Alcohol affects the ability to judge depth and distance. Drinking drivers perceive something as far away when it is really very close. They cannot tell where the cars around them really are or how far away road signs or signals are.

Speed perception Drinking drivers often cannot tell how fast another car is approaching or how far away an oncoming car is. Drinking drivers also have no sense of how fast they are going, which is not surprising when you consider that alcohol can severely dull the senses.

An intoxicated driver will have difficulty focusing on the pen as the officer moves it. ▶

Blurred or double vision is often the result of a driver's having had too much to drink.

Vision Alcohol affects the eyes' reflex action that controls the size of the pupils. The reflex causes the pupils to become smaller in bright light and larger as the light diminishes. Drinkers' eyes are not protected against headlight glare, because their pupils do not return to normal size quickly enough once the headlights have passed. Temporary blindness results. Alcohol also impairs side vision and color vision and may cause double vision.

The Mental Effects of Alcohol

Alcohol doesn't just affect the part of your brain that controls your physical reactions. It also affects the part of the brain that controls the ability to reason.

As if that isn't bad enough, alcohol affects your judgment and, consequently, can make you feel as if you are thinking more clearly than usual. This false message makes drinking drivers even more dangerous, because they don't have the judgment to realize that something is wrong. A driver in this condition is apt to make poor decisions—even fatal ones.

Alcohol affects your *inhibitions*, the elements of your personality that stop you from behaving without regard to possible consequences. In drivers, the loss of inhibition can be very dangerous.

What Are the Laws About and the Tests and Penalties for Drinking and Driving?

Drinking and driving cause countless tragedies. All states have laws regulating the minimum drinking age and laws against drinking and driving. In all states, it is illegal for persons under age 21 to buy, possess, or drink alcoholic beverages.

In 29 states, your driver's license can be suspended if you refuse to take a test for blood alcohol concentration or if you fail the test. This is in addition to any fines or penalties connected with conviction for driving while intoxicated or driving under the influence.

Implied Consent Laws

When you use public roads, you agree to give law enforcement officials permission to test you for alcohol use if you are arrested on suspicion of driving and drinking. This permission is known as *implied consent,* and it is the law in all 50 states. The test will determine your BAC, or *blood-alcohol concentration.*

Drinking and driving is stupid, and it's illegal. In many states, adult drivers with a BAC of 0.10 percent or higher can be charged with driving while intoxicated (DWI). Some states call it driving under the influence (DUI).

Tests for Intoxication

Chemical analysis of blood or urine can measure a person's BAC, or a breath-testing device can measure the percentage of alcohol in the breath. In an increasing number of states, a reading of 0.08 percent or higher is enough to convict adult drivers of DWI or DUI and to take away their license. For teenage drivers, a BAC of 0.01 percent or higher is enough for conviction in many states.

Even if a driver's BAC is lower than the legal limit, he or she can still be charged with DWI or DUI. A police officer can stop anyone whose car appears to be out of control. The officer can give a field sobriety test by asking the driver to perform simple tasks, such as closing the eyes and touching the nose with the index finger.

If you are ever stopped for suspicion of DWI or DUI, be courteous and cooperate with the police officer. Drivers who refuse to submit to a chemical test for BAC can have their licenses suspended whether they are convicted or not.

Penalties

The penalties for DWI or DUI are different from state to state. A driver's license can be suspended, a fine can be assessed, or a jail term can be assigned. If a death results from a collision while drinking, the driver could be prosecuted for vehicular manslaughter. Drivers convicted of DWI or DUI also have to pay higher insurance premiums once their licenses are restored.

WHAT WOULD YOU DO?

The driver has been drinking steadily. How can his companions get home? What is their responsibility to the driver?

CHECKPOINT

4. How does alcohol affect a driver?
5. What should you know about the laws, tests, and penalties for driving while intoxicated?

Alcohol is not the only drug that can impair your ability to drive. Almost any drug can have a harmful effect on your driving skill.

There are many different kinds of drugs. Some can be bought only by prescription. Others can be bought over the counter without a prescription. Some drugs are against the law but can be bought illegally.

What Drugs Affect Driving Ability?

How a drug affects you depends on the drug itself. Some drugs can decrease your ability to make sound decisions and respond well to situations. Other drugs can change the way you think. It's important that you know about these drugs and their effects on driving. Once you understand the danger of combining drugs and driving, you can take steps to avoid putting yourself and others at risk.

Over-the-Counter Drugs

Over-the-counter drugs are drugs that can be purchased legally without a doctor's prescription. You may not even think of them as drugs. They are used for colds, headaches, allergies, and the like. It's important to read the package label of these drugs, which may warn that use will "cause drowsiness or dizziness," or "Do not drive after using." Pay attention to these warnings! It's your responsibility as a driver to know what side effects any medications you are taking might cause.

◀
Many of the capsules, tablets, and syrups commonly found in medicine cabinets are over-the-counter drugs.

Tips for New Drivers

Under the Influence

Be aware of signs that other drivers on the road may be under the influence of alcohol or other drugs. Various signs indicate possible problems.

Traveling at erratic speeds—either too fast or too slow   Alcohol-impaired drivers often have trouble driving at a steady speed.

Running over curbs or turning into the wrong lane   Alcohol-impaired drivers are often unable to turn smoothly.

Weaving from side to side   Alcohol-impaired drivers suffer from loss of coordination, which affects their ability to steer smoothly.

Ignoring or overshooting traffic signs   Alcohol-impaired drivers suffer impaired reflexes and vision loss.

If you find yourself on the same roadway as a driver who shows any of these signs, increase the amount of space between your cars. Be alert to the fact that there is an impaired driver sharing the roadway with you. If possible, inform a police officer of what you have noticed.

Marijuana masks the feeling of nausea that accompanies intoxication. Drinkers who mix marijuana and alcohol may not realize how much alcohol they have consumed. They may continue drinking until they suffer alcohol poisoning, which can result in coma, or even death.

Prescription Drugs

You can buy prescription drugs at a pharmacy if your doctor orders them for you. A prescription is required by law because these drugs can have powerful effects on your body. If your doctor orders a prescription drug for you, be sure to ask your doctor or pharmacist if you can drive safely while taking it.

Many prescription drugs have warnings on the bottle. Look carefully. It's your responsibility as a driver to know what drugs you are taking and what effects they can have.

Depressants

Depressants slow down, or depress, the central nervous system. Doctors order depressants for patients who are experiencing a lot of tension, who are very anxious, or who are being treated for high blood pressure.

Narcotics	Depressants	Stimulants	Hallucinogens
heroin	alcohol	amphetamines (speed)	marijuana
cocaine (including crack or rock)	barbiturates		LSD
	methadone		PCP (angel dust)
codeine	sleeping pills		hashish
morphine	tranquilizers		

While depressants can help with these symptoms, they also slow down the patient's mental and physical activity. Like alcohol, which is also a depressant, these drugs slow down reflexes and have a harmful effect on coordination. A driver who takes depressants can act like a driver who drinks alcohol.

Stimulants

Stimulants speed up, or stimulate, the central nervous system. Some drivers misuse these drugs and take them to keep awake when driving long distances.

Stimulants can give users a false feeling of well-being and make them think that they are superalert. These drugs often cause drivers to take foolish and life-threatening risks. When the effect of stimulants wears off, which can happen very suddenly, users can become very tired quickly. Many stimulants are illegal.

Hallucinogens

Hallucinogens are so dangerous that selling or using them is against the law. They are called mind-altering drugs for a good reason. Hallucinogens change the way a person thinks, sees, and acts.

Marijuana Marijuana may make a user drowsy. It can affect people's awareness of how fast they are driving and their ability to judge time and space. People who use marijuana may just sit and stare at something for a long time and be completely unaware of anything else that is going on around them.

No one really knows when the effects of marijuana wear off. The chemicals in this drug can stay in the body for as long as four to six weeks. Drivers may think that the effects have worn off when they are still under the influence of marijuana.

LSD and PCP The strongest hallucinogens are LSD and PCP (angel dust). While using LSD or PCP, people can forget who they are, where they are, and what they are doing. These drugs can cause drivers to lose the ability to judge space and the speed at which they are driving.

Narcotics

Narcotics have a strong depressant effect. They can cause stupor, coma, and even death. *It is illegal for you to buy or possess narcotics.*

CHECKPOINT

6. What kinds of drugs affect your driving ability?

WHAT WOULD YOU DO?

You are taking a prescription medicine. Can you drive your sister to the movies? How will you decide if it is safe for you to drive?

Distractions Can Increase Driving Risk

▲
Wearing headphones while you drive prevents you from hearing the sirens of emergency vehicles and police cars.

There's so much to pay attention to when you drive. You have to see what is going on around you. You need to be sure that other drivers know where you are and what you plan to do. You have to keep adjusting your speed and vehicle position to driving conditions. You have to be alert to any surprises that might turn into emergencies.

With all this going on, you need to be sure that no distractions inside your car will take your attention away from your driving and increase your risk.

How Can Distractions Hinder Your Driving Ability?

Imagine that you are driving along on a busy highway. Suddenly you see an old-fashioned car driving beside you. You have never seen a car like this before, so you take your eyes off the road ahead for just a second to get a closer look. Just then another car pulls ahead of you, and you have to brake hard. You have let yourself become distracted from your driving responsibilities. You almost crashed into another car.

Lots of events can distract you as you drive. It's important to be aware of these distractions so that you can be a safe and responsible driver.

A Car Radio Can Distract You

Most cars have radios and tape decks, but don't let yourself become so interested in the music that you forget to pay attention to your driving. Don't forget, too, that loud music can mask useful information.

Sometimes a radio can be distracting because there might be static on a station that you want to hear. Looking for and changing tapes or CDs is also distracting—and very dangerous. You are taking your eyes off the road and are driving with only one hand on the wheel. You're not paying full attention to your driving. If the static bothers you, turn off the radio. Your concentration must be focused on driving, not on listening to music.

Headphones Can Be Dangerous

In most states, it's against the law to wear stereo headphones while you drive. This is a good law because you need as much information as possible when you drive—and that includes what you may hear.

If you're wearing headphones, you may not be able to hear another car honking its horn at you. You might lose your concentration if you're too absorbed in what you're hearing on your headphones. Put them away— you can listen to your personal stereo at another time. Your job now is to pay attention to your driving.

Passengers Can Distract You

Sometimes the people in your car want you to pay more attention to them than to your driving. They might ask you to turn around and look at what they're doing. Sometimes they can be talking so loudly that you can't even hear yourself think. At other times, passengers may try to roughhouse in the car or hang out the windows.

You are responsible for the safety of your passengers, and it's your responsibility to tell them to sit still or be quiet. You can explain that you'll pay attention to them when you get where you're going. You're not being rude—you're being a safe, responsible driver.

Little children can become restless on long trips. They can start fighting with each other or try to take off their safety belts. You can make sure that children behave by telling them the rules before you start driving and by keeping them quietly occupied.

You also have to think about children's needs. To avoid boredom, children need to have something to do. Make sure you have some tape cassettes for them to listen to in the car

or quiet games for them to play. You can also stop more often than you normally would and let the children get out and stretch their legs.

Other Distractions

Driving with animals in the car can be dangerous. A dog can suddenly jump on your lap, or a cat can crawl under your feet and land on the gas pedal. You have to plan ahead if you are going to take an animal in your car. Think about putting the animal in a carrying case, or ask a friend to come with you and hold the animal by its leash. If you travel with pets frequently, you should be aware that pet safety belts are available at specialty shops.

Many drivers become distracted in traffic jams. They get stuck for a long time and lose their concentration. Remember, even when you are stopped, it is important to pay attention to everything that is going on around you.

When driving with infants and small children, be sure they are in safety seats and that the seats are securely placed in the car.

Don't let passengers distract you. Tell them how you expect them to behave before they enter your car.
▼

Advice From the Experts

Robert Anastas, *Executive Director,* Students Against Driving Drunk/Student Athletes Detest Drugs

Robert Anastas

Traffic crashes, especially alcohol-related collisions, are the greatest cause of death and injury of young people. You should avoid driving and riding situations that involve drinking. You do not have a right to hurt your friends, yourself, or others.

The best insurance against teens driving drunk is to make a Contract for Life. It promises parents to rule out social pressure and helps parents cope with teen activities. Teens who sign their name to a contract show love and respect for parents, family, and friends.

WHAT WOULD YOU DO?

What steps can the driver take to avoid distractions on a long trip?

When you are driving on a toll road, you will need change to pay the toll. Make sure you know how much change you will need, and look for change *before* you start out on your trip. Plan ahead. Have a container with plenty of change in it within reach so that you don't have to search through your pockets when you should be concentrating on driving. You could also put a passenger in charge of finding the correct change.

Drivers who smoke can be distracted when they are searching for and lighting cigars, cigarettes, or pipes. A lighted cigarette falling to the seat or in the driver's lap is dangerous as well. Don't smoke while you drive—especially in a closed car where passengers can inhale the fumes.

Remember, your job is to concentrate on your driving. Being prepared to handle distractions is part of that job.

CHECKPOINT

7. What distractions can hinder your driving ability?

CHAPTER 3 REVIEW

KEY POINTS

LESSON ONE

1. Drinking alcohol can change people's actions, thoughts, and feelings. It can become addictive so that the need for alcohol becomes more important than friends, family, and future plans.

2. Your responsibilities include not letting anyone, including yourself, who has been drinking to drive, realizing that serving liquor makes you legally responsible for the actions of your guests if they drive while drunk, and knowing about support groups such as Alcoholics Anonymous and Alateen.

3. Some symptoms that indicate a problem-drinker are loss of initiative, frequent lateness and absence from school, loss of friends, trouble with the law, secretiveness, sleeplessness, and memory loss.

LESSON TWO

4. Some ways alcohol affects driving ability are that it removes inhibitions, reduces ability to react quickly, impairs coordination and has a bad effect on a driver's judgment.

5. When you use public roads, you agree to give law enforcement officials the right to test you for alcohol use if they suspect you of drinking and driving. This is the law of implied consent. In many states, a driver is considered intoxicated if his or her blood alcohol concentration is 0.08 percent or greater. Penalties for DWI or DUI may include driver's license suspension, assessment of a fine, or a term in jail.

LESSON THREE

6. Over-the-counter drugs, prescription drugs, depressants, stimulants, hallucinogens, and narcotics can affect driving ability. Over-the-counter drugs can be purchased without a doctor's order. Prescription drugs must be ordered by a doctor. Depressants slow down the central nervous system; stimulants speed it up. Hallucinogens are illegal mind-altering drugs. Narcotics are illegal drugs that have a strong depressant effect.

LESSON FOUR

7. Distractions can hinder your driving ability by drawing your attention away from the roadway. Distractions include car radios and tape decks, stereo headphones, noisy passengers, disruptive children, animals, traffic jams, toll payments, and smoking.

PROJECTS

1. Many organizations work to educate drivers about the dangers of drinking and driving. Two of the best known are Mothers Against Drunk Driving (MADD) and Students Against Driving Drunk (SADD). You have read about MADD. Find out about SADD. Learn how you can start a chapter in your community.

2. Use your state driver's manual or interview a police officer. Discover the circumstances under which a teenage driver can be convicted of DUI or DWI in your state. Find out about the penalties for conviction as well.

CHAPTER 3 REVIEW

BUILDING MAP SKILLS

Using the Mileage Chart

Suppose you are planning to drive from Abiline to El Paso. How many miles would you be traveling? One way to find out would be to use a mileage chart like the one on this page. Using a mileage chart is easy.

First look at the names of cities down the left side of the chart. Find Abiline, and put your left finger over it.

Then look at the cities across the top of the chart. Put your right finger on El Paso.

Now move your left finger across the chart until it reaches the box below El Paso. The number in the box is the distance in miles between Abilene and El Paso. The distance is 450 miles. That's quite a trip.

To estimate how long it will take you if you drive at an average of 55 miles per hour, divide 450 by 55. The trip will take between 8 and 9 hours. But don't forget to add in some time for rest stops. So you can figure on about a 10-hour trip.

Try It Yourself

1. How many miles is it between San Angelo and Eagle Pass?

2. If you are traveling at 55 miles an hour, about how long will it take you to drive from El Paso to Pecos?

3. Which trip would be longer—from Odessa to Houston, or from Lubbock to San Antonio?

MILEAGE CHART

	Abilene	Amarillo	Dallas	Eagle Pass	El Paso	Houston	Lubbock	Midland	Odessa	Pecos	San Angelo	San Antonio
Abilene		273	180	302	450	355	171	148	180	245	92	250
Amarillo	273		351	517	421	597	134	237	258	330	310	513
El Paso	450	421	646	479		751	345	312	289	210	415	555
Lubbock	171	134	318	394	345	530		121	142	219	202	406
Odessa	180	258	352	301	289	507	142	20		75	132	345
San Angelo	92	310	262	215	415	374	202	113	132	210		215

CHAPTER 3 REVIEW

CHAPTER TEST

Write the letter of the answer that best completes each sentence.

1. Distractions can
   a. slow reflexes.
   b. decrease risk.
   c. increase risk.
2. Drinking alcohol
   a. does not affect your mental abilities.
   b. often helps you think more clearly.
   c. slows down the part of your brain that controls muscles and reflexes.
3. Over-the-counter drugs
   a. may be used when driving short distances.
   b. may impair driving ability.
   c. must be ordered for you by a doctor.
4. You can reduce the effects of alcohol if you
   a. take a very cold shower.
   b. exercise.
   c. allow several hours to pass.
5. *Implied consent* means that you
   a. agree to be tested if you are suspected of drinking and driving.
   b. agree to obey the rules of the road.
   c. have the right to refuse a test if you are stopped by police.
6. You can avoid distractions while driving by
   a. putting on a set of personel stereo headphones.
   b. looking at the scenery.
   c. turning off your radio and asking passengers to be more quiet.
7. One way to handle a drinking problem is to
   a. just drink once a week.
   b. just drink beer.
   c. join a support group.
8. Alcohol is
   a. a harmless substance.
   b. a powerful drug.
   c. non-addictive.
9. Adults are considered intoxicated if the alcohol in their bloodstream is more than
   a. 0.10 percent
   b. 0.04 percent
   c. 0.07 percent
10. Even a small amount of alcohol can affect your
    a. long-term memory.
    b. ability to judge depth, distance, and speed.
    c. hearing.

Write the word or phrase that best completes each sentence.

| prescription | stimulants | concentrate |
| peer pressure | inhibitions | depressants |

11. _____ stop you from behaving without regard to possible consequences.

12. Drugs that slow down the central nervous system are called _____ .

13. _____ drugs must be ordered by a doctor.

14. _____ often give drivers a false sense of self-confidence and cause them to take foolish and life-threatening risks.

15. The influence of your friends is called _____ .

DRIVER'S LOG

In this chapter, you have learned about how social pressures can cause you to behave in ways that will put you and others at risk. Imagine that a friend has been drinking and wants to drive you home. Your friend says, "Don't worry, I'm just fine." What would you say? How might your friend respond? Write a dialogue showing what might happen.

CUMULATIVE REVIEW

UNIT 1

This review tests your knowledge of the material in Chapters 1–3. Use the review to help you study for your state driving test. Choose the answer that best suits the question.

1. The best way to fight fatigue is to
   a. use a stimulant.
   b. rest.
   c. look at the scenery.
   d. drink coffee.

2. *BAC* stands for
   a. brain alcohol content.
   b. blood alcohol concentration.
   c. basic automobile collision.
   d. body alcohol content.

3. In one hour the adult human body can burn about
   a. $\frac{1}{2}$ ounce of alcohol.
   b. 1 ounce of alcohol.
   c. 3 ounces of alcohol.
   d. 0.08 ounce of alcohol.

4. Traffic laws are enforced by
   a. the CIA.
   b. state and local police.
   c. the department of motor vehicles.
   d. United States marshals.

5. Almost half of all collisions
   a. result in fatalities.
   b. involve only one car.
   c. are "fender-benders."
   d. involve pedestrians.

6. Marijuana remains in the body
   a. up to 24 hours.
   b. up to six hours.
   c. up to six weeks.
   d. up to one week.

7. A visual acuity test measures
   a. how well you can see.
   b. pupil dilation.
   c. convex vision.
   d. headlight power.

8. Over-the-counter medications
   a. never affect driving ability.
   b. sometimes produce side effects.
   c. improve concentration.
   d. must be prescribed by a doctor.

9. The area of vision directly ahead of a person is called
   a. side vision.
   b. convex vision.
   c. the area of central vision.
   d. peripheral vision.

10. The chance of injury to oneself or others is called
    a. risk.
    b. carelessness.
    c. luck.
    d. responsibility.

11. A driver can compensate for color blindness by
    a. wearing tinted contact lenses.
    b. learning the shapes and meanings of signs, signals, and markings.
    c. only driving at night.
    d. using stereo headphones.

12. Each year, a driver's chance of being involved in a collision is
    a. 1 in 5.
    b. 1 in 10.
    c. 1 in 3.
    d. 1 in 2.

13. The influence of one's friends is called
    a. maturity.
    b. peer pressure.
    c. HTS.
    d. SIPDE.

14. One way to reduce driving risk is to
    a. anticipate the actions of others.
    b. always use high-beam headlights.
    c. join a support group.
    d. close the windows.

15. Through driver education students learn
   a. how to maneuver and control a car.
   b. the traffic laws of all 50 states.
   c. how to drive without paying attention.
   d. how to join a support group.

16. If you are temporarily blinded by headlight glare, you should
   a. look down.
   b. see a doctor.
   c. reduce your speed.
   d. close your eyes.

17. Some physically disabled people are able to drive by using
   a. prosthetic devices.
   b. breathylizers.
   c. peripheral vision.
   d. narcotics.

18. A person traveling by foot is a
   a. cyclist
   b. pedestrian.
   c. jaywalker.
   d. driver.

19. Alcohol affects
   a. your judgment.
   b. traffic laws.
   c. the HTS.
   d. the automobile industry.

20. A person who is feeling angry or upset should
   a. let someone else drive.
   b. turn on the radio.
   c. talk to passengers.
   d. sing.

21. You can gain insight into how drugs and alcohol impair driving through
   a. the Smith System.
   b. the SIPDE process.
   c. driver education.
   d. the Uniform Vehicle Code.

22. Prescription drugs
   a. can be purchased by anyone.
   b. can be ordered only by a doctor.
   c. are illegal.
   d. are always safe to use before driving.

23. Stereo headphones
   a. can distract your attention.
   b. can help you to concentrate.
   c. are built into many new cars.
   d. help some drivers hear better.

24. A driving strategy that requires you to look at the "big picture" is
   a. the SIPDE process.
   b. the Smith System.
   c. the HTS.
   d. visual acuity.

25. The maximum speed limit on interstate highways in most areas of the country is
   a. 60 mph.
   b. 50 mph.
   c. 55 mph.
   d. 70 mph.

26. Roads are part of the
   a. Highway Transportation System.
   b. Smith System.
   c. Administrative System.
   d. Uniform Vehicle Network.

27. Stimulants
   a. improve concentration.
   b. impair judgment.
   c. depress the central nervous system.
   d. improve reflexes.

28. One problem common to night driving is
   a. moon blindness.
   b. pedestrians.
   c. headlight glare.
   d. color blindness.

29. A collision is another term for
   a. momentum.
   b. an injury.
   c. vehicle failure.
   d. a crash.

30. To make wise driving decisions, use
   a. the SIPDE process.
   b. the Uniform Vehicle Code.
   c. an HTS.
   d. risk.

UNIT

LEARNING THE BASICS

The fundamentals of driving are second nature to good drivers. These basics will become second nature to you as well. This unit will help you learn the first steps toward becoming a good driver.

UNIT CONTENTS

SIGNS, SIGNALS, AND MARKINGS

Good drivers understand the role of communication. The signs, signals, and markings you see on the roadway are a vital means of communication. It is important that you understand the messages that they communicate.

CHAPTER 4 OBJECTIVES

LESSON ONE

Understanding Regulatory and Warning Signs

1. Identify and describe the purpose of regulatory signs.
2. Describe the actions to take at regulatory signs.
3. Identify the purpose of warning signs.
4. Describe how to respond to warning signs.

LESSON TWO

Guide and International Signs

5. Identify and describe the purpose of informational or guide signs.
6. Identify and describe the design and function of three international signs used in the United States.

LESSON THREE

Understanding the Purpose of Pavement Markings

7. Identify the meaning of yellow and white roadway lane markings.
8. Describe the meaning of arrows and other nonlane roadway markings.

LESSON FOUR

Responding to Traffic Control Signals

9. Describe traffic signals and the meanings of the colors.
10. Describe the colors and meanings of lane-use lights.

Understanding Regulatory and Warning Signs

A *no-standing zone* is an area where a car is not allowed to stop for any reason. Examples of no-standing zones are bus stops, fire stations, and in front of hospital emergency rooms. Stopping in a no-standing zone is likely to earn you a ticket and get your car towed away.

Stop signs are most frequently placed at one or more corners of an intersection.

Highways and streets would be difficult to use without signs that give information, warnings, and tell drivers what to do and what not to do. If there were no signs, how would you know you were on the right road? How would you manage risk if you didn't know the speed limit or when to stop or yield? Roadway signs provide important information about where you are, where you're going, and what rules or laws to follow.

What Are Regulatory Signs?

Regulatory signs regulate or control the movement of traffic. These signs tell you and other drivers what you must do and what you must not do when you drive. Regulatory signs are red, white, black, green on white, or white on black. Most regulatory signs have a vertical, rectangular shape. A red circle with a red slash on any of these signs means *NO*. You can recognize regulatory signs by their color and shape.

What Actions Should You Take at Regulatory Signs?

Regulatory signs give commands or set limits. When you see a stop sign, you must stop. When you see a yield sign, you must slow and yield right of way to traffic on the cross road or the road into which you are merging. A speed limit sign indicates the maximum speed you may drive under ideal conditions.

Stop Signs

Most often you will see a stop sign at the intersection of two roadways. There may be stop signs on all four corners or on only one or two corners of an intersection. In some places stop signs are located in the middle of the block; these indicate crosswalks.

You must come to a full stop at a stop sign. Often a white stop line is painted on the pavement in line with the sign. There may be two white lines indicating a pedestrian crosswalk just beyond the stop line, or there may be walk lines and no stop line. You are required to stop in front of the first white line you come to. If there are no lines, stop just in front of or in line with the sign.

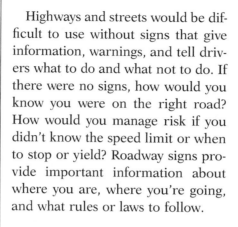

Yield sign
Triangle
Red

Speed limit
Vertical rectangle
White

One way
Horizontal rectangle
Black

General regulatory sign
Vertical rectangle
White

Do not enter
Square
Red

Stop sign
Octagon
Red

General regulatory signs
Square
White

Reduced speed limit
Vertical rectangle
Yellow

Wrong way
Horizontal rectangle
Red

Railroad crossing
Crossbuck
White

General regulatory signs
Square and Horizontal rectangle
White

After you stop, if there is no traffic from the right or left you may proceed. When there is traffic on the other roadway, you must decide what to do. If there are stop signs for cross traffic and another car has reached its stop sign before you reach yours, you must let it go first. If you and the other car arrive at the same time, the car on the right must be given right of way. If the other car is on your left, make sure it is going to wait. Then proceed cautiously.

Yield Signs

At a yield sign, you move from one roadway onto or across another one. As you approach the yield sign, slow down and check oncoming traffic and the traffic behind you. Scan right and left for cross and oncoming traffic. If a vehicle is coming toward you, you'll have to judge its distance and speed and decide whether you can safely enter or cross the road. You may need to stop and wait until the roadway is clear of traffic before you proceed.

Speed Limit Signs

Speed limit signs show the maximum, or fastest, speed allowed on a roadway. Driving faster than the posted speed is illegal. Some speed limit signs also post minimum speeds. These signs are usually on expressways. You should not travel slower than the minimum speed posted, unless road or weather conditions make it unsafe to travel at that speed.

Railroad Crossbuck

A railroad crossing crossbuck is located where railroad tracks cross the roadway. On multiple-lane roadways and in heavy-traffic areas, signal bells, flashing red lights, and railroad gates may also warn and protect drivers. Regardless of whether or not lights or gates are present, if a train is coming, you must stop.

What Are Warning Signs?

Warning signs alert you to changes in the condition or use of the road

Be careful at intersections. Always be prepared to yield to another car, even if you are legally permitted to proceed. If the situation looks dangerous, yield.

Approximately 120 people are killed each year in the United States in collisions with deer. It is estimated that at least that many people are killed trying to miss colliding with deer.

Tell you what to expect ahead.

   Intersections

   Changes in width

   Traffic

   Crossings

   Conditions

   Curves

 **Construction**

?

WHAT WOULD YOU DO?

What does the sign mean? What would you do in this situation?

ahead. Warning signs include those that tell you about road construction and maintenance, school zones and crossings, railroad crossings, curves, intersections, changes in road width, and deer crossings. All warning signs are either yellow or orange with black symbols or letters, and most are diamond-shaped.

What Actions Should You Take at Warning Signs?

When you see a warning sign, increase your level of alertness to changes in the roadway, in traffic, or in environmental conditions. Always proceed with caution. Be especially careful when you see a school zone sign or a railroad advance warning sign.

School Area Signs

When you see a school zone or school crossing sign, you must slow down and proceed with caution. Children may be playing nearby and may dart into the street. At a school crossing sign, give right of way to children crossing the roadway.

Railroad Advance Warning Signs

Be especially careful when you come to a railroad advance warning sign. Be sure to slow down before you reach the tracks, and look in both directions to see if a train is approaching.

CHECKPOINT

1. How can you tell which signs are regulatory signs?
2. What should you do when you see a stop sign? A yield sign? A railroad crossbuck?
3. How do you know which signs are warning signs?
4. How should you proceed at school zone signs and railroad advance warning signs?

Guide and International Signs

Highway signs do more than just warn you and tell you what you can and cannot do. Signs can provide information about where you are, where you're going, how to get there, how far you have to go, and what services and sites are available to help make your trip comfortable and enjoyable.

As you drive, you will see signs that convey information through color, shape, and symbols instead of words.

What Are the Functions of Guide Signs?

As you travel along the roadways, you'll see four kinds of guide signs. These signs give information about roadways and routes; the mileage to certain destinations; roadside services such as rest stops, service stations, and campsites; and recreational areas and nearby points of interest.

Route Makers

Routes are the numbered roadways that crisscross the continent. Interstate routes that lead *into* cities have three digits and begin with an odd digit. If a three-digit route begins with an even digit, the route goes *around* a city.

Destination and Mileage Signs

You'll often see destination and mileage signs mounted over highway lanes. They tell you where you are, which lane to take to get to your destination, what exits are coming up, and how far away the exits are. Smaller signs on the side of the road also tell you how far you are from

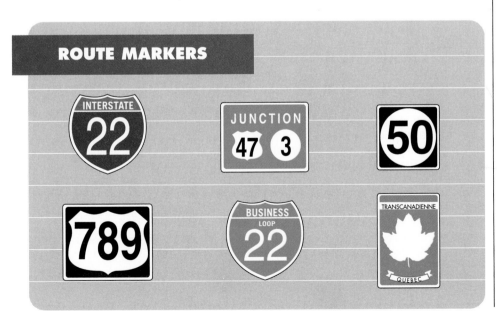

ROUTE MARKERS

INTERSTATE 22

JUNCTION 47 3

50

789

BUSINESS LOOP 22

TRANSCANADIENNE QUEBEC

  **Destination and mileage**

US 38 5
Greenville 40
St Louis 125

44 EXIT

22 EAST 7 Marion
EAST 7 Norge

  **Roadside services**

CAMPING

H HOSPITAL

SCENIC AREA

 **Recreation areas**

ROCKY MOUNTAIN NAT'L PARK 6 MILES

ROCKY MOUNTAIN NAT'L PARK

CULTURAL CROSSROADS

THE
SOCIAL STUDIES CONNECTION

One of the most important traffic safety devices is the automatic traffic signal. It is responsible for the orderly movement of millions of automobiles and pedestrians in today's cities and towns. The 3-way traffic signal was invented in 1923 by Garrett A. Morgan. He sold the rights to his invention to the General Electric Company for $40,000.

Morgan earned a far more important reward for another of his safety devices. In 1916, two dozen men were trapped by an explosion in a tunnel 228 feet below Lake Erie in Cleveland, Ohio. The tunnel was filled with smoke, natural gases, dust, and debris. The men seemed doomed since no one could get down into the tunnel and survive. However, using his new invention—the gas inhalator, an early gas mask—Morgan was able to lead a rescue party to reach the men and save many of their lives. In 1963, the city of Cleveland awarded this courageous African American a gold medal for his heroism.

INTERNATIONAL TRAFFIC SIGNS

 No bicycles

 Falling rocks

 No U-turn

 First aid station

 **Telephone**

 **Gas station**

different places. Destination and mileage signs are either white or green.

Roadside Services

When you want to stop for gas or food or make a phone call, look for the blue signs with white lettering.

Recreational Areas

Some informational signs are brown with white lettering. These signs guide you to state and national parks, historic sites, and other places of interest.

What International Signs Are Used in the United States?

International signs are those that you can understand without knowing another language. The meaning is conveyed by their color, shape, symbols, and numbers.

CHECKPOINT

5. Which signs are guide signs?
6. What kinds of international signs are used in the United States?

WHAT WOULD YOU DO?

What does the sign mean? What should you be alert to when you see this sign?

Understanding the Purpose of Pavement Markings

You've probably noticed lines, arrows, and words painted on streets and highways. These markings give drivers and pedestrians important information, directions, and warnings about roadway travel. You need to understand pavement markings in order to control and reduce risk.

What Do the Yellow or White Lines on the Roadway Mean?

Yellow and white roadway lines provide directions or warnings for drivers. Yellow lines divide traffic traveling in opposite directions. White lines parallel to the roadway separate same-direction traffic into lanes. White lines perpendicular to the roadway indicate crosswalks, railroad crossings, and stop signs at intersections.

Yellow Lines

Traffic that is traveling in opposite directions on a roadway is separated by double solid yellow lines, a broken yellow line, or a combination of broken and solid yellow lines. On

Double broken yellow lines mark lanes in which traffic changes direction at different times of the day. ▶

You may not pass on a two-way road divided by solid yellow lines. ▶

The broken white lines indicate that you may change lanes or pass.

divided highways, a single, solid yellow line marks the left edge of the roadway.

If the solid line of the combination solid-broken yellow lines is the first one to your left, you may not cross it to pass another vehicle. If the broken yellow line is the first one to your left, you may cross it (and the solid yellow line) to pass a vehicle when it is safe to do so. When two solid yellow lines divide a road, you cannot cross them to pass another vehicle. You may, however, turn across them to turn into a driveway.

White Lines

White lines that are parallel to the roadway mark the lanes for traffic moving in the same direction. If the lines are broken, you can move from lane to lane when it is safe to do so. Single white lines between lanes of traffic moving in the same direction

are meant to discourage passing at high-risk locations but do not prohibit passing.

Solid white lines are used to indicate the right side of the roadway. These lines are especially helpful at night because they mark the outer edges of the road, which are other-

This solid white line marks a breakdown lane. You should not travel in a breakdown lane.

Shared Left-Turn Lane

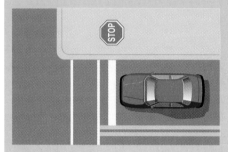

Stop Line

Pedestrian Crosswalk

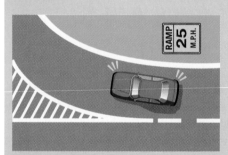

Road Exit Ramp

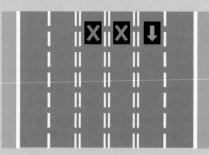

Reversible Lane ▪ at different times of day may be used by traffic moving in opposite directions

High Occupancy Vehicle (HOV) ▪ lane for use by vehicles carrying 2 or more passengers

Disabled Driver Parking

Tips for New Drivers

Shared Left-turn Lanes

Here are tips for using shared left-turn lanes safely.
- Don't get in the lane too soon. The longer you stay in the lane, the more likely it is you will meet someone coming in the opposite direction.
- Watch for cars pulling out of entrances and side streets. They may cross in front of you, cutting you off.
- Don't use a shared left-turn lane for anything but turning left.

wise hard to see. A solid white line may also mark a bicycle or breakdown lane beside the roadway.

What Do Other Markings on the Roadway Mean?

Other roadway markings may include lines, arrows, symbols, and lettering designed to guide drivers and pedestrians.

Arrows

White arrows on the roadway direct you into lanes from which you can drive straight ahead or turn right or left. On some three-lane roadways, the center lane is marked by parallel solid and broken yellow lines with white arrows that point alternately left and right. These lanes are *shared left-turn lanes*. Vehicles moving in either direction can use these lanes to make left turns into another road or entrance. Drivers who want to make left turns onto the roadway can also move into the shared left turn lane and wait for a gap in traffic.

Other Markings

On the opposite page are other pavement markings whose meaning and purpose you should know.

CHECKPOINT

7. Which pavement markings let you know that it is legal to pass? That it is illegal to pass?
8. How is a shared left-turn lane marked? How would you use it?

WHAT WOULD YOU DO?

You are driving alone. Are you allowed to use this lane? Why or why not?

Responding to Traffic Control Signals

Traffic control signals keep traffic moving in an orderly manner and to indicate right of way. Except in large cities, most signals operate automatically, using a timer system to change the lights through the green-yellow-red sequence. In many large cities, signals are linked electronically to and are controlled by computer. This sets up a gridwork that allows traffic to move smoothly and adjusts to changes in traffic volume.

How Do You Know When to Stop or Move Your Car Through Traffic?

As a user of the highway transportation system, your movement, whether you're a driver or pedestrian, is controlled by a series of traffic signals, arrows, flashing lights, pedestrian signals, or the directions of a traffic officer.

NERGY TIPS

Save fuel by letting up on the accelerator well in advance of a red light, stop sign, or yield sign.

TRAFFIC CONTROL SIGNALS

RED
STOP (Right turn on red after stop permitted in nearly all states)

YELLOW
DO NOT ENTER THE INTERSECTION

GREEN
GO (When safe to do so)

ARROW
YOU CAN GO ONLY IN THE DIRECTION IN WHICH THE ARROW POINTS

FLASHING RED
You must stop and proceed only when it is safe to do so.

FLASHING YELLOW
Slow down and proceed with caution.

GREEN ARROW
Traffic moving in the direction of the arrow may proceed if clear.

YELLOW ARROW
Appears after green arrow to indicate light is about to change.

RED ARROW
Used to indicate traffic is not allowed in direction of arrow.

RED   YELLOW   GREEN

STEADY WALK
Pedestrians may proceed across street.

 FLASHING WALK
Be alert for change in signal.

 STEADY DON'T WALK
Pedestrians should not enter street.

 FLASHING DON'T WALK
Pedestrians in street may proceed across street; others should not start.

Lane-Use Lights

 RED X
You must never drive in a lane under a RED X signal.

 YELLOW X
A steady YELLOW X indicates the driver should safely vacate this lane—because it soon will be controlled by a RED X.

 GREEN ARROW
You are permitted to drive in a lane under a GREEN ARROW or GREEN X signal.

 FLASHING YELLOW X
A flashing YELLOW X indicates the lane is to be used, with caution, for left turn movements only.

Traffic Signals

Traffic signals are located at intersections where the level of risk increases. Special-use signals may operate at certain times or on demand at school zones, fire stations, or factories. Traffic signals may be vertical or horizontal, with from one to five or more separate lenses that give information to roadway users.

The most common lenses are red, yellow, and green circles.

At a flashing signal you must either stop or slow down, depending on the color of the light. A flashing red signal means that you should come to a full stop. You must slow at a flashing yellow signal.

Pedestrian Signals

In the city, you'll find pedestrian signals at busy intersections. Some are also located in the middle of the block. They may have either words or signals telling pedestrians how to proceed. If you're driving and the pedestrian signal starts to flash an orange "don't walk," you can expect that your traffic signal is going to turn from green to yellow to red. However, don't just watch the pedestrian signals. Pay attention to the pedestrians and your own traffic signal.

Traffic Officer's Signals

Keep in mind that a police officer can take the place of and overrule

James E. Weaver, Highway Engineer, Traffic Control Division, Federal Highway Administration

James E. Weaver

Highway and traffic engineers design traffic control devices to convey a uniform, clear, and simple message to all highway users. It is your responsibility as a driver to recognize and fully understand the meaning of these devices by their color, shape, legend, and placement. This is important so that you will be able to respond properly and take the actions needed to maneuver your car safely in different traffic, terrain, and weather conditions.

❓ WHAT WOULD YOU DO?

You are stopped at a red light and want to turn right. Should you make the turn now?

traffic control signals. So, when an officer *is* present, you should follow the officer's signals even if they go against those of an automatic traffic signal or stop sign.

Are There Signals that Let You Know Which Lanes You Can Use?

On heavily traveled multiple-lane roadways, you may see *lane-use lights* mounted above the roadway. It is important for you to know what to do in response to these signals, because they are used when lane traffic is reversed during rush hours. Lane-use lights indicate which lane you can use at any given time.

CHECKPOINT

9. What are the colors and the meanings of the colors of traffic signals?
10. What are the meanings of the different colors of lane-use lights?

CHAPTER 4 REVIEW

KEY POINTS

LESSON ONE

1. Regulatory signs control the movement of traffic. They can be red, white, black, green on white, or white on black. A red circle with a red slash on any of these signs means *NO*.

2. You must come to a full stop at stop signs, yield right of way to cross traffic at yield signs, drive no faster than the limit posted on speed limit signs, and stop at railroad crossbuck signs.

3. Warning signs alert you to changes in road conditions. They are black on yellow or orange and are usually diamond shaped. Some warning signs are construction, school area, and railroad advance warning signs.

4. Respond to warning signs by increasing your level of alertness, slowing down, and proceeding with caution.

LESSON TWO

5. Informational, or guide, signs include route signs, destination and mileage signs, roadside service signs, and recreational area signs.

6. International signs communicate their meaning by symbols. Some international signs used in the United States are First Aid Station, and Telephone.

LESSON THREE

7. Yellow lane markings divide traffic moving in opposite directions. White lane markings separate traffic traveling in the same direction. If the first line on the pavement to your left is a yellow or white broken line, you may pass another vehicle; if the line is solid, you may not pass.

8. Arrows direct drivers into lanes from which they can turn. Other road markings include lines, symbols, and words to guide drivers and pedestrians in crossing intersections, parking areas, road exit ramps, reversible lanes, and stop lines.

LESSON FOUR

9. Traffic signals have from one to three or more lenses. Those with three lenses can be either vertical or horizontal. The most common lenses are red (Stop), yellow (Do not enter intersection), and green (Go when safe to do so).

10. A red X signal prohibits driving in that lane. A green arrow indicates that you are permitted to drive in that lane. A steady yellow X indicates that you should vacate the lane when it is safe to do so, and a flashing yellow X indicates that the lane may be used with caution.

PROJECTS

1. Find out how intersections in your state are marked where right turn on red is prohibited. Describe what you believe to be the advantages and disadvantages of right turn on red. Try also to discover what there is in common among intersections where right on red is prohibited.

2. Do you find certain signs, signals, or pavement markings confusing? How would you improve them? How would you change their location, shape, size, color, symbols, lettering, numbering, timing, and how often they appear?

CHAPTER 4 REVIEW

BUILDING MATH SKILLS

Reading and Interpreting a Bar Graph

A bar graph presents information in a way that makes it easy to compare quantities.

The bar graph below shows the number of licensed vehicle drivers in different years. The numbers along the vertical axis, going up the left side of the graph, stand for tens of millions. So 1 equals 10 million, 5 equals 50 million, and so on.

The years in which the number of drivers are being compared are written along the bottom of the graph, on the horizontal axis.

Try It Yourself

1. About how many licensed drivers were there in 1962?

2. About how many more licensed drivers were there in 1975 than in 1955? About how many more were there in 1975 than in 1962?

3. Which year shown on the graph had the fewest number of new drivers from the previous year shown?

4. Between which two years shown did the number of licensed drivers nearly double?

5. What is the approximate average number of new licensed drivers each year? (Figure the difference between the last and the first years shown. Then divide by the number of years.)

6. If the trend in numbers of licensed drivers continued, about how many would you expect there were in 1990?

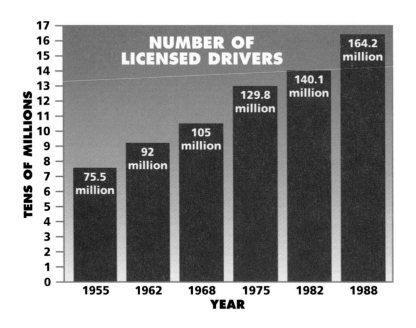

CHAPTER 4 REVIEW

CHAPTER TEST

Write the letter of the answer that best completes each sentence.

1. White lines parallel to the road separate
   a. traffic moving in the same direction.
   b. traffic moving in opposite directions.
   c. cars from trucks.
2. When a police officer is giving hand signals at an intersection, you should
   a. always follow the officer's direction.
   b. follow the officer's directions only if they agree with traffic signals.
   c. proceed with caution.
3. A yield sign indicates that a driver
   a. has the right of way.
   b. may need to stop and wait until the roadway is clear of traffic before proceeding.
   c. must move to a different lane.
4. You approach a stop sign and observe that there are no other vehicles around. You
   a. slow down but continue moving past the sign.
   b. come to a full stop at the sign.
   c. blow your horn and increase your speed.
5. Two solid yellow lines on a roadway indicate that
   a. passing is permitted in either direction.
   b. the left lane may be used only for left turns.
   c. no passing is permitted.
6. When approaching a flashing red traffic signal, you should
   a. slow and proceed with caution.
   b. respond as if it were a stop sign.
   c. immediately turn right.
7. A steady yellow "X" posted above a highway lane indicates that
   a. vehicles should move slowly.
   b. vehicles should move to a different lane.
   c. the lane will become an exit ramp.
8. Blue signs with white lettering indicate
   a. roadside services.
   b. roadway conditions.
   c. construction areas.
9. Shared left-turn lanes are marked by
   a. solid yellow lines.
   b. white arrows pointing in the same direction.
   c. parallel broken yellow lines with white arrows that point left and right.
10. A red arrow indicates
    a. a detour.
    b. a one-way street.
    c. traffic is not allowed in the direction of the arrow.

Write the word or phrase that best completes each sentence.

advance warning   pavement markings
regulatory   high-occupancy vehicle
breakdown lanes   reversible lanes

11. You may be permitted to drive in _____ lanes if your car has two or more passengers.

12. A _____ sign indicates what a driver must or must not do.

13. Lane-use lights are mounted above _____ .

14. Traffic signals, signs, and _____ provide drivers with information.

15. A railroad _____ sign is round and yellow with black markings.

DRIVER'S LOG

In this chapter you have learned about the signs, signals, and markings that communicate information to drivers. Take five minutes to list all that you can remember and tell what they mean. Which ones did you leave out? Write about how you will remember them in the future.

RULES OF THE ROAD

Drivers belong to the society of roadway users. In a smooth running society, members agree to follow the rules. It is important that you learn the rules of the road in order to be a responsible member of the roadway community.

LESSON ONE

Each State Has Administrative Laws

1. Identify the procedures that are regulated by administrative laws.
2. Describe how to comply with administrative laws.

LESSON TWO

Right-of-Way Rules Are Essential

3. Define the meaning of the term *right of way.*
4. Identify when you should yield right of way.

LESSON THREE

Speed Limits Help in Reducing Risk

5. Define the meaning of the following kinds of speed limits: fixed, advisory, and day and night.
6. Explain under what conditions posted speed limits do not apply.

LESSON FOUR

If You Are Involved in a Collision

7. Describe the actions that you should take if you are involved in a collision.

LESSON ONE — Each State Has Administrative Laws

Rules and laws are vital to a smooth-running society. Before you can join the society of drivers, you need to know about its laws and ordinances.

Traffic laws are important for a variety of reasons.

◆ They provide rules for the behavior of drivers.
◆ They help drivers predict what others on the road will do.
◆ They serve as a guide to police and courts.
◆ They promote the orderly flow of traffic and help prevent collisions.

What Are Administrative Laws?

Each state has laws that enable state officials to control the operation of the state's highway transportation system. Among the laws are *administrative laws*, which establish the procedures for:

◆ issuing driver's licenses and learner's permits
◆ registering motor vehicles
◆ financial responsibilities of drivers and owners
◆ minimum safety equipment and care of an automobile

How Do You Comply with Administrative Laws?

To drive and own a car, you must obey your state's motor vehicle laws —beginning with obtaining a license to drive.

Excessive speed can cost you points. Excessive speed also wastes fuel. Be responsible!

Getting a Driver's License

Granting a license to operate any motor vehicle on public highways is a function of state government. The licensing of drivers serves to identify who is a driver, to improve traffic safety, and to provide funding to operate various programs.

In order to be allowed to have a driver's license, you must pass a series of tests. Each state tests people's knowledge of signs, signals, and markings; traffic laws; and safe driving practices. The tests may be written or computerized.

All states test for minimum visual requirements and typically raise questions concerning hearing or special physical conditions. In most states, the last step is a driving test, sometimes called a road or in-vehicle test. You take the driving test to demonstrate that you have vehicle control skills. If you pass these tests and pay the necessary fees, you will receive a driver's license.

Because states have the power to issue licenses, states also have the power to take them away. States can suspend, or take away, licenses for a specified period of time—usually for 30 to 90 days, but less than 365 days. States can also revoke licenses. This means states can take licenses away for a year or more, after which the person whose license has been revoked can apply for another license. Revocation is sometimes permanent for habitual offenders, that is, drivers who repeatedly commit serious traffic violations.

Violations and the Point System

How does the state decide when to take away a person's driver's license? Most states use a *point system*. Various traffic violations "cost" a number of points, depending on their seriousness. When a driver is ticketed for violating a traffic law and is convicted, a report is sent to the state's department of motor vehicles. The points are then put on the driver's record.

If a driver whose license has been suspended continues to get points when the suspension is lifted, the license can be revoked. Some violations are so serious that offenders can lose their licenses immediately upon conviction. These violations include the following:

◆ driving under the influence of alcohol or other drugs
◆ leaving the scene of an accident in which there has been an injury
◆ using a motor vehicle in the commission of a crime

Certificate of Title

States issue a certificate of title when you buy a car. This certificate is proof that you own the car. The state keeps a copy of this title. Anyone selling a car must supply a certificate of title to the buyer. The certificate of title lists the name of the owner and the make, style, vehicle identification number (VIN), and engine number of the car.

Vehicle Registration

Once you purchase a car, you must register it with the state. Once you do so, you will receive a vehicle registration form and license plates. In states where liability insurance is required, you must provide the name of the company who insures your automobile. Registration must be renewed yearly. You should always have your registration in the car.

Insurance

Part of the responsibility of driving is the ability to prove financial responsibility. This means that you must show that you can pay for damages you may cause if you are in a crash that results in death, injury, or property damage to others. You will learn more about automobile insurance in Chapter 15.

CHECKPOINT

1. What administrative laws does every state have?
2. What do administrative laws require you to do?

WHAT WOULD YOU DO?

Where is a good place to keep your car's registration?

Right-of-Way Rules Are Essential

When you drive, sometimes one or more drivers or pedestrians will want to use the same roadway space at the same time that you do. How can you avoid a collision? You can determine who should go first and who should wait. To do so, you need to know the rules about right of way.

What Is Right of Way?

As a good driver, you will sometimes have to yield right of way, or let others go first. *Never assume that you automatically have the right of way.* Right of way is always given by someone. Right-of-way laws are very clear in identifying who shall yield to whom in almost every situation. However, human beings make mistakes. The rule that you must yield right of way in order to avoid a collision overrides all the others.

Right-of-way laws of all states are based on the Uniform Vehicle Code. Therefore, the laws about when drivers should yield the right of way are the same from state to state.

When Should You Yield the Right of Way?

Here are three situations in which you must yield right of way.

◆ You must yield to any emergency vehicle, such as an ambulance, that has its sirens on and its lights flashing. Move to the far right of the road and stop if you are on a two-way, two-lane roadway or on a multilane

highway going in the same direction as the emergency vehicle. If you are going in the opposite direction on a multilane road, you do not have to stop, but you should move to the right.

◆ You must yield to blind persons carrying a white cane or using a guide dog, no matter where they cross.

◆ You must yield to any pedestrians at crosswalks.

On the following pages, you will find some of the right-of-way situations that come up most often. In each picture, the red car must yield. In all these situations, drivers must yield to pedestrians who are crossing at crosswalks.

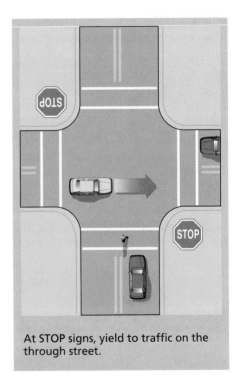

At STOP signs, yield to traffic on the through street.

When you are on a side street approaching a well-traveled road, stop at the intersection even if a stop sign is not present. Proceed when you are sure you have enough time and space to do so.

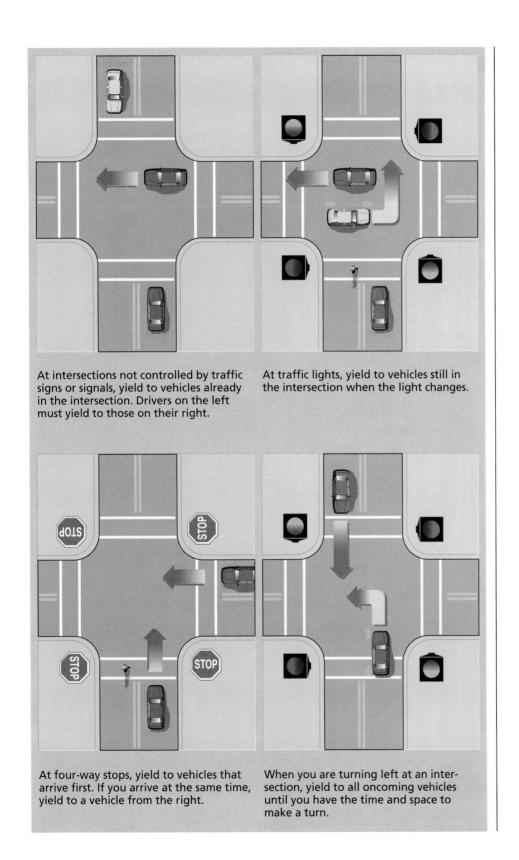

At intersections not controlled by traffic signs or signals, yield to vehicles already in the intersection. Drivers on the left must yield to those on their right.

At traffic lights, yield to vehicles still in the intersection when the light changes.

At four-way stops, yield to vehicles that arrive first. If you arrive at the same time, yield to a vehicle from the right.

When you are turning left at an intersection, yield to all oncoming vehicles until you have the time and space to make a turn.

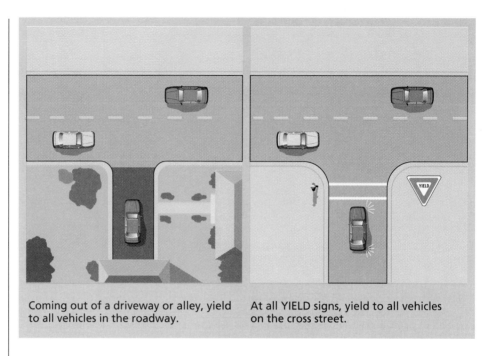

Coming out of a driveway or alley, yield to all vehicles in the roadway.

At all YIELD signs, yield to all vehicles on the cross street.

WHAT WOULD YOU DO?

To whom would you yield? Why?

One of the most common violations in fatal collisions involving more than one car is a driver's failure to yield right of way. Remember, just because you are on a major street or are on the right at a four-way stop, don't assume that others will yield to you. Be alert! Sometimes it is safer to yield even if the other driver is required by law to yield. To manage risk, you should remember that others will not always obey traffic signs and signals. Make yourself visible and identify an escape route in case something goes wrong.

When signaling a move left or right into a lane being used by other drivers, you must yield to any vehicle that is passing or appears to be so close that it presents a danger.

On a nondivided highway, drivers must stop when meeting or overtaking a school bus that is loading or unloading children. Laws vary from state to state, so it is important to know the school bus laws for states in which you will be traveling.

CHECKPOINT

3. What does *right of way* mean?
4. In which situations should you yield the right of way?

Speed Limits Help in Reducing Risk

The most important requirements for safe driving are visibility, time, and space. Together they determine the speed at which you can travel safely. What is a safe speed? Posted maximum speed limits give guidelines to answer this question, but only under ideal conditions.

Speed limits are chosen carefully to protect you and other drivers. Traffic engineers study road conditions and evaluate the road surface, the average amount of traffic, and any hidden dangers. They also know how many collisions have happened at any given location. A speed limit is decided upon only after all these factors have been taken into consideration. Further studies may also be conducted to see if limits should be lowered as congestion increases.

What Kinds of Speed Limits Are There?

All states post speed limits on their roadways. These speed-limit signs reflect the *maximum* speed at which you can drive under the best of conditions. For example, you would not drive at the maximum allowable speed in the middle of a snowstorm, but you might do so on a clear day.

Posted speed limits do not tell you at what speed to drive. They only say you cannot safely go faster or, in special cases, slower than the speed shown. Most states have speed limits posted even off interstate highways. All states also have basic speed limits

that mean you cannot drive at speeds slower or faster than conditions safely permit. What does this mean to you as a driver?

Fixed Speed Limits

Fixed speed limits are the maximum and minimum speeds that a car may be driven on a particular roadway. Drivers may never travel at a speed faster than the maximum posted speed. Drivers whose speed is greater than the posted maximum speed can be arrested and, if convicted, made to pay a fine.

Drivers can also be arrested and ticketed for driving too slowly. A car traveling below the minimum posted speed limit can be dangerous to other drivers who must suddenly slow down when they approach this car. Slow drivers can also make other drivers nervous or angry and cause traffic tie-ups and congestion.

Tips for New Drivers

Being Pulled Over

What should you do if you are pulled over by the police?

- Stay calm.
- Remain in your car, keeping your hands visible.
- Produce requested documents quickly and efficiently.
- Be courteous. Do not argue with, insult, or touch the officer.
- Do not lie, cry, or make excuses.
- *Never* try to bribe the officer. Bribery is illegal!

Note the advisory speed limit sign. You cannot exceed 35 mph on this curve. ▶

Advisory Speed Limits

All roads are not straight and flat. There are hills, curves, and other changes in the roadway. Drivers need to adjust their speed for these chang-es. Advisory speed limits interrupt normal driving speed for a limited time. They provide guidelines for adjusting speed.

For example, a warning sign is usually posted before a sharp curve on two-lane highways and exit ramps. If the curve is very sharp, a square yellow advisory speed sign may be posted beneath the warning sign to advise you of the maximum safe speed for that curve. In addition, chevron-shaped markings may be used to emphasize the risk. Like all speed limits, advisory limits are based on ideal road conditions.

Day and Night Speed Limits

Some states have lower speed limits at night. Night driving is more dangerous because it is hard to see in the dark. Driving at a lower speed gives drivers more time to search for visual clues and to identify objects or conditions that could increase risk.

THE SOCIAL STUDIES CONNECTION

If you drive in Mexico or Canada, you will see signs in Spanish or French. In both countries, another "language" is used on signs as well. It is the "language" of the metric system of measurement.

Distances on destination signs in Mexico and Canada are given in kilometers rather than in miles. Similarly, speed limit signs refer not to *miles per hour* but to *kilometers per hour*. The speed limit sign you see here means 100 kilometers per hour (km/h), or about 65 miles per hour. You can figure out whether you are traveling within the allowable speed limit by converting kilometers per hour to miles per hour. To make a rough estimate, take half of the posted speed limit and add a little more. Half of 100 is 50, and a little more is 60 or 65. For a closer estimate, take $\frac{5}{8}$ of the posted speed limit. Then check your speedometer to see whether you are traveling between 60 and 65 miles per hour.

When you drive in another country, make sure you know whether that country uses the metric system of measurement. If it does, remember to account for that fact. To help you out, the speedometers in many car models record speeds both in miles per hour and in kilometers per hour.

What Are Basic Speed Laws?

No matter what speed limit is posted, all states have a basic speed rule in their traffic laws that says: *Always drive at a speed that is reasonable and proper for existing conditions.*

A safe speed at any time is determined by the type and condition of the road and by such factors as the traffic, weather, and light. Your ability to manage visibility, time, and space also determines what is a safe speed at any given time.

By law, drivers must go slower than the minimum posted speed if poor road or traffic conditions make that speed unsafe. In such cases, the arresting officer must show that the driver was going too fast for the weather, road, or traffic conditions at that time.

Driving faster than the posted speed limit is never safe or reasonable and is always illegal.

Take note of these facts about speed. The higher the speed:

◆ the less time the driver has to spot hazards and take action
◆ the greater the time and distance it takes to stop a vehicle
◆ the greater the chance the car will skid or roll over on a turn
◆ the greater the force of impact will be in a collision
◆ the greater the personal injuries and property damage will be in a collision

Drivers can also be arrested for driving too slowly. In these cases, the officer must show that the speed was so slow that it caused danger to other drivers going at a reasonable speed.

◀ *A speed of 30 mph may not be reasonable and proper in snowy weather.*

CHECKPOINT

5. What are the different kinds of speed limits?
6. What are the basic speed laws?

WHAT WOULD YOU DO?

It's raining, and you see this sign. At what speed would you drive? Why?

If You Are Involved in a Collision

No matter how good a driver you are, there is no guarantee that you can always avoid a collision. Human suffering, loss of time, legal problems, and great expense can result from a collision regardless of who is at fault.

What Should You Do If You Are in a Collision?

After a collision some people may panic or react in strange ways. They may also be in a state of shock. If you are in a collision, you should try to remain calm. Remember that the collision scene is no place to begin arguing with the other driver or with the police. Do not accuse anyone of causing the collision and do not admit fault yourself. Sign only forms given to you by the police. Do not sign any other statements at the scene. You have the legal right to consult an attorney before making any statement.

If you are involved in a collision, you should:

Stop immediately Drivers who do not stop when involved in a collision are breaking the law. Unless someone was seriously injured or killed, and if you can still drive your car, try to move it off the roadway and out of traffic. Turn off the ignition to prevent the risk of fire.

Warn others if possible If you can't move your car out of traffic, you must do everything you can to notify other drivers that there is a problem ahead. Turn on your hazard flashers. If you have flares or reflecting triangles, set them up at least 100 feet ahead of and behind the collision scene. If you don't have them, ask someone, possibly another driver who offers to help, to stand at the side of the road out of traffic and wave a flashlight or light-colored cloth to warn oncoming traffic.

Give aid to the injured Check for injured persons. Try to make them comfortable, but do not move them unless you know what you are doing. Moving an injured person can result in more serious injury. Do

Collisions are frightening, but knowing what to do if you are involved in one can help you to stay calm.

what you can to provide first aid. (You will learn more about first aid in Chapter 14.)

Try to get medical help If you or someone who has stopped to help has a car phone or a CB, use it to call an ambulance. Or try to flag down another driver to go for aid or call the appropriate emergency services.

Call the police By law, a collision resulting in injury, death, or property damage above a given dollar value must be reported to the police. A few states require that all collisions be reported no matter what the damages are.

Exchange information Drivers involved in collisions should exchange information with the other driver and any passengers. You should exchange drivers' and passengers' names and addresses, driver's license information, names of insurance companies, and vehicle registration information. If you are involved in a collision with a parked car, you should try to locate the owner. If you cannot, leave a note under the windshield wiper blades containing the same information that you would exchange at any other collision scene. For your records, write down the license number of the car that is struck.

Get names and addresses of witnesses You have already exchanged information with the other driver and passengers. If there are witnesses at the scene, write down their names and addresses too. You might need them to verify your account of the collision.

Stay at the scene If you are uninjured, remain at the scene of the collision until your help is no longer needed. If people have been seriously

injured or killed, remain at the scene until the police allow you to leave.

Make accident reports Drivers involved in any collision that results in injury should make a written report to the police and to the department of motor vehicles. States have different laws about reporting property damage under certain amounts. Know what your state law requires. Check your state driver's manual or motor vehicle department to get this information. If you do not file a report, your driver's license could be suspended regardless of whether or not the collision was your fault. Of course, you should also inform your insurance company.

See a doctor. Even if you have been treated at the scene of the collision, be sure to see your own doctor. Some injuries do not appear right away. Be safe and get yourself checked out thoroughly.

▲
Make a written accident report to the police, even if you have talked with them at the collision scene.

Death rates are higher for occupants of small pickup trucks and small utility vehicles than for any other type of passenger vehicles, including the smallest cars.

W. Randall Leader, Trooper II
Nebraska State Patrol

W. Randall Leader

Over 200 people die each day because someone didn't know or simply chose not to obey a traffic law. Traffic laws have created an order on our roads.

As a state trooper, I have seen what happens when traffic laws are not obeyed. Because I have seen the destruction caused by crashes, I feel it is my duty to not only explain laws to motorists, but also to enforce laws whenever it is necessary. As a motorist, it is *your* duty to reduce the risk of injury or death by knowing and obeying all traffic laws.

WHAT WOULD YOU DO?

You have had a collision. The other driver says that there's no need to get the police involved. What would you tell the driver?

Legal consequences of a collision can be very serious. If a collision is the result of your having broken a traffic law, you may, depending on the severity of the crash:

◆ be fined and have to pay court costs.

◆ have your license suspended or revoked.

◆ be sent to jail.

If it is found that you were intoxicated or under the influence of drugs at the time of the collision, the penalties are even more severe.

If you pass a collision scene and help appears needed, you should stop well off the roadway and offer whatever assistance that you can. However, if the situation appears under control, keep going. Stopping at the scene of a collision when it is unnecessary for you to do so can cause additional hazards for others who are using the roadway.

CHECKPOINT

7. What are your responsibilities if you are in a collision?

CHAPTER 5 REVIEW

KEY POINTS

LESSON ONE

1. Every state has administrative laws that set standards for issuing driver's licenses and learner's permits, certificates of title, motor vehicle registration, and financial responsibility requirements.

2. To comply with the administrative laws, drivers must obtain a driver's license, maintain an acceptable driving record, obtain a certificate of title when buying a car, register the vehicle, and prove financial responsibility by obtaining automobile insurance.

LESSON TWO

3. *Right of way* means that one driver is required to yield when making a move in traffic.

4. You must yield the right of way to emergency vehicles, blind persons, and pedestrians in crosswalks. At intersections not controlled by signals or signs, yield to vehicles already in the intersection. At stop or yield signs, yield to traffic on the cross street. At four-way stops, yield to vehicles that arrive first; if you arrive at the same time, yield to the vehicle at the right. Coming out of a driveway or alley, yield to all vehicles in the roadway. At traffic lights, vehicles still in the intersection when the light changes must be given the right of way. When moving into a lane used by other drivers, yield to passing vehicles. Stop when a school bus stops.

LESSON THREE

5. Fixed speed limits are the maximum and minimum speeds that a car may be driven on a particular roadway. Advisory speed limits provide guidelines when an adjustment in speed is needed, such as when approaching a sharp curve in the road. Day and night speed limits take into account the increased difficulty of night driving. A lower speed limit is posted for night driving.

6. The basic speed law states, *Always drive at a speed that is reasonable and proper for existing conditions.* For example, if the weather is bad or the road condition is poor or traffic is heavy, a driver can be arrested for speeding even if that driver is within the posted maximum speed.

LESSON FOUR

7. Drivers involved in a collision must stop immediately and turn off the ignition, warn others if possible, give aid to the injured, try to get medical help, call the police, exchange relevant information, get names and addresses of witnesses, stay at the scene, make accident reports, and see a doctor to check out any possible injuries.

PROJECTS

1. Find out the location of your area's department of motor vehicles. Visit it or write a letter asking for a copy of your state's driver's manual. Do the same with two neighboring states. Report on laws that are the same as the laws in your state and those that are different.

2. Ask at least four drivers if they can name five facts about speed. Prepare a report on your findings. You may want to compare your report with those of others in your class and put together a combined report on drivers' attitudes and knowledge about speeding and speed laws.

BUILDING MAP SKILLS

Using Coordinates

You want to find Port Allen, Louisiana, on the map. How can you do that quickly?

First find Port Allen on the map index. It is listed alphabetically. Beside the name you will see H-12. These are *coordinates*.

Look at the map. There are letters along the left side and numbers along the bottom. Find the H and put your left finger on it. Now find the 12. Move your left finger straight across the map until it is above the 12. Port Allen is in that area.

Notice the ● beside Port Allen. This means it is a county seat. A ● stands for a town, a ● stands for a city, and * stands for the state capital. If you scan the map quickly, you can see that the names of cities and towns are written in different-size type. The larger the type, the greater the population.

Try It Yourself

1. Find Denson on the map. Is its population greater or less than the population of Port Allen?

2. Find Franklinton and Watson. Which is a county seat?

3. Find Baton Rouge and New Orleans. Which is the capital of Louisiana? Which has the smaller population?

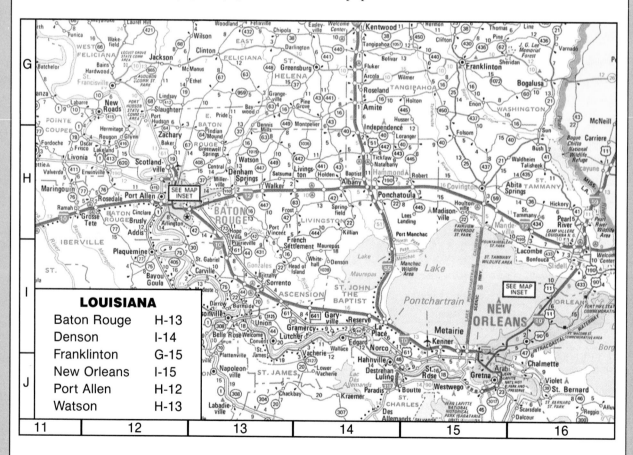

LOUISIANA

Baton Rouge	H-13
Denson	I-14
Franklinton	G-15
New Orleans	I-15
Port Allen	H-12
Watson	H-13

CHAPTER 5 REVIEW

CHAPTER TEST

Write the letter of the answer that best completes each sentence.

1. If you are in a collision and the other driver is injured, you should
   a. go home and call an ambulance.
   b. stay at the scene until police arrive.
   c. run away as fast as you can.
2. Posted speed limits
   a. tell you at what speed you must drive.
   b. are only on interstate highways.
   c. indicate you cannot safely go faster or slower than certain speeds.
3. The higher the speed, the more likely it is that a vehicle will
   a. develop engine problems.
   b. roll over on a turn.
   c. get excellent gas mileage.
4. Administrative laws set standards for
   a. rules of the road.
   b. minimum speed allowed.
   c. motor vehicle registration.
5. On a two-lane street, an ambulance is coming from behind with its siren blaring. You should
   a. pull over to the left and stop.
   b. pull over to the right and stop.
   c. increase your speed.
6. At an intersection, a person with a guide dog steps off the curb. You
   a. tap your horn and continue forward.
   b. stop to yield right of way.
   c. drive around the person.
7. Your driver's license can be revoked if you
   a. are convicted of DUI or DWI.
   b. get into a collision.
   c. drive below the minimum speed limit.

8. Two drivers who have been in a collision should
   a. avoid any contact with each other or witnesses.
   b. split the cost of any damages.
   c. exchange names, addresses, and other information.
9. Right-of-way rules determine
   a. minimum speed limits in each state.
   b. procedures for turning right.
   c. who should yield right of way.
10. You must pass a series of tests in order to
    a. increase your number of driving points.
    b. obtain a driver's license.
    c. obtain a certificate of title.

Write the word or phrase that best completes each sentence.

advisory speed limits   Uniform Vehicle Code
        basic speed rule   accident report
vehicle registration information   point system

11. The _____ states that you should always drive at a speed that is reasonable and proper for existing conditions.

12. If you are involved in a collision, you should make a(n) _____ .

13. Most states use a _____ to keep track of traffic violations by individual drivers.

14. All states have right-of-way laws that are based on the _____ .

15. _____ provide guidelines for adjusting speed to roadway conditions.

DRIVER'S LOG

In this chapter, you have learned about the rules and laws that govern the roadways and the motorists who use them. Write about the five rules you think you will have the most trouble remembering. Explain what you will do to jog your memory.

GETTING TO KNOW YOUR CAR

It is important for you to know and understand your car's systems and the checks you should make before you start driving. Understanding the function and purpose of each system and what the lights and gauges can tell you will help you to manage risk.

CHAPTER 6 OBJECTIVES

LESSON ONE

Comfort and Control Systems and Risk Management

1. Describe four devices that help make you comfortable in a car.
2. List six devices that enable you to control a car and explain what each does.

LESSON TWO

The Visibility and Protective Systems of Your Car

3. Name at least five aids to visibility.
4. Describe four features that are designed to protect you and your passengers from injury.
5. Name three antitheft devices.

LESSON THREE

Information and Communication Systems

6. Name at least seven devices that provide information about your car.
7. Name and describe how at least five devices let you communicate with drivers and pedestrians.

LESSON FOUR

Checks and Procedures to Use Before Driving

8. Describe six checks you should make before entering your car.
9. Describe five checks you should make after entering your car.

Comfort and Control Systems and Risk Management

Suppose you're driving along and suddenly you see a light blink on your control panel. What does it mean? If you don't know the answer, it means that you don't know your car. Not knowing puts you, your passengers, and other drivers at risk.

Cars are equipped with a variety of comfort and control devices. Before you begin to drive, you have to know what these devices do, where they are located, and how they operate. For specific information, refer to the owner's manual.

What Devices Help Make You Comfortable in a Car?

You must concentrate while driving, and being uncomfortable can distract you from the driving task. Cars have comfort devices to help you, but you have to know how to use them to their best advantage. Some comfort devices help to reduce muscle strain. Others control the interior climate of your car and make driving less tiring.

Seat-Position Controls

The driver's seat must be comfortable and it must suit the driver. It should provide good visibility and access to the controls.

Many cars have power seat-adjustment controls, which allow you to adjust the seat up or down, forward or back, or tilt the seat to better fit the car to the driver.

In cars without power seats, the seat-adjustment lever is usually located on the lower left side or front of the driver's seat. Pulling back or up on the lever allows the driver to adjust the seat forward or back for better access to car controls and switches.

Steering Wheel

Many cars have an adjustable (tilt-wheel) steering wheel. Drivers can adjust the steering wheel to a position that provides maximum comfort and control.

Air Conditioner and Heater

Use the air conditioner to cool the car and lower the humidity, and use the heater to warm the car interior and clear fogged windows. Never overheat your car. An overheated car can cause drowsiness.

Air Vents

Adjustable vents allow outside air to flow into the car. They are usually located on the dashboard or on the front lower left and right sides.

How Can You Control the Movement of Your Car?

The parts of a car's control system enable you to start and stop the car and control its speed and direction.

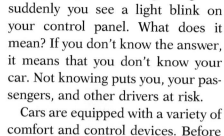

The refrigerated truck was patented in 1949 by Frederick McKinley Jones, an African-American inventor. Until that time, fresh produce and other perishable food had to be transported by railroad. The refrigerated truck made it possible for towns not on railroad routes to receive regular deliveries of these products.

Ignition Switch

Inserting and turning the key in a car's ignition switch starts the engine. This switch is usually found on the steering column. The ignition switch normally has five positions: Accessory, Lock, Off, On, and Start.

Selector Lever for Automatic Transmission

On cars having an automatic transmission, you choose the gear you want by moving the gear selector lever. The gear selector lever is located either on the steering column or

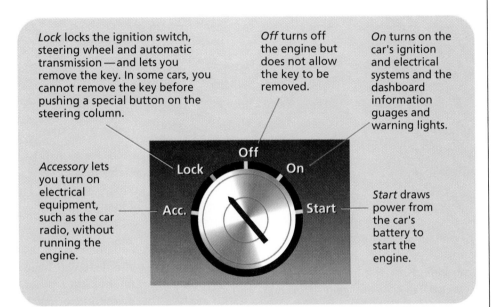

Lock locks the ignition switch, steering wheel and automatic transmission—and lets you remove the key. In some cars, you cannot remove the key before pushing a special button on the steering column.

Off turns off the engine but does not allow the key to be removed.

On turns on the car's ignition and electrical systems and the dashboard information guages and warning lights.

Accessory lets you turn on electrical equipment, such as the car radio, without running the engine.

Start draws power from the car's battery to start the engine.

When a car with power steering stalls, the power steering is lost. If the car cannot be started and needs to be rolled off the road, the steering wheel will be very difficult to turn.

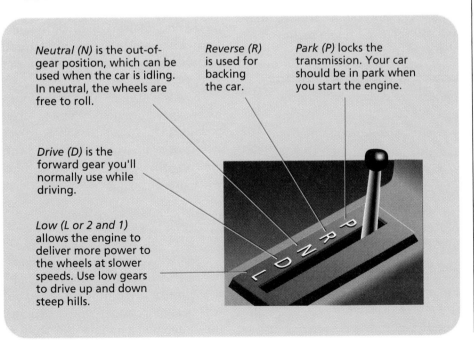

Neutral (N) is the out-of-gear position, which can be used when the car is idling. In neutral, the wheels are free to roll.

Reverse (R) is used for backing the car.

Park (P) locks the transmission. Your car should be in park when you start the engine.

Drive (D) is the forward gear you'll normally use while driving.

Low (L or 2 and 1) allows the engine to deliver more power to the wheels at slower speeds. Use low gears to drive up and down steep hills.

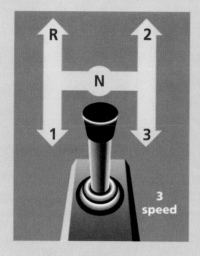
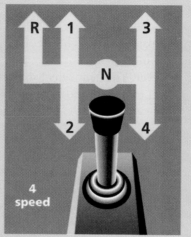
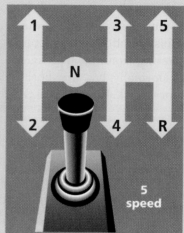

Cars with a manual transmission have a gearshift instead of a selector lever. The gearshift can have 3, 4, or 5 speeds.

on the floor to the right of the driver's seat.

A vehicle with automatic transmission will start only in Park or Neutral. Usually drivers start from Park, because Park is the gear in which they leave the car. In this position, a vehicle will not roll. A car in Neutral *will* roll if parked on an incline.

Braking in an Emergency

If your foot brakes fail, use your parking brake to stop the car in an emergency. First:

1. Downshift.

2. Then *gradually* use your parking brake until the car comes to a stop.

Using the parking brake to stop your car may damage the braking system, so use it *only* in an emergency.

Gearshift for Manual Transmission

On cars having a manual transmission, you choose the gear you need by stepping down on the clutch pedal and moving the gearshift (or stick shift). The gearshift is usually located on the floor to the right of the driver's seat, although occasionally you'll find the gearshift on the side of the steering column.

The gearshift may have three, four, or five speed positions, plus a reverse position. The fifth gear serves as an *overdrive* gear, which allows the engine to run more slowly and fuel-efficiently at high speeds.

Clutch Pedal

Cars with manual transmissions have a clutch pedal located to the left of the brake pedal. In Chapter 7 you will read more about how to operate the clutch pedal and the gearshift.

Steering Wheel

You control the direction of your front wheels by turning the steering wheel. In cars equipped with *power steering*, it takes little effort to turn the steering wheel.

Accelerator or Gas Pedal

You move the car and control its speed by pressing on the accelerator, or gas pedal, with your right foot. The greater the pressure you put on the accelerator, the more fuel the carburetor or fuel injectors feed to the engine. The more fuel that flows into the engine, the faster the car will go.

Cruise Control

Cruise (or *speed*) *control* is an optional car feature that lets you maintain a desired speed without keeping your foot on the accelerator. Cruise control is intended for highway driving, in situations where you can maintain a constant rate of speed.

To use cruise control, first accelerate to the speed of the traffic, then reduce speed by 2 or 3 mph. Set the control button or switch located on the turn-indicator arm or on the steering wheel. You can switch off cruise control whenever you choose, or you can cancel it by tapping the brake pedal.

Although cruise control is a convenience, think when you use it. Cruise control may lead you to be less alert than you should be. It lessens your ability to reduce speed by easing up on the accelerator and can also cause a skid if you must suddenly brake on a slick surface.

Brake Pedal

You slow or stop the car by pressing down on the brake pedal. *Power* (or *power-assisted*) *brakes* require less foot pressure to operate than nonpower brakes. However, power brakes do *not* shorten the distance needed to stop the car.

Parking Brake

The parking brake, also called an *emergency* or *hand brake*, is used to keep a parked car from rolling. The parking-brake control can be a small pedal located to the left side of the floor panel, a hand lever located under the left side of the dashboard, or a floor-mounted hand lever located to the right of the driver's seat.

CHECKPOINT

1. What equipment is designed to make drivers comfortable?
2. What devices control the car? What does each one do?

Cruise control wastes fuel if used in areas with steep hills or mountains.

WHAT WOULD YOU DO?

You're driving in the right lane at 50 mph. What actions would you take to minimize risk? What car controls will come into play?

The Visibility and Protective Systems of Your Car

Always be sure that your head- and taillights are clean. Dirty lights reduce visibility.

Some safety features reduce driving risk by aiding visibility. Others reduce or control risk by protecting the driver and passengers from injury. Still others guard the car against theft.

What Devices Aid Visibility?

Seeing and being seen are critical to controlling risk and making driving easier and safer. A car's visibility system better enables you to see the roadway and maximizes the ability of others to see you.

Lights

Using your headlights helps other roadway users to see you both at night and during the day. Headlights help you to see better at night, in dim light, and in bad weather. Taillights and side-marker lights better enable drivers and other highway users to see your car.

Headlights can be switched to either *low* or more intense *high beams*. Most of the time you'll be using the low beams.

The switch to turn on your lights is found either on the dashboard or on a stem to the left side of the steering column. In most cars, you pull the lever toward you to change to high beams. In some older cars, the high-/low-beam switch is a button located on the left side of the floor panel.

When you turn on your headlights, your taillights and side-marker lights also come on. In addition, the dashboard gauges, dials, and controls light up. You can dim or brighten these dashboard lights by turning a knob located on the instrument panel or turn-indicator lever.

In many cars, the same light switch knob used to turn on exterior lights can also control the dashboard-light brightness and turn on the interior dome light.

Windshield Wipers and Washer

Cars normally have two-, three-, or variable-speed front-windshield wipers. Some cars also have a rear-window wiper.

A variable-speed wiper allows the driver to set the wipers to move at a very slow or very rapid rate. This feature is useful when just an occasional wipe is needed to keep the window clear, as during a light drizzle. It is also helpful during a driving rain when a faster rate is needed.

The windshield washer squirts water or an antifreeze solution onto the windshield. The liquid is stored in a container under the hood.

Sun Visors

Sun visors can be moved up and down and turned to the side to prevent the sun from shining into the driver's eyes. However, be careful not to let the visors interfere with your view of the roadway or traffic to the side.

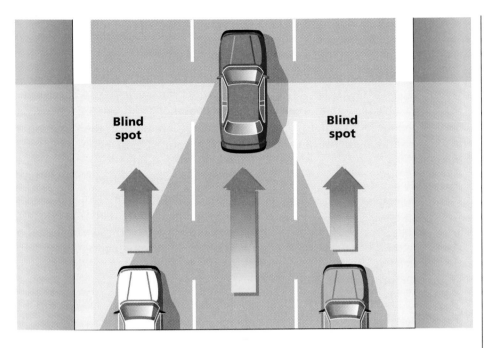

◄

Look over your shoulder for traffic in your blind spots before changing lanes, and try never to travel in another driver's blind spots.

Defroster (Defogger)

Use the defroster—sometimes called the defogger—to clear moisture or frost from the front, rear, and side windows. Heat from the defroster can also make it easier to scrape ice from the windows. In most cars, front and rear defrosters have separate controls.

Rearview and Side-View Mirrors

Your car's rearview and side-view mirrors provide vision to the rear and sides of the roadway. Even when correctly adjusted, however, they cannot eliminate all *blind spots*—areas of the road that you cannot see in the mirrors. For this reason, you should

THE SCIENCE CONNECTION

When you are planning to change lanes, you must be certain your blind spots are clear. One way you can check your blind spots is by using a convex mirror.

A convex mirror is a curved mirror in which reflection takes place on the outer surface. Its center bulges out toward the viewer. Most large auto-supply stores and hardware stores sell these mirrors.

To use a convex mirror, fasten it to the corner of the side-view mirror on the driver's side. (Many convex mirrors have adhesive backing so they can be placed directly on the side-view mirror.)

With the convex mirror, you can see along the entire driver's side of the car. However, be aware that what you see in a convex mirror is actually closer than it appears. Use a convex mirror to help you see along the side better. Remember, however, that it is only an aid in reducing the size of your blind spots. You still need to check over your shoulders.

never rely exclusively on your mirrors when backing, changing lanes, or making turns. You need to turn your head and look over both shoulders to scan the road fully.

For night driving, many rearview mirrors can be adjusted to reduce the glare from headlights of cars behind you.

What Features Protect You and Your Passengers from Injury?

Your car's protective features help to reduce risk by guarding you and your passengers against injury in case of a collision or sudden emergency maneuver.

Some safety features, such as air bags, are *passive* devices. Passive devices operate without the user having to do anything. Other features, such as manual safety belts, require riders to take some action to protect themselves.

Safety Belts

Drivers and passengers should always wear safety belts—preferably, shoulder-lap belts—whenever the car is in motion. If you are wearing a shoulder-lap belt at the time of a crash, your risk of being killed is reduced by about *50 percent.*

Safety belts protect the wearer against injury in a collision. They lessen the chance that you or your passengers will be thrown against the dashboard, through the windshield, or out a door that has sprung open in a crash. In addition, safety belts help keep you behind the wheel and in control of the car if you have to swerve or brake abruptly or are struck by another vehicle.

A growing number of states have passed laws that require the driver and front-seat passengers to wear safety belts. All 50 states have laws requiring very young children to ride only in special safety-tested and approved car seats.

Glancing often in your rearview and side-view mirrors helps you to scan all around your car. ▶

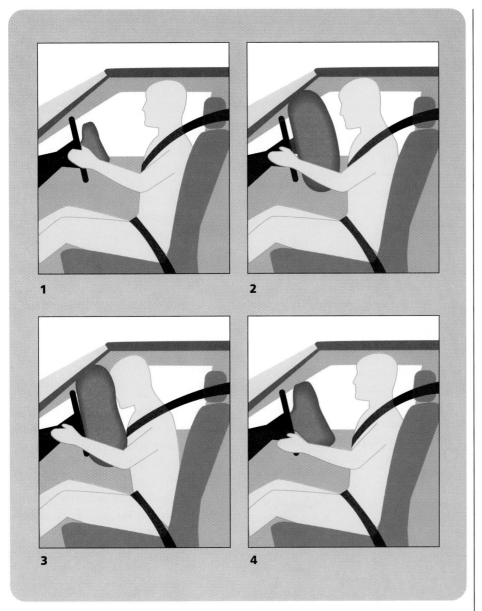

◀

In less than one second, airbags (1) begin to inflate on impact, (2) become fully inflated, (3) cushion the driver from the frontal blow, and (4) deflate.

Air Bags

An increasing number of cars are now equipped with air bags, which inflate automatically in a frontal crash, then deflate again in a mere fraction of a second. Air bags are extremely effective in preventing injuries in front-end collisions. They do not reduce the need for wearing a safety belt.

Head Restraints

Head restraints are standard equipment on front-seat backs and optional on the rear seats of some cars. These padded restraints protect against whiplash (neck injury), especially when your car is hit from behind. To get the maximum benefit from head restraints, make sure that they are properly adjusted. Head

Nearly one out of seven recovered stolen cars still have the keys in them!

WHAT WOULD YOU DO?

What is the driver doing wrong? What would you tell her?

restraints should be high enough to make contact with the back of your head, not the base of your skull.

Door Locks

Keep car doors locked. Locked doors not only are less likely to open in a crash, but they also help prevent uninvited people from entering your car when you're stopped.

Structural Features

Car makers build a wide range of safety features into their cars. Safety features include tempered safety glass windows, impact-resistant bumpers, protective padding on the dashboard and roof, and energy-absorbing steering columns and instrument panels, and childproof door locks that are controlled by the driver. Other factors, such as a car's size and weight, also help determine how well occupants are protected in a crash.

What Devices Guard Against Car Theft?

Car theft is a nationwide problem. Various devices help to protect your car against thieves and vandals.

Ignition Buzzer

When your key is in the ignition switch and you open the driver's door, you will hear a buzz or other sound to remind you to take your key with you when you leave the car.

Locks

Cars are equipped with various locks, including door locks, a steering-column lock, and locks on the trunk, hood, and gas tank.

Alarms and Other Antitheft Devices

A wide range of antitheft devices is available for cars, ranging from elaborate alarm systems to disabling devices that keep the car from starting or prevent the steering wheel from turning. Some car security systems can be turned on or off by remote control using a keychain transmitter. There are even car-tracking systems, which use transmitters concealed in the car to enable police to locate the vehicle if it is stolen.

CHECKPOINT

3. What devices aid your ability to see and be seen?
4. What features help protect you and your passengers from injury in the event of a collision?
5. What devices might prevent the theft of a car?

As you drive, you gather information about other roadway users, the roadway itself, and off-road conditions by scanning in all directions. You get information about the workings of your own car by checking the instruments, gauges, and lights on the dashboard.

While you gather information, you're also communicating information. That is, you're letting other roadway users know where you are and what you intend to do.

What Devices Provide Information About Your Car?

Drivers need to know how fast they are going, how far they have gone, and how their car systems are working. The instruments, gauges, and lights on your dashboard can give you this information.

Speedometer and Odometer

The speedometer shows, in miles per hour and kilometers per hour, how fast your car is moving. Keep track of how fast you're going by checking your speedometer frequently.

The odometer keeps track of the total number of miles the car has been driven. Some cars also have a separate trip odometer, which records the distance driven between two places or over a certain period of time.

Fuel Gauge

Your fuel gauge shows how close to full—or empty—your fuel tank is. Consult your owner's manual to find out exactly how many gallons your tank will hold.

Alternator Gauge or Warning Light

Your car's alternator provides electricity to keep the engine running, recharge the battery, and operate such equipment as lights and radio. If the alternator does not produce enough power, the electricity stored in your battery will be drained. When that starts to happen, the alternator gauge will indicate "discharge" or a red warning light will come on.

When the alternator does not work properly, turn off unnecessary elec-

A warning light flashing on alerts you to a problem, but does not tell you what is wrong. Take your car to a mechanic as soon as possible. Do not drive any farther than you absolutely must.

It is time to refuel when the needle on your fuel gauge reaches the red area.
▼

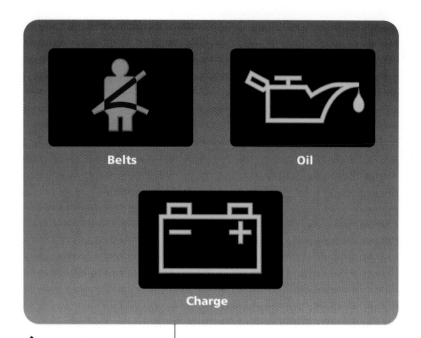

Belts

Oil

Charge

▲
The safety-belt light turns red when you start the car to remind you to buckle up.

Brake Warning Light

Most cars have a brake warning light. When it goes on, you might be low on brake fluid, the fluid is leaking, or the brakes are not working properly. Check with a mechanic immediately.

Other Dashboard Lights

Your *parking-brake light* reminds you to release the parking brake before moving the car. A *high-beam indicator light* shows when your car's high-beam headlights are on, and a *safety-belt warning light and buzzer* remind you to fasten your safety belt.

trical devices and check with a mechanic as soon as possible. If you delay, your battery will die.

Temperature Gauge or Warning Light

The temperature gauge or light lets you know if your engine temperature is too high. Overheating can damage your engine. If it overheats, get off the road as soon as possible and have the problem checked.

Oil-Pressure Gauge or Warning Light

The oil-pressure gauge warns you when the pressure at which oil is being pumped to the engine is low. To avoid serious engine damage, stop driving as soon as possible and consult a mechanic.

Note that the oil-pressure gauge or light does not indicate how much oil is in the engine. You need to check the oil dipstick for that information.

How Can You Communicate with Other Roadway Users?

Other drivers need to know where you are and what you are planning to do. You can't talk to them verbally, but your car has a number of devices that you can use to communicate with other roadway users. Get to know these devices.

Taillights

Like headlights and side-marker lights, taillights help other drivers and pedestrians to see your car. Taillights also help communicate your intentions.

In addition to red taillights that come on when you turn on your headlights or parking lights, the back of your car is equipped with red *brake lights*, white *backup lights*, and red or amber *turn indicators*. All cars manufactured since 1986 also have a third red brake light located in the bottom or over the top center of the rear window.

Brake lights go on when you step on the brake, to warn other drivers that you are slowing or stopping. The backup lights signal that you've shifted into reverse and intend to back up.

One other light on the back of your car is the *license-plate light*, which comes on with headlights and parking lights. This light is required by law and aids in identifying vehicles.

Directional (Turn) Signals

Your flashing red or amber directional, or turn, signals—sometimes called "blink lights" or "blinkers"—tell other drivers that you plan to turn or change lanes. To operate the signals, move the turn-indicator arm up for right or down for left.

Normally, the signal lever clicks into position, then clicks back again when you straighten the wheel. If the signal doesn't stop flashing, move the lever back manually.

Emergency Flashers (Hazard Lights)

The emergency-flasher switch is usually located on the steering column or dashboard. Emergency flashers make all four turn-signal lights flash at the same time.

Use your emergency flashers to warn other drivers that your car is stopped on or near the road or that you are moving very slowly.

Parking Lights

In addition to low- and high-beam headlights, your car is equipped with parking lights. Use parking lights (or emergency flashers) to help other drivers see you when your car is stopped along the road. Parking lights are *not* designed to light the roadway when your car is in motion. In some states it is illegal to drive with parking lights on.

Horn

Use your car's horn to alert drivers, pedestrians, or cyclists to your presence or warn them of danger.

The horn is generally located on the steering wheel, but its exact position varies from car to car. Before driving any car, it's wise to locate and try the horn. In an emergency, you won't have time to search for it.

CHECKPOINT

6. What devices provide information about your car?
7. What devices enable you to communicate with other roadway users?

WHAT WOULD YOU DO?

You want to turn left, then pull over to the right side of the road. How would you communicate to others what you plan to do?

Checks and Procedures to Use Before Driving

If you were a pilot, you wouldn't dream of taking off without thoroughly checking your airplane first. Safety and equipment checks are equally important when you're about to drive a car. The best time to find out about a problem or potential problem is *before* your car is moving.

What Should You Check Before Entering Your Car?

You should inspect the car and the area around it before you enter your car. If you need to step into the roadway, check carefully for approaching traffic.

Surrounding Area

◆ Look for children playing nearby.

Each year about 200 children under the age of six are killed while playing in the family driveway.

◆ Look for animals that may be hiding under or walking or sleeping near the car.

◆ Look for objects in the area of the car and on the roadway that may interfere with safe movement or damage the tires.

◆ Check under the car for fresh stains that could be indications of fluid leaks.

Wheels

◆ Check for underinflated tires and for tire wear or damage.

◆ Note which way your front wheels are turned. This is the direction in which your car will go as soon as it begins moving.

On a warm day, condensation from a car's air-conditioning unit may form a puddle under the car. It's important to be able to distinguish this puddle from those formed by fluid leaks.

Check under your car for leaks, objects, and animals every time you plan to drive. ▶

◀
Adjust mirrors and seats, fasten your safety belt, and lock the doors before you move into traffic.

Car Body

◆ Check for damaged or missing parts and that all lights and windows are clean and undamaged.
◆ In winter, scrape off snow and ice.

Under the Hood

◆ At least once a week or when you stop for gas, check the levels of the engine oil, radiator coolant, and battery, brake, transmission, and windshield-washer fluids.
◆ Check the battery connection. Are the cables tight? Are the terminals free from corrosion?

Getting Into the Car

Now you're ready to get into your car. Do it safely.
◆ Load packages and have passengers enter from the curb side.
◆ Look carefully for approaching traffic before stepping into the roadway. Have your keys in hand.

◆ Walk around the front of the car, facing oncoming traffic.
◆ Wait for a break in traffic before opening the door, and open it only far enough and long enough to allow you to get in the car.

What Should You Check After Entering the Car?

Get into the habit of making safety checks and adjustments as soon as you get into the car. In addition to the following guidelines, consult your owner's manual for additional information.

Inside-the-Car Checks and Procedures

◆ Close and lock all doors.
◆ Place the key in the ignition.
◆ Adjust the seat so that you can clearly see the roadway and comfortably reach the floor pedals and other car controls.

Charles A. Butler, Manager,
Driver Safety Services

Charles A. Butler

How well you manage risk is determined by what you do before you start driving. Make sure all vehicle system devices are working properly, and know how to use and adjust them—especially mirrors, seat, lights, steering wheel, and occupant restraints. Vehicle system devices improve visibility and improve your ability to steer, accelerate, and brake. They also protect you in the event of a crash. Good risk managers always make pre-driving vehicle systems checks.

? WHAT WOULD YOU DO?

You have never driven this car before. What checks and procedures will you use before entering and driving the car?

◆ Adjust the head restraint. Have passengers adjust theirs.

◆ Adjust the rear- and left side-view mirrors so that you can use them with just your eyes and do not need to move your head. Adjust the right side-view mirror for the best vision with the least head movement.

◆ Check the inside of the windows. Clean, defog, or defrost as necessary.

◆ Make sure there are no objects inside the car that will block your view or tumble about as you drive.

◆ Familiarize yourself with the controls for any devices you may need to use. *While moving, minimize the time you take to use any of these devices. Make any adjustments when traffic and roadway conditions do not pose a threat.*

◆ Fasten your safety belt and make sure all passengers have fastened theirs.

CHECKPOINT

8. What should you check before getting into your car?
9. What should you check once you are inside the car?

CHAPTER 6 REVIEW

KEY POINTS

LESSON ONE

1. Devices that help make you comfortable in a car include seat-position controls, adjustable steering, heater, air conditioner, and air vents.

2. Devices that enable you to control a car include the ignition switch which starts and stops the engine, gear-selector lever or gearshift which puts the transmission into the gear you select, steering wheel which controls the direction of the front wheels, cruise control which lets you maintain a desired speed without keeping your foot on the accelerator, accelerator which moves the car and controls the speed by feeding fuel to the engine, brake pedal which slows or stops the car, parking brake which keeps a parked car from rolling.

LESSON TWO

3. Devices that aid visibility include lights, windshield wipers and washer, sun visors, defroster, and rear and sideview mirrors.

4. Car features that protect you and your passengers from injury include safety belts, air bags, head restraints, door locks, and various structural features such as safety-glass windows, impact resistant bumpers, protective padding on the dashboard.

5. Devices such as locks, alarms, and the audible key reminder can help prevent the theft of a car.

LESSON THREE

6. The speedometer, odometer, fuel gauge, alternator gauge, temperature gauge, oil-pressure gauge, brake warning lights, and various dashboard lights provide information about your car.

7. Taillights, directional signals, emergency flashers, parking lights, and horn let you communicate with others.

LESSON FOUR

8. Before entering your car you should check the surrounding area for children, animals, objects, or fluid leaks; check the condition and direction of the tires; inspect the body of the car for damage and clean the lights and windows; and regularly check the fluid levels and battery connection.

9. After entering the car, lock the doors; adjust the seat, head restraint, and mirrors; clear the windows; reposition any objects inside the car that may block your view; familiarize yourself with all controls; fasten your safety belt; and make sure passengers have fastened theirs.

PROJECTS

1. Obtain a car owner's manual and read through the contents. Find the sections that deal with the various kinds of systems you've read about in this chapter. What information can you obtain from an owner's manual that you won't find in a textbook?

2. Research and report on the comparative safety of different makes and models of motor vehicles. Try to find out specific reasons why some vehicles are safer than others. Your librarian can help you identify sources of information. You may also want to discuss this subject with insurance agents, mechanics, and other knowledgeable people.

BUILDING SOCIAL STUDIES SKILLS

Making a Circle Graph

A poll is a way of finding out what a group of people think about a certain topic. You've probably seen or heard of polls showing what people think about political events, celebrities, and economic situations.

Conduct a poll to find out what members of your class think are their chances of being involved in a collision.

Try It Yourself

Follow these steps.

1. Count the number of people in your class. This number represents 100 percent of the class.

2. Ask each person this question: *What do you think the chances are of your being in a car collision?* Then ask each one to choose one of the following as a response:
   a. 1 in 5, b. 1 in 10, c. 1 in 50,
   d. 1 in 100, e. 1 in 500, f. 1 in 1000, g. don't know

3. Tally the number of responses to each choice.

4. Divide the number of responses to a choice by the total number of people in the class to give you the percent of people who responded to that choice. For example, if four people said "1 in 10" and there are 27 people in the class, the fraction would be $\frac{4}{27}$, or about 15 percent.

5. Make a circle graph to show the results. A full circle represents the whole class, or 100 percent. First divide the circle into fourths. Each fourth represents 25 percent. Then mark segments of the circle to show the approximate percent of people who responded to each choice.

6. Your finished graph might look something like the one below.

The chances of being in a traffic collision in any given year are actually 1 in 5. In a poll of 1,506 people, only 1 person out of 10 chose that rate. How does your class compare?

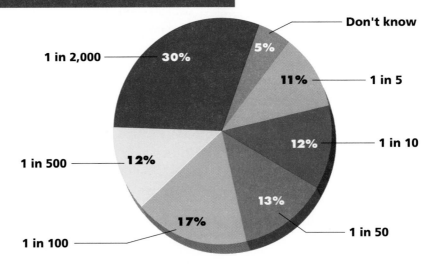

PERCEPTION OF RISK

1 in 2,000 — 30%
Don't know — 5%
11% — 1 in 5
1 in 500 — 12%
12% — 1 in 10
13% — 1 in 50
17%
1 in 100

CHAPTER 6 REVIEW

CHAPTER TEST

Write the letter of the answer that best completes each sentence.

1. Three features that improve visibility are
   a. sun visors, bucket seats, and headlights.
   b. defroster, windshield wipers, and side-view mirrors.
   c. sunroof, air bags, and brake lights.
2. Head restraints should be adjusted to make contact with
   a. the base of your skull.
   b. the top of your head.
   c. the back of your head.
3. Cruise control
   a. increases your control of a car.
   b. may lead you to be less alert than you should be.
   c. is best used in heavy inner-city traffic.
4. An odometer indicates
   a. the distance a vehicle has traveled.
   b. the speed at which a vehicle is traveling.
   c. the amount of current in your battery.
5. Three devices that control the speed and direction of your car are the
   a. gearshift, brake pedal, and steering wheel.
   b. engine, battery, and accelerator.
   c. tires, air conditioner, and ignition switch.
6. Ice has collected on your windshield. You try to remove it, but it is frozen solid. You should
   a. pull the sun visor into the "up" position.
   b. turn on the air conditioner.
   c. turn on the defroster.
7. Each year approximately 200 children under six are killed while playing
   a. on highways.
   b. in driveways.
   c. on sidewalks.
8. Taillights, emergency flashers, and parking lights
   a. are parts of a car's communications system.
   b. can be activated with the ignition in the "off" position.
   c. are parts of a car's information system.
9. Using a safety belt will
   a. protect you from getting whiplash.
   b. increase your chances of surviving a collision.
   c. decrease your chances of surviving a collision.
10. Directional signals
    a. are controlled by the turn-indicator arm.
    b. are controlled by a button on the dashboard.
    c. become activated whenever you turn the steering wheel.

Write the word or phrase that best completes each sentence.

air bags	blind spots	safety check
automatic	manual	antitheft devices

11. You should look over your shoulder when turning to detect anything in your _____ .

12. Cars that have a(n) _____ transmission require you to use a clutch pedal.

13. _____ are considered passive safety devices because they operate automatically.

14. A _____ enables you to find out about a problem before your car is moving.

15. Alarm systems and audible key reminders are examples of _____ .

DRIVER'S LOG

In this chapter, you have learned about the different systems of your car and the checks you should make before and after entering your car. When you become a driver, what will you do to be sure that you don't forget to make these checks—even if you feel you're in too much of a hurry to take the time? Write a paragraph telling what you will do.

STARTING, STEERING, STOPPING

Basic driving procedures are second-nature to good drivers. It is important that you learn these procedures so that you can manage them safely and smoothly. Mastering the basics is crucial to the driving task.

CHAPTER 7 OBJECTIVES

Basic Operating Procedures: Automatic Transmission

1. Describe how to start a car with automatic transmission and put the car in motion.
2. Describe how to slow and stop a car with automatic transmission.

Basic Operating Procedures: Manual Transmission

3. Explain how manual and automatic transmissions differ.
4. Describe how to start and move a car with manual transmission.
5. Explain how to use each forward gear.

Acceleration, Deceleration, and Speed

6. Define *acceleration* and *deceleration* and explain how they are related to speed.

Learning How to Steer the Car

7. Describe the procedures for steering straight ahead and when turning.
8. Explain how to steer in reverse gear.

Basic Operating Procedures: Automatic Transmission

In Chapter 1 you learned a basic principle of responsible driving: to reduce risk, you need to manage visibility, time, and space. Your ability to put this principle into practice depends on how well you can control your car. You control a car through a set of gears called a transmission. The transmission enables you to move your car forward or backward. The gear you select determines the direction.

When you follow the steps for starting your car, warning lights come on briefly.
▼

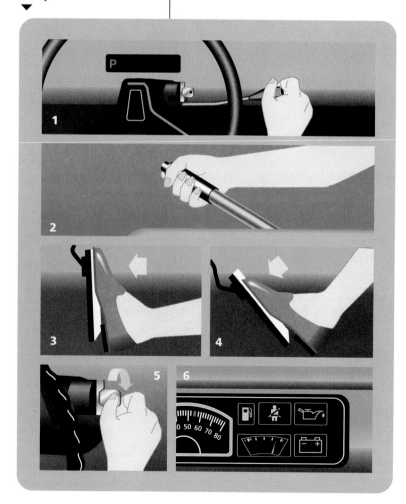

Whether you drive a car with automatic transmission or one with a manual transmission, the key to becoming a skilled driver is the same: *practice.*

How Do You Start and Move a Car with Automatic Transmission?

It's important to start your car's engine properly to avoid damaging the starter system or wasting fuel.

To start the engine of a car with automatic transmission, follow the steps below, one at a time. Practice doing these steps until they become habit.

1. Make sure the gear selector lever is in Park. If the selector lever is in Neutral, the car may roll if the parking brake has not been set.
2. Check that the parking brake is set.

    Note: If your car has an electronic fuel-injection system, or if the engine is warm from driving or very cold from the weather, steps 3 and 4 may vary or may not be required at all. Check your car's owner's manual for details.
3. Set the automatic choke by pressing the accelerator (gas pedal) once to the floor and releasing it.
4. Press the accelerator lightly with your right foot and hold it.
5. Turn the ignition key to the *start* position. Release the key *as soon as* the engine starts.

◀ *To put a car in motion, accelerate gently to avoid "jackrabbit" starts.*

6. As the engine idles (runs with no pressure on the accelerator), check the gauges and warning lights to be sure that the oil-pressure system and other systems are working properly.

Putting the Car in Motion

Once your engine is running and you've checked the gauges, you're ready to put the car in motion. Follow these steps:

1. Press down firmly on the brake pedal. While most drivers use their right foot to brake, some use their left foot. Follow the advice of your driving instructor.

2. Use your right hand to shift the gear selector lever to Drive or Reverse, depending on which way you intend to move.

3. Release the parking brake.

4. Turn on your directional signal to indicate the direction you want to move.

5. Check for traffic in your rear-view and side-view mirrors. Be prepared to accelerate into the desired lane once the roadway is clear.

6. Look over your shoulder to check blind spots.

7. Remove your foot from the brake, and apply gradual pressure to the accelerator.

Working the accelerator properly takes practice if you use your right foot for both accelerating and braking. For best control of both the accelerator and brake pedals, rest the heel of your right foot on the floor in a position that lets you keep it there while pivoting back and forth between the two pedals. The forward

Who works to find the fuel that powers your car? Nettie S. Strange, an African-American, examines oil-well bore samples for indications of the presence of oil. She graduated from Virginia State College and received her master's degree in geology from the University of Texas.

Identify in advance the need to stop by using the SIPDE process. ▶

Allowing your engine to run unnecessarily while your car is stopped or parked wastes fuel and pollutes the air. In some cities, doing so is also against the law.

part of your foot should fall comfortably on both pedals.

Moving forward after stopping on an uphill grade requires extra practice. To keep from rolling back, use your left foot to press the brake pedal while gently accelerating with your right foot. As soon as the car starts to pull forward, take your left foot off the brake. (An alternative is to hold the car in place by setting the parking brake, then release the brake as you accelerate.)

How Do You Slow and Stop a Car with Automatic Transmission?

You will often have to slow down and stop your car under both planned and unexpected circumstances. Red lights, stop signs, pedestrians running across streets, cars cutting in front of you—these and countless other situations will require you to apply your brakes.

Braking

For smooth braking, you need to develop a sense of timing and get a feel for applying the right amount of pressure on the brake pedal. Your goal is to stop in time, neither overshooting nor undershooting your desired stopping point. Moreover, whenever possible, you want to stop your car gradually, not abruptly.

The amount of foot pressure required to brake to a stop depends on the size and weight of the car, its type of brakes, your maneuvering space, and the road surface. As you practice driving and become more experienced, you'll become increasingly skilled at judging the distance needed to bring your car to a smooth stop.

For effective control of brake pressure, position the heel of your foot between and in front of the accelerator and brake pedals. In this way, you'll be able to apply pressure with your toes, and you can easily increase or decrease pressure as needed.

Follow these steps when braking to stop:

1. Check your mirrors for any cars that may be following. If time permits, lightly tap the brake pedal: your flashing brake lights will warn drivers behind you that you intend to stop.
2. Apply smooth, steady, firm pressure to the brake pedal, easing up slightly as you come to a halt.
3. Leave the transmission in *drive* if you plan to move ahead within a minute or so, as when stopped for a red light. If you'll be stopped longer, follow the parking procedures described in Chapter 9, and turn off your engine.

Emergency Braking

The procedures for stopping under emergency conditions differ slightly. If a driver or pedestrian suddenly enters your path of travel, you may need to stop the car as quickly as possible. However, you don't want to slam on the brakes so hard that the wheels lock (stop turning). Locked wheels may increase your stopping distance, and can also cause you to lose steering control and go into a skid.

To prevent the wheels from locking, press, or "squeeze," the brake pedal firmly to a point just *before* the wheels lock, and hold there. This is called *threshold braking.* If the wheels start to skid, reduce pressure very slightly, then add pressure again as needed. Release pressure as the car comes to a stop. For more guidelines on braking and skid control, see Chapter 13.

When purchasing a car, consider buying one that has *anti-lock brakes.* An anti-lock brake system is designed to keep a car's wheels from locking when the driver brakes abruptly.

CHECKPOINT

1. What steps would you follow to start and move a car with automatic transmission?
2. How would you use your brakes to slow and stop a car with automatic transmission? How would you stop in an emergency?

WHAT WOULD YOU DO?

How can you enter the flow of traffic safely and smoothly?

Basic Operating Procedures: Manual Transmission

Many people drive cars with manual transmissions simply because they enjoy shifting gears with a stick shift. Others prefer manual-shift cars because they usually cost less than the same model with automatic transmissions and, when properly driven, may reduce fuel consumption.

How Do Manual and Automatic Transmissions Differ?

There are usually four or five gears in forward and one in reverse. In manual transmissions, the choice of the forward gear determines the power delivered by the engine to the drive wheels.

An automatic transmission set in Drive will shift the forward gears for you. When you operate a stick shift, you must change gears by hand. You start in low gear and shift to higher gears as you pick up speed. As you slow down, you shift back down from high to low.

To change gears, you break the connection between the engine and the transmission by pressing the clutch pedal to the floor. When the clutch pedal is up, the engine is again engaged to the transmission.

How Do You Operate a Car with Manual Transmission?

Learning to drive a car equipped with a manual transmission is easier if you already know how to operate an automatic-transmission car. The key to driving a stick-shift car is mastering the clutch, which you'll use each time you shift gears.

Starting the Engine

As when starting an automatic-transmission car, make sure the parking brake is set. Press the clutch pedal to the floor with your left foot, press the brake pedal with your right foot, and then shift into *neutral.* (There is no gear position equivalent to Park on the gearshift for a manual-transmission car.) Now turn the ignition key to start.

Putting the Car in Motion

In order to get a manual-shift car moving—and keep it moving—you must learn to coordinate the use of the clutch with that of the gearshift and the accelerator. Reading about how to do this will help you to understand the process. Only through actual practice, however, can you gain the experience needed to master stick-shift driving.

Clutching and shifting actions should come to feel so natural to you that you scarcely need to think about them. After all, once you're on the roadway, you can't be looking down at your feet and hands. Your full attention must be focused on traffic.

The key to smooth clutch operation is learning to sense the *friction point.* This is the point when, as you let up the clutch pedal, the engine

Below are the gearshift positions for 4-speed and 5-speed manual transmissions.

▼

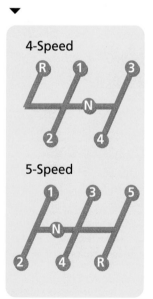

4-Speed

5-Speed

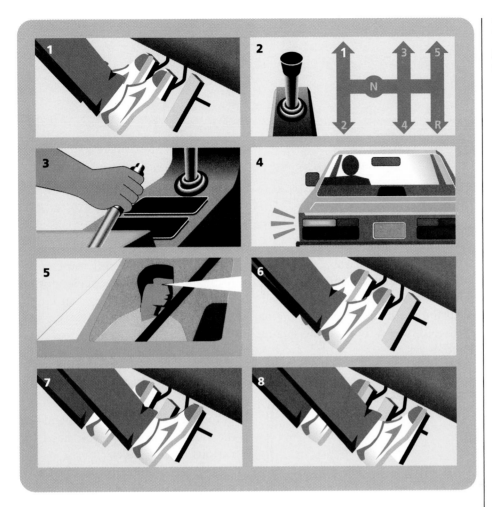

◀
You use both feet when you shift and move a car with a manual transmission.

and the transmission engage. As you continue to let up the clutch, you must match the forward (or backward) motion of the car with an increase in pressure on the gas pedal.

The easiest way to get a feel for the friction point is to practice by using reverse gear. Because reverse is a lower gear than first, you'll find it easier to sense the friction point.

Follow these steps to put the car in motion:

1. Press the brake pedal with your right foot. With your left foot, press the clutch pedal to the floor.
2. Shift into First gear.
3. Release the parking brake.
4. Switch on your turn signal to indicate the direction you plan to move.
5. Check for traffic in your rear-view and side-view mirrors. Look over your shoulder to check blind spots.
6. Slowly let the clutch up to the friction point. Remember: look at the roadway, not down at your feet or hands!
7. Move your right foot from the brake to the accelerator.
8. As you press down gently on the accelerator, slowly let up the clutch pedal all the way.

It takes plenty of practice to use the clutch pedal to shift smoothly. ▶

If the car jerks forward, you either released the clutch too abruptly, or you pressed too hard on the gas pedal. If the car lurches and the engine stalls out, you've not fed the engine enough gas.

Tips for New Drivers

Holding the Car in Place

Learning to move a manual-shift car forward after stopping on an uphill grade takes practice. To keep the car from rolling backward:

1. Set the parking brake.
2. Press the clutch to the floor, and shift into First gear.
3. Let the clutch pedal up to the friction point, and press gently on the accelerator.
4. Release the parking brake as you begin to feel the car pulling forward.
5. Press the accelerator as you let up the clutch pedal.
6. Accelerate in First gear until you have gained enough speed to shift into Second gear.

Don't hold your car in place on a hill by pressing the gas pedal slightly while keeping the clutch near the friction point. "Riding the clutch" this way wears your clutch needlessly. Always brake to keep your car from rolling back.

Keep practicing until you can co-ordinate clutch and accelerator. A good place to practice is an empty parking lot.

How Can You Use Each Forward Gear?

Your selection of gears depends on the power and speed you need for various driving tasks.

Low, or First, gear gives the power needed to set a car in motion.

Second gear lets you go as fast as 15 to 25 mph, depending on the horsepower of the engine and on whether the transmission is 3-, 4- or 5-speed. You can also use Second gear to start on ice or drive in heavy snow.

Third gear, in cars with 3-speed transmissions, is used for all speeds over about 25 mph. If a car has a 4- or 5-speed transmission and a small engine, Third is used at speeds up to 30 or 40 mph.

Use Fourth gear for driving above 35 mph on flat roadway. When driving uphill, you may have to achieve 40 mph or more before shifting to Fourth or Fifth gear.

Keep in mind that power, speed, and the gear in use are strictly related. At a given speed, the power of an engine is greater in lower gear. For example, when starting up a steep grade, you generally shift to a lower gear to maintain power. When the roadway levels out, you can shift to a higher gear and keep up the same speed with less power.

Shifting to a Higher Gear

To shift to a higher gear, follow these steps:

1. Accelerate to a speed appropriate for the gear you want to be in.
2. Press the clutch pedal to the floor.
3. Release the accelerator.
4. Shift to the next higher gear.
5. Press again on the accelerator. Release the clutch pedal part way.

6. Let the clutch pedal up all the way.

Downshifting

There are several reasons to *downshift,* or shift from a higher to a lower gear: to gain power, to accelerate, to steer effectively, to brake the car on a downslope (except when the road is slippery), and to slow down or stop.

To shift to a lower gear, follow these steps:

1. Release the accelerator. (If you also want to slow down, press the brake pedal.)
2. Press the clutch pedal to the floor.
3. Shift to the next lower gear. (A sudden decrease in speed may require you to shift to an even lower gear—as when braking sharply

◀
Coordinate using the clutch, gearshift, and gas pedal to shift gears.

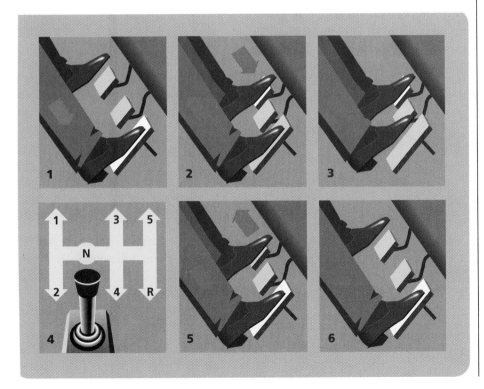

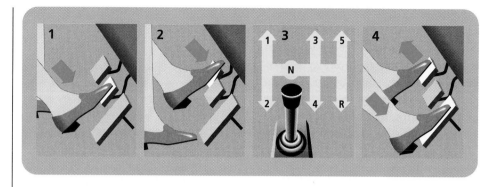

To downshift, brake. Then press the clutch to the floor, shift to the next lower gear, and press the accelerator. ▶

and downshifting from Fourth gear to Second.)

4. Release the clutch pedal to the friction point. Press down on the accelerator as necessary.

Note that you do not have to downshift through each lower gear as you slow down or stop. In fact, routinely downshifting to stop will cause unnecessary wear on the clutch, an expensive part to replace.

Bear in mind, too, that it is easy to downshift from Fifth, Fourth, and Third gears to lower gears, but difficult to shift from Second to First. To downshift to first gear, you have to bring the car almost to a complete stop.

Stopping

To stop from a low gear, follow these steps:

1. Check your mirrors for traffic that may be following.
2. Tap the brake pedal to flash your brake lights and signal drivers behind you that you intend to stop.
3. Press the clutch pedal to the floor. (Doing this keeps the car from jerking or stalling.)
4. Move your right foot to the brake pedal. Apply smooth, constant pressure until the car comes to a stop.
5. Keep your foot on the brake pedal and shift to Neutral.

To make an emergency stop, press the clutch pedal to the floor, and use threshold-braking.

?

WHAT WOULD YOU DO?

What actions would you take with the brake, the clutch, and the gear shift as you approach, then pass through, this intersection?

CHECKPOINT

3. How is a manual transmission different from an automatic transmission?
4. What steps would you follow to start and move a car with manual transmission?
5. How would you use the forward gears of a vehicle that has a manual transmission?

To minimize driving risk, you must be able to maneuver your car safely. To do so, you have to know your car's capabilities and limitations. When changing lanes or passing, for example, you need to judge how much time and distance your car will require to move ahead of other vehicles. Learning about acceleration, deceleration, and speed can help you judge time and space more accurately thus helping you to be a safe driver.

How Are Acceleration, Deceleration, and Speed Related?

Speed and acceleration are closely linked. When drivers say their car has good *acceleration* (or "pickup"), they mean the car is able to increase speed relatively quickly. The time it takes to accelerate from one speed to another is the *rate of acceleration*.

Deceleration, on the other hand, refers to decreasing speed, or slowing down. The time it takes to decel-erate from one speed to another is the *rate of deceleration*.

Several factors affect a car's acceleration, including the power of the engine, the transmission and differential gear ratios, adhesion between the drive wheels and the road surface, and the weight the engine is pulling. Your ability to drive safely and effectively depends in large part on the knowledgeable use of your car's acceleration.

Acceleration and Deceleration Rates Vary

Rate of acceleration varies with speed. At higher speeds, a car's rate of acceleration is lower. As a result, it will generally take more time to accelerate from 45 mph to 55 mph than from 20 mph to 30 mph.

Understanding this principle is important for risk management. For example, the lower acceleration rate at high speeds means you must allow more time to pass when traveling at 50 mph than when moving at 30 mph.

If you sometimes wear high-heeled shoes, keep a pair of low-heeled shoes in the car to put on when you drive. Driving in low-heeled shoes will give you better control of the accelerator and brake pedals.

A speedometer tells you how fast you're traveling at a given moment, but to find out your average speed for a particular distance, you'll need to do a little math.

Average speed equals total distance traveled divided by total time traveled. Suppose, for example, the distance from your home to the beach is 70 miles. One afternoon, it takes you an hour and a half to drive there. Your average speed equals 70 (total miles driven) divided by $1\frac{1}{2}$ (total time), or just over 46 miles per hour.

Tips for New Drivers

Accelerating

- For best control when accelerating, rest the heel of your foot on the floor, and press the pedal gently with your toes.
- As a general rule, accelerate gradually. Beginning drivers sometimes make errors when they increase speed quickly. Accelerating gradually also saves fuel.
- No two cars accelerate exactly the same way. When driving an unfamiliar car, allow yourself time to get used to the feel of the gas pedal and to the car's acceleration capability.

Equally important to keep in mind is that deceleration rates, like acceleration rates, vary with speed. At higher speeds, your car's rate of deceleration is lower. So a car traveling at 60 mph needs a great deal more time and space to slow and brake to a stop than the same car traveling at 30 mph.

A vehicle's rates of acceleration and deceleration also vary with weight. A heavy truck, for example,

needs much more time and distance to accelerate or decelerate than does a passenger car.

Maintaining a Constant Speed

The ability of vehicles to maintain a given speed varies greatly. Large passenger cars with high-horsepower, 6- or 8-cylinder engines and mid-size and sporty sedans with turbocharged small engines generally have good acceleration and can maintain their speed climbing a hill. An underpowered subcompact car, however, may not be able to hold its speed because of its small engine.

Many large vehicles, too, have difficulty maintaining their speed. Tractor-trailer rigs and interstate buses have huge engines, but these large vehicles accelerate very slowly.

Monitoring Your Speed

New drivers generally find it difficult to estimate speed accurately. Keep track of your car's speed by checking the speedometer. Do so by using quick glances, as traffic condi-

The greater the speed, the greater the distance needed to brake the car to a stop. ▶

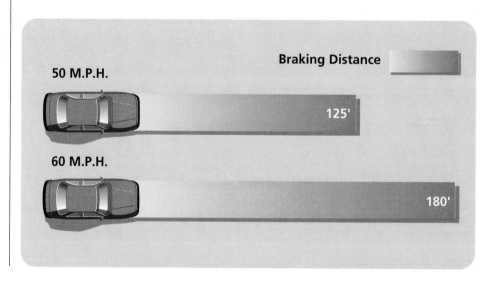

Braking Distance

50 M.P.H.

125'

60 M.P.H.

180'

◄
New drivers often increase speed without realizing it, so check your speedometer frequently.

tions permit. Never take your eyes off the road to watch the speedometer.

With experience, you should become more aware of how speed affects the function and feel of your car. You'll notice, for example, that as speed varies, there's a difference in the car's vibration and in the level of sound from the tires, the wind, and the engine. Drivers of manual-transmission cars must make a special effort to learn to judge speed, because they have to make speed-related decisions about shifting gears.

Note that it's harder to estimate your car's speed immediately after you've made a sharp change in speed. If, for example, you've been driving at 20 mph and rapidly accelerate to 45 mph, you'll feel as though you're moving faster than you actually are.

On the other hand, if you've been traveling at highway speeds and suddenly enter a 25-mph zone, your tendency may be to slow down less than you should because you've become accustomed to moving at higher speeds. The best way to prevent yourself from speeding in such an instance is to check your speedometer.

CHECKPOINT

6. What is *acceleration?* How are acceleration and speed related?

❓

WHAT WOULD YOU DO?

Which vehicle probably needs more time and distance to accelerate: the truck or the car? How would knowing this help you manage time and space to reduce risk?

Learning How to Steer the Car

Many new drivers assume that they know all they need to know about steering a car. After all, they think, they've been steering bicycles and sleds since they were children. Such activities do share elements in common with steering an automobile. However, there are important differences new drivers must learn.

For one thing, unlike a bike or sled, a motor vehicle has power independent of the driver's own efforts—a great deal of power. Moreover, steering is not simply a matter of pointing the car in the direction you want to go. Steering is a basic means of risk management.

Think of the steering wheel as the face of a clock so that you can position your hands correctly.

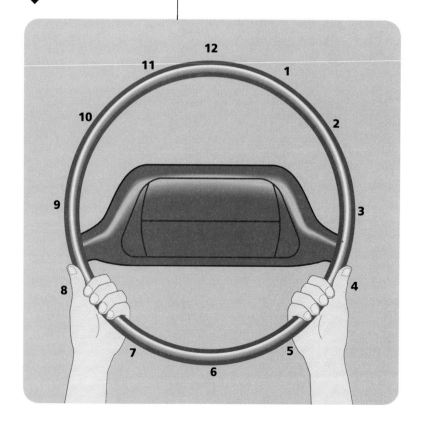

How Can You Steer Your Car Forward and Through Turns?

Suppose you're about to drive through an intersection. Suddenly another car crosses in front of you. The best way to avoid a collision is to brake your car, right?

Not necessarily. It often takes less time and space to steer away from an object than to brake to avoid hitting it. (Of course, in order to avoid a collision by steering, you must have previously identified an area into which you can safely steer.)

Steering plays a particularly important part in risk management when you're traveling at speeds over 25 or 30 mph. At such speeds, steering may often be your only way to avoid a collision, because higher speeds increase the distance and time needed to stop the car.

Holding the Steering Wheel

When steering in a straight line or through a moderate curve, grasp the steering wheel firmly with your fingers. For efficient handling, position your hands on the lower part of the wheel, preferably in the 7 o'clock and 5 o'clock positions or the 8 o'clock and 4 o'clock positions. Many experienced drivers place their hands at 10 o'clock and 2 o'clock or at 9 o'clock and 3 o'clock. Follow the recommendations of your instructor. No matter which hand position you use, your thumbs should rest on the wheel.

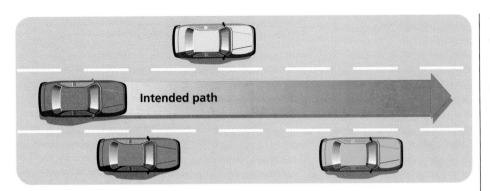

◄
Always look and steer toward a point in the center of your intended path of travel.

Tracking and Steering

Keeping your car moving on the path of travel that you have chosen is called *tracking*. Tracking requires a driver to make whatever steering adjustments are needed to hold the desired course.

To track smoothly, learn to direct your attention to points well ahead along your intended path of travel. Choose these points on the basis of where you want to go and traffic conditions.

If you're like many new drivers, you'll find steering a car more challenging than you'd anticipated, particularly when traveling on curved, winding roads. At first, you may not notice small changes in your car's position in a traffic lane. You may fail to adjust your steering in time and then tend to overcorrect, causing the car to zigzag rather than move in a straight line or smooth curve. With practice and concentration, though, you'll soon improve your ability to keep your car on track with only minor steering adjustments.

Steering in a Straight Line

The steering adjustments you must make on a straight road are small but critical. Be on the alert for gradual changes in the position of your car. It shouldn't "wander" in its lane. Avoid turning the steering wheel more than absolutely necessary.

Steer toward a point in the center of your path of travel, looking well ahead as you drive. When you look to the point where you will steer, you will automatically steer in the proper direction.

As you steer, check your inside and outside mirrors frequently. Doing this is especially important whenever you spot something along your intended path of travel that may cause you to change your speed or position.

To look in your rear-view mirror, move just your eyes. To look in your side-view mirror, turn your head only slightly.

Steering to Turn

Steering through a turn requires more steering-wheel movement than does lane positioning. To turn corners smoothly and safely, you need to develop a good sense of timing and make a habit of searching a wider area.

When steering through a turn, keep in mind that your car's rear wheels do not follow the same path as the front wheels. They have a

The average driver takes one-half to three-fourths of a second to step on the brake after identifying a dangerous situation. Thus, even at 20 mph, your car would travel at least 20 feet before you could step on the brake.

If you are not too tall or somewhat stout, you may find push-pull steering more comfortable. ▶

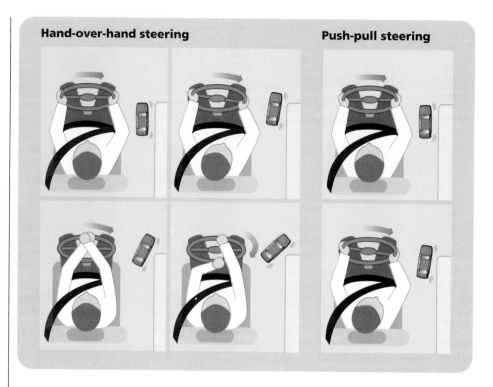

Hand-over-hand steering

Push-pull steering

smaller turning radius, so you must allow ample space along the path you're turning. Without this space, your rear wheels may hit the curb or other objects.

Two specific steering techniques are effective for turning the wheel: hand-over-hand and push-pull. The following procedures describe how to make a right turn; to make a left turn, reverse the movements.

Hand-over-hand steering When you need to turn right, use your left hand to push the steering wheel up, around, and down. At the same time, bring your right hand across your left forearm to grip the wheel on the far side. Then use your right hand to pull the side of the wheel up, around, and down. Repeat this series of movements as often as needed to complete the turn, making any left or right steering corrections that may be required.

Hand-over-hand steering provides effective car control when you're steering through tight-radius turns, such as hard turns and hairpin turns.

Push-pull steering When you use push-pull steering, the palms of both hands should be facing you. To turn right, firmly grasp the steering wheel with your left hand at about the 7 o'clock position. Push the wheel until your hand is at about 11:00 o'clock. Slide your right hand up to about 12:00 and pull the steering wheel down while moving your left hand back down to 7 o'clock. Continue pushing and pulling the wheel as you complete the turn.

Using push-pull steering, both your hands will be on the wheel at all times. You will never have to cross your hands or arms when you turn.

Whichever steering method you choose, use the following guidelines when making a turn.

◆ Look beyond the turn to the point you want to reach. Identify this point before you start to turn.

◆ Always use your directional signal. Check the roadway ahead and both mirrors before starting to turn. Check the mirrors again after completing the turn, waiting if possible until you've straightened the wheels.

◆ On a hard turn, slow down enough to maintain steering control as you enter the curve. Accelerate gently about halfway through to pull out of the curve.

◆ With your eyes on the point you want to reach, start to steer back to the straight-ahead position when you're about midway through a turn. Do this by reversing the hand-over-hand or push-pull movements.

How Do You Steer in Reverse?

When steering in reverse gear, you have to learn where to look and how to control direction and speed. Always back up slowly and carefully. When you steer backward, the car's movement is more abrupt.

Moreover, visibility through the rear window is very limited, and head restraints and passengers may further block your view. If you were to back up while looking into the rear-view mirror—*not* a good idea—your view would be even more restricted.

To maximize your ability to see, turn your head and shoulders so that you can look back in the direction you want to move. When you back up, the *rear* of your car moves in the *same* direction that you turn the steering wheel, while the *front* swings in the *opposite* direction.

Note, too, that when you back a car, the two points most likely to hit something are the rear side of the car in the direction you're turning and the front side of the car opposite the direction you're turning.

Steering to the Rear

Follow these steps when backing.

1. With your foot on the brake, shift into Reverse gear. If you are backing straight, place your left hand on the top of the steering wheel and your right arm across the top of the seat. Look over your right shoulder. If you are backing to the right or left, keep both hands on the wheel and look over your shoulder in the direction you want to move.

2. Ease pressure off the brake slowly. Give yourself plenty of time to

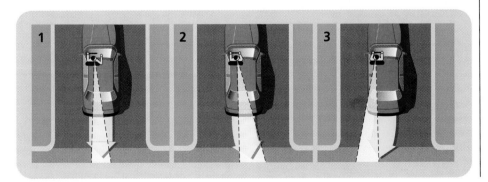

◄ Don't forget to look over both shoulders when you steer to the rear.

Judy Walters, Driver Education Instructor, Spokane, Washington

Judy Walters

Begin now to practice patience. It is an attitude and habit of mind you can practice in the car that allows you to perform at your peak in any situation.

- Don't "gun" the engine.
- Think "gradual" to accelerate or brake.
- Slow down to less than 10 mph to make well-tracked turns.
- Make sure you have enough time and space to enter and cross an intersection.
- Signal and check mirrors and blind spots before gradually changing lanes.

❓ WHAT WOULD YOU DO?

What procedures would you follow to back out of this driveway? What safety precautions should you take before moving the car?

monitor the rear and front of your car. To move the car slowly, apply only slight pressure, if any, to the accelerator.

3. Look at the point where you want to go, so that you can identify and correct steering errors early. Turn the wheel as needed. If, for example, the car wanders left, turn the wheel slightly right, then back to center.

4. Concentrate your visual search out the rear window, with quick, repeated glances to the front. Keep alert to ensure that the car is moving in the right direction and that the front end is not about to strike anything.

5. Continue to look out the rear window as you bring the car to a stop. If you turn toward the front before you're finished backing, you may hit something with the rear of your car.

CHECKPOINT

7. What procedures would you follow to steer a car straight ahead? To turn?

8. How do you back a car?

CHAPTER 7 REVIEW

KEY POINTS

LESSON ONE

1. To start a car with automatic transmission, put the gear selector in Park. Set the automatic choke. Then press the accelerator and turn the key. To move the car, step on the brake and shift to Drive or Reverse. Release the parking brake, take your foot off the brake, and accelerate gradually.

2. To slow and stop a car with automatic transmission, check your mirrors, tap your brake pedal, and apply steady pressure to the brake pedal, easing up slightly as you come to a halt.

LESSON TWO

3. You need to change forward gears by manually shifting up or down in a manual transmission. An automatic transmission set in Drive will shift the forward gears for you.

4. To start a car with manual transmission, set the parking brake. Press the clutch to the floor, step on the brake, shift into Neutral, and turn the key. To move the car, shift into First and release the parking brake. As you let the clutch up, move your right foot from the brake to the accelerator and press gently. To stop the car, press the clutch to the floor, and move your right foot to the brake. Apply smooth pressure until the car stops.

5. First gear sets the car in motion. Second gear is used for speeds up to 15 to 25 mph or to start on ice or drive in heavy snow. Third gear is used for speeds over 25 mph (3-speed transmissions) or speeds up to 30 or 40 mph (4- or 5-speed transmissions). Fourth or Fifth gear is used for driving at higher speeds.

LESSON THREE

6. *Acceleration* is an increase of speed. *Deceleration* means slowing down. The rate of acceleration or deceleration varies with speed. At higher speeds, a car's acceleration and deceleration rates are lower.

LESSON FOUR

7. To steer your car straight ahead, steer toward a point in the center of your path of travel. When steering to turn, look beyond the turn to the point you want to reach. Use the hand-over-hand or push-pull steering method.

8. When backing, look over your right shoulder, place your left hand at the top of the steering wheel, and steer in the direction you want the car to move. Proceed slowly and carefully, monitoring both the rear and front of your car.

PROJECTS

1. Talk to someone who's been driving for at least several years. Ask what important lessons this driver has learned through experience, and what tips he or she might offer you as a beginning driver.

2. Explain and demonstrate to a friend or relative the difference between the hand-over-hand and push-pull steering methods. Which technique seems easier to you? Why? Survey several drivers to find out which method they use and why.

BUILDING MAP SKILLS

Understanding Roadway Classifications

Maps help you get where you're going. They also tell about the kinds of roads you can use to get there. Most maps have a key like this one. Find 🛡91 at coordinates D,5 on the map. The map key tells that this is a free limited-access highway. There are no tolls on this highway. See the dots along Route 9? The key tells you this is a scenic route. The key also tells you that Route 9 is a paved secondary road that is not divided.

Try It Yourself

1. What can you tell about Route 7 between Pittsfield and Stockbridge?

2. What kind of road connects Adams and Savoy Center?

3. Describe the different kinds of roads you can take from Southampton to Pittsfield.

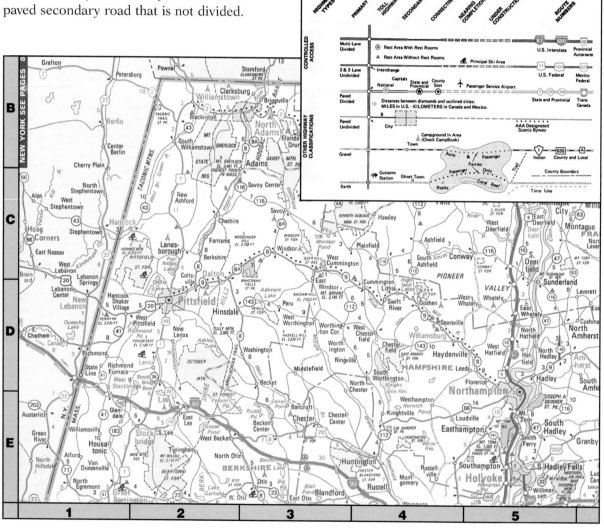

CHAPTER 7 REVIEW

CHAPTER TEST

Write the letter of the answer that best completes each sentence.

1. You can set an automatic choke by
   a. pumping the brake pedal.
   b. pressing the gas pedal once to the floor and then releasing it.
   c. turning the ignition key to "on."
2. One advantage of push-pull steering is that
   a. your hands are on the wheel at all times.
   b. your hands are free to adjust the mirrors.
   c. you can back up more easily.
3. In manual transmissions the speed of the car determines
   a. the tightness of a car's turning radius.
   b. the choice of forward gear.
   c. the need for an occasional fuel injection.
4. A car's rate of acceleration is lower at
   a. warmer engine temperatures.
   b. high speeds.
   c. low speeds.
5. To avoid rolling backwards when starting from an uphill grade you should
   a. set your parking brake firmly.
   b. lock the brakes.
   c. start the engine in third gear.
6. As you drive you will develop the ability to estimate your speed by
   a. sensing the vehicle's friction point.
   b. riding the clutch.
   c. sensing a difference in the car's vibrations.
7. To start a car with an automatic transmission,
   a. first shift into second gear.
   b. keep your foot on the brake pedal.
   c. make sure the gear selector lever is in Park.

8. In order to change gears you must
   a. press the clutch pedal to the floor.
   b. engage in threshold braking.
   c. rapidly decelerate.
9. When turning, always
   a. press on the clutch pedal.
   b. use your directional signal.
   c. shift into Reverse.
10. When driving around a curve you should focus
    a. beyond the turn, on the point you want to reach.
    b. on the road directly in front of you.
    c. on objects in your rearview mirror.

Write the word or phrase that best completes each sentence.

> rate of deceleration   tracking   clutch
> acceleration   manual transmission
> high-hazard   automatic

11. _____ means an increase of speed.
12. A car's _____ can have four or five forward gears.
13. The key to smooth _____ operation is sensing the friction point.
14. _____ means keeping your car moving on the path that you have chosen to travel.
15. The time it takes for a car to slow down is the _____ .

DRIVER'S LOG

In this chapter, you have learned about the basic procedures you need to learn in order to operate a vehicle. Write at least two paragraphs giving your ideas about why these procedures are almost second nature to experienced drivers and why they should become second nature to you.

BASIC DRIVING SKILLS

Minimizing risk on the roadway depends upon drivers' mastery of basic driving skills such as passing, changing lanes, and moving to and from curbs. Understanding how to safely execute these skills is vital to all drivers.

CHAPTER 8 OBJECTIVES

Moving from a Curb into Traffic and Out of Traffic to a Curb

1. Describe procedures for steering away from the curb and entering traffic.
2. Describe procedures for steering out of traffic and moving toward a curb.

Managing Power and Speed on Hills and Mountains

3. Describe how to drive uphill and downhill.
4. Describe safe procedures for driving on mountain roadways.

Managing Visibility, Time, and Space when Changing Lanes

5. Describe several factors involved in making a lane change correctly.

Passing Another Vehicle and Being Passed

6. Name conditions you should be aware of when you want to pass another vehicle.
7. Describe the procedure for passing another vehicle.
8. Describe what to do when another vehicle passes you.

Moving From a Curb into Traffic and Out of Traffic to a Curb

Basic driving skills include moving your car away from the curb and into traffic, as well as moving the car out of traffic and to the curb.

Anytime you are moving into or out of the flow of traffic, not with it, you face increased risks. You have to make judgments about visibility, time, and space. For example: Can you see well enough to make this move safely? How fast are other vehicles moving? Is there time enough and space enough to make the move?

What Is the Procedure for Leaving a Curb and Entering Traffic?

When you leave a curb, you are going from a stopped position to a moving position. This procedure in- volves planning how you will move, then actually making the move.

Advance Planning

Visibility, time, and space are im- portant factors in planning your move away from a curb.

Visibility Check your view of on- coming traffic, and also of traffic ahead of you and behind you. Notice any traffic signals, signs, and road markings.

Time Be aware of the speed limit on the roadway and how fast the vehicles in your lane are moving. Will you have enough time to move into your lane? Will vehicles behind you have to slow down or stop when you merge into traffic?

Space Check the space in front of and behind your vehicle. Decide

As with any driving maneuver, you must plan ahead before leaving a curb and entering traffic. ▶

◄
Once you have prepared in advance, you are ready to move into the traffic flow.

whether you have room to pull out of your parked position in one smooth move or whether you'll have to maneuver back and forth to clear the vehicle in front of you. Make sure you have room to enter the roadway and still keep a safe distance between your car and the one in front of you.

Making the Move

Once you've made your plan, follow these steps for making the move.
1. Use your side- and rearview mirrors to check traffic around you.
2. Turn to your left and look over your shoulder to check traffic in your blind spot.

Parking Beyond an Intersection

Be especially careful if you have decided to park in a space or make a turn just beyond an intersection. Follow these steps.

1. Don't signal right or left as you approach the intersection. Other drivers may think you're going to turn at the intersection.
2. If other cars are near the intersection, move carefully into the correct lane and slow down.
3. Use your signals only after you have entered the intersection.

3. When you've decided it is safe to move into traffic, signal your intention to leave the curb.
4. Steer away from the curb and directly into the nearest lane of traffic, accelerating moderately. If traffic is heavy, you may want to use an arm signal. (See Chapter 9 for instructions on how and when to use arm signals.)

What Is the Procedure for Steering to the Curb?

Steering your car out of traffic and toward a curb also requires advance planning before you actually make the move.

Advance Planning

You need to make plans in advance whenever you move your vehicle out of traffic.

WHAT WOULD YOU DO?

You hear an emergency vehicle approaching as you are about to pull away from the curb. What steps would you take?

As with moving away from a curb, visibility, time, and space are key factors in your plan to move *toward* the curb.

Visibility   Pick out the spot where you want to stop. Scan the traffic scene in front of you, and use your mirrors to check traffic behind you and to your sides.

Time   Note the speed of the traffic you're in. Consider how much you'll have to slow down in order to make the move.

Space   Notice the amount of room available to you to move into another lane, if you need to do so in order to get to the curb. Is there space to move your car directly into the parking area, or will you need to parallel park?

Making the Move

After you've planned your move and decided it's safe to move toward the curb, follow these steps.

1. Signal your intent to move.
2. Tap your brakes lightly, signaling to drivers behind you that you are going to stop.
3. Apply gradual pressure on the brakes to reduce speed.
4. Steer out of the traffic lane to where you want to go, using your brakes as needed to stop the car.

CHECKPOINT

1. What are some factors to consider when moving your car away from a curb and into the flow of traffic?
2. How can your wish to park near an intersection affect the way you exit from the flow of traffic?

Managing Power and Speed on Hills and Mountains

Whenever you drive, you always have an invisible passenger with you. That passenger is the force of gravity. Gravity works both inside and outside your car at the same time.

If you're driving uphill, the force of gravity works against your car, so you need to use more power. If you're driving downhill, gravity is working with you, so you need to use less power, and you may have to use your brakes. For more information about gravity and how it affects your car, see Chapter 13.

How Do You Drive Uphill and Downhill?

Driving on hills takes special effort, regardless of whether your car has an automatic transmission or a manual transmission.

Driving Uphill

As you drive uphill, your car needs more power in order to keep moving at the same speed. How you provide

ENERGY TIPS

If your car is equipped with cruise control, don't use it when you're driving uphill or downhill. It wastes gas. Save it for flat, straight roadways.

Whether you are driving uphill or downhill, the force of gravity is pulling on your car.
▼

▲
Shift to a lower gear to control speed when driving down a long, steep hill.

SAFETY TIPS

Be especially alert when you're driving through a falling rock zone. Be prepared to brake suddenly or take other evasive maneuvers.

that power depends on whether your car has an automatic or a manual transmission.

Automatic transmission Before your car begins to lose speed by moving uphill, slowly increase the amount of pressure you're putting on the gas pedal. Notice your speedometer. When you've reached the speed you want to maintain, keep your foot at that point until you need to slow down for any reason.

Manual transmission Before your car begins to lose power and speed, downshift to a lower gear in order to increase the engine's pulling power. (For more information on downshifting, see Chapter 7.)

Driving Downhill

As you drive downhill, your car will gain speed, so you need to decrease the engine power.

Automatic Transmission Ease off the pressure you're applying to the gas pedal. Your car will begin to

coast. If it begins to pick up too much speed, press the brake pedal lightly to slow down. If you're going down a long steep hill, it is best to move the selector lever to a lower gear. Doing so gives you better control of your speed and steering, and saves on braking. If you need to use the brake, use light pressure. Don't ride the brake pedal.

Manual transmission If you're going down a long hill, it may be best to downshift to a lower gear before you start down the hill. Doing so gives you more control over the speed of your car by allowing you to use engine drag. If you wait to shift until you are moving downhill and picking up speed, you will need to apply the brakes lightly while shifting to the next lower gear. If the hill is steep, your engine's braking power may not be enough to slow the car unless you continue to apply the brakes. If this is the case, quickly downshift again. Use the brakes to slow down even more if you need to.

How Do You Drive on Mountains?

Driving up or down mountains presents special problems. The roads are curved, sometimes sharply, and the uphill and downhill grades are steep. You need to use extra care to be able to control your car under these conditions.

Special Roadway and Traffic Problems

Sharp curves, steep grades, and other vehicles limit how much of the road ahead you can see at one time.

When you come to a curve where it's difficult to see oncoming traffic, slow down. If necessary, tap your horn and flash your lights to warn approaching drivers.

If you are behind a truck or car with a trailer, slow down even more than you would behind another car and increase your following distance. Pay very careful attention to signs and pavement markings.

Effects of Weather and Altitude

Rain, snow, haze, and fog are especially dangerous when you're driving in the mountains. Try to find out about the weather conditions in the area before you begin a mountain drive.

In high altitudes, the air contains less oxygen. Lack of oxygen can cause you to feel short of breath and sleepy. Your heart might beat faster and you may get a headache. If any of these symptoms occur, change drivers, stop driving, or find a route at a lesser altitude, if possible.

Mountain air also affects your car's engine. It doesn't get as much oxygen and loses power. It heats up faster, and gas may vaporize in the fuel line, causing the engine to sputter and stall. Keep an eye on the temperature gauge when driving in the mountains. If it shows red or hot, stop and allow the engine to cool off.

Driving Up a Mountain

If your car has an automatic transmission, use the same procedure to drive up a mountain as you would use if you were driving up a hill. The transmission will downshift automat-ically. If you have a manual transmission, you may need to downshift often to go up steep inclines.

Driving Down a Mountain

If you're driving with an automatic transmission, downshift manually for better control when going down a mountain. Don't ride the brake pedal. Use light pressure on the brakes to slow down gradually. If you're driving with a manual shift, downshift often to reduce speed, maintain control, and save on braking.

CHECKPOINT

3. How are procedures for driving uphill different from those for driving downhill?
4. How can high altitude affect you and your car if you're driving in the mountains?

WHAT WOULD YOU DO?

Your car has automatic transmission, and you've been using the Drive gear. Describe your procedure as you are about to head up a hill.

Managing Visibility, Time, and Space when Changing Lanes

The oldest known network of roads for commercial use was established in China during the Chou Dynasty, which ruled from 1122 to 221 B.C. Traffic was so heavy that laws were passed decreeing a uniform wheel size, the prohibition of reckless driving, and the establishment of traffic regulations at busy intersections.

You should take road conditions into account before you decide to change lanes.
▼

You have probably seen drivers who are constantly changing lanes, swooping between other cars on the highway. Chances are they're exceeding the speed limit and endangering lives. Of course, there are times when you and other drivers need to change lanes. You can minimize risk by learning the right way to do it.

What Is the Safest Way to Change Lanes?

As with other safe driving procedures, changing lanes involves two major phases: advance planning and making the change.

Advance Planning

You may have a number of reasons for changing lanes. You may need to change lanes to make a turn, pass another vehicle, avoid an obstacle in your lane, park, or exit a road. Whatever the reason for changing lanes, you need to plan ahead in order to make the move safely. Planning includes knowing where you are now, where you want to go, and what the road conditions are between the two. Check these items as you plan your move.

Visibility   What is the path of travel like in the lane you are in? Note if there are vehicles in the path ahead and what they are doing. Use your mirrors to check for vehicles behind you. What is the path of travel like in the lane you want to enter? Scan ahead 20 to 30 seconds and to the sides and rear.

Are other vehicles signaling to move into the lane you want to move to? If there are, wait until the other vehicles have changed lanes. Then check again.

Time   How fast are you going? If you need to speed up to change lanes, make sure you can do so without exceeding the speed limit.

Space   Do you have room to make the move safely? Make sure there is a gap between vehicles that you can move into safely.

Making the Change

When you've checked out your plan to change lanes and are ready to make the move, follow these steps.

1. Check your mirrors again.
2. Signal your intent to move right or left.

Tips for New Drivers

Communicating with Other Drivers

Your safety, the safety of your passengers, and the safety of other roadway users depends to a large extent on how well you communicate with other drivers and with pedestrians. Good roadway communication involves giving clear signals and warnings, paying attention to signals and warnings given by other drivers, and noticing where pedestrians are and what they're doing.

Drivers exchange four basic kinds of communication.

Intentions plan to turn left or right; slowing down; plan to pass (please move over); plan to back up

Warnings trouble ahead in my lane; need to stop suddenly; danger in your lane; headlights are blinding

Presence parked car; disabled car

Feedback recognizing another driver's signal; recognizing the presence of a pedestrian; thanks to a driver for allowing you to pass

Here is how to communicate.

Electronic signals turn signal lights, brake lights, backup lights, emergency hazard flashers; horn (short, sharp, or steady blasts); headlights (flash on and off, switch from high to low beams)

Body gestures hand signals; nodding up and down; shaking head sideways; smiling; puzzled or confused look; raised eyebrows

?

WHAT WOULD YOU DO?

You want to move into the right hand lane. How would you manage visibility, time, and space?

3. Check over your shoulder nearest the lane you want to enter for vehicles in your blind spot.
4. Adjust your speed up or down as necessary.
5. Move only when you have the time and space to do so.
6. Steer smoothly into the next lane. Push/pull steering is best. (For more information on push/pull steering, see Chapter 7.) After you've steered into the next lane, turn off your signals.

CHECKPOINT

5. Describe what you would check before you change lanes.

Passing Another Vehicle and Being Passed

Passing another vehicle on a two-lane, two-way roadway can be one of the most dangerous movements in driving.

What Conditions Will Help You Decide if You Should or Should Not Pass?

Before you pass another vehicle on a road with one lane of traffic in each direction, you need to know whether or not passing is legal. If passing is legal, you then need to decide if it makes sense to pass under existing traffic, weather, and road conditions. Finally, you need to decide if your speed, the speed of the car ahead of you, and the speed limit make it possible for you to pass safely.

Road Signs and Pavement Markings

Warning signs and roadway markings will tell you if passing is allowed in the area in which you're driving. (See Chapter 4.)

Atmospheric Conditions

Bright sunlight, rain, snow, sleet, hail, and fog add to the danger of passing. If you're driving under these conditions, it is wiser to slow down, proceed with caution, and perhaps avoid passing even if road signs and markings indicate that passing is allowed.

Nighttime visibility and the condition of the road surface can also add to the danger of passing. If you can't see ahead to the place where you will reenter the lane after passing, don't attempt to pass. If the road surface seems rough or in poor condition, avoid passing.

Your Speed and the Other Vehicle's Speed

As you approach a vehicle in front of you, note your speed. You may have to slow down to keep a margin of safety between your car and the vehicle ahead. Estimate how fast the vehicle is moving. If it is going 5 to 10 miles per hour slower than you were

If you're driving a car at 50 miles per hour, it will take you about 16 seconds to pass another car traveling at 40 miles per hour.

THE MATH CONNECTION

How fast are you really traveling when you're in a car?

MILES PER HOUR	FEET PER SECOND
30	44
40	58
50	73

The fastest human runners can run a mile in about 4 minutes. That's about 22 feet per second.

before you began to slow down, you might decide to pass.

You must also be aware of the speed limit on the roadway. You will typically need to accelerate to at least 10 miles per hour faster than the vehicle in front of you in order to pass it. However, you cannot legally exceed the speed limit to pass another vehicle.

How Do You Pass Another Vehicle?

Once you know it's legal to pass, and it makes sense to pass in the situation, follow this procedure.

1. Check the path ahead, the off-road areas, behind you, and the lane you want to enter. Make sure no other vehicles are signaling to move into the lane. If you are on a two-lane, two-way road, check that there are no oncoming vehicles. If there are, make sure that they are far enough away to allow you to complete passing safely. If you have any doubt, don't pass.
2. If the way is clear, signal your intent to move left. Flash your headlights. Use your turn signals.
3. Check over your left shoulder for cars in your blind spot. Adjust your speed upward as necessary, and steer smoothly into the passing lane. Use very slight controlled movement of the wheel— usually not more than one-eighth of a turn.
4. Accelerate firmly. If you're on a road with a single lane in each direction, keep watching for oncoming traffic.
5. Check your rearview mirror

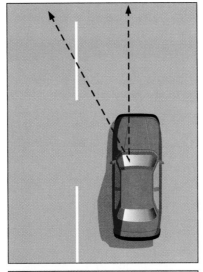

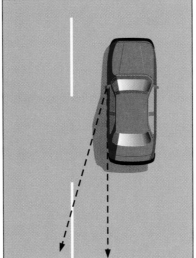

quickly. When you see both headlights of the vehicle you've passed in the mirror, signal your intent to return to the right lane and steer gradually in that direction. Turn off your signal and maintain an appropriate speed.

What Should You Do if You're Being Passed?

Drivers of vehicles that are passing you assume the responsibility for

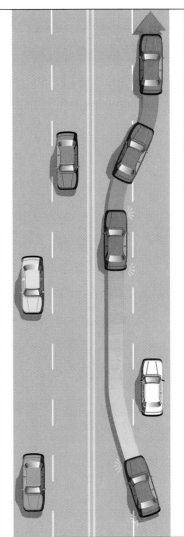

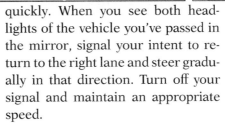

Before you pass, check your path ahead and to the sides and rear. Signal, pass, and signal again before returning to your lane.

*Barry Caruso, Coordinator
Traffic Safety Education,
Wayne County Public
Schools, Ohio*

Barry Caruso

Basic on-road procedures—such as moving to and from the curb, driving on grades, changing lanes, and passing—never change. The better you perform these procedures, the more predictable you are. A good driver is very predictable. A predictable driver communicates every move. Once you have perfected basic on-road procedures, you need to tell other drivers what you are doing.

Remember, as the driver you are responsible for the action of your vehicle. Be as good a driver as you can, and THINK!

WHAT WOULD YOU DO?

Does it make sense for the driver of the car to try to pass the van?

their safety and yours, but you can often protect yourself and be of help to the passing driver.

By regularly checking your side- and rearview mirrors, you can remain aware of the movement of vehicles behind you and alongside of you. When you see that you're being passed, stay to the right in your lane. Do not speed up: It's illegal to do so when you're being passed.

Remain aware of the traffic situation around you. Sometimes a passing vehicle will decide to drop back rather than complete the pass. Don't accelerate unless it is necessary to give the vehicle more room to get back behind you.

CHECKPOINT

6. What should you consider before deciding to pass another vehicle?
7. How are visibility, time, and space important when passing another vehicle?
8. How can you help another driver who is passing you?

CHAPTER 8 REVIEW

KEY POINTS

LESSON ONE

1. To move your car away from a curb and into the flow of traffic, check traffic in front and in back of you, the speed of vehicles already on the roadway, and the space available to you for moving away from the curb.

2. To move your car out of traffic and toward the curb, prepare the move well in advance. Check traffic behind you, signal your intention, steer toward the curb, and brake as needed.

LESSON TWO

3. To drive up or down hills, downshift and accelerate or brake as necessary.

4. Use your horn and lights to signal your presence when you can't see around a sharp curve ahead. Increase your following distance, and be aware of the effects of low oxygen on your body and your car.

LESSON THREE

5. To change lanes correctly, plan your move in advance, communicate your intent to other drivers, check your blind spot, and begin and complete the move. Adjust your speed to meet the situation.

LESSON FOUR

6. Before you pass another vehicle, note whether passing is legal. Consider the effects of weather and road conditions on your ability to manage visibility, time, and space.

7. To pass another vehicle, make sure you have a clear path of travel, signal your intent, check your blind spot, and begin the pass. Accelerate, and return to the lane when you see both headlights of the vehicle you've passed in your rearview mirror.

8. If you are being passed, pay particular attention to the movement of the passing vehicle. You can help a driver who is passing you by giving the vehicle enough time and space, remaining aware of the movement of other vehicles, and not speeding up.

PROJECTS

1. Take a ride as a passenger and record the different forms of communication you notice between drivers. Include communication by mechanical or electronic signals and by body signals. What kinds of information do drivers communicate by each method?

2. Can you tell from reading your state's driver's manual whether or not your state is one that has many mountain roads? How much space does the manual devote to mountain driving? Interview a traffic control officer or state trooper to find out whether more crashes occur in hill or mountain driving than in lowland driving.

CHAPTER 8 REVIEW

BUILDING LANGUAGE SKILLS

Using Prefixes and Combining Forms

The vocabulary describing vehicles and road-ways is full of interesting words. Several of these words are formed by using a prefix and a root word.

A prefix is a word part that has a meaning of its own but cannot stand alone as a word by itself. Here are some examples of prefixes and their meanings:

anti—not, against
de—removed, reversed
dis—apart, away from
inter—between, among
re—again
trans—across, beyond, or through
un—not

The vocabulary of driving also includes words that begin with a combining form. This is a word part that can act like a prefix, but it can also join another combining form to make a word, such as *photo + graphy.* Two common combining forms are *auto,* meaning "self," and *semi,* meaning "half" or "partly."

Knowing the meanings and uses of prefixes and combining forms can help you figure out the meanings of new words.

Try It Yourself

Choose a prefix or combining form from those above in order to complete each word or term below. Define the words and terms, using what you already know and what you've learned about prefixes and combining forms. If you don't know what a word or term means, ask someone or look it up.

1. __ celeration
2. __ preciation
3. __ national symbols
4. __ action time
5. __ abled
6. __ protected left turn
7. __ change
8. __ section
9. __ alignment
10. __ lock brakes
11. __ freeze
12. __ fogger
13. __ theft device
14. __ tread
15. __ mission

-national -lock -section re-
un- dis-
anti- de- -mission
-freeze trans. inter-

CHAPTER 8 REVIEW

CHAPTER TEST

Write the letter of the answer that best completes each sentence.

1. When passing another vehicle you must
   a. drive 5 mph above the speed limit.
   b. must typically accelerate to at least 10 mph faster than the other vehicle.
   c. must briefly flash your emergency lights.
2. In order to complete a pass safely, you should
   a. see the other vehicle's headlights in your rearview mirror.
   b. have at least five seconds total passing time.
   c. tap your horn lightly.
3. You see a parking space across an intersection. You should
   a. cross the intersection, signal, and park.
   b. signal, cross the intersection, and park.
   c. cross the intersection, park, and signal.
4. When driving downhill in a car with a manual transmission you should
   a. downshift to gain more control.
   b. upshift to decrease engine power.
   c. ride the clutch to maintain an even speed.
5. Driving on mountain roads can cause you to
   a. become short of breath and feel sleepy.
   b. lose control of the gears.
   c. lose the effects of gravity.
6. When changing lanes,
   a. turn off the radio.
   b. make sure you are not on a one-way street.
   c. use push/pull steering.
7. Drivers exchange information about
   a. intentions.
   b. communications.
   c. markings.

8. You can help another driver to pass you on a two-way, two-lane road by
   a. moving to the right.
   b. speeding up.
   c. putting on your high beams.
9. In moving from a curb, you must
   a. quickly accelerate and join the flow of traffic.
   b. avoid using hand signals.
   c. make judgments about visibility, time, and space.
10. When you come to a curve where you can't see oncoming traffic, you should
    a. tap your horn and flash your lights.
    b. change lanes.
    c. use both your side and rearview mirrors.

Write the word or phrase that best completes each sentence.

communicate   gravity   altitudes
atmospheric conditions   advance planning

11. You should avoid passing in rain, snow, or other dangerous _____ .

12. Driving at high _____ can affect the performance of your car.

13. You can _____ with other drivers with electric signals or body gestures.

14. When driving downhill, _____ causes a car to speed up.

15. Checking mirrors, the roadway, your path of travel, and traffic behind you are all part of _____ .

DRIVER'S LOG

In this chapter, you have learned about some basic driving skills, such as moving to and from a curb, changing lanes, and passing. Which do you think will be hardest for you? Write two paragraphs explaining why and what you will do to gain confidence in your ability to execute the manuever.

CUMULATIVE REVIEW

This review tests your knowledge of the material in Chapters 1–8. Use the review to help you study for your state driving test. Choose the answer that best suits the question.

1. A driver gathers the most information through
   a. hearing.
   b. vision.
   c. touch.
   d. memory.

2. Administrative laws require
   a. car owners to be financially responsible.
   b. manufacturers to buy insurance.
   c. the governor to make traffic laws.
   d. the federal government to set car prices.

3. Drugs that slow down your reflexes are
   a. stimulants.
   b. depressants.
   c. hallucinogens.
   d. prosthetic.

4. When being passed on the left,
   a. speed up slightly.
   b. stay in the right side of the lane.
   c. stay in the left side of the lane.
   d. change lanes.

5. If you are involved in a collision,
   a. stop immediately.
   b. go home and call the police.
   c. find witnesses.
   d. sign documents at the scene.

6. Traffic control signals are typically located
   a. on expressways.
   b. at intersections.
   c. at interchanges.
   d. on the dashboard.

7. A dangerous drug that changes the way you see, think, and act is a
   a. stimulant.
   b. hallucinogen.
   c. depressant.
   d. prescription.

8. Strong emotions can
   a. improve your driving ability.
   b. cause you to be inattentive.
   c. help you to stay alert.
   d. improve your judgment.

9. A car with manual transmission has a
   a. clutch pedal.
   b. choke pedal.
   c. gear selector lever.
   d. Smith System.

10. When a driver's license is taken away permanently, it is
    a. revoked.
    b. suspended.
    c. intoxicated.
    d. inhibited.

11. Traffic moving in opposite directions is separated by
    a. white lines.
    b. yellow lines.
    c. regulatory signs.
    d. shock absorbers.

12. Alcohol is absorbed into the bloodstream through the
    a. skin.
    b. stomach wall.
    c. adrenal gland.
    d. tongue.

13. The basic speed rule states that you should
    a. adjust your car's speed to weather and road conditions.
    b. drive at one-half the posted speed limit.
    c. drive at the posted speed limit.
    d. check your car's speedometer every few seconds.

14. The direction of a car's front wheels is controlled by the
    a. accelerator.
    b. steering wheel.
    c. clutch.
    d. alternator.

15. Warning signs are usually
  a. yellow or orange.
  b. blue and white.
  c. green or blue.
  d. black and white.

16. HOV lanes are for use by
  a. cyclists.
  b. pedestrians.
  c. vehicles carrying 2 or more passengers.
  d. emergency vehicles.

17. To start a car with an automatic transmission, the gear selector lever should be in
  a. Park.
  b. choke.
  c. Neutral.
  d. First gear.

18. Using headlights during daylight
  a. can increase your visibility to others.
  b. is a waste of energy.
  c. is illegal in some states.
  d. can increase your risk of a collision.

19. This sign STOP requires that you
  a. proceed with caution.
  b. come to a full stop.
  c. yield to vehicles in the cross street.
  d. slow down.

20. You can prove ownership of a car with a
  a. birth certificate.
  b. certificate of title.
  c. certificate of registration.
  d. driver's license.

21. A car's engine will run more efficiently at high speeds when in
  a. Reverse gear.
  b. Low gear.
  c. First gear.
  d. Overdrive gear.

22. When driving down a mountain,
  a. shift to a lower gear.
  b. shift into reverse.
  c. lock the brakes.
  d. exceed the speed limit.

23. A driver can usually sense a clutch's friction point best in
  a. first gear.
  b. third gear.
  c. Reverse gear.
  d. Neutral gear.

24. To keep a parked car from rolling, use
  a. cruise control.
  b. the accelerator.
  c. the emergency brake.
  d. the SIPDE process.

25. Regulatory signs
  a. control the flow of traffic.
  b. warn of changes in roadway conditions.
  c. are usually spaced 100 feet apart.
  d. are usually green or brown.

26. To prevent locking a car's wheels, use
  a. the Smith System.
  b. threshold braking.
  c. the ignition switch.
  d. motor oil.

27. Recreational area signs are
  a. brown.
  b. blue.
  c. green.
  d. red.

28. At high altitudes, a car runs a risk of
  a. exploding.
  b. overheating.
  c. hydroplaning.
  d. locking.

29. To warn others that your car is stopped on the side of the road, use
  a. the dome light.
  b. a dipstick.
  c. an emergency brake warning light.
  d. emergency flashers.

30. Large trucks
  a. gain speed slowly.
  b. gain speed quickly.
  c. frequently roll over.
  d. usually have four-cylinder engines.

MOVING ONTO THE ROAD

Once you are behind the wheel, you need to perform many complicated maneuvers. This unit will help you understand these maneuvers in order to become a responsible driver.

UNIT CONTENTS

TURNING AND PARKING

The ability to execute turns and parking maneuvers properly requires practice, good judgment, and knowledge of traffic laws. It is important that you learn the techniques that will enable you to perform these maneuvers safely.

CHAPTER 9 OBJECTIVES

How to Prepare for and Execute a Right Turn

1. List the procedures to follow when preparing to turn right at an intersection.
2. Describe the steps needed to execute a right turn.

How to Prepare for and Execute a Left Turn

3. Describe how to prepare for a left turn.
4. State how to make a left turn from a one-way street and from a two-way street.

Planning and Executing a Reverse in Direction

5. Describe how to prepare to make a turnabout.
6. Describe four ways to make a turnabout.

How to Prepare for and Execute a Parking Maneuver

7. Describe how to angle park and perpendicular park.
8. Describe how to parallel park.
9. Describe how to park in a driveway, in a garage, and on a hill.

How to Prepare for and Execute a Right Turn

Manage risk. Be aware that more than one-third of all collisions occur at intersections.

Suppose that you are driving along the roadway and want to turn right at the next intersection. What should you do? To answer that question, you need to learn the basics of control and visual search and make good use of time and space.

How Do You Prepare to Make a Right Turn?

Before you execute a right turn at an intersection, check the roadway, choose the correct lane, communicate your intentions, and position the car correctly. Prepare for the turn 200 to 300 feet in advance of the intersection.

Check

Check for signs and markings that control your movement. Is a traffic signal, a yield sign, or a stop sign present? Are turns allowed? If so, are

they restricted to certain times of day or to certain types of vehicles? Are there special turning lanes?

Choose

Choose the correct lane. Move into the lane, after you make sure that it is clear, and reduce your speed.

Communicate

Let other drivers know that you plan to turn by signaling early. A flashing brake light will warn drivers behind you that you plan to turn. Use your turn signal 150 feet in advance of the turn.

Position the Car

Position your car to the right side of the right lane, 3 to 5 feet from the curb or shoulder. Check other traffic in, at, and approaching the intersection. Make sure no cyclists are to

Make right turns from the lane closest to the right curb unless they are allowed from other lanes. Turn into the lane corresponding to the one you just left. ▶

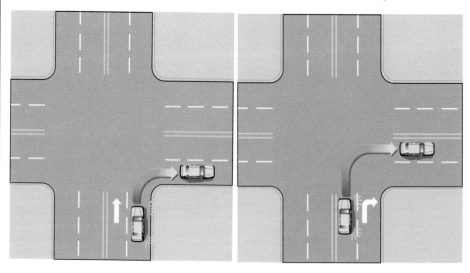

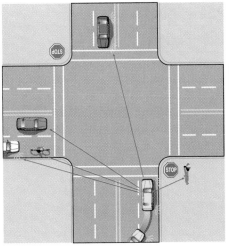

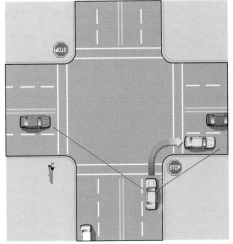

◀

Move to the right lane in advance of a right turn. Check for pedestrians and other vehicles, including those across the intersection, before turning.

your right. If you are at a stop sign or red signal, stop before the crosswalk. If necessary, move up to a point where you can see cross traffic. Be prepared to yield to pedestrians.

How Do You Execute a Right Turn?

The steps for executing a right turn are the same whether you are turning onto a one-way or a two-way street. After you have positioned yourself correctly and signaled your intentions, check again for cross traffic. Then follow these steps.

1. If there is no traffic signal or stop sign, find a 7- to 8-second gap in traffic to your left. Just before turning, scan the intersection again to the left.

2. When your front wheels are opposite the point where the curb begins to curve, look through the turn along your intended path of travel. Begin the turn, using hand-over-hand or push/pull steering.

3. Follow the general curve of the curb as you turn. Stay in the right

lane by looking through the turn along the intended driving path.

4. Complete the turn by reversing your steering. Make sure the turn signal is off.

CHECKPOINT

1. What should you do before you turn right at an intersection?

2. How do you make a right turn?

WHAT WOULD YOU DO?

You want to turn right at the next intersection. How will you proceed?

How to Prepare for and Execute a Left Turn

SAFETY TIPS

When you are turning either right or left at an intersection, be very careful not to signal too early if there are other places to turn before the intersection. A driver in another roadway who believes you intend to turn somewhere else could pull out in front of you.

Position your car in advance of a left turn. Check for pedestrians and other vehicles in and across the intersection.

When you make a left turn, you follow many of the same procedures you use to make right turns. However, be aware that a driver turning left *must* yield right of way to any cross traffic and to vehicles approaching from the opposite direction.

How Do You Prepare for a Left Turn?

To prepare for a left turn, check the roadway, choose the correct lane, communicate your intentions by signaling, and position your car correctly. Remember to reduce speed before making your turn.

Check

Check for traffic signs and signals, and traffic ahead and to the left and right. Be sure no one is about to pass you on your left side.

Choose the Correct Lane

Signal and move into the correct lane. Stop behind the stop line if there is one. Keep your wheels straight.

Communicate Your Intentions

Don't forget to signal your turn 150 feet in advance of the intersection. Flash your brake lights by tapping the brake pedal. Use your turn signal.

Position the Car

Position your car just to the right of the center line or, on a one-way street, the left curb.

How Can You Execute a Left Turn?

The steps for executing a left turn depend on the type of street you are

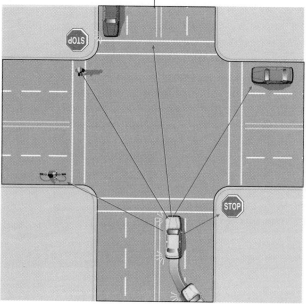

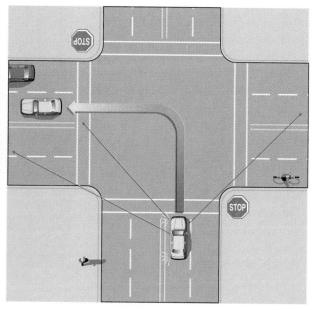

Use an arm (or hand) signal to communicate better with drivers behind you.

Left Turn   **Right Turn**   **Stop**

on and the type of street you are turning onto.

Turning Left from a Two-Way Street onto a Two-Way Street

1. Check that there are no vehicles, pedestrians, or other obstacles in your intended path of travel.
2. Find a 9-second gap to your right and a 7-second gap to your left.
3. Proceed into the intersection until you are about one lane width away from its center. Yield to any approaching traffic and pedestrians in the intersection. Keep your wheels straight.
4. Look through the turn along your intended path of travel. Begin the turn, using hand-over-hand or push/pull steering.
5. Follow the path of travel so that you arrive in the lane just to the right of the center line. Complete the turn by reversing your steering. Be sure the turn signal is off.

THE SOCIAL STUDIES CONNECTION

In 1983, President Ronald Reagan made a historic appointment to his cabinet. For the first time, a woman was named Secretary of Transportation. The woman was Elizabeth Hanford Dole and, in her position, she was the "boss" of 102,000 employees with a yearly budget of over $28 billion. As Secretary of Transportation, she was in charge of coordinating programs that provide safe, economical, and efficient transportation on land, sea, and in the air.

Elizabeth Dole began her public-service career in the third grade in Salisbury, North Carolina. She was elected president of the Bird Club. She says that the election lit a spark that never died. "Liddy" Dole went to Duke University and then Harvard Law School. She remembers being shocked at Harvard to discover that only 4 percent of the students in her class were women and being angrily told by a male classmate that she had no right to be there. "You're taking the place of a qualified man," he said.

In her position at the Department of Transportation, Mrs. Dole introduced a nine-point plan to promote the women who had made up only 19 percent of the Department. She also made sure that a billion dollars' worth of transportation contracts were awarded to minority-owned businesses. Elizabeth Dole is now President of the American Red Cross.

CULTURAL CROSSROADS

You need to learn which lane to enter when turning left from a one-way street onto another one-way street and onto a two-way street. ▶

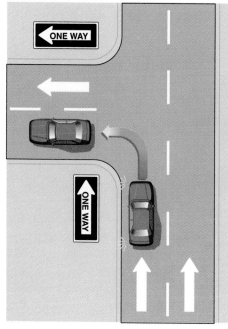

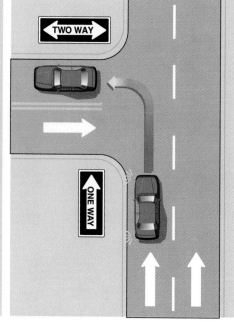

WHAT WOULD YOU DO?

You want to turn left. How will you prepare for the turn? To whom will you yield right of way?

Turning Left from a Two-Way Street onto a One-Way Street

Turning onto a one-way street is like turning onto a two-way street, except that you enter the lane of traffic closest to the intersection.

Turning Left from a One-Way Street Onto a One-Way Street

Making a left turn from one one-way street onto another is similar to making other left turns. However, you will not have to cross a lane of traffic coming toward you.

Turning Left from a One-Way Street onto a Two-Way Street

If you are turning left from a one-way street onto a two-way street, position your car in the far left-hand lane. Then turn into the first lane of traffic going in your direction.

CHECKPOINT

3. What should you do *before* you make a left turn?
4. How would you make a left turn from a two-way street onto another two-way street?

Planning and Executing a Reverse in Direction

No matter how skillful a driver you are, you may sometimes miss a street or building you are looking for. If so, you may have no choice but to turn around, or make a *turnabout*.

How Should You Prepare to Make a Turnabout?

As in all maneuvers you make with your car, careful preparation is a key to managing risk. Before you make a turnabout, consider the following.

◆ Are there signs that prohibit the turnabout, such as *No U Turn* signs?
◆ Are there specific laws that prohibit the turnabout when there are no signs?
◆ Is there at least 500 feet of visibility in each direction?
◆ Are you near hills, curves, or within 200 feet of an intersection?
◆ Is there heavy traffic?
◆ Do you have enough space to complete the maneuver?
◆ Are there traffic and pedestrians in your path?

How Can You Make a Turnabout?

You can make a turnabout in one of the four ways below. Use the method that best suits traffic conditions, the street, and local traffic laws.

Two-Point Turns

The two-point turn is one method to use when making a turnabout.

Either head into or back into a driveway to reverse direction.

Backing into a driveway Back into a driveway when there is no traffic close behind you in your lane and there is a clear driveway on your right.

1. Signal early. Flash your brake lights to alert following drivers. Check for objects or children in the driveway as you drive past.
2. Stop about 3 feet from the curb, with your rear bumper just beyond the driveway you will enter. With your foot on the brake, shift into Reverse. Check again for obstacles in your intended path.

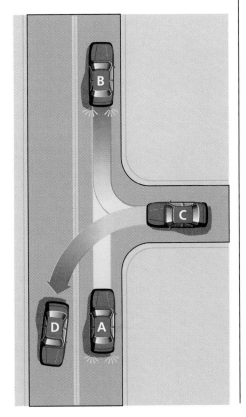

◀

If you can't go around the block, make a turnabout by backing into a driveway.

By backing into a driveway rather than heading in, you can see in both directions to better assess risk when you prepare to reenter traffic.

You can make a turnabout by heading into a driveway on the left (below) or on the right (below right).

▼

3. When it is clear, look over your right shoulder. Back up slowly, turning the wheel rapidly all the way to the right. As the rear of the car enters the driveway, turn the wheel to the left, centering the car in the driveway. Stop when the front of the car is clear of the curb.

4. Shift to Drive, signal, check traffic, and leave the driveway when it is safe to do so.

Heading into a driveway on the left When you head into a driveway, you will have to back into the street. Select a driveway on the left that affords good visibility. Make sure there are no hedges or other objects along the driveway that will obscure your view of the road.

1. Signal a left turn. Check for traffic, flash your brake lights, and stop if necessary. When the driveway is clear, turn into it as close to the right side as you can. This allows more room for the front of the car to swing left as you back out to the right.

2. When the rear bumper clears the edge of the roadway, stop with your front wheels straight. With your foot on the brake, shift into Reverse gear.

3. Look in all directions for pedestrians and over your right shoulder for traffic in your planned path. Back up slowly, rechecking traffic, and stop before crossing the curb.

4. Turn the wheel quickly all the way to the right. Keep your car in the first lane of traffic. Halfway through the turn, start to straighten the steering wheel.

5. Stop when the front wheels are straight. Check mirrors and over your shoulder, signal, shift to Drive, and accelerate to traffic speed.

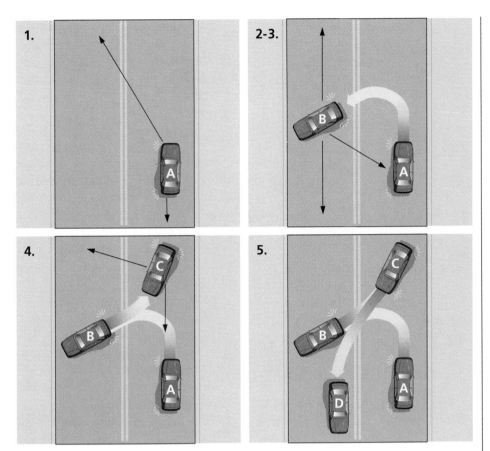

◀

You need to have a good sense of speed and steering control to make a three-point turn.

Heading into a driveway on the right Heading into a driveway on the right in order to make a turnabout is very dangerous because a driver must back across two lanes of traffic before moving forward. You should make this maneuver only in low-speed, low-traffic residential areas. Follow the steps for heading into a driveway on the left, but reverse the directions in steps 1, 3, and 4.

Three-Point Turns

One of the hardest turnabouts for the new driver is the three-point turn. To minimize risk, make a three-point turn only when the street is narrow, there are no driveways to turn into, you have very good visibility, traffic is very light, and you can't drive around the block. To make a three-point turn, follow these steps.

1. Stop as close to the right edge of the curb as possible. Check for traffic in both directions. Wait until you have a 20- to 30-second gap to complete the turn.

2. Signal a left turn. Look over your left shoulder for any cars in your blind spot. Then move the car slowly while turning the steering wheel rapidly to the left to bring the car into the opposite lane. Hold this position.

3. When the front wheels are almost to the curb (about 4 feet away), turn the wheel rapidly to the right. Stop the car just short of the curb.

4. Check traffic to your left, then

Never make a three-point turn near the top of a hill, on a curve, near an intersection, or near trees, hydrants, or other such objects.

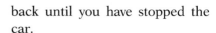

To make a U-turn, move your car slowly, but turn the steering wheel rapidly. ▶

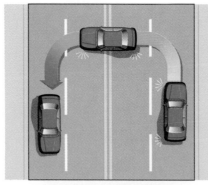

WHAT WOULD YOU DO?

You are driving north and need to turn around. How will you make the turnabout? Why?

over your right shoulder. Shift into Reverse and, while backing slowly, turn the wheel to the extreme right position. About 4 feet before stopping, turn the wheel quickly to the left. Keep looking

back until you have stopped the car.

5. Shift into Drive. Check traffic. Signal and accelerate to normal speed.

U-Turns

To make a U-turn, you do not back up, and therefore you need a wide street in which to make the turn. Be aware that U-turns are illegal in some places.

Here is how to make a U-turn on a two-lane road after first making sure the turn is legal.

1. Stop your car close to the right edge of the curb. Check for traffic in both directions. Signal a left turn. Check over your left shoulder again before starting the turn. Do not start the turn if you will interfere with traffic.

2. Turn the steering wheel rapidly all the way to the left, moving the car slowly until it is facing in the opposite direction.

3. When the turn is almost completed, straighten the wheels, and proceed in the proper lane at normal speed.

Around the Block

The fourth way to reverse direction is to drive around the block. This method is often the easiest and safest to use.

CHECKPOINT

5. What should you consider before making a turnabout?

6. How can you reverse your car's direction?

How to Prepare for and Execute a Parking Maneuver

Parking can be one of the most exasperating experiences of driving. Sometimes you feel the only way you can get into a space is by bumping nearby cars out of the way. So, how can you park easily?

Parking is an art. To park quickly, easily, and safely, you need good control of your car, accurate judgment of space, and a good understanding of steering.

In order to park safely, you need to understand the different ways to park. They are *angle parking*, *perpendicular parking*, and *parallel parking*.

How Do You Angle Park and Perpendicular Park?

When you park at an angle, you have little room to maneuver and cannot see very well. So you must be very careful when entering and leaving angled and perpendicular parking spaces.

Left- or Right-Angle Parking

You may have seen angled parking spaces in parking lots or along the streets of towns and smaller cities. The spaces are set at an angle from 30 degrees to 90 degrees to the curb or line.

To angle park on the right, follow these steps.
1. Stay 5 or 6 feet from parked cars to give yourself room to see and maneuver. Observe traffic in all directions and be alert for cars

about to leave nearby spaces. Signal for a right turn.
2. Proceed until you can see along the left side of the car to the right of the space you will enter. Steer sharply right. Creep ahead at 3 to 5 mph into the space midway between the lines. Check the left front and right rear of your car to make sure you have clearance.
3. As you straighten the wheels, move forward until the front of your car is aligned with those on both sides.

Angle parking on the left is similar to that on the right. In this case, start turning the steering wheel to the left when you can see along the right side of the car parked to the left of your chosen space. Now you must keep

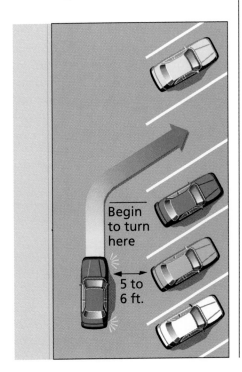

Begin to turn here

5 to 6 ft.

Do not park just around a curve or just over the crest of a hill. Drivers approaching from the rear may not see you until it is too late. To avoid colliding with you, they may have to steer into the oncoming lane.

◄

You need to position your car carefully before you enter an angled parking space.

Check that your left front fender doesn't scrape the car on the left when you exit an angled space. ▶

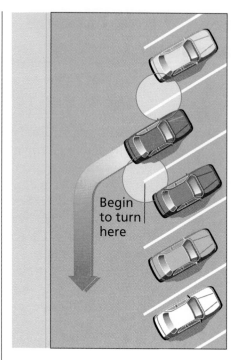

Begin to turn here

Do not park in a space next to a poorly parked car. You may find it hard to maneuver your car into and out of the space, and the other car may scrape yours when it is exiting.

Whether entering or leaving a perpendicular space, keep your car positioned 7 to 8 feet from the row of parked cars. ▶

to see at that angle and there is very little room for maneuvering.

To enter a perpendicular parking space on the right, follow these steps.

1. Stay 7 to 8 feet from parked cars for best visibility. Observe all traffic conditions and check for cars about to back out of a space. Signal for a right turn.

2. Slow to 3 to 5 mph. Start turning right when your front bumper lines up with the left side of the car to the right of your chosen space. Steer sharply right. Proceed slowly, checking for clearance of your left front bumper. Check your right rear fender to see it does not scrape the rear of the car on your right.

3. As you straighten the wheels and center in your space, move forward slowly and stop just short of the curb or in line with the cars parked beside you.

Entering a perpendicular parking space on the left is similar to entering one on the right. In this case you turn the steering wheel in the opposite direction and keep track of the right front bumper and the left rear fender.

track of the right front bumper and the left rear fender.

Perpendicular Parking

Many parking lots have parking spaces that are marked at 90 degrees to the curb or line. These are perpendicular parking spaces. Perpendicular parking is risky because it is hard

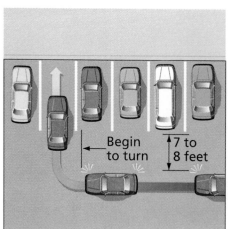

Begin to turn

7 to 8 feet

Begin to turn when your winshield is here

Exiting an Angled or a Perpendicular Parking Space

To leave an angled or a perpendicular space, follow these rules.

1. With your foot on the brake, shift into Reverse. Check all traffic around you. Back very slowly with your wheels straight, looking to your left and over your right shoulder. Keep checking the back and sides for obstacles. Yield to any oncoming traffic.

2. To exit from an angled space, turn the steering wheel sharply right when your front fender will clear the rear of the car to your right.

3. When you exit from a perpendicular space, turn the wheel slightly right or left when your windshield lines up with the rear bumpers of the cars on both sides. Make sure your front fender clears the rear of the car opposite to the direction you are turning.

4. As the car enters the traffic lane, quickly turn the steering wheel in the opposite direction to straighten the front wheels. Keep looking out the rear window until the car stops.

5. Shift into Drive, accelerate, and move into traffic.

How Do You Parallel Park?

You parallel park most often along the side of a street. Parallel parking may seem hard at first, and you'll have to practice to become expert at it. To parallel park, you need a space at least 5 feet longer than the length of your car.

Parallel Parking

Here is how to parallel park.

1. Approach the parking space in the proper lane. Check traffic behind you. Signal and flash your brake lights to alert following drivers of your intention to stop.

2. Move parallel to the car in front of the space, leaving about 3 feet between cars. Stop when the center posts of the two cars are even. Keep your foot on the brake and shift into Reverse.

3. Back up, steering sharply to the right. Align the door post with the rear bumper of the car in front.

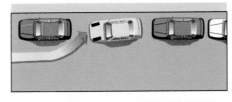

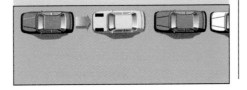

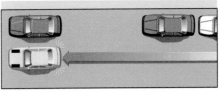

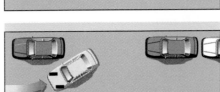

When parallel parking spaces are marked, they are typically 22 to 26 feet long and 8 feet wide. The average car length is 15 feet.

◀

It takes a great deal of practice to be able to parallel park efficiently.

ENERGY TIPS

Remember to adjust the driver's seat and all mirrors, lock the door, and fasten your safety belt *before* you start your car to save fuel.

Continue backing slowly, straightening your front wheels, until your front bumper lines up with the rear bumper of the car in front.

4. Back up, steering rapidly to the left. Stop before making contact with the bumper of the car behind the space.

5. With your foot on the brake, shift into Drive or first gear. Move forward slowly, centering your car in the parking space. Stop and set the parking brake.

To exit from a parallel parking space, follow these steps.

1. Shift into Reverse. Back slowly, straightening your wheels. When your car is about 1 foot from the car behind you, turn the wheel rapidly to the left and stop.

2. With your foot on the brake, shift into Drive or first gear. Signal a left turn. Check your blind spots. Move forward slowly, steering rapidly the rest of the way to the left.

3. Yield to approaching traffic. Then move forward slowly. When your center door post is even with the rear bumper of the car in front of you, turn the wheel right until the front wheels point straight ahead.

4. Check the position of the car to your right, being careful not to scrape it. When your rear bumper is opposite its rear bumper, accelerate gently and steer right as necessary into traffic.

How Would You Park in Other Areas?

Parking lots and city streets are not the only areas where you park. You might have to park in a driveway or a garage, or on a steep hill.

Parking in a Driveway

At times, you may have to park in a driveway. Driveways may have trees and shrubbery or fences and buildings on either side. Centering your car is especially important in a narrow driveway. Furthermore, because many driveways are often sloped downward, you should make sure to set your parking brake.

Parking in a Garage

Parking in a garage is also similar to perpendicular parking. You must make sure to center your car, either between the walls of the garage or between the sides of the garage door opening. Good positioning and the ability to judge space to your sides are important in parking in a garage. Remember to check both fenders for clearance as you back slowly out of the garage.

Parking on a Hill

Parking on a hill is similar to parking on a flat surface. However, you must make sure your car will not roll into traffic after you leave it. The procedures described here are for parking on the right side of the street. To park on the left side, make appropriate right-left adjustments.

Parking downhill with a curb To make sure your car does not roll, take these precautions.

1. Bring the car to its normal parallel-parked position. Turn the steering wheel sharply right and move slowly forward.

2. Stop the car when the front right wheel touches the curb. Set the parking brake. If your car has a manual transmission, shift into Reverse.

Parking downhill without a curb You may need to park facing downhill on a roadway that has no curb. Follow the same procedure for parking downhill with a curb, but move as close to the shoulder as possible.

Parking uphill with a curb Follow these guidelines to park facing uphill when there is a curb at the edge of the roadway.

1. Bring the car to a normal parallel-parked position.
2. Move forward slowly, turning the wheels sharply left as far as they will go. Move about 3 feet and stop.
3. In Neutral, with your foot covering the brake, allow the car to roll back slowly with the wheels cramped left until the rear of the

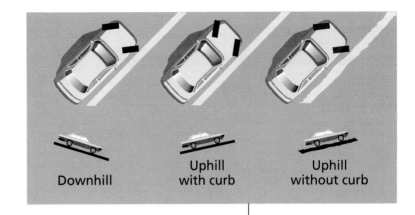

Downhill   Uphill with curb   Uphill without curb

right front tire touches the curb. Set the parking brake. If your car has a manual transmission, shift to first gear.

Parking uphill without a curb To park uphill on a road without a curb, follow the procedure for uphill parking with a curb. However, center the car in the space with the front wheels turned to the right so that if the car begins to roll, it will move off the roadway.

▲
When you park on a hill, position the front wheels so that the car cannot roll into the roadway.

ips for New Drivers

Leaving a Car Safely

Don't be careless. Learn the safe way to leave your car.
- With your foot firmly on the brake pedal, shift into Park (automatic) or Reverse (manual).
- Set the parking brake.
- Close all windows.
- Turn the key to the lock position, and remove it from the ignition switch. Turn your steering wheel slightly to lock it too.
- Check for approaching traffic. Look in your mirrors *and* check your blind spot.
- Wait for a break in traffic before opening the door. Then open it only far enough and long enough to get out of the car.
- Lock the door. Then, keeping an eye on traffic, move quickly around the rear of the car toward the curb.
- Whenever possible, have passengers exit from the curb side of the car.

Advice From the Experts

Carolyne Wilmoth
Classroom Driver Education Instructor
AAA Colorado

Carolyne Wilmoth

You use the same techniques to park, make turnabouts, and turn at intersections. The maneuvers you can make are not always the same. So, you need to understand signs, signals, and pavement markings. You must also practice proper techniques for visual search, steering, speed-control, and space management.

While low-speed and close-quarter maneuvers are rarely associated with serious injuries or deaths, it is still worthwhile always to use the correct procedures.

WHAT WOULD YOU DO?

What procedures will you follow in order to park on the hill?

Restrictions on Parking

Every state has its own parking restrictions. Before you decide to park your car anywhere, make sure that you will be parked legally. Parking laws may differ from state to state. However, in most states it is illegal to park in these areas:

- ◆ at a bus stop
- ◆ in a loading zone
- ◆ in the traffic lane beside another vehicle (double parking)
- ◆ on a sidewalk
- ◆ half in, half out of a driveway
- ◆ across someone else's driveway
- ◆ within a given distance of a fire hydrant
- ◆ in the fire zone in front of schools and in front of other public and private buildings
- ◆ in a no-standing zone

CHECKPOINT

7. What should you do when entering an angled parking space?
8. How would you parallel park?
9. What should you do when parking on a hill or in a driveway or in a garage?

CHAPTER 9 REVIEW

KEY POINTS

LESSON ONE

1. To prepare for a right turn, check the roadway, choose the correct lane, and communicate by signaling well in advance of the turn. Position your car to the right side of the right lane.

2. To execute a right turn, find a gap in traffic to your left, look along your intended path of travel, and turn the car, following the curve of the curb.

LESSON TWO

3. To prepare for a left turn at an intersection, check the roadway, choose the correct lane, and communicate your intentions. Position your car just to the right of the center line or, on a one-way street, the left curb.

4. When turning left, check for other vehicles, pedestrians, and cars across the intersection. Look for a 9-second gap to your right and a 7-second gap to your left. Look through the turn along your intended path of travel, and turn the car.

LESSON THREE

5. To prepare to make a turnabout, consider its legality in the situation, the amont of visibility, the amount and position of traffic, and the space available.

6. To turn your car around, you can make a two-point turn by heading into or backing into a driveway, make a three-point turn, make a U-turn, or drive around the block. The method you use depends on its legality and on traffic and roadway conditions.

LESSON FOUR

7. To perform a perpendicular or angle parking maneuver, position your car correctly for best visibility; check for traffic and obstructions and signal; turn into the space when you have clearance on all sides.

8. To parallel park, move parallel to the car in front of the space; back slowly into the space; and center your car in the space.

9. Be aware of objects on either side when you park in a driveway or garage. Centering your car is especially important. To park uphill or downhill, position the front wheels in such a way that your car cannot roll into the roadway.

PROJECTS

1. Observe a spot where turnabouts are permitted on a well-traveled road. Prepare a chart showing the kinds of turnabouts you observed drivers making and the frequency of each type of turnabout. Note any problems the drivers had in making the turnabouts. Discuss your observations with your class.

2. Observe several cars parked uphill and downhill. Record how each car's front wheels are positioned. Make a diagram showing how each car would move if it started to roll. Determine which cars had their wheels positioned correctly.

BUILDING MAP SKILLS

Using Junctions and Interchanges

Roadways that are numbered routes meet, or intersect, at *junctions*. On a map, junctions may be marked by a ○, in the same way that towns are. On an expressway, junctions are *interchanges*, shown by a ◇ on the map. You need to know about junctions and interchanges in order to get from one roadway to another.

Suppose you are in Oswego and want to travel to Rome. You might drive south on Route 481 until you reach the junctions of Routes 481 and 90, at an interchange. Then you would drive east on Route 90 to the interchange that is the junction of Routes 90 and 365. You would drive north on Route 365 to Rome.

Try It Yourself

1. Is there a junction of Routes 20 and 90?

2. How would you drive from Chittenango to Eaton?

3. How would you drive from Florence to Parish, stopping in Williamstown? How many junctions are there? Where are they?

4. Describe how you would travel from Hannibal to Syracuse. How many junctions are there? How many interchanges?

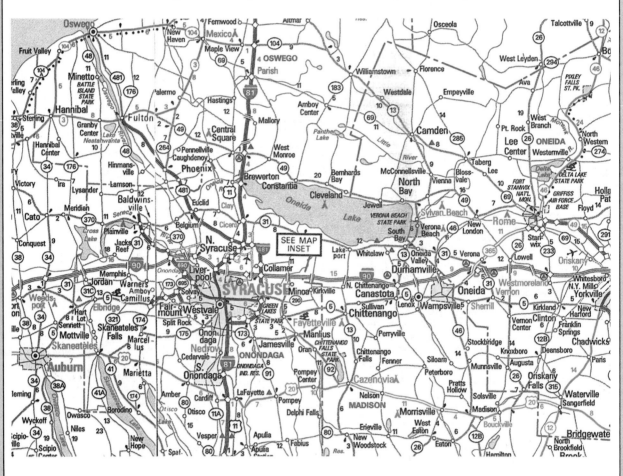

CHAPTER 9 REVIEW

CHAPTER TEST

Write the letter of the answer that best completes each sentence.

1. When you park uphill against a curb on the right, your car's front wheels should be
   a. turned to the right.
   b. turned to the left.
   c. positioned straight ahead.
2. The safest way to reverse direction is to
   a. make a U-turn.
   b. drive around the block.
   c. make a three-point turn.
3. You should signal for a right or left turn
   a. 200 to 300 feet in advance.
   b. 7 to 8 feet in advance.
   c. at least 150 feet in advance.
4. To parallel park, move your car parallel to the car in front of the space, at a distance of
   a. 1 to 2 feet.
   b. about 3 feet.
   c. about 5 feet.
5. The steps for making a right turn
   a. are the same whether turning onto a one- or two-way street.
   b. depend on the kind of street you turn into.
   c. depend on the presence of traffic in the cross street.
6. To turn left, the gap in traffic should be
   a. 7 to 8 seconds in both directions.
   b. 9 seconds to the right and 7 seconds to the left.
   c. 200 to 300 feet in either direction.
7. To make a two-point turn, you
   a. drive around the block.
   b. head into or back into a driveway.
   c. shift to Neutral.

8. To exit from an angled parking space, first
   a. turn the steering wheel sharply right.
   b. shift into Reverse.
   c. move parallel to the car in front.
9. If you park downhill in a car with a manual transmission,
   a. shift into Reverse.
   b. shift into Neutral.
   c. shift into First gear.
10. Your car should be positioned next to the center line before
    a. making a right turn from a one-way street.
    b. making a left turn from a two-way street.
    c. moving straight across an intersection.

Write the word or phrase that best completes each sentence.

three-point turn   perpendicular
roundabout   travel path
turnabout   right turn

11. A _____ parking space is set at 90° to the curb.

12. To make a _____ , position your car to the right side of the right lane.

13. One example of a _____ is the U-turn.

14. Make a _____ only when the street is narrow, you have good visibility, and traffic is light.

15. When turning at an intersection, look through the turn along your intended _____ .

DRIVER'S LOG

In this chapter, you have learned about preparing for and executing maneuvers such as making right and left turns and turnabouts and parking. Which of these maneuvers do you think will be hardest? What will you do to help you overcome the difficulty? Write two paragraphs to explain your ideas. You can draw a diagram to help you.

DRIVING ENVIRONMENTS

Whether you drive on a quiet country road or a busy four-lane highway, you must be alert to the probability of risk. Learning how to manage visibility, time, and space in different environments will help you to minimize risk.

CHAPTER 10 OBJECTIVES

LESSON ONE

Managing Visibility, Time and Space

1. Describe how to manage visibility as a driver.
2. Describe ways that you can manage time as a driver.
3. Describe how to manage space as a driver.

LESSON TWO

Visibility, Time and Space on Urban Streets

4. Describe the special factors that affect driving on city streets.
5. List ways to manage visibility, time, and space when driving in the city.

LESSON THREE

Visibility, Time and Space on Rural Roads

6. Describe the special factors that affect driving on rural roads.
7. List ways to manage visibility, time, and space when driving on rural roads.

LESSON FOUR

Visibility, Time and Space on Multiple-Lane Highways

8. Describe the special factors that affect driving on multiple-lane and limited-access highways.
9. List ways to manage visibility, time, and space when driving on multiple-lane and limited-access highways.

Whenever you drive, the risk of collision is always present. However, you can minimize that risk by learning to manage visibility, time, and space.

As you read about visibility, time, and space, keep in mind that they are closely related. To become a safe driver, you must understand how visibility, time, and space work together in all driving situations.

How Can You Manage Visibility?

Visibility refers to your ability to see the roadway and to be seen by other drivers and pedestrians. You can take specific actions to maximize visibility both before you begin driving and once you're on the road.

Advance Preparations

Take these steps to manage visibility before you begin driving.

◆ Clear and clean the inside and outside of your car windows.
◆ Make sure all car lights are clean and in good working order.
◆ Make sure your defroster and windshield wipers and washer work properly.
◆ Adjust rearview and side-view mirrors for maximum visibility. Also adjust the driver's seat properly.
◆ Obtain and keep handy any items you might need to improve visibility, such as sunglasses, a flashlight, and a scraper.
◆ Remove obstructions inside the car, such as ornaments that hang from the rearview mirror or packages that block your view.

Behind-the-Wheel Actions

The first step to managing visibility while driving is to turn on your headlights, day or night. Driving with your low beams on in daylight makes your car visible to drivers and pedestrians about 2,200 feet sooner than it would be with no headlights.

Maximize your visibility to other roadway users by signaling your intentions well in advance. Also, avoid driving in another driver's blind spot.

To help ensure your ability to see the roadway, always wear glasses or contact lenses if you need them. To shield your eyes from glare, put on sunglasses or use your sun visors.

Dirty headlights limit visibility. Road grime on the headlights can reduce illumination as much as 90 percent.

To reduce risk and manage visibility, clean your headlights regularly.
▼

How Can You Manage Time?

By managing time wisely, you increase your control over driving situations and help to reduce risk. Decreasing or increasing your car's speed, for instance, can enable you to avoid colliding with a vehicle or pedestrian.

To manage time effectively while driving, always keep in mind that time, speed, and distance are closely linked. For example, the amount of time and distance you need to stop your car increases with your speed. Similarly, the time and distance required to pass a car depends on how fast your car and the other car are traveling.

Initial driver reaction time to a roadway problem is one-half to three-quarters of a second. During that time, your car continues to move forward. The *braking distance* is the distance your car covers until it stops, once you apply your brakes. Total *stopping distance* includes both the distance traveled from the moment you see and react to the problem and the distance traveled after braking.

In Chapter 1 you learned how you can use the SIPDE process to reduce risk. By helping you to identify threatening objects or conditions as early as possible, the SIPDE process maximizes the amount of time available for you to take whatever evasive action may be required.

Here are some guidelines for managing time. Note how managing time and space, or distance, are the same.

Scan ahead 20 to 30 seconds as you drive for information that can help

you select a safe path of travel. Twenty to 30 seconds equals about $1\frac{1}{2}$ to 2 blocks at 25 to 30 mph in the city, and about one-half mile at 50 to 65 mph on the highway.

Identify objects or conditions within 12 to 15 seconds ahead that

▲
Drive with your low-beams on, even in the daytime, to enable other drivers to see you better.

Managing Time

Effective time management begins before you get behind the wheel. Here are some tips:

- Make a conscious effort to understand and learn to judge time and speed factors. Try to develop a sense, for example, of how much longer it takes a car to slow down and stop when moving at 50 mph than at 20 mph.
- Plan your route in advance, and always allow yourself plenty of time to reach your destination.
- Get traffic information from the radio or other source to help you plan the best route of travel.

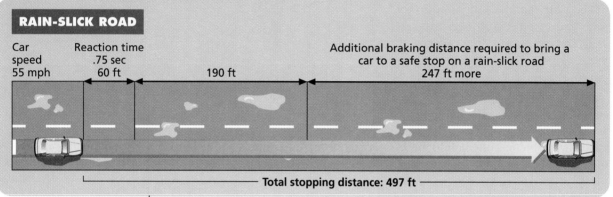

BRAKING DISTANCE

DRY ROAD

Car speed 55 mph

Reaction time .75 sec 60 ft

Braking distance on a dry road 190 ft

Total stopping distance: 250 ft

RAIN-SLICK ROAD

Car speed 55 mph

Reaction time .75 sec 60 ft

190 ft

Additional braking distance required to bring a car to a safe stop on a rain-slick road 247 ft more

Total stopping distance: 497 ft

▲

Braking distance depends on many factors, including the size of your car, the condition of the road, and the car's speed.

could increase the level of risk. Objects or conditions 12 to 15 seconds ahead are at a distance equal to about 1 city block or one-quarter mile when you're on the highway.

Keep a minimum 2- to 3-second following distance between your car and the car ahead. You need at least 2 to 3 seconds to steer evasively. To figure the distance between your car and the vehicle ahead, notice when the rear of the vehicle passes a fixed point, such as a sign or tree. Count "one-second-one, two-seconds-two." If the front of your car passes the point before you finish "two-seconds-two," you're following too closely.

How Can You Manage Space?

Managing space when you drive means managing the distance between your car and the vehicles ahead, behind, and to the sides. Your goal is to allow yourself enough space to maneuver safely at all times. By managing space wisely, you also increase your ability to see and be seen.

Consider Time, Distance and Speed

In learning to manage time, you've already learned a great deal about managing space. For example, by maintaining a minimum following distance of 2 to 3 seconds, you're managing both time *and* space.

The close link between managing time and space is also clear in terms of your car's speed. The faster you're traveling, the more time *and* distance you need to brake to a stop.

In fact, if you double your speed, you need *four* times the distance to stop. Moving at 30 mph on a dry road, for instance, you need about 44 feet to stop. At 60 mph, however, you need about 176 feet (4 × 44). In mathematical terms, the braking distance increase (in feet) equals the square of the increase in speed.

Assess and Adjust the Space Around Your Car

Having ample space around your car is important because space gives you time to observe, think, decide, and act or react. By adjusting your car's position to maintain a safe margin of space, you can generally avoid the need to brake, accelerate, or swerve suddenly. A cushion of space also gives you room to steer in case of emergency.

Here are some guidelines for managing space.

Adjust your following distance as needed. Two to 3 seconds is the minimum, but leave 4 to 5 seconds at speeds of 40 mph or more and 5 to 6 seconds if the road is slippery or you're following a vehicle large enough to block your view.

Try to keep a 2-second distance behind your car. Distance behind your car is the hardest to maintain because other vehicles may *tailgate*, or follow too closely. If you're being tailgated, increase—do *not* decrease—the space between you and the car ahead. If possible, let the tailgater pass.

Whenever possible, try to keep as much as 8 feet on either side of you. At the very least, keep a car's width to one side of you. The more room you have around your car, the more space you have to react to threatening situations.

If there is insufficient space ahead, behind, or to the side of your car, take prompt action to increase the space. For example, if you're boxed in by cars, adjust your speed to move away from the pack.

CHECKPOINT

1. In what ways can you manage visibility while driving?
2. How can you manage time while driving?
3. What actions can you take to manage space when you drive?

WHAT WOULD YOU DO?

What are some ways you can manage visibility, time, and space before driving this car? What steps would you take while driving?

LESSON TWO | Visibility, Time and Space on Urban Streets

The hustle and bustle of city streets can make driving a real challenge, especially for new drivers. By understanding the factors that affect driving in the city and by managing visibility, time, and space effectively, you can meet the demands of urban driving.

What Special Factors Affect City Driving?

Cities can be hectic places. Pedestrians fill the sidewalks while cars, buses, and other vehicles crowd the streets. Double-parked vehicles often block visibility, and potholes may interrupt traffic flow.

Traffic Density

In city traffic, you will be driving among many more vehicles than you will in suburban or highway driving. The traffic is dense and often slow moving, and threatening situations occur more frequently. Maintaining a margin of space around your car can be difficult.

Number of Pedestrians

Cities seem to overflow with people: workers, shoppers, children, and others. Expect to encounter pedestrians anywhere and everywhere. Never assume that pedestrians will see you or that they will obey traffic rules or signals.

ENERGY TIPS

Avoid "jackrabbit" starts when traffic signals turn green. Accelerating gradually saves fuel—and is safer.

City streets, crowded with vehicles and pedestrians, demand an extra degree of driver alertness. ▶

Intersections

Cities are filled with intersections. In the city, intersections are typically jammed with both vehicles and pedestrians moving in all directions. When approaching or crossing a city intersection, you need to use maximum care.

Slow or Irregular Traffic Flow

In congested city streets, vehicles often move in packs or lines. The movement may be in a steady stream or with frequent starts and stops.

Cars stopping to park or parked cars pulling away from the curb may interrupt the flow of traffic. Roadwork or construction can also slow traffic. While you may move more slowly than you'd like to when you drive in a city, it is usually dangerous to try to move any faster.

Lower Speed Limits

City speed limits are lower than suburban or highway speed limits. In addition, they may change in different parts of a city.

Sight Obstructions

Several factors tend to limit visibility in city driving. Parked and double-parked vehicles can partially block your view, as can nearby buses, trucks, and vans. Smog and pollution also may reduce your ability to see.

Potholes and Other Road Defects

In cities with heavy traffic, streets take a lot of wear and tear. Potholes and rough surfaces may develop.

They slow traffic and pose a potential danger to drivers, pedestrians, and cyclists.

How Can You Manage Visibility, Time, and Space in City Driving?

By knowing the special factors to be alert for when driving in the city, you can manage visibility, time, and space to minimize risk.

Guidelines for Managing Visibility in the City

Here are some guidelines to help you manage visibility on urban streets.

◆ Scan one to two blocks ahead and from one side of the street to the other. Don't focus on any one object in your path.
◆ Keep your low-beam headlights on at all times.

▲
Double-parked cars on urban streets severely limit your ability to scan ahead.

Never speed up to "beat" a changing traffic signal. If an impatient driver accelerates into the intersection just as the red light turns green, your cars will collide.

Rear-end crashes are more common than any other kind. Leave enough following distance. Too often drivers follow more closely than they should and are unable to stop in time.

◆ Check your rearview and sideview mirrors to monitor traffic, especially as you approach an intersection or when you intend to stop.

◆ Signal your intention to turn or pull over well ahead of time.

◆ Keep alert to the taillights of vehicles ahead of you so that you can anticipate when other drivers are braking or planning to turn. However, always be prepared for unexpected stops or turns.

◆ Be ready for pedestrians darting out from between parked cars or crossing streets illegally.

◆ Be on the lookout for warning signs and signals. Also be alert for the sirens and flashing lights of police cars, ambulances, fire engines, and other emergency vehicles.

◆ Be aware of entrances and exits for apartment buildings, parking

lots, and the like. Often they are not visible until the last moment.

Guidelines for Managing Time in the City

Follow these guidelines for managing time while driving in the city.

◆ Reduce speed. Use the SIPDE process to help you identify threatening conditions early, particularly as you approach intersections.

◆ Dense traffic can make drivers tense and impatient—and sometimes reckless. Always be ready to stop or steer to avoid a collision.

◆ Often braking is the only response you can make in city traffic to avoid a collision. When you spot a possible threatening condition but are not sure if you'll have to stop, take your foot off the accelerator and place it just over the brake pedal without pushing down. By "covering the brake" in this manner, you're ready to slow or stop if you need to.

◆ To give drivers and pedestrians maximum time to see and react to you, drive with your low-beam headlights on and always signal your intentions well in advance.

◆ Give yourself extra time for driving in city traffic, particularly during rush hours and other busy periods. Know what route you'll be traveling, and listen to the radio for traffic information before setting out.

Guidelines for Managing Space in the City

Use these guidelines to manage space in city traffic.

◆ Do not follow other vehicles too closely, even in bumper-to-bumper

Problem Behavior

When you scan the roadway, observe the behavior of other drivers for clues to potential problems. Watch for drivers:

• taking their eyes off the road while talking with others
• using cellular phones
• smoking, eating, reading, or looking at a map
• with unusual postures at the wheel, which may indicate intoxication
• signaling late or not at all
• moving too slowly or too rapidly or following too closely (tailgating)
• drifting from side to side in their lane
• whose view may be obstructed by packages, objects, or tall passengers
• with out-of-state license plates, who may be searching for an address or unaccustomed to driving in your area

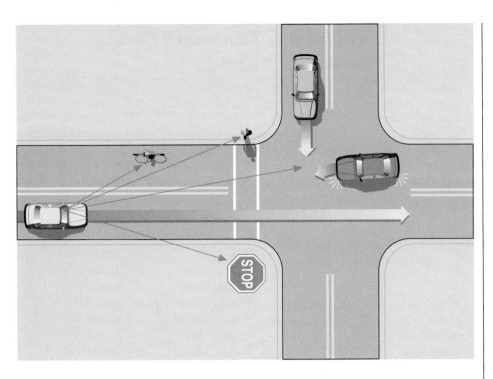

In the city, scan carefully for pedestrians, cyclists and other cars at intersections.

traffic. Never follow less than 2 seconds behind.

◆ When stopped behind a car, wait for that car to move well ahead before you move forward. Always leave a margin of space in case the car stops suddenly.

◆ Keep as wide a margin of space as possible between your car and parked cars. Watch for people leaving parked cars and for cars pulling out suddenly.

◆ Avoid driving side-by-side with other cars on multiple-lane streets. Either move ahead of the other cars or drop back.

◆ Keep as much space as you can between your car and vehicles in the oncoming lanes.

◆ Before you enter an intersection, make sure there are no cars or people blocking your intended path of travel. Otherwise, you may be caught in the intersection when the light changes.

CHECKPOINT

4. What are some special factors that affect city driving?
5. What actions can you take to manage visibility, time, and space when you drive in the city?

WHAT WOULD YOU DO?

You are driving through the city during rush hour. What steps would you take to manage visibility, time, and space?

LESSON THREE | Visibility, Time and Space on Rural Roads

In some ways, country driving is easier than city driving. Traffic is generally lighter, and there are fewer pedestrians and not as many distractions. Still, driving in rural areas poses its own particular challenges.

What Special Factors Affect Driving on Rural Roads?

When driving on rural roads, be especially alert for roadway conditions that limit your ability to see or maneuver.

Road Conditions

Many rural roads are two-lane, two-way roadways. Curves may be sharper and hills may be steeper than on many city streets. Roads may have concrete, asphalt, gravel, or dirt surfaces, with or without a shoulder. Some rural roads may even have drainage ditches alongside. At night, many rural roads are poorly lighted —or not lighted at all.

Such road conditions can prove hazardous. Drivers must exercise special care, for example, when passing other vehicles and when driving on loose, low-traction road surfaces.

Higher Speed, Fewer Controls

Sound judgment is more important than ever when driving in rural areas. Country roads typically have higher speed limits than city streets.

Snow on the road and a ditch alongside make maneuvering on this roadway difficult. ▶

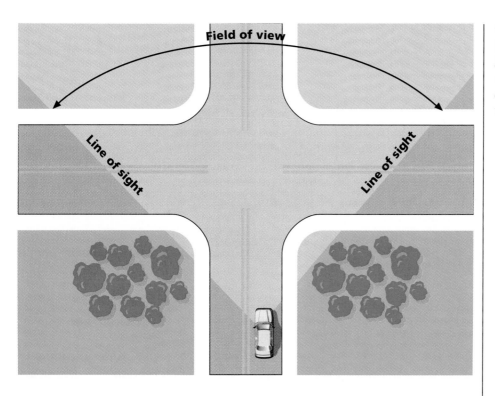

Trees close to the road limit visibility. To have a wider field of view, the driver must move closer to the intersection.

Moreover, you'll encounter fewer traffic lights and stop signs on rural roads than on city streets. At railroad crossings, there may be no signs, signals, or gates. Drivers must remain alert for traffic crossing the roadway.

Slow-Moving Vehicles

Tractors and other farm vehicles do not travel at the same speeds as cars do. As a result, drivers on rural roads often have to pass such slow-moving vehicles. Some farm vehicles, such as harvesters, are very wide, limiting the visibility of following drivers and making passing extremely difficult, if not impossible.

Sight Obstructions

Trees, bushes, and tall crops growing close by the road all limit visibility for drivers on country roads. These obstructions can make driving even more challenging on narrow, winding, or sharply curving roads, many of which are common in rural areas.

Hills, too, can reduce visibility. As you near the top of a hill, your view of the road ahead will be limited. The steeper the grade, the less you can see.

Animals and Objects on the Road

Deer, raccoons, cows, and other animals, both wild and domestic, frequently cross rural roads. To learn more about the very real dangers posed by animals on the roadway, see Chapter 12. Other possible threatening conditions on rural roads include fallen rocks and tree branches and wet leaves.

SAFETY TIPS

Don't underestimate the risks of rural driving. In the city, there is a greater danger of colliding with another vehicle. In the country, there is a greater chance of your car going out of control and colliding with a fixed object or overturning. Drive cautiously at all times.

How Can You Manage Visibility, Time, and Space in Rural Driving?

Rural driving may seem more peaceful than urban driving, but you must remain fully attentive at all times. Just as you would when you're driving on city streets, use the SIPDE process, and be ready to deal with the unexpected.

Guidelines for Managing Visibility in Rural Areas

Here are some guidelines to help you manage visibility on country roads.

◆ Always drive with your low beams on. Use your high beams at night on very dark roads when there are no other cars around.

◆ Scan ahead 20 to 30 seconds, looking for vehicles, pedestrians, animals, and objects on or near the roadway. If road or weather conditions limit your visual search time, reduce your speed.

◆ Identify objects or conditions within 12 to 15 seconds ahead that may pose a danger. If you can't see that far, slow down until your visual path clears. Be ready to cover your brake.

◆ Drive at a speed that will let you respond safely to threatening conditions that may be just over a hill or around a curve.

◆ Don't follow large vehicles so closely that they block your view of potential dangers.

◆ Always signal your intention to turn, to pull over, to pass, and to get back into your lane.

Guidelines for Managing Time in Rural Areas

Use these guidelines to help you manage time on rural roads.

◆ Watch for slow-moving vehicles. Adjust your speed as needed.

◆ Reduce your speed as you approach intersections, particularly those without traffic control devices. Be prepared to slow down further or even stop.

◆ Allow extra time for driving on unfamiliar roads. Plan your route in advance.

◆ Reduce your speed when driving on gravel, dirt, or other low-traction road surfaces.

◆ When approaching or passing an animal on or near the road, drive slowly in case the animal bolts across your path.

$AFETY TIPS

Scan the roadway and off-road area ahead. If you see a rider on horseback, reduce your speed and pass slowly, giving horse and rider as much leeway as possible. *Never* sound your horn to warn of your approach.

You may encounter slow-moving vehicles more frequently in rural areas. ▼

◄

When driving on low-traction roadways, lower your speed to manage risk.

Guidelines for Managing Space in Rural Areas

Follow these guidelines for managing space on rural roads.

◆ Adjust your following distance for your speed and for road conditions. Remember that you'll need a minimum of 2 to 3 seconds to steer evasively.

◆ If a vehicle is tailgating you, give it as much space as possible to pass and pull in front of you. If there's a car ahead of you, increase your following distance.

◆ On two-lane roads, keep as much space as possible between your car and oncoming traffic.

◆ Never pass on any uphill grade when you don't have a clear path ahead in which to complete the pass.

◆ As you search the road for vehicles, animals, or objects that could threaten your safety, weigh the consequences of acting to avoid the threat against the danger of collision.

CHECKPOINT

6. What are some special factors that affect rural driving?
7. What actions can you take to manage visibility, time, and space when you drive on rural roads?

?

WHAT WOULD YOU DO?

You are traveling on a two-way hilly road that has many sharp curves. What special factors affect visibility? What are some ways to manage time and space?

Visibility, Time and Space on Multiple-Lane Highways

Traveling on multiple-lane highways and expressways is usually faster than traveling on local roads. Driving at higher speeds is demanding, however. You need to concentrate fully in order to manage visibility, time, and space.

This section focuses on expressways and other multiple-lane and limited-access highways, including freeways, interstate highways, parkways, and turnpikes and other toll roads. *Limited-* or *controlled-access* highways allow vehicles to enter and exit only at specific places.

What Special Factors Affect Driving on Multiple-Lane Highways?

Driving on an expressway or other high-speed road is very different from driving on urban streets or rural roads. There may be one or more lanes of traffic moving in the same direction that you are. Cars, trucks, and other vehicles zip past you at high speeds. The scenery seems to whiz by—along with route markers and other road signs containing all sorts of information.

Higher Speed Limits

Expressway speed limits are generally higher than those on city streets or rural roads. Higher speeds mean that drivers must manage time and space with particular care when following and passing vehicles, changing lanes, and reducing speed. High-speed collisions are far more damaging than those occurring at lower speeds.

At highway speeds of 40 to 65 mph, you'll need 4 to 5 seconds to react to a threatening situation and brake your car to a stop. Therefore, you must be able to see ahead at all times an absolute minimum of 4 to 5 seconds.

Traveling on multiple-lane, high-speed highways poses special challenges for the driver. ▶

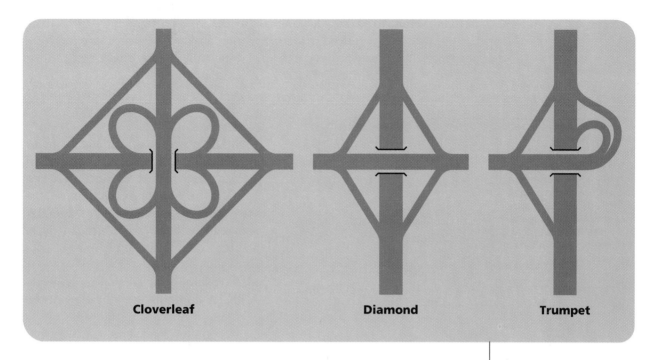

Cloverleaf   **Diamond**   **Trumpet**

Limited Entrances and Exits

Entrance and exit ramps on controlled-access highways may be many miles apart. Entrances and exits are usually made from the extreme right-hand lane. However, there are many entrance and exit ramps located in the extreme left-hand lane.

Signs posted along the highway tell drivers when they are approaching an exit or *interchange*. Interchanges are points where you can enter or leave the expressway or connect with a highway going in another direction.

Interchanges are made up of through lanes, ramps, and speed-change lanes. Ramps are short, one-way roads connecting two highways. Speed limits on ramps typically range from 25 to 45 mph. Speed-change lanes are short lanes next to the main travel lanes of a highway. A deceleration lane allows vehicles to reduce speed to exit; an acceleration lane lets vehicles increase speed to merge with traffic.

Frequent Passing

Passing other vehicles and having other vehicles pass you is an integral part of driving on multiple-lane highways. Depending on the roadway and on your lane position and speed, you may find yourself being passed on your left, on your right, or on both sides simultaneously.

Trucks and Other Large Vehicles

Trucks, tractor-trailers, buses, and other large vehicles add additional challenge to driving on multiple-lane highways because they hamper visibility. Large vehicles can also buffet your car with wind gusts as they rumble past.

▲
Three common interchange designs are the cloverleaf, the diamond and the trumpet.

Sometimes the same lane is used for both entering and exiting a highway. It may be less risky to let the vehicle getting on the highway go first, but be prepared to yield whether you are the one who is exiting or the one who is entering.

There may be more lanes at toll plazas than on the highway itself. Choose a lane with a green signal well in advance and *stay in that lane*. Be especially alert to drivers ahead of you who switch lanes suddenly.

Because of their larger size, you need more time to pass a truck or bus than to pass a car. Indeed, traveling at 50 mph, it may take you as much as 7 seconds longer to pass a tractor-trailer than a car!

How Can You Manage Visibility, Time and Space on Multiple-Lane Highways?

Safe and responsible driving on multiple-lane highways and expressways requires careful decision making on the part of the driver. You should focus on managing visibility, time, and space to reduce the risk of a collision or other mishap.

Guidelines for Managing Visibility on Highways

Here are guidelines for managing visibility on multiple-lane and limited-access highways.

◆ Scan 20 to 30 seconds ahead for vehicles, objects, animals, and even pedestrians on or near the roadway.
◆ Be alert for the special dangers of highway entrances and exits. Drivers can merge too slowly or without looking or cut across lanes at the last moment.

◆ Check your rearview and side-view mirrors frequently to monitor the position of traffic around you, especially before changing lanes or exiting a highway.
◆ Always signal your intention to change lanes, merge, or exit well in advance of the move.
◆ Drive with your low beams on at all times. Use your high beams on very dark highways, but only when there are no other vehicles around.
◆ Check the taillights of vehicles ahead to know when other drivers are slowing down or planning to pass or change lanes.
◆ Position your car so that large vehicles do not block your view of the roadway ahead or to the sides.
◆ Look for road signs to learn what the speed limit is and to know when your exit is approaching and which side it's on.

Guidelines for Managing Time on Highways

Use these guidelines to help you manage time on highways.

◆ Use the SIPDE process to help you identify threatening conditions within 12 to 15 seconds ahead.
◆ Always adjust your speed and fol-

The roadways that connect cities and towns have many names, which vary somewhat in meaning. A *highway* is a main public roadway, especially one that runs between cities. An *expressway* is a divided highway with limited access that has more than one lane running in each direction. A *turnpike* is a road, usually an expressway, that requires drivers to pay a toll. *Freeway* is generally a synonym for *expressway,* but it can also refer to a highway that is not a toll road. A *beltway* is a highway that goes around an urban area. A *parkway* is a wide, landscaped highway that may be limited to non-commercial vehicles.

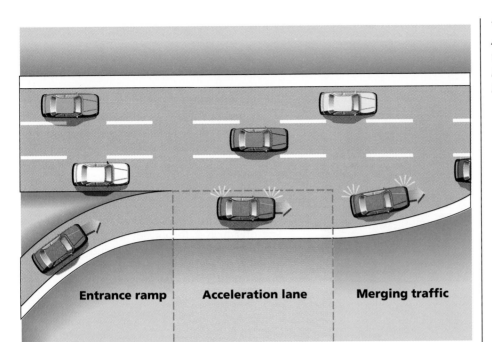

Entrance ramp | **Acceleration lane** | **Merging traffic**

◀
Always signal while still in the acceleration lane and before merging into highway traffic.

lowing distance so that you have at least 4 to 5 seconds to stop in case of an emergency.

◆ When you merge into traffic, try to enter the stream of vehicles at the speed they are traveling.

◆ When exiting an expressway, move over toward the exit lane as soon as you can. Wait until you're actually in the exit lane before reducing your speed.

◆ Adjust your speed to avoid traveling in packs of cars.

◆ Watch for vehicles that may have trouble keeping up with the speed of traffic. Adjust your speed or position in advance.

◆ Plan your route ahead of time. Know which highways you'll be traveling on and where to exit.

◆ Avoid driving on congested highways during peak traffic periods or in bad weather. Listen to the radio for roadway information before starting out. Allow extra time if you must drive.

Guidelines for Managing Space on Highways

Follow these guidelines to manage space on multiple-lane and limited-access roadways.

◆ Adjust your car's position for the speed that you and other drivers are traveling and for road and weather conditions. Allow yourself a margin of space to accelerate, brake, and steer.

◆ Allow yourself a gap of at least 4 seconds when merging with other traffic, changing lanes, or entering an expressway from an entrance lane.

◆ To change lanes, turn the steering wheel gradually. Oversteering, or steering too sharply into another lane, can lead to loss of control at higher speeds.

◆ If you must cross several lanes, move over one lane at a time, signaling each time.

◆ Make room for cars entering expressways. If there are no vehicles in

When passing a vehicle in the center lane of a highway that has three or more lanes of traffic traveling in the same direction, be careful of cars passing on the vehicle's *other* side. They may wind up in your intended travel path.

Bill Wen, Director, ATE Ryder, Alexandria, Virginia

Bill Wen

Ask yourself three questions while driving: 1) What can I do to reduce the probability of a dangerous event? 2) How can I increase my opportunity to manage a dangerous event should one occur? and 3) If a collision is unavoidable, how can I reduce its consequences?

Regardless of the driving environment, the first objective is to prevent a high-risk situation from developing by improving your visibility to others and by giving yourself more time and space to deal with it.

? WHAT WOULD YOU DO?

You are in the left lane of a crowded multiple-lane highway. Suddenly you realize your exit is approaching, all the way on the right. How would you handle this?

the lane next to you, move over a lane before you approach an entrance ramp.

◆ If a vehicle is tailgating you, change lanes—when it's safe—to let the vehicle pass. In the meantime, increase your following distance behind cars ahead.

◆ Never cut in too soon in front of a vehicle you're passing.

◆ When passing a truck or other wide vehicle, keep in mind that you have less space to the side between your car and the vehicle than you do when passing a car.

◆ Be alert for places where highways may narrow—when approaching tunnels or bridges, for example. Reduce your speed and proceed cautiously.

CHECKPOINT

8. What factors affect driving on multiple-lane and limited-access highways?
9. What actions can a driver take to manage visibility, time, and space on an expressway?

CHAPTER 10 REVIEW

KEYPOINTS

LESSON ONE

1. In addition to making advance preparations, you can manage visibility by keeping your low beams on (even in daylight), signaling intentions well in advance, and avoiding driving in another driver's blind spots.

2. You can manage time by being aware of the link among time, speed, and distance, and by using the SIPDE process.

3. You can manage space by allowing enough distance between your car and other vehicles to the front, rear, and sides.

LESSON TWO

4. Special factors that affect city driving are traffic density, number of pedestrians, number of intersections, slow or irregular traffic flow, lower speed limits, sight obstructions, and potholes and other road defects.

5. Some ways to manage visibility, time, and space on city streets are to scan one to two blocks ahead, use your mirrors to monitor traffic, signal early, be ready for pedestrians and hidden exits, always be ready to steer or stop, use the SIPDE process, and keep a margin of space around your car.

LESSON THREE

6. Factors that affect driving on rural roads are road conditions, higher speeds, fewer traffic controls, slow-moving vehicles, sight obstructions, and animals and objects on the road.

7. Among the ways to manage visibility, time, and space on rural roads are to identify dangerous objects 12 to 15 seconds ahead, drive slowly if an animal is nearby, avoid passing on an uphill grade if your view is not clear, and use the SIPDE process.

LESSON FOUR

8. Special factors that affect visibility, time, and space on multiple-lane and limited-access highways are higher speed limits, limited entrances and exits, frequent passing, and the presence of trucks and other large vehicles.

9. Some ways to manage visibility, time, and space on multiple-lane and limited-access highways are to use the SIPDE process, signal when changing lanes, position your car so that you can see and be seen, adjust your speed to avoid traveling in packs, and plan your route ahead of time.

PROJECTS

1. Use a road map to plan a trip from one city to another. List the highways you would travel on, and write the numbers of the highway exits you would use. If possible, take the trip as a driver or passenger, and compare the accuracy of your plan to what you actually experience on the trip.

2. Make your own comparison between city driving and driving on a rural road or highway. Observe differences in road surfaces, traffic signs and signals, density of traffic, and visibility.

BUILDING CRITICAL THINKING SKILLS

America's First "Highway Transportation System"

Imagine a bustling town carved into a canyon in the desert. Fields of corn, squash, and beans grow in once-dry fields made fertile by an irrigation system of rainwater channeled over high cliffs and running into the canyon. Imagine an 800-room multistory sandstone dwelling that houses over 1,000 people built against the side of the canyon. The rooms of the dwelling face inward toward a system of patios and plazas that provide access to circular chambers used as meeting halls. Then imagine a series of roadways leading out of the canyon. It is more than 1,000 years ago and you are in Pueblo Bonito in Chaco Canyon, located in what is now New Mexico.

Long before Europeans came to the Americas, Pueblo Bonito was the center of one of the most sophisticated settlements in the prehistoric southwest. From around A.D. 900 to the middle of the 15th century, a civilization called the Anasazi or "Ancient Ones" lived in settlements in what is now called the Four-Corners region, with Pueblo Bonito at their hub.

Almost four centuries before the voyages of Columbus, the Anasazi were using a network of wide roadways connecting Pueblo Bonito with nearly 100 outlying communities such as Pueblo Alta. Goods were carried across what might very well be one of the first highway transportation systems between Pueblo Bonito and outlying settlements scattered over 40,000 square miles.

The remarkable civilization of the Anasazi left Chaco Canyon in the mid 1200s. Their descendants still live nearby. They are the Navajo.

What Do You Think Now?

How does what you have read about the peoples of Chaco Canyon change your ideas of America before the arrival of Christopher Columbus?

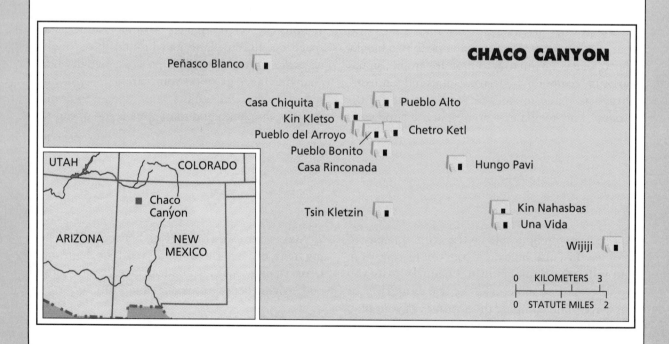

CHAPTER 10 REVIEW

CHAPTER TEST

Write the letter of the answer that best completes each sentence.

1. A limited access highway
   a. allows vehicles to enter or exit only at certain places.
   b. does not permit trucks or buses.
   c. has no shoulders.

2. When you spot a threatening traffic condition in city traffic, you should
   a. shut your windows.
   b. cover the brake.
   c. use the total stopping method.

3. One way to manage time and space is to
   a. drive parallel to other cars on multiple-lane streets.
   b. ride a bicycle.
   c. maintain a margin of space around your car.

4. Speed limits on country roads are typically
   a. lower than those on urban roads.
   b. higher than those on urban roads.
   c. between 15 and 30 miles per hour.

5. Managing space while you drive means
   a. managing the distance between your car and vehicles around you.
   b. reaching your destination quickly and safely.
   c. successfully passing other vehicles on multiple-lane highways.

6. As you near the top of a hill
   a. your view of the road ahead is limited.
   b. your view of the road behind you is limited.
   c. you should accelerate.

7. When driving on a dirt or gravel road, you should
   a. pull over to the right side.
   b. increase your speed.
   c. reduce your speed.

8. The first step to managing visibility while driving is to
   a. stay away from large obstructions.
   b. turn on your low-beam headlights.
   c. look in your blind spots.

9. During urban driving, you should
   a. look at least 1 block ahead.
   b. look at least 5 blocks ahead.
   c. use your high-beam headlights.

10. On multiple-lane highways, passing other vehicles
    a. should be avoided.
    b. is an integral part of driving.
    c. is a method of staying alert.

Write the word or phrase that best completes each sentence.

distance   expressway   interchanges
lead time   margin of space   rural roads

11. The faster you travel, the more time and _____ you need to come to a stop.

12. Always keep a _____ around your car.

13. Some _____ may have drainage ditches alongside.

14. A freeway is one example of a(n) _____ .

15. _____ are made up of through lanes, ramps, and speed-change lanes.

DRIVER'S LOG

In this chapter, you have learned about managing visibility, time, and space in different driving environments. Write two paragraphs in response to this question:

In which driving environment do you think you will have the most difficulty managing visibility, time, and space? What steps will you take to overcome this difficulty?

LIGHT AND WEATHER CONDITIONS

Good drivers are prepared for any kind of light or weather conditions. It is important for you to understand how to manage visibility, time, and space in order to minimize the risk caused by poor light or inclement weather.

CHAPTER 11 OBJECTIVES

Driving Safely in Low Light and at Night

1. Describe how visibility is affected by low light conditions.
2. Explain how to drive safely in low light and at night.

Visibility, Bright Light and Glare

3. Describe the conditions that create glare from the sun.
4. Explain how you can drive safely in the glare of the sun.

Minimizing Risk in Rain and Snow

5. Explain how to manage visibility, time, and space in rain and snow.
6. Explain how to minimize risk in snow and rain.

Other Hazardous Weather Conditions

7. Describe five hazardous weather conditions other than snow and rain and the risks involved in driving in each.

LESSON ONE — Driving Safely in Low Light and at Night

Visibility on the roadway is decreased at night and just before sunrise or after sunset. As visibility decreases, your risk of being in a collision increases. To lessen risk, you must understand how reduced light limits visibility and how to manage the driving task in low light conditions.

How Do Low Light Conditions Affect Visibility?

Your ability to see and to be seen diminishes when the amount of available light is lessened.

Reduced sunlight during dusk and dawn hours makes it difficult to see the roadway and vehicles traveling on it. Other drivers as well as pedestrians have difficulty seeing your car, particularly if you don't have your headlights on.

Night driving presents special challenges. At night, darkness limits your view of the road ahead and the surrounding area. Even with your headlights on, your ability to see ahead when turning or driving around a curve is severely reduced. Also, the glare of other vehicles' headlights can be distracting—or blinding.

How Can You Drive Safely When the Amount of Light Is Low?

To drive safely in low light conditions, you must maximize visibility and manage time and space wisely.

Fifty percent of all teenage motor vehicle fatalities occur between 9 P.M. and 6 A.M.

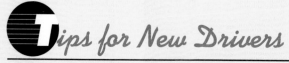

Tips for New Drivers

More Suggestions for Dealing with Visibility Problems at Night

Slow down. Remember that your visibility is limited.

Avoid looking directly into the headlights of oncoming cars. When necessary to maintain your bearings, glance down at the right edge of your traffic lane beyond the oncoming car.

To remind an approaching driver that his or her high beams are on, quickly switch your own headlights from low to high and back again.

If you can adjust your rear view mirror for night driving, do so to cut glare from the headlights of vehicles behind you.

If you must stop along the road, use your emergency flashers to enable other drivers to see you.

Watch for animals, joggers, bicyclists, and obstacles in the road.

Always remove sunglasses once the sun sets.

When your view of the road is limited, slow down. Maximize your ability to see and maneuver. Always keep your low-beam headlights on, day and night. Your headlights and taillights help to illuminate your car, making it easier for others to see you in all kinds of light.

During Dusk and Dawn Hours

All states require that you use your headlights either from sunset to sunrise or between a half hour after sunset and a half hour before sunrise. Using your headlights makes it easier to see and be seen in the dim light of dusk and dawn. Do *not* use your parking lights. They are not designed to light the road ahead but to indicate your status when you are parked safely off the roadway.

At dawn or dusk, increase the distance between your car and the one ahead, and use your turn signals well in advance.

At Night

Night driving requires extra concentration and a greater level of awareness. With darkness limiting visibility, it is wise to drive more slowly at night than you do during the day and to leave more distance between your car and the car ahead.

Use low beams and high beams correctly. On very dark roads with no other cars around, use your high beams to increase visibility. Be sure to switch back to low beams as soon as you spot the headlights or taillights of a car ahead of you. The glare of your high beams can momentarily blind another driver.

Don't overdrive your headlights. At night, drive at a speed that will allow you to stop within the range of your lights—that is, within the distance you can see. Driving faster than that is called *overdriving your headlights,* and makes you vulnerable to unseen hazards.

Use the 3- or 4-second rules you have already learned to help you judge a safe following distance.

Look beyond your headlights. Get into the habit of looking for objects just beyond your headlight beams to see possible threatening conditions. Looking beyond your headlights is essential when making turns or rounding curves.

CHECKPOINT

1. Describe how visibility is affected by low light conditions.
2. What can you do to minimize risk when driving at night?

WHAT WOULD YOU DO?

What kinds of visibility problems do you face in this situation? How can you manage time and space to reduce the risk of collision?

Visibility, Bright Light and Glare

SAFETY TIPS

When the sun is directly behind you, it may shine on your rearview mirror and make seeing behind you impossible. Be aware that this is happening to the driver in front of you as well, and increase your following distance.

Glare decreases visibility and causes you to become more easily fatigued.

▼

Think of a bright summer morning. The sky is cloudless and everything is bathed in sunlight. That's a pretty picture for a day at the beach, but it's not always so pretty when you're behind the wheel of a car. The glow of that sunlight can turn to dangerous glare.

What Conditions Create Glare from the Sun?

Sunshine increases visibility, but the glare caused when the sun hits your windshield can act in the opposite way—it can diminish visibility. The sun's glare is most dangerous at certain times.

In the morning or late afternoon, for example, when the sun is low on the horizon, glare can make it hard to see the road ahead. Glare can also reduce your ability to see the brake lights of other vehicles, especially if you're driving toward the sun and its rays shine directly in your eyes.

How Can You Drive Safely in the Glare of the Sun?

As in all driving situations, advance preparation can help you minimize the risk of glare. As part of your predriving check, you should always make sure that your car's windshield is clean. As part of your overall car maintenance, you should replace the windshield if it is badly scratched. Glare is worse through a dirty or scratched windshield.

Have sunglasses handy. As soon as you begin to squint, slip them on to shield your eyes. Reduce speed, increase your following distance, and adjust your sun visor to block out the sun. However, be careful that the visor does not hinder your view in any way.

Use the SIPDE process to help you manage risk in glare situations. Give yourself an extra margin of safety by leaving more distance between your car and other vehicles. Check carefully for pedestrians—remember, they are having trouble seeing too. Even if you have your sunglasses on and can see road signs and signals, keep in mind that others on the road-

The reflection of sunlight off snow and ice causes wide areas of glare.

way may not be able to see as clearly. Always be alert for the sudden, careless, or unsafe actions of other drivers and pedestrians.

Keep in mind that if you are having trouble seeing, so are the drivers around you. The sun shining on the back of your car may make it very difficult for the driver behind you to see your brake lights or directional signals. For this reason, it's wise to tap the brake pedal to flash your taillights, to use your turn signals well in advance, *and* to use hand or arm signals as well to communicate your intentions.

Keep in mind, too, that when the sun is behind you, oncoming drivers have the sun's glare in *their* eyes and may have trouble seeing you. Drive with your low-beam headlights on to make your car more visible, and signal well in advance your intention to turn or change lanes.

CHECKPOINT

3. Describe the circumstances in which the sun's light can create dangerous glare.
4. What steps would you take to minimize risk in a glare situation?

? WHAT WOULD YOU DO?

The sun is shining behind you. What can you do to minimize risk for both yourself and the driver behind you?

Minimizing Risk in Rain and Snow

It might be pleasant if you could just stay indoors when it is raining or snowing outside. However, most of the time you can't. If you have to drive somewhere in rainy or snowy weather, you must understand and manage the risk that driving in such weather presents.

How Can You Manage Visibility, Time, and Space in Rain and Snow?

Rain and snow decrease your ability to see not only ahead of you but all around you as well. Decreased visibility, in turn, makes it difficult for you to judge distances and to manage time and space well. Bad weather conditions also make it much harder for other drivers and pedestrians to see your car.

Heavy rain or snow can limit your view so much that you can't see very far ahead or even the edges of the roadway. Snow and sleet collecting on your windshield can produce blind areas that your windshield wipers can't reach. Snowy or rainy weather can also make the roadway slick, reducing the ability of your tires to grip the road, and increasing your risk of collision. Here are some steps you can take to minimize risk.

Prepare in advance. Start by cleaning your car's windows and lights. Check the tread and pressure of your tires. Check the headlights, windshield wipers, defroster, and other equipment to make sure they are in good working condition.

Allow for extra margin of safety. Drive more slowly and leave extra space between your car and other vehicles.

Even though they may be necessary during winter months, snow tires reduce fuel economy. Remove them as soon as winter is over.

THE SCIENCE CONNECTION

In some regions you may see a roadway sign that says "Bridge Freezes Before Roadway" posted on the approach to a bridge or overpass. In winter, the temperature of the ground beneath a road is often higher than the air temperature. The roadway on a bridge or overpass, however, has no ground directly beneath it. As a result, cold air circulates freely both above and below the bridge, which can cause it to freeze before the roads on either side of it. Bridges and overpasses also tend to remain frozen longer than the connecting roads.

When you see a sign like the one just described, reduce speed and proceed with care. An unexpected patch of ice could cause your car to skid.

When the temperature is near freezing and roads are wet, exercise similar caution when driving on shady sections of any sunlit roadway. The sun's warmth may have kept most of the road ice-free, but ice may have formed in the lower temperatures of the shade.

Drive in the tracks of the vehicle ahead of you. Those tracks are drier than the surrounding surface and offer better traction.

Give other drivers plenty of advance notice. When you intend to slow down or turn, communicate your intentions early so that other drivers have time to react accordingly.

Be alert. Be on the watch for pedestrians dashing for shelter.

Keep your low-beam headlights on. Increase the distance you can see and make your car more visible to other drivers and pedestrians.

Ease your way into turns and curves. Avoid sudden acceleration, starts, or stops.

If rain becomes so heavy that not even your windshield wipers' highest speed can keep up with the downpour, signal, then pull well off the road in a protected area and wait for the storm to lessen in intensity. Remember to switch on your emergency flashers so that other drivers can see your car.

You may also need to pull over if, in snow or sleet, your windshield wipers become crusted with ice, or if accumulating snow or sleet creates blind areas on your windshield. Use a scraper and brush to remove all of the buildup, and run your defroster before you resume driving. If you can, aim the heat at the windshield.

How Can You Minimize Risk in Snow and Rain?

If you've ever gone sledding, skiing, or ice-skating, you know just how slippery a snow- or ice-covered surface can be. Imagine trying to maneuver a heavy, fast-moving car on such a surface. One way to avoid risk entirely is to postpone driving until the weather clears. Whenever possible, wait until the roads are plowed and sanded or salted before venturing out on them.

Sometimes, of course, you cannot postpone a trip. If you do have to drive under snowy or icy conditions, be aware that there is a great danger of skidding. Drive slowly and extremely cautiously. Allow yourself an extra large margin of safety. When you do want to slow down, stop, or turn, maneuver the car gently and gradually.

Tips for New Drivers

Stuck in the Snow?

If you get stuck in snow, you may be able to free your car by "rocking" it. Follow the steps below.

1. Keep your front wheels pointed straight ahead, if possible. The car will move more easily in a straight line.
2. Shift back and forth between Drive (or first gear) and Reverse. Accelerate forward slowly and steadily. When the car will move forward no farther, press firmly on the brake to stop and hold the car while you quickly shift to Reverse.
3. Release the brake and accelerate with gentle pressure as far back as the car will go until the wheels start to spin. Step on the brake again and hold it while shifting to Drive.
4. Repeat as necessary. Do *not* spin your wheels: You'll only dig yourself in more deeply.

Repeat these shifts as quickly and smoothly as possible, but be sure to use the brake to hold the car at a stop while shifting gears. Each forward-and-backward movement should take the car a little farther in one direction or the other.

When rocking a car, proceed cautiously. If the tires do suddenly grip, the car may lurch forward, backward, or sideways. Warn bystanders to keep their distance, and take care not to strike nearby cars or objects.

If you are approaching a large vehicle on a slush-covered roadway, turn on your windshield washers and wipers about 30 seconds before you meet. This gets the glass wet and will help to clean the glass quickly after you pass.

Avoid using your high beams in heavy rain, sleet, or snow. Under such conditions, light is reflected back into your eyes, decreasing your ability to see.

WHAT WOULD YOU DO?

How would you get your car out of the snowdrift?

Anticipate and Prevent Skids

If you change speed or direction gradually and smoothly rather than abruptly, you will minimize the risk of skidding. In Chapter 13 you will learn what to do if your car does go into a skid.

Anticipate situations in which skids are likely, and take steps to maintain control of your car. For example, when driving on a wet road when the temperature is near freezing, allow yourself extra time and space to brake and steer. If you're approaching a sharp curve or steep hill, slow down well in advance and keep a firm grip on the steering wheel. When you have to turn the wheel, do so slowly and only as much as necessary.

When you know that you'll have to stop for a stop sign or red signal light on an ice- or snow-packed roadway, shift to Neutral and press the brake pedal down gently. Shifting to Neutral helps you to brake and to prevent skidding by eliminating the thrust effect of the wheels.

Anticipate and Prevent Hydroplaning

During the first 10 to 15 minutes of a rainfall, the roads are at their slickest. This occurs because the rain's moisture mixes with surface dirt and oil to form a slippery film. This film greatly reduces the ability of your tires to grip the road.

At speeds as low as 35 mph, the tires of a vehicle will begin to skim along the wet surface of the road, much like a water-skier zipping across the surface of a lake. The car may completely lose contact with the road and be moving on a thin film of water. This is called *hydroplaning.* Hydroplaning is very dangerous because it severely limits your ability to control your car. To prevent hydroplaning, don't exceed a speed of 30 mph when driving on wet roadways.

Keep on hand the cold-weather items you may need, such as a windshield scraper and brush, a shovel, jumper cables, emergency flares and gloves.

CHECKPOINT

5. What strategies can you use to manage visibility, time, and space in rainy or snowy weather?
6. What risks can you anticipate when driving in rain or snow? What steps can you take to minimize them?

Fog rolling in off the water, industrial smog, or a sudden dust or sand storm can diminish the light of a bright, clear day. Strong gusts of wind can blow your car off the road. You can learn to minimize risk under these conditions.

How Can You Minimize Risk in Other Hazardous Weather Conditions?

Just as you must understand and learn how to manage the risks of driving in rain and snow, you must also understand and learn how to manage the risks posed by other weather hazards.

Fog or Smog

Dense fog poses unique hazards. Scattered patches of thick fog may occur so suddenly that your field of vision is cut without warning. If the humidity is high enough, moisture can accumulate both inside and outside your windshield, further reducing your already limited visibility. Turn on your windshield wipers and defogger as necessary.

Your low-beam headlights are essential when driving in fog, both to help you see and to enable others to see you. If the fog is thick, you may also want to switch on your emergency flashers, to further increase your ability to be seen.

Resist the temptation to put on your high beams. The small droplets of water in fog reflect light back into your eyes, making visibility much poorer with high beams than with low beams.

To better manage time and space when driving in fog, reduce speed, increase your following distance, and remain alert for sudden movements.

If fog is very dense, the wisest thing to do is to signal and pull off the road to a protected area and wait for driving conditions to improve. If you do pull over, turn on your emergency flashers to make your car visible to other drivers.

In some areas, industrial smoke and other kinds of air pollution create smog that decreases drivers' visibility as much as does fog. Methods described for driving in fog are equally useful for smog conditions.

Sand and Dust

In some parts of the country, sand and dust cause serious visibility problems. In desert areas, for example, sandstorms and dust storms can make it all but impossible to see. This severe decrease in visibility greatly increases the risk of a collision.

If possible, avoid driving in sandstorms and dust storms. If you're caught in such a storm, signal, pull off the road, turn on your emergency flashers, and wait for the storm to pass.

If you must drive, use your low-beam headlights, and proceed slowly and very cautiously.

In ancient Babylonia more than 4,000 years ago, a 3,000 foot long tunnel was built under the Euphrates River. The tunnel connected the royal palace with the temple of the gods. The Babylonians were able to build the tunnel by re-routing the river during the dry season. The tunnel was lined with brick and was used only by pedestrians.

Gary Guzouskas, Administrator, New Hampshire Department of Education

Gary Guzouskas

As you drive you may encounter various conditions that affect your ability to see and operate your car safely. To reduce risk, use your headlights every time you drive and keep them clean and aligned. Be alert to changing environmental and roadway conditions. When buying a car, consider one whose design limits blind spots and whose color enhances its ability to be seen.

Whenever visibility becomes limited, adjust your speed and position to provide more space between your car and other highway users.

Wind

Depending on the size and weight of the car you're driving, high winds can be a nuisance—or downright dangerous. Wind can buffet cars traveling on a highway like boats tossed in stormy seas. A strong enough gust of wind can actually push a lightweight car right out of its lane!

Under windy conditions, reduce speed and grip the steering wheel firmly to maintain control of your car. Leave extra space between your car and nearby vehicles, especially those that are likely to be affected by the wind, such as vans, recreational vehicles, and cars pulling trailers.

Be aware that nature is not the only source of wind. When a bus, truck, or tractor-trailer speeds by your car—in either direction—you'll feel a powerful blast as it passes. Always allow as much distance as possible to the side between your car and a passing large vehicle. In this way, you can minimize the force of the resulting wind gust. On a two-lane highway, for example, hug the right edge of the road.

? WHAT WOULD YOU DO?

Explain how you would manage risk in this situation.

CHECKPOINT

7. What weather conditions other than snow and rain pose dangers for drivers? What risks would you anticipate in these conditions?

CHAPTER 11 REVIEW

KEY POINTS

LESSON ONE

1. Reduced light during dusk and dawn and at night makes it harder for you to see and for other drivers and pedestrians to see you. At night, your view of the roadway and off-road areas is limited, and you have to cope with glare from the lights of oncoming vehicles.

2. When driving in low light, reduce speed, increase following distance, signal turns well in advance, and use your low or high beams as appropriate. At night, look beyond your headlights, but drive at a speed that will allow you to stop within their range.

LESSON TWO

3. In the morning or late afternoon, when the sun is low on the horizon, glare makes it hard to see the road and the brake lights of other vehicles.

4. To minimize the risk from sun glare, wear sunglasses and use your sun visor. Reduce speed and increase your following distance.

LESSON THREE

5. Steps you can take to manage visibility, time, and space in rain or snow are to prepare in advance, leave an extra margin of safety, drive in the tracks of the vehicle ahead of you, signal other drivers early, keep your low-beam headlights on, and ease your way into turns and curves.

6. To minimize risk in rain or snow, postpone driving until the weather is clear, maneuver the car gently and gradually to prevent skids, allow extra time for braking and steering, and drive slowly to avoid hydroplaning.

LESSON FOUR

7. Fog and smog decrease visibility. When driving in these conditions, keep on low-beam headlights, reduce speed, and increase following distance. If the fog or smog is very dense, pull off the road and use your emergency flashers.

Sand and dust storms can make it impossible to see. During such storms it is best to pull off the road and use emergency flashers to alert other drivers of your presence. If you must drive, use low-beam headlights and proceed with caution.

In heavy winds, reduce speed and grip the steering wheel firmly to control the car; increase the distance between you and other vehicles, especially RVs, vans, and cars pulling trailers. When being passed by a large vehicle, allow as much distance between your car and it to minimize the force of the resulting wind gust.

PROJECTS

1. The laws governing when and when not to use headlights and parking lights vary from state to state. Find out what the rules are in your state. Take an informal survey of drivers you know. How many are aware of your state's regulations?

2. Automotive stores sell various products designed to help drivers cope with winter driving. Visit an automotive store and evaluate the usefulness of several such products. Which would you buy? Which would you avoid? Why? Discuss your findings with the class.

CHAPTER 11 REVIEW

BUILDING MAP SKILLS

Using a Triptik

A *Triptik* is a continuous series of strip maps in booklet form put out by the American Automobile Association (AAA). A Triptik provides detailed routing from the place you are traveling from to the place you want to go. All you have to do is flip the strips.

The front page of each strip map shows a section of a through, cross-country route and all necessary highway details (Map A). The centerfold contains an area map (Map B). It shows the area surrounding the major route, so that you can deviate from the marked route if you choose. The back page ordinarily shows detailed maps of cities along the marked route (Map C).

Try It Yourself

1. On which map would you find the route highlighted for best travel through Baltimore? What route is this? What else does the map tell you about this route?

2. You are at the corner of Bentwood Avenue, heading west on Chase Street. Describe how you would get to the Baltimore Arena. Which map would you use?

3. Suppose you are north of Baltimore, traveling south on Route 83. You want to take Route 45 into the city. Which map would you use? How would you get to Route 45?

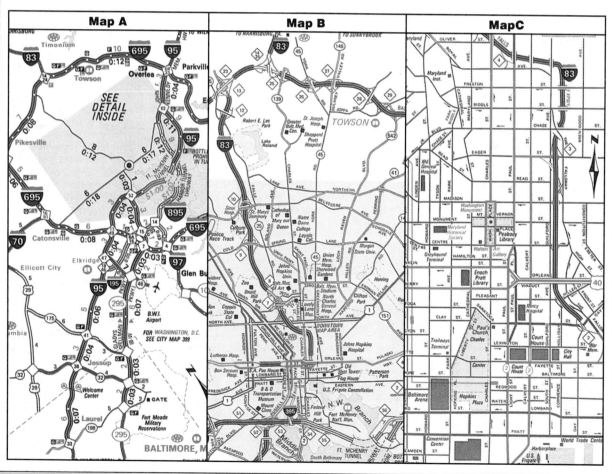

| Map A | Map B | Map C |

CHAPTER 11 REVIEW

CHAPTER TEST

Write the letter of the answer that best completes each sentence.

1. You can lessen the risk created by the sun's glare by
   a. opening your sunroof.
   b. using your high beams.
   c. wearing sunglasses.
2. You should keep your low-beam headlights on
   a. at all times, day or night.
   b. from dusk until dawn.
   c. only when you cannot see.
3. As visibility decreases
   a. your risk of being involved in a collision decreases.
   b. your risk of being involved in a collision increases.
   c. the barometer rises.
4. Using your high beams in fog can
   a. increase visibility by as much as 250 feet.
   b. decrease your ability to see.
   c. warn other drivers of your approach.
5. A dirty or scratched windshield
   a. can cause you to skid in bad weather.
   b. can worsen the effects of glare.
   c. has no effect on glare.
6. During dusk and dawn hours, it is
   a. more difficult for other drivers and pedestrians to see you.
   b. easier to hydroplane.
   c. easier to see the roadway.
7. To brake safely on a snow-packed road,
   a. quickly press the brake all the way to the floor.
   b. shift to Neutral and press the brake gradually.
   c. shift to Overdrive and press the brake.

8. Dense fog can
   a. permanently affect the surface of your windshield.
   b. cause moisture to accumulate on the inside of your windshield.
   c. cause elevated roadways to freeze.
9. If you are caught in a sand storm, you should
   a. use your windshield wipers.
   b. pull off the road and put on your emergency flashers.
   c. use your high beams.
10. A car traveling on a wet road at 35 mph can
    a. get increased gas mileage.
    b. lose contact with the road entirely.
    c. develop engine trouble.

Write the word or phrase that best completes each sentence.

| sun visor | temperature | smog |
| hydroplane | windshield | taillights |

11. When you _____ , your car skims along the surface of water on the roadway.

12. Your headlights and _____ help to illuminate your car.

13. One way to avoid glare is to use your _____ .

14. Air pollution and smoke can create _____ that decreases drivers' visibility as much as does fog.

15. Glare caused when the sun hits your _____ can diminish visibility.

DRIVER'S LOG

In this chapter, you have learned how different light and weather conditions affect the driving task. Imagine the weather is between 25 and 35 degrees and it is beginning to rain. Write a weather advisory for drivers that gives hints on driving safely in these conditions and what conditions drivers might expect later in the day.

CHAPTER ◆ 12

SHARING THE ROADWAY

The society of roadway users includes motorists, pedestrians, and cyclists. It is important to learn how to interact safely with others on the roadways. Good drivers do this by communicating with and anticipating the actions of others.

CHAPTER 12 OBJECTIVES

Sharing the Roadway with Pedestrians and Animals

1. Describe problems that pedestrians can pose.
2. Tell how to avoid collisions with pedestrians.
3. Describe pedestrian responsibilities.
4. Identify ways drivers can avoid collisions with animals.

Sharing the Roadway with Motorcycles and Bicycles

5. Identify high-risk situations involving cyclists and explain actions that drivers can take to reduce the risk of collision with them.
6. Describe the responsibilities of motorcyclists on the roadway.

Sharing the Roadway with Other Vehicles

7. Describe ways to share the roadway with three vehicles other than cars and cycles.
8. Describe at least three precautions you should take around slow-moving vehicles.

Safe Driving Procedures at Railroad Crossings

9. Explain how to drive safely through a railroad crossing.

Sharing the Roadway with Pedestrians and Animals

Be on the lookout for pedestrians who may need extra time to cross the street. ▶

Drivers must be alert to all roadway users, not just other motorists. Other roadway users such as pedestrians and animals can present special problems. Anticipating these problems can help you to protect yourself and others.

What Problems Do Pedestrians Pose to Drivers?

Every year, there are some 8,000 pedestrians killed and 80,000 injured in the United States.

Intersections are the most common scene of collisions with pedestrians. Drivers who must concentrate on traffic, signs, and signals, as well as other roadway users, often fail to check for pedestrians until the last moment, when it's too late.

Also, pedestrians may be distracted and cross streets without looking both ways. They might run across streets either against a red light or just as a light is turning red.

Jaywalking, crossing without regard for traffic rules or signals, is a common pedestrian error, as is walking into the street from between parked cars.

When traffic is light, pedestrians might cross at places other than intersections, because they assume no cars are coming. In areas without sidewalks, pedestrians walk in the street or roadway, posing an additional risk to drivers.

Children

Children are at a disadvantage as pedestrians because they're smaller and less visible to drivers. They are

More than 70 percent of collisions with pedestrians happen in urban areas. However, the likelihood of a *fatal* collision is greater in rural areas. The chance of a death occurring in an urban pedestrian collision is about 1 in 13. In a rural collision, it is 1 in 5.

also less capable than adults of judging when it's safe to cross a street and less likely to fully understand the consequences of their misjudgment.

In many urban and suburban areas, children use the street as their playground. When playing on sidewalks, children tend to forget about traffic and dart into the street, often between parked cars.

Children on skateboards, sleds, roller skates, or bicycles sometimes lose control and shoot over the edge of a sidewalk into the street.

Adults

Adults should know better than children, but they don't always act that way. Adults commonly jaywalk, particularly when rushing to get somewhere or to escape harsh weather. Adults often assume not only that drivers will see them, but that the drivers will always grant them the right of way. Making these two assumptions can prove fatal.

How Can You Avoid Collisions with Pedestrians?

The SIPDE procedure—particularly the first step, Search—is essential to drivers in avoiding and preventing collisions with pedestrians.

Scan the roadway and sides of the road continuously as you drive. Watch for children on or near the roadway. Also look for clues that children may be present. Playground and school-crossing signs, toys in a front yard, or a tricycle in a driveway all indicate that children may be nearby.

In residential areas, reduce speed and drive as far away from the curb or parked cars as you safely can. Use *ground viewing*, which means scanning beneath parked vehicles, for any sign of movement.

▲ Be on the alert for children on bicycles in suburban areas.

ips for New Drivers

Pedestrians to Watch For

Certain pedestrians require drivers to pay special attention

- Elderly pedestrians may have impaired eyesight or hearing. They may move and react slowly and require extra time to cross streets.
- The physically challenged, such as blind people and people in wheelchairs, may need extra time to cross streets.
- Pedestrians with strollers or carriages may need extra time to move onto or off a sidewalk.
- Joggers running with their backs to traffic can pose a hazard. Many do not wear reflective clothing, which makes them difficult to see when visibility is low.
- People on the job, such as mail carriers, delivery people, or roadway maintenance workers, may be distracted by their work and step out into the roadway without checking traffic.

▲
Because of their size, buses can block your view of pedestrians who are about to cross the street.

take evasive action. To warn a pedestrian of your approach, tap your horn. Blasting a horn may frighten pedestrians into doing something dangerous. Always yield pedestrians the right of way, even if the pedestrian is crossing illegally.

What Responsibilities Do Pedestrians Have?

Like drivers, pedestrians, too, must pay attention to rules, signals, and signs. Pedestrians must learn to judge gaps in traffic, and then cross streets only when and where it is safe—and legal—to do so.

◆ Never assume that a driver will see you and stop.
◆ Cross only at intersections.
◆ Cross only when the light is green or red and yellow, or when a pedestrian signal shows a *walk* symbol.
◆ Do not step off the curb while waiting for the light to change.
◆ Pause before crossing to look and listen for approaching traffic.
◆ When walking on or near a roadway, walk facing traffic.
◆ When walking or jogging on or near a roadway, wear reflective clothing, especially when visibility is reduced. In addition, do not wear headphones.
◆ When walking with young children, always take them by the hand when crossing streets.

Most pedestrians who are hit at intersections are struck just as they step into the street.

When stopped at a red signal at an intersection, do *not* start moving the instant the light changes: first check for pedestrians and vehicles in the intersection.

Exercise special care at intersections, particularly when you're making a turn. Be alert for people crossing against the light, stepping off a curb prematurely, or rushing to beat a changing light. Watch, too, for pedestrians who need more time to cross a street than the "Walk" signal allows them. Although not exactly a pedestrian, someone riding a skateboard or on roller skates should deserve your attention, especially near intersections.

Be alert for adults and children near bus stops, train stations, in school zones, near parks, and in shopping areas.

When backing up, never rely on your rearview mirror alone. Before backing, make certain there is no one behind or next to your car. This is particularly important with regard to children, who may be too small for you to see them when you are behind the wheel.

Never assume a pedestrian sees your car. A preoccupied pedestrian, or one who has been drinking, may not notice you. Always be ready to

How Can Drivers Avoid Collisions With Animals?

The dangers posed by animals on the roadway should not be taken lightly. Smashing into a 150-pound deer at 50 miles per hour, for example, will not only kill the animal, but will also wreck the car and may well kill the passengers.

The problem of animals on the roadway is particularly severe during the hours between sunset and sunrise, when light conditions limit visibility. Fog can also contribute to vehicle-animal collisions.

Small Animals

Whether it's a cat darting across a city street or a raccoon crossing a highway, small animals cause a surprising number of collisions. In trying to avoid the animal, the driver might swerve and strike another vehicle or a fixed object along the road. Or, the driver might slam on the brakes—and be struck in the rear by the car behind.

Large Animals

Hitting a large animal can prove fatal for both the animal and the car's occupants. Deer are the large animals most often struck, but drivers also have collisions with horses, cows, and other farm animals.

Using SIPDE to Avoid Collisions with Animals

Whether you're driving on city streets or along country roads, using the SIPDE procedure will help you avoid collisions with animals.

Be especially cautious when driving through farmland or any wooded areas where you are likely to encounter deer or other animals along the road. Search for movement along the sides of the road. At night, search for sudden, unusual spots of light which may be identified as the reflection of your headlights off animals' eyes.

SAFETY TIPS

While hitchhiking may be legal in some areas, it is not a safe practice. The hitchhiker has no idea what kind of person the driver is, and there is no guarantee that the hitchhiker will not be robbed or assaulted by the driver.

Each year motor vehicles kill thousands of deer, antelope, and other wild animals. In 1990, in Pennsylvania alone, *more than 43,000* deer were killed in collisions with motor vehicles.

◀

Slow down when you see a deer on the side of the road. It may panic and bolt in front of you.

You can buy and attach to your car an ultrasonic animal warning device. Studies show that such devices can prevent up to 80 percent of vehicle-animal collisions.

WHAT WOULD YOU DO?

What possible unseen hazards may be present in this situation? How can you manage risk?

As you're driving, predict what you might do if an animal suddenly darts across the road.

What you decide to do, if you encounter an animal, will depend on the kind of road you're on, traffic conditions, and other factors. As a general rule, try to position yourself so that you can avoid executing a move hastily. If you're driving on a two-lane road, drive with your headlights on and move toward the center line to improve visibility. That way, you'll have more room to spot an animal on the side of the road without having to swerve immediately to avoid it. When driving near the center of the road, however, avoid swerving to the left into the path of oncoming cars.

Be especially careful when driving at night and in fog. During dusk and dawn, deer move around to feed, and these are also the times during the day when visibility is reduced. If you do spot an animal near or on the road, slow down and be prepared to stop. Leave as wide a safety margin as you can when driving around or past an animal. Also, if you spot one animal, assume that others are nearby.

If it appears impossible to avoid striking a large animal, brake firmly and steer to strike it at an angle. Let up on the brake pedal just before hitting the animal. This will cause the front of the car to rise and reduce the chance that the animal will come through the windshield.

If you see signs that say "Cattle Crossing" or "Open Range" or signs that warn of horseback riders, keep a lookout for animals on or near the roadway. Reduce speed as soon as you catch sight of an animal.

Always drive past any animal slowly and cautiously; a frightened animal may bolt in any direction.

Finally, keep in mind that in certain situations you have no real choice but to strike an animal rather than try to evade it. For example, if a squirrel darts in front of your car, and swerving or hard braking might cause a collision with a pedestrian or other vehicle, you must choose the less serious of the two collisions.

CHECKPOINT

1. What are some pedestrian behaviors that lead to collisions with vehicles?
2. What precautions can drivers take to avoid collisions with children?
3. What are some of the basic safety rules pedestrians should follow?
4. If you can't avoid hitting a large animal, what steps should you take to minimize the damage to your car?

Sharing the Roadway with Motorcycles and Bicycles

In 1990, 850 bicyclists and 3,120 motorcyclists were killed in collisions in the United States. As the number of people riding bikes and motorcycles increases, the number of collisions with cars and other large vehicles may increase, too.

As a driver, you should recognize the potential risk of collisions posed by cyclists and take precautions to minimize the risk.

How Can You Recognize and Reduce the Risk of Problems Caused by Cyclists?

Both motorcycles and bicycles are smaller, less stable, and less visible than cars. Two wheels provide less stability than four, making these vehicles harder to steer and handle than many people realize. As a car driver, you need to be aware of cyclists and of how the roadway problems they face are different from yours.

Watching Out for Cyclists

Two-wheeled vehicles, particularly bicycles, are much more difficult than cars for drivers to spot, especially when they approach from behind or from the side. A moped is a low-powered two-wheeled vehicle that shares some of the same visibility problems as a bicycle or motorcycle and is most commonly driven on city streets. On highways a motorcycle

◀

Cyclists should be especially careful to stay out of a driver's blind spots.

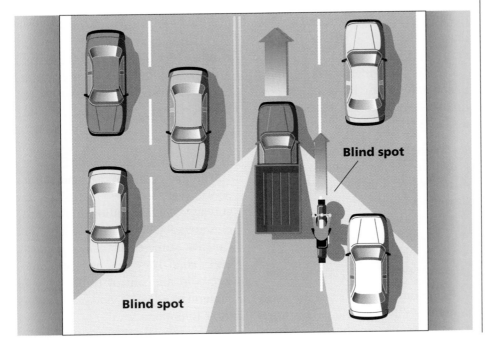

Blind spot

Blind spot

does not take up an entire lane and may easily drop out of sight in a driver's blind spot. In addition, drivers tend not to look for cyclists.

Motorcycles and bicycles also are easily hidden from drivers' sight by larger vehicles sharing the roadway. The small handlebar mirrors on both motorcycles and bicycles offer their drivers only a limited view to the rear. In addition, cyclists have no windshield wipers to aid visibility in case of a sudden shower.

Always make cyclists aware of your intentions and position. Drive with your headlights on, and signal well in advance when turning, changing lanes, or stopping. Tap your horn to warn a cyclist of your approach.

Dangerous Roadway Conditions

Drivers must be aware of the problems that cyclists face in order to anticipate situations in which a cyclist might veer or skid into the path of a car, or might suddenly slow down, steer widely left or right, or stop suddenly.

Cyclists must make a much more major adjustment in speed or position than a driver in situations such as these:

◆ encountering a storm drain, a gravel surface, or a pothole
◆ driving on a rain-slicked road or through a large puddle
◆ getting caught in an unexpected rain or snow shower
◆ being blown by a sudden strong gust of wind

To minimize risk, scan the roadway ahead for problems that may cause a cyclist to change speed or direction, skid, or make a sudden stop. Anticipate potential risk by allowing cyclists as much maneuvering space as possible. When driving behind a cyclist, increase your following distance. *Never* try to pass a cyclist in a tight space.

If a cyclist is carrying a passenger, be especially careful. A passenger leaning the wrong way can throw a motorcycle or bicycle off balance.

Use your mirrors to check for cyclists approaching from the rear. They often squeeze between cars traveling in parallel lanes. Always check your blind spots, too, before changing lanes. Be on the lookout for cyclists approaching intersections and coming around curves.

Lack of Protection

Unlike drivers, who have the protection of their cars, cyclists are unprotected. In the event of a mishap—collision, skid, blowout—the risk of serious or fatal injury is high to the cyclist. Keep this in mind when dealing with cyclists.

When driving through residential areas, watch for bicycles and motorcycles entering the roadway from driveways and side streets.

Failure to Obey Traffic Laws

Human error or ignorance accounts for countless collisions involving cyclists. Although motorcycles are subject to the same laws that cars are, some cyclists seem to break every rule. They ride between lanes, weave in and out of traffic, ride in drivers' blind spots, and fail to signal their intentions.

Some bicyclists show an equal disregard for safety. They ride on the wrong side of the road, shoot through stop signs and red lights, and cut in front of cars. Children on bikes, unconcerned with traffic laws, may ride up one-way streets or sail through intersections with barely a glance to either side.

Such careless riding poses a danger not just to the cyclist but to all roadway users. You should be alert to the possibility that cyclists may not follow traffic laws, and you should always be prepared to take evasive action if necessary.

On the other hand, you should follow all traffic laws so that you do not endanger cyclists and other users of the roadway.

Irresponsible Drivers

Many collisions involving cyclists occur because drivers have difficulty seeing motorcycles and bicycles. However, some cyclists become the victims of careless or inconsiderate drivers. These drivers may tailgate cyclists, cut them off, or pass too close for safety. Such reckless actions put both driver and cyclist at risk.

What Special Responsibilities Do Motorcyclists Have?

Motorcyclists have as much right to ride on the highways as any other drivers. They also have the responsibility of driving safely and watching out for drivers of other vehicles.

Motorcyclists should not take advantage of the smaller size of their vehicles to weave in and out of lanes of traffic at high speeds. This behav-

ior is highly dangerous to the cyclist. Motorcyclists should take care to stay out of other drivers' blind spots. Other drivers might not be as aware as they should about looking in their mirrors for motorcycles to begin with, so it is important that a motorcylist never be in a spot that is not visible to nearby vehicles.

CHECKPOINT

5. Describe problems that cyclists can cause for a driver. Explain how you would manage risk in each circumstance.
6. What should motorcylists do on the roadway?

?

WHAT WOULD YOU DO?

The motorcyclist reduces speed, but does not stop. Now you can pass the cyclist safely. What potential hazards should you watch for?

Tractor-trailer mirrors are mounted high, so the driver loses sight of your car if you travel alongside the trailer. ▶

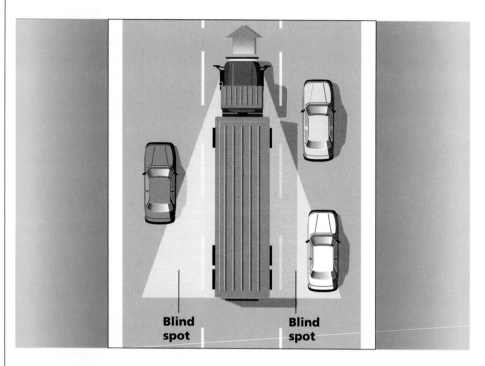

Blind spot　　**Blind spot**

A truck weighing 80,000 pounds traveling at 55 mph takes about 300 feet, or the length of a football field, to stop.

Whether driving on city streets or superhighways, you'll share the roadway with vehicles that range in size from two-wheel, 30-pound bicycles to 18-wheel, 80,000-pound tractor-trailers. You've already explored some problems you might encounter with bicycles and motorcycles. To manage time and space near larger vehicles, you need to understand their characteristics and limitations.

How Can You Safely Share the Roadway with Other Vehicles?

Keep in mind that differences in size, shape, and weight of a vehicle affect handling ability as well as the amount of visibility a driver has.

Trucks and Tractor-Trailers

Trucks on the road today can be up to 120 feet long and weigh up to 60 tons. That's about four times as long as the average car and 40 times heavier. Put yourself in the truck driver's place. Being aware of problems they face will help you manage risk.

Visibility Truck drivers sit high above the surface of the roadway and have excellent visibility ahead. However, it is hard for them to see what is to the side of and behind the truck. Despite the use of side-view mirrors, a car may be all but invisible to a truck driver.

Trucks create visibility problems for other drivers. With a truck blocking your view, you can't see traffic or the roadway ahead.

Time Handling a truck is more difficult than handling a car. Weighed down with cargo, a truck accelerates slowly and tends to lose speed when climbing an uphill road. Going downhill, however, a truck's momentum causes it to pick up speed.

When you're passing a truck, allow much more time than you'd need in order to pass a car. Not only is the truck longer, but its bulk creates a wind factor that you'll also have to be aware of as you steer around the vehicle.

Space Trucks, of course, take up much more room on the roadway than do cars. As a result, it's much harder to see around one when you're following it. Increase your following distance when you're behind a truck. Remember that a truck requires a wide turning space and more time and space to stop than cars do. When you approach a truck in an oncoming lane, leave as much space as possible between the truck and your car.

Buses

The same visibility and handling factors that pertain to trucks also apply to buses. Allow buses an equal amount of "elbow room," and follow the same 4-second-distance rule when following a bus. Remember that local buses stop frequently to pick up and discharge passengers, often disrupting traffic flow in the process.

You should be especially careful when you approach or pass a stopped bus. Reduce speed and keep alert for pedestrians rushing to catch the bus and discharged passengers hurrying across streets in front of the bus. Always be ready to stop.

Remember, drivers traveling in either direction on a nondivided roadway must stop for a school bus that has flashing red lights to indicate it is picking up or dropping off children.

Small Cars

There are more small cars on the road today than ever before. While these cars may cost less to buy and operate than larger cars, they have some drawbacks.

Small cars may have less power than larger cars. As a result, a small car may have difficulty passing other

Save fuel by using public transportation, such as buses, or riding a bicycle whenever possible.

How to Safely Share the Roadway with a Truck

Always allow at least a 4-second following distance to make you visible to the truck and allow you to see more of the roadway.

When stopping behind a truck stopped at a sign or signal, allow extra distance in case the truck rolls back when starting.

Allow yourself extra time and space when passing. When a large truck is about to pass you, steer to adjust to the gust of air caused by the truck.

If a truck is bearing down on you as you drive downhill, move into another lane or pull over to let the truck pass.

Try not to drive on the right side of a truck, especially just below the right-front passenger side. This is a blind spot for the truck driver.

Never try to drive by the right side of a truck at an intersection if the truck's right-hand signal is on, even if the truck is in the left lane. Large trucks make very wide right-hand turns.

Never pass a truck on the right side on the roadway.

After passing a truck, do not pull right in front of it after you clear it. Leave plenty of room in case you have to hit your brakes.

vehicles. Small cars may also have to strain to climb a steep hill.

When driving a small car, allow yourself extra space and time to pass another vehicle. If a small car is passing you, give the driver ample space and time to maneuver.

Also give small cars extra room when roads are slippery or there are strong winds. Lightweight cars tend to skid more easily on slick roadways.

Other Kinds of Vehicles

You may encounter other kinds of vehicles on the roadway.

Emergency vehicles When you meet ambulances, police cars, and fire trucks with lights flashing or sirens on, you should yield the right of way. Pull to the right and stop, or otherwise provide a clear path for the emergency vehicle.

Snowmobiles Snowmobiles are allowed on certain roads in some states. They are hard to see, and are difficult for their drivers to handle and to stop. Allow extra time and space to adjust to any maneuver that a snowmobile makes.

Recreational vehicles Recreational vehicles are harder than cars for drivers to handle because of their size and weight. Allow an added margin of safety if you encounter one, especially in a strong wind. Remember that its driver has limited visibility to the rear and to the sides.

Ice cream trucks Approach ice cream trucks cautiously. Watch for children darting into the street and emerging from between parked cars. In some states, drivers must stop for an ice cream truck equipped with flashing red lights and must yield the right of way to pedestrians going to and from the truck. Check your state drivers' manual.

THE HISTORY CONNECTION

In Japan in the year 1635, a law was passed that caused Japanese lords and thousands of their household staff to take to the roadways of that island nation. The law required that the nation's lords, known as *daimyo* or "great names," build mansions in the capital city of Edo, now known as Tokyo. The lords were to keep their families in Edo, and spend every other year at the court of the ruler, or *Shogun*.

Because of this law, the daimyo had to travel once a year to or from their country estates and Edo. Moreover, the daimyo were told how many of their household staff must travel with them, what equipment to take, and what route to follow. The wealthiest daimyo had to bring 1,000 or more of their household staff both to and from Edo.

Since there were over 250 daimyo to which the law applied, there would be many great processions criss-crossing Japanese roads in all seasons. These groups, known as *Daimyo Gyoretsu* or "Processions of the Lords," were on the roadways for several weeks. Each night they would stop at one of a huge network of inns established along the national roadways to accommodate the travelers in this procession. In no other country of the world was there such an extensive and elaborate system of overnight accommodations at this time.

Maintenance vehicles Road work involves vehicles of many sizes and shapes with the potential to disrupt traffic. Drivers need to be alert to such vehicles and to adjust speed and position to accommodate sudden moves.

How Do You Deal With Slow-Moving Vehicles?

Slow-moving vehicles, such as farm tractors, horse-drawn wagons, and various special-purpose vehicles, move at a slow speed because they don't have the power to move any faster.

Try to spot a slow-moving vehicle as early as possible, because your car will approach the vehicle more rapidly than a vehicle traveling at a normal rate of speed. These vehicles often, but not always, display special signs identifying them as slow-moving. If the vehicle is especially wide, it may carry a "wide load" sign on the rear. Once you identify such

◄

Allow a wide vehicle more room to maneuver, especially on turns.

You may encounter slow-moving maintenance vehicles in city traffic. ▶

?

WHAT WOULD YOU DO?

The driver of the truck wants to pass. What should you do?

a vehicle, reduce speed and follow at a safe distance.

Before passing, consider the driver's likely actions. For example, the driver of a construction vehicle may drive on the roadway for only a short distance before turning off. A road-maintenance or utility truck may stop or pull over to the side.

If you decide to pass, do so safely and only where it is legal to pass. Be especially careful on single-lane country roads, where you're more likely to encounter a slow-moving vehicle. Visibility is limited on such roads, and if the vehicle you're following is large, you'll have added difficulty seeing past it.

If you see a slow-moving vehicle traveling in the opposite direction, be alert for oncoming cars moving into your path as they pass the vehicle.

CHECKPOINT

7. Name three types of motor vehicles with which you might share the roadway. Explain how you can reduce risk when interacting with these vehicles.

8. When you are sharing the roadway with a slow-moving vehicle, what are three precautions you should take?

Despite warning signs and signals, many collisions occur at railroad crossings each year. Among the causes of these crashes are driver impatience and poor judgment.

How Can You Drive Through a Railroad Crossing Safely?

Too many drivers forget, or ignore, safe-driving procedures at railroad crossings, often with fatal consequences. This lesson describes those procedures.

Determine When It's Safe to Cross

Slow down as you approach a railroad crossing. Look for warning lights or signals or lowered crossing gates.

Stop no closer than 15 feet from a railroad crossing if a train is approaching. *Never* attempt to cross a track if warning lights are flashing.

Even if warning lights are not flashing, look both ways and listen to make sure no train is coming before crossing. Never rely solely on mechanical warning equipment—it could be broken.

If there are no lights or crossing gates present at a railroad crossing, proceed with extra caution. Stop, look, and listen for approaching trains before moving ahead.

After a train has passed, check in both directions to see that no other trains are coming before you start across the tracks.

Always wait for the vehicle ahead of you to clear the tracks before you start across.

Stay Alert

Drivers who travel the same route day in and day out tend to pay less

◀

Be patient and very cautious at railroad crossings. Never think you can beat the train to the crossing.

Harvey LaCount, Coordinator of Driver and Traffic Safety Education, Florida A&M University

Harvey LaCount

Because drivers and pedestrians often act without thinking or communicating their intentions, you must learn to predict what they might do. Drivers must be alert and use their eyes properly to spot clues from others, such as inattention, changing lanes without signaling, and following too closely. Spotting these clues early will help you take steps to protect yourself and others. Remember, driving is a full-time job. Always provide enough time and space between your vehicle and other highway users to allow for their mistakes.

? WHAT WOULD YOU DO?

The train has just about passed. Describe your procedure as you get ready to resume movement.

attention to their surroundings. Such inattention can have tragic consequences at a railroad crossing.

Don't take familiar crossings for granted. Never assume that the track is clear: stop, look, and listen for trains.

Don't Panic If Your Car Stalls

Never stop your car on railroad tracks for any reason whatsoever. In the rare event that your car stalls on the tracks, don't panic.

Immediately check in both directions for approaching trains. If a train is coming, leave your car at once, and move away from the tracks. If no train is approaching *and* you have a clear view of the track in both directions, try to restart your engine. Continue to check for trains.

If you can't start your car and you're sure no trains are coming, try to push your car off—and well away from—the tracks.

CHECKPOINT

9. What must you do to negotiate a railroad crossing safely?

CHAPTER 12 REVIEW

KEY POINTS

1. Pedestrian problems include people who cross a roadway without regard for rules or signals, children who run into the street and who play in the street, adults who have been drinking, people who need extra time to cross, and joggers.

2. To prevent collisions with pedestrians, use SIPDE to develop effective visual search habits. Position your car for maximum visibility, take special care at intersections and when backing, and never assume a pedestrian sees your car.

3. Pedestrians should obey all rules, signals, and signs, walk facing traffic if walking on the roadway, wear reflective clothing when jogging, hold children by the hand, cross streets only when and where it is safe and legal to do so, never assuming that a driver will see them.

4. To avoid collisions with animals, be careful when driving through wooded areas, especially when visibility is reduced. Watch for signs indicating that animals may be nearby.

LESSON TWO

5. Cyclists pose different problems than a driver because cycles have less stability and protection than automobiles. To reduce the risk of collision with cyclists, anticipate problems they may have, and adjust your speed or position. Always make cyclists aware of your position and intentions.

6. Motorcyclists should not weave in and out of traffic at high speeds and should be careful to make themselves visible to drivers.

LESSON THREE

7. Trucks and tractor trailers: when passing allow extra time; when you approach a truck in an oncoming lane, leave plenty of space between it and your car. Buses: react as you would to a truck, but approaching and passing requires special care as buses maybe picking up or discharging passengers. Small cars: allow extra room on slippery roads or windy days; give drivers ample time and space to manuever.

8. Try to spot a slow-moving vehicle early. Reduce your speed and follow at a safe distance. Pass only where it is legal.

LESSON FOUR

9. Slow down as you approach a railroad crossing. Look for warning lights or signals or lowered gates. Before you cross, stop, look, and listen for trains. Never assume the track is clear.

PROJECTS

1. Observe the interaction between pedestrians and traffic at a busy intersection for about 15 minutes. Make note of unsafe actions taken by both pedestrians and drivers. Discuss your observations with the class.

2. Visit a bicycle shop or sporting goods store. What products does the store sell to help make cyclists, joggers, and others more visible in dim light?

BUILDING MATH SKILLS

Figuring Travel Time

Travel involves rate of speed, distance, and time. To find how long it will take you to get somewhere when you know your distance and speed, divide the distance by the speed. (To get an exact answer, you may have to change miles per hour to miles per minute by dividing mph by 60.)

$T = D \div S$, where T = time, D = distance, and S = speed.

For example, suppose you will drive 270 miles at an average speed of 45 mph. How long will the trip take?

$$T = 270 \div 45$$
$$T = 6$$

The trip will take 6 hours.

Figure the time for each distance and speed below.

TIME	DISTANCE	SPEED
?	20 miles	30 mph
?	40 miles	35 mph
?	115 miles	50 mph

To estimate distance when you know speed and time, multiply the speed and the time.

$$D = S \times T$$

How far can you travel in 5 hours at an average speed of 35 mph?

$$D = 35 \times 5$$
$$D = 175$$

You can travel about 175 miles.

Figure the distance for each speed and time below. Round your answer to the nearest whole mile.

DISTANCE	SPEED	TIME
?	25 mph	30 minutes
?	45 mph	2 1/4 hour
?	30 mph	1 hour 20 minutes

Now look back at each problem. If you wanted an estimate instead of an exact answer, what shortcuts could you take?

Try It Yourself

1. Traveling at local speeds, about how many miles away is someplace 20 minutes from your house?

2. Use a map to plan a trip from one city to another. Estimate the amount of time it will take to travel the distance between the two cities.

3. Use a map to figure out which cities or towns are about 3 hours away from your house.

CHAPTER 12 REVIEW

CHAPTER TEST

Write the letter of the answer that best completes each sentence.

1. When driving behind a tractor-trailer,
   a. allow at least a 4-second following distance.
   b. attempt to pass.
   c. tap your horn lightly.
2. Collisions with pedestrians occur most often
   a. at intersections.
   b. on highways.
   c. on weekends.
3. Drivers who travel the same route every day,
   a. have fewer collisions than other drivers.
   b. pay less attention to their surroundings.
   c. fall asleep at the wheel more often.
4. As the use of cycles increases,
   a. the number of collisions involving cars will decrease.
   b. air pollution will decrease.
   c. the number of collisions with cars might increase, too.
5. Drivers use *ground viewing* to
   a. scan the road for animals.
   b. scan beneath parked vehicles for signs of movement.
   c. avoid large puddles.
6. Because truck drivers sit high above the surface of the roadway, they
   a. don't have any blind spots.
   b. have great visibility of the road ahead.
   c. are able to see above fog.
7. If it appears impossible to avoid striking a large animal, you should
   a. accelerate and move forward.
   b. turn off your car's engine.
   c. steer to strike it at an angle.

8. When driving behind a cyclist you should
   a. increase your following distance.
   b. pass at the first opportunity.
   c. turn on your high beams.
9. Most small cars have
   a. more power than larger cars.
   b. the ability to pass easily.
   c. less power than larger cars.
10. If you approach a railroad crossing when a train is coming, you should
    a. stop at least 15 feet from the crossing.
    b. stop directly in front of the crossing signal.
    c. try to cross the tracks, if the gate is open.

Write the word or phrase that best completes each sentence.

traffic flow   parallel   hazard
stability   stalls   jaywalking

11. Crossing a street without regard for traffic rules or signals is called _____ .

12. Motorcycles are harder to steer than people realize, because two wheels provide less _____ than four.

13. If your car _____ on railroad tracks while a train is coming, you should leave your car at once.

14. Cyclists often squeeze between cars traveling in _____ lanes.

15. Local buses stop frequently to pick up and discharge passengers, often disrupting _____ in the process.

DRIVER'S LOG

In this chapter, you have learned about the responsibilities and risks of sharing the roadway with motorists, pedestrians, cyclists, and animals.

Write what you think are the five most important responsibilities a driver has when sharing the roadway.

NATURAL LAWS
AND DRIVING

The natural laws, which include inertia, gravity, and momentum, affect the driving task. It is important to understand natural laws so that you can use your knowledge of them to help you manage risk in different driving situations.

CHAPTER 13 OBJECTIVES

Natural Laws and the Movement of Your Car

1. Describe the natural laws of inertia, friction, momentum, kinetic energy, and gravity, and explain each one's relationship to driving.

Natural Laws and Steering and Braking

2. Explain how natural laws affect a car's stopping distance.
3. Identify the factors that affect steering.
4. Name the ways that natural laws affect steering around a curve.
5. Describe how gravity and the contour of the road affect steering.

Using Natural Laws to Manage Skids

6. List factors that can cause your car to skid.
7. Name and describe the kinds of skids there are.
8. Describe how to manage risk in responding to a skid.

Natural Laws, Risk Management, and Collisions

9. Explain how speed control can help you avoid a collision.
10. Describe how knowledge of natural laws can help you avoid a collision.
11. Tell how to minimize the risks of a collision.

Natural Laws and the Movement of Your Car

Does this sound familiar? You're in a car and the driver brakes. The car stops, but your books on the backseat continue moving forward onto the floor. Why did this happen? A natural law is the culprit.

What Are Natural Laws?

Natural laws are always at work. Some of these laws are inertia, friction, momentum, kinetic energy, and gravity.

Inertia

Inertia causes your books on the backseat to continue moving forward even after you brake. Two aspects govern inertia. One is that objects at rest do not move unless some force acts on them. The other is that moving objects continue to move in a straight line.

All things have inertia. As the car was moving, so were your books. When the driver braked, it exerted a force to make the car stop, but your books kept moving forward in a straight line. Then they fell to the floor.

You have to know about inertia when you drive because you and your passengers have inertia. If you brake the car hard, everyone will tend to keep moving forward. Drivers must manage risk by anticipating how to reduce inertia's effects.

One way to do this is to wear safety belts. These belts provide a force that acts against inertia. If you don't wear safety belts, you may be thrown forward against the windshield or dashboard if the brakes are applied hard.

Another way to manage risk is to be sure to secure all loose objects, such as your books.

Friction

Press your foot down hard on a carpeted floor. Keep it pressed down as hard as you can and try to move across the carpet. Does it feel as if some kind of force is trying to stop your foot from moving, almost as if your foot and the carpet are sticking together?

The force that seems to try to make the surface of your shoe "stick" to the surface of the carpet is *friction*. Friction is a force between two surfaces that resists the movement of one surface across the other. You can make your foot move across the car-

Tips for New Drivers

Drying the Brakes

Wet brakes do not work as efficiently as dry brakes. After you have driven through heavy rain or deep puddles, check for wet brakes. If you apply the brakes lightly and the car pulls to one side or does not slow, your brakes are probably wet. Dry the brakes by applying light pressure to them. The friction created will generate heat, which will dry the brakes.

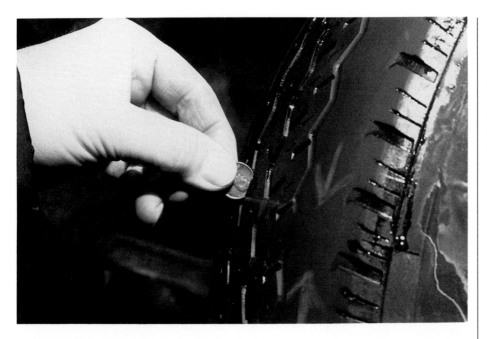

◄

The minimum safe tread depth for your tires is $\frac{1}{16}$ inch. To check your tire's tread depth, place a Lincoln-head penny in the tread. If the tread does not come at least to Lincoln's head, replace the tire.

pet by applying more force than friction can resist or overcome.

Just as friction tries to make your foot stick to the carpet, it tries to make the surface of your tires "stick" to the surface of the road. Your car has to overcome friction in order to move. Your car stays on the road, however, because a certain amount of friction is always present.

Friction between the road and your tires is called *traction,* or *adhesion,* which means "sticking together." Adhesion or traction holds your car on the road. Here are some factors affecting traction.

Tire pressure   Tires are made with grooved surfaces treads, that grip the road. For best traction, inflate tires to the pressure recommended by the manufacturer. Properly inflated tires grip the road evenly. Under- or over-inflation reduces traction. If you underinflate your tires, only the outer edges grip the road. If you overinflate them, only the centers tend to contact the road.

Tire condition   Would you try to walk on slippery packed snow or ice with rubber boots worn smooth? Of course not! You would slide all over. The same concept applies to tires. At 55 mph, a car can lose contact with the road surface if the water is as shallow as $\frac{1}{12}$ inch. Bald tires—tires with very little or no tread—provide almost no traction on wet, icy, or snow-covered roads. Even on dry roads, bald or badly worn tires increase your stopping distance, reduce directional control, and are more apt to get punctured.

Rain   When the road is wet, water gets between the surface of the road and the tires. Water provides a smooth surface for the tires to move across, and a smooth surface does not provide good traction. If tires are properly inflated and have good tread, much of the water will go into the grooves between the treads. This means that the treads themselves will come in contact with less water and more road surface.

Snow and ice make a roadway slick, reducing friction between your car and the road's surface. ▶

Ice and snow Ice and snow can reduce traction more than rain. Traction is poorest near 32°F, when snow and ice start to become a slippery, watery slush. Any road is dangerous when covered with ice or snow, so don't drive at these times unless absolutely necessary.

Snow tires help to increase traction in snow, but not necessarily on ice. Chains are helpful in increasing traction on ice, but they provide poor traction on pavement. In states where they are allowed, studded tires can give the same results as chains. All-weather tires are a good choice for most drivers.

Road condition Road condition also affects traction. Rough roads and potholes make your car bounce up and down, reducing traction. Wet leaves on the road also reduce friction, causing the wheels to lose traction and slide.

Momentum

If a 12-pound bowling ball and an 16-pound bowling ball were rolling toward an object at the same speed, which ball would cause more damage? Because it is heavier, the 16-pound bowling ball would.

Momentum is the product of weight and speed. It provides an explanation for what seems obvious in the bowling ball example. All objects in motion have momentum. The greater the momentum of the vehicles, the greater the damage in a collision might be.

A vehicle's momentum depends on weight and its speed. If either the weight or the speed doubles, so does the vehicle's momentum. If the weight or the speed triples, so does the momentum.

In short, as speed increases, so does the likelihood of damage in case of a collision. The lighter your car, the greater the likelihood that it will be damaged.

Kinetic Energy

All objects in motion have *kinetic energy* as well as momentum. Kinetic energy is the energy of motion. The faster a car moves, the more energy of motion it has.

What does this mean to you as a driver? You need to know that the more energy of motion a car has, the more time and distance it will take to stop.

The heavier a car is, the more energy of motion it has. If a car's weight doubles, its stopping distance doubles as well.

Here is what kinetic energy and momentum can mean when you are accelerating or braking.

Acceleration Suppose that you drive a station wagon and usually carry one or two passengers and light packages. You are aware of how your car accelerates when you enter an expressway. Now suppose that you are going on a trip with four other people, and the back of the wagon is fully packed. You have increased the weight of your car. It will not accelerate as quickly. Thus, you will not be able to enter an expressway as quickly as you usually do. You may need to manage time and space differently. You might want to press down more on the accelerator to compensate for the extra weight and wait for a larger gap in traffic before entering the roadway.

Braking Once you are moving on the expressway, the car's momentum and kinetic energy have increased because its weight and speed have been increased. Its stopping distance has also increased. Reduce risk by leaving a greater distance between your car and the one in front of you.

Gravity

If you toss a ball into the air, it comes down. The ball falls because of *gravity*. Gravity is a force that pulls all objects toward the center of the Earth. Because gravity affects all objects, it can make a car speed up or slow down.

Don't overload your car. Every 100 miles that you travel with extra weight costs you 1 mile per gallon.

THE MATH CONNECTION

It's a mathematical fact that the faster you drive, the more the braking distance increases.

Use the following formula to prove this. If S is the speed, the formula is:

$(S \times \frac{1}{10} S) \div 2$ = braking distance in feet

Braking distance at a speed of 50 miles per hour can be calculated as:

$(50 \times 5) \div 2$
$250 \div 2 = 125$ feet

You don't have to do the calculations as you drive to realize that the faster you are traveling, the more space you have to leave in front of you in case you have to brake suddenly.

An overpacked car-top carrier can make a car less stable by changing its center of gravity. ▶

?

WHAT WOULD YOU DO?

What would you say to the passengers about wearing safety belts?

When you drive uphill, gravity acts to slow your car. To maintain speed, accelerate just before the car begins to climb the hill. When you drive downhill, gravity acts with your car. As a result, your speed increases. To prevent the car from moving too fast, you could use your brakes or downshift.

Center of Gravity

Gravity gives objects their weight. The weight of an object, such as your car, is distributed evenly about a point. This point is called the object's *center of gravity.*

The lower an object's center of gravity, the more stable the object. Most cars are designed to have a low center of gravity in order to handle well in turns and during quick maneuvers. Changes in a car's center of gravity affect how well the car handles. A car-top carrier loaded with heavy objects raises the car's center of gravity, making it less stable and difficult to control on turns and curves and during sudden changes in braking, acceleration, and direction. Vehicles that have a high center of gravity, such as vans, also have these problems.

CHECKPOINT

1. What affects traction? How?

Natural Laws and Steering and Braking

Natural laws affect stopping distance, braking, and steering. Understanding the relationships between natural laws and driving can help you to be a better and a safer driver.

How Do Natural Laws Influence Braking Distance?

The laws of nature affect all vehicles the same way, but people react differently. Thus, you may not stop within the same distance another driver in the same car will. The distance your car takes to stop is its *total stopping distance*. Perception distance, reaction distance, plus braking distance make up total stopping distance. A good rule of thumb for estimating stopping distance is to use the 2- or 4-second rule. See Chapter 10 for more information.

In order to stop, you must (1) identify a need to stop (this is your *perception distance*), (2) react by braking (your *reaction distance*), and (3) slow your car to a stop (your *braking distance*). Each of these actions takes time. Time means distance, and speed affects your stopping distance.

Natural Laws and Braking

Braking is a result of friction between the brake linings and the wheel drums or wheel discs and pads. This friction slows the rotation of the wheels and tires and increases adhesion between the tires and the road. As you brake, you decrease your car's momentum and kinetic energy.

Factors Affecting Braking Distance

The following factors can increase braking distance.

Speed The greater the speed, the longer the braking distance.

Condition of the vehicle Worn brakes, tires, or shock absorbers reduce traction. Reduced traction increases braking distance.

Condition of the roadway Braking distance is greater when the friction on the roadway surface is reduced, such as during bad weather or if the road is unpaved or rough.

Hills and mountains Gravity affects the time and space needed to stop a car going downhill. Because a car going downhill tends to go faster, the braking distance increases.

What Factors and Natural Laws Affect Steering?

Your ability to steer a car depends on many factors. The steering mechanism, tires, and suspension are three mechanical factors. Wheel alignment and road conditions are also important in steering, as is the way you load the car.

Friction helps to keep your car on the road. As you know, the friction between the road and tires is usually called traction. When a driver turns

Telephone poles are about 100 feet apart. Use this measure to help you estimate distance while you are driving.

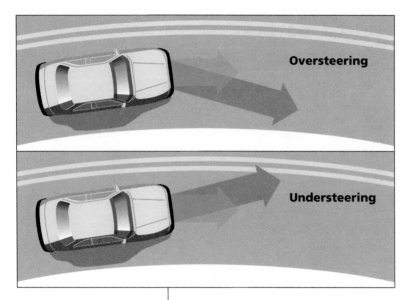

Oversteering

Understeering

Hand position is another factor that affects car control. Hold the steering wheel firmly, but with your fingers rather than the palms of your hands. Keep your thumbs along the face of the steering wheel, not wrapped around it. This gives a more sensitive touch and better control. Adjust your seat so your hands rest in a balanced position on opposite sides of the wheel.

How Do Natural Laws Affect Steering Around a Curve?

Inertia tends to keep a car moving in a straight path. As you enter a curve or turn, you must overcome the effects of inertia by turning the steering wheel. You are moving the car out of its straight path. At the same time, you feel as if you are being pulled toward the door into the curve. What you feel is *centrifugal force.*

As you slow down and enter the curve or turn, you turn the wheel. Friction between the tires and the road acts against centrifugal force and allows the car to follow a curved path. As long as there is enough friction to overcome centrifugal force, you can make the turn. As you turn the wheel, the front tires provide the traction needed to turn the car.

Slow your car as you enter a curve or turn. The faster you go, the more difficult it is for traction to overcome inertia.

If your speed is too high or you turn the steering wheel too sharply or not enough when entering a curve, you may understeer or over-steer. If you understeer on right

▲
Monitor your speed as you enter a curve so that you neither oversteer nor understeer.

the steering wheel, the front tires provide the traction to turn the car.

Because of inertia, a moving car will tend to go in a straight line. Because cars and roads are all different, the car may tend to wander. Thus, you must be able to steer straight. *Directional control* refers to a car's ability to hold a straight line. If your car has good directional control, you will have an easy time keeping the car moving in the direction you steer it.

Turning the steering wheel enables friction to overcome centrifugal force.
▼

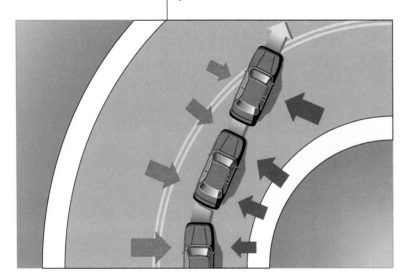

turns or curves, you may find yourself driving in the opposite lane, facing oncoming traffic. If you oversteer, you can pull the car entirely off the roadway. The opposite results are true on left turns or curves.

How Do Gravity and the Contour of the Road Affect Steering?

Gravity in relation to the contour of the road affects how well a car will take a curve.

Banked Roads

Have you ever seen the Indy 500 auto race? The track is *banked*, or higher on the outside of curves than on the inside. On a properly banked curve, the roadway tilts down toward the inside of the curve. Although a car tends to move toward the outside of a curve, the downward tilt of a banked curve improves steering control by working with the force of gravity. If the banking or downward tilt was toward the outside of the curve, gravity and inertia would tend to pull the car off the road, making steering more difficult.

Crowned Roads

Crowned roads are higher in the center than at either of the edges to facilitate drainage. When driving in the right lane on a two-way crowned road, gravity will tend to pull your car to the right, off the roadway. You must counteract the effect of gravitational pull by exerting more force on the steering wheel to keep the car on the road.

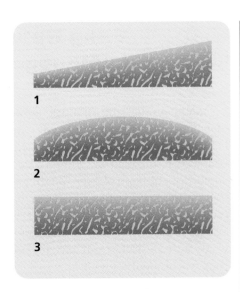

◀ *A car handles differently on (1) banked roads, (2) crowned roads, and (3) flat roads.*

CHECKPOINT

2. How do speed, traction, and gravity affect braking distance?
3. Describe how steering is affected by traction and inertia.
4. What role do friction and centrifugal force play in steering around a curve?
5. How does gravity affect steering on a banked or crowned road? How should you respond?

?

WHAT WOULD YOU DO?

You are driving at 30 mph. Explain what you would do before you enter the curve.

Understanding the natural laws that affect the control of your car can help you regain that control when you lose it through skidding. *Skidding* is loss of control over the direction your car is moving because of reduced traction. If you skid, you are not helpless. Once you understand what causes a skid, you're already on your way to dealing with one.

What Can Make Your Car Skid?

Whenever you skid, one of three things happened: traction was reduced, you tried to change speed too quickly or you changed direction too quickly.

Reduced Traction

A loss of traction or a reduction in traction can be frightening and dangerous for the inexperienced driver. When traction is reduced, your tires lose their grip on the road's surface and the car begins to slide. Drivers should always be aware of conditions that could result in reduced traction. See Chapter 11 for more information on driving in conditions of reduced traction.

Changing Speed Too Quickly

You are on a slippery road and you want to slow down. You step firmly on the brake pedal and your car starts to skid. What happened? You tried to change speed too quickly. Traction could not overcome the car's kinetic energy and momentum as fast as you wanted it to.

Changing Direction Too Quickly

Turning a car quickly is like a large football player trying to make a sharp turn at a full gallop. Sometimes it works, but sometimes it doesn't. If you're driving at a high speed, your car has a tremendous amount of momentum and kinetic energy. Inertia is also at work, trying to force your car to move in a straight path. Tire traction may not be great enough to compensate for momentum, kinetic energy, and inertia when you turn or enter a sharp curve.

How fast is a high speed? It depends on the road. Look at the speed limit signs posted just below the warning signs as you near a curve. They tell you the maximum safe

SAFETY TIPS

When driving on slick roads, make gradual and smooth changes in speed. Ease off the gas pedal and shift to neutral gear. Press the brake pedal down gradually. In neutral, all four wheels brake equally, since none is receiving power. So, traction is increased overall and so is braking efficiency.

Tips for New Drivers

Dealing with Skids

Skidding can be frightening. You can minimize trouble, however, by remembering the following points.

- The most important thing you must do is respond quickly and correctly. Concentrate. Do not panic.
- Do not brake. This will only make the skid worse.
- Look in the direction you want to go.
- Make steering corrections quickly but smoothly.
- Don't give up. Keep steering.

speed you should use to enter the curve. Then you need to adjust speed downward according to conditions.

What Are the Kinds of Skids?

Knowing the kind of skid you are experiencing will help you to manage the risk involved, and may even help you to prevent skidding.

There are four basic kinds of skids: braking, power, cornering, and blowout. If you know the causes and re-sults of these kinds of skids, and the conditions under which they occur, you can deal with them safely.

- ◆ A *braking skid* occurs when you apply the brakes so hard that one or more of the wheels lock.
- ◆ A *power skid* occurs when you suddenly press on the accelerator too hard.
- ◆ A *cornering skid* occurs when you lose steering control in a turn.
- ◆ In a *blowout skid*, a tire suddenly loses air pressure.

	KINDS OF SKIDS			
Type	**Braking skid**	**Power skid**	**Cornering skid**	**Blowout skid**
Reason	The brakes are applied so hard that one or more wheels lock.	The gas pedal is pressed suddenly, too hard.	The tires lose traction in a turn.	A tire suddenly loses air pressure.
Conditions	a sudden stop a wet, slippery, or uneven road	a sudden, hard acceleration a slippery road surface	a turn made too fast poor tires or a slippery road surface	a punctured, worn, or overinflated tire an overloaded vehicle
What Can Happen	Steering control is lost. If the front wheels lock, the car skids straight ahead. If only the rear wheels lock, they slide sideways. The car might spin around.	A car with front-wheel drive plows straight ahead. In a car with rear-wheel drive, the back end can skid to the side. The car might spin around.	Steering control is lost. The rear wheels skid away from the turn The car keeps going straight ahead.	There is a strong pull toward the side on which a front tire has blown out. A rear-tire blowout might cause a pull toward the blowout, side-to-side swaying, or fishtailing.
What To Do	Take your foot off the brake pedal. Steer. When the wheels start turning again and moving forward, steering control will return.	Ease up on the gas pedal until the wheels stop spinning. Steer to straighten the car. Countersteer if the car starts to spin.	Take your foot all the way off the accelerator. Steer to straighten the car.	Do not brake. Make firm, steady steering corrections. Do not change speed suddenly. Slow down gradually and drive off the road.

Accelerate and brake gradually to reduce the risk of skidding on snowy roadways. ▶

?

WHAT WOULD YOU DO?

You have a blowout. What is likely to happen? What should you do? Why?

How Do You Respond to a Skid?

Suppose you are driving carefully on an ice-covered roadway. There are cars parked alongside the traffic lane, and traffic is heavy in both directions.

Suddenly your car begins to skid. How can you manage the risk of a skid and drive out of it?

1. If you have time, ease off the gas pedal and shift into Neutral. Stay off the brake.
2. With your foot off the pedals, steer in the direction you want the car to go.
3. Each time the skid changes direction, turn the wheel smoothly and quickly in the direction you want the car to go.
4. Keep steering until you are out of the skid.

CHECKPOINT

6. What conditions can make your car skid?
7. Describe four kinds of skids.
8. Describe how to safely steer out of a skid.

Natural Laws, Risk Management, and Collisions

The goal of any driver is to avoid collisions and injuries. Good drivers understand how to use accelerating, braking, and steering to help them achieve this goal.

How Can You Use Speed Control to Avoid a Collision?

Braking is a natural reaction to avoid a collision. However, it is not always the correct evasive action.

Accelerating

Speeding up may sometimes be your only means of reducing risk. These situations occur most often at intersections or in merging traffic. For example, you may be in an intersection when a car comes at you rapidly from one side. Braking may leave you directly in the car's path. Steering to the side may take too much time or may not be possible if there are objects on both sides of you. If the road ahead is clear, a quick increase in speed may bring you to safety.

Braking

In some situations, steering to the side or accelerating may not be possible. At speeds under 25 mph, it takes less time and distance to stop than to steer into another lane.

When braking, you want to stop fast without making the wheels lock, or stop turning. Locking the wheels reduces traction and increases stopping distance. To brake quickly, use the threshold/squeeze braking method. With this method, you use your entire body to sense how the brakes are working. Keep your heel on the floor and your foot on the brake so that the metatarsal joint just above the ball of the foot rests on the brake pedal. "Squeeze" the pedal down with a steady, firm pressure until just before the brakes lock. If they lock, ease up about 2 or 3 degrees. Immediately squeeze down again, but not as firmly. Continue until you reach your desired speed. This type of braking allows you to maintain steering control.

The *antilock brake system* is optional equipment that eliminates the problem of locked brakes. This system has sensors that detect if a wheel stops turning. If this happens, pressure on the wheel's brakes is reduced

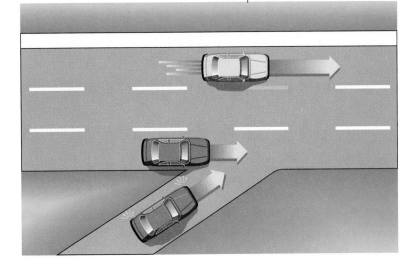

The driver in the left lane accelerated to avoid the possible collision in the right lane.
▼

For best braking control, squeeze the brake pedal with your toes. ▶

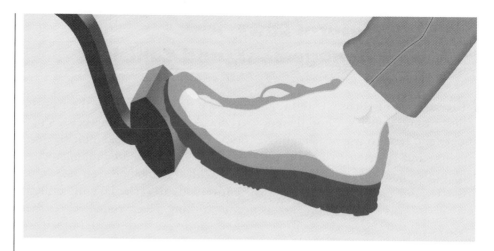

SAFETY TIPS

When you are making a left turn across oncoming traffic, do not turn your steering wheel to the left until the traffic clears. If you did turn the wheel and then were bumped from behind, you could be pushed into a head-on collision with traffic in the oncoming lane.

until the wheel starts turning again. This action is independent of the pressure the driver applies to the brake pedal. Antilock brakes permit maximum brake pressure while retaining steering control.

How Can Knowledge of Natural Laws Help You to Avoid a Collision?

A knowledge of natural laws is vital to car control. Knowing how natural laws work is also important when making evasive maneuvers.

Steering to Avoid a Collision

You are driving at 55 mph. As you reach the top of a hill, you see a car with a flat tire stopped in your lane about 3 seconds ahead. You are going too fast to stop in time. At 55 mph and normal traction, it takes about 4 seconds to stop the car. You have only 3. What can you do?

In this case, you should steer to the right. To do this:
1. Turn the steering wheel as much as half a turn to the right.

2. Immediately turn it back about twice the amount you turned it to the right.
3. Turn the wheel right to bring the car back into its original path.

You use what you know about traction to steer out of trouble. If you turn the wheel more than half a turn, your speed might be too high for traction to overcome centrifugal force.

Controlled Off-Road Recovery

Traffic is heavy but moving at 55 mph. You see a car that is passing a bus coming toward you. You realize the car will not return to its lane in time. You steer to the right. The car passes you safely on the left, but now your two right wheels are on the unpaved shoulder. You want to get back on the road. This is a case when traction is especially important.

Tires rolling on different surfaces have different amounts of grip. The tires on the paved area have more traction than the tires on the unpaved area. Applying the brakes in this situation may cause the car to skid. Turning the wheel sharply could cause your car to skid out of control, flip over on the road, or shoot back across the roadway.

The correct maneuver consists of three steps.

1. Allow the car to move right until the wheels on the shoulder are about 12 to 18 inches from the road edge.
2. Move the steering wheel about a quarter turn to the left. As soon as you feel the right front tire contact the road edge, steer back to the right about half a turn.
3. Immediately turn the steering wheel straight ahead. Do this without braking or accelerating.

This maneuver is called *controlled off-road recovery*.

How Can You Minimize the Risk and Consequences of a Collision?

Unfortunately, it is not always possible to avoid a collision. By knowing what to do before a collision happens, however, you will help to minimize its effects. You should understand the factors that contribute to the force of impact of a collision.

Force of Impact

The force with which a moving car hits another object is called the *force of impact*. Three factors affect the force of impact.

Speed of the car The force of impact at 20 mph is four times that at 10 mph. And the force of impact at 30 mph is nine times that at 10 mph.

Weight of the car The heavier a car is, the harder it will hit any other object.

Impact distance The force of impact also depends on the distance a moving vehicle travels between first impact with an object and the point where the vehicle comes to a full stop. When a car hits an unmoving solid object, the impact distance is short. The object does not "cave in" at impact, and so kinetic energy is spent immediately on impact. The shorter the impact distance, the greater the damage.

Reducing the Force of Impact

You reduce the force of impact if you increase the impact distance. The following energy-absorbing features help increase impact distance.

Sand canisters You often see canisters filled with sand in front of concrete barriers on highways. If a car hits these canisters, they break apart. The sand helps reduce the car's force of impact. The car would slow more gradually than if it hit the concrete barrier.

Car features New cars include a number of features that help increase impact distance by absorbing energy. These features include air bags; crumple zones; automatic safety belts; head restraints; energy-absorbing bumpers, steering columns, and wheels; padded dashboards; safety-glass windshields; and reinforced sides. See Chapter 6 for more information about energy-absorbing features.

If a Collision Is Unavoidable

Suppose a collision seems unavoidable. What should you do? If you can increase the impact distance, you will lessen the force of impact, which

In the 1400s, the Inca Empire stretched from the border of Colombia-Ecuador to central Chile in South America. From Cuzco, the capital, well-constructed roads ran to all parts of the empire. The total length of this road system was about 9,500 miles, and was designed for people on foot. Relay runners were stationed at posts along the road to carry messages and parcels quickly to and from the capital.

Bruce Reichel, Driving
Instructor, Bill Scott
Racing (BSR), Inc.

Bruce Reichel

If you understand the factors involved when a vehicle is in motion, you can learn how to adjust the speed and position of the vehicle to work with the natural laws.

Controlling a car is controlling its energy, and its weight and speed determine the car's energy. A car weighing 2,000 pounds traveling at 30 mph has half the energy of a 4,000-pound car traveling at the same speed. A 2,000-pound car traveling at 60 mph has four times the energy of the same car traveling at 30 mph.

WHAT WOULD YOU DO?

A car has lost control and is swerving into your lane. What should you do?

in turn will reduce the risk of serious damage or injury.

Head-on A head-on collision with another vehicle or an immovable object, such as a large tree, is the worst type of collision. If you can reduce your speed, the force of impact will be less. Driving into something that is movable, such as a bush or a snowbank, will also reduce the force of impact.

Side Suppose you are about to be broadsided in an intersection and cannot avoid it. How can you minimize the damage? You can accelerate to make impact behind the passenger compartment or with the rear end of your car. This will help minimize damage or injury, since impact will occur behind the passengers.

CHECKPOINT

9. Under what conditions can accelerating or braking help you avoid a collision?
10. How can traction and steering help you avoid a collision?
11. How would you use knowledge of force of impact to respond to a head-on or side collision?

CHAPTER 13 REVIEW

KEY POINTS

LESSON ONE

1. Natural laws include inertia, friction, momentum, kinetic energy, and gravity. Inertia causes objects and passengers in a vehicle to keep moving forward when the vehicle is stopped abruptly. Friction between the road and a car's tires holds the car on the road. Momentum determines the extent of damage in a collision. Kinetic energy affects braking and acceleration. Gravity can slow your car when driving uphill, or increase the speed of a car going downhill.

LESSON TWO

2. Braking is a result of friction between the brake linings and the wheel drums. It slows the rotation of the wheels and tires and increases adhesion between the tires and the road.

3. Friction and inertia affect steering, as do road conditions and a car's tires, steering mechanism, suspension, and wheel alignment.

4. As you enter a curve, inertia and centrifugal force can be overcome by the friction between the tires and roadway.

5. Gravity pulls a car into the curve on an inwardly banked curve, thus improving steering control. If the banking is toward the outer part of the curve, gravity pulls the car away from the curve, making steering more difficult.

LESSON THREE

6. Reduced traction and too rapid changes in either speed or direction can cause skidding.

7. Four kinds of skids are braking, power, cornering, and blowout.

8. To respond to a skid, do not brake. Look in the direction you want to go. Steer smoothly and quickly into the skid.

LESSON FOUR

9. It is possible to avoid some collisions by accelerating and steering if the roadway is clear. At speeds under 25 mph, braking can help to avoid a collision.

10. You may be able to avoid a collision by understanding the relationship between steering, speed, and friction.

11. Reducing speed, choosing something that will "cave in," and protecting the passenger compartment are three ways to reduce the force of impact and minimize the risk of a collision.

PROJECTS

1. Make a photo display of potential low-traction areas in your community. Label each photo and list the potential danger. If possible, return to the area to check out your suspicion. If you do, make sure to position yourself so you are safe and will not become a danger to traffic.

2. Check the shoulders and off-road areas of some local highways. Are they well designed and maintained? Do they provide an escape path in an emergency? What dangers do they pose to drivers? How do you think they could be improved?

BUILDING MAP SKILLS

Using the Distance Numbers

The distance numbers shown on a map can give you a more accurate idea than the map scale of how far apart two places are. On this map, distance numbers are either black or red. The numbers indicate the distance in miles between towns, junctions, and interchanges.

Here's an example of how the numbers work. Find Plainview and Floydada on the road map. Along the highway running between the two cities, you'll see a black number 29 (just below the *w* in Plainview). This means that Plainview and Floydada are 29 miles apart.

Along Interstate 27 between Plainview and Lubbock, you'll see the red number 47. It tells you that it's about 47 miles from Plainview to Lubbock.

If you add the numbers—29 + 47—the sum is 76. So, the distance by road from Floydada to Lubbock, going through Plainview, is about 76 miles.

In general, you can estimate driving time more accurately by using distance numbers rather than the map scale, especially if the road to be driven has many curves and loops. Keep in mind, though, that distance numbers indicate only the mileage, not the condition of the road. Six miles of travel along a twisting back road can take twice as long as ten miles of highway driving!

Try It Yourself

1. You're going from Crosbyton to Guthrie. How far is it?

2. How many miles is it from Plainview to Farwell along Routes 84 and 70?

3. What is the shortest route going from Matador to Morton?

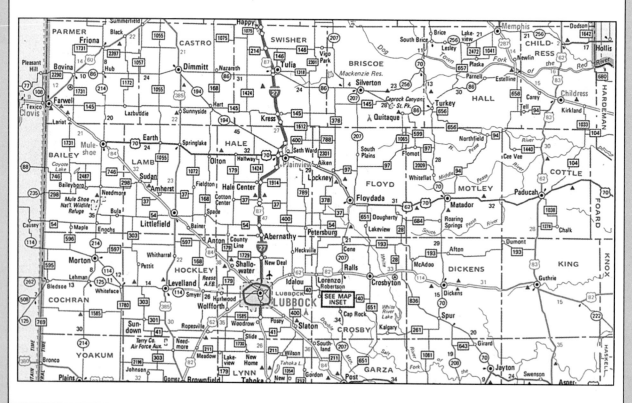

CHAPTER 13 REVIEW

CHAPTER TEST

Write the letter of the answer that best completes each sentence.

1. A vehicle's momentum depends on its
   a. kinetic energy.
   b. speed and weight.
   c. center of gravity.
2. If only the outer edges of a tire grip the road,
   a. the tire is properly inflated.
   b. the tire is overinflated.
   c. the tire is underinflated.
3. Three factors that affect braking distance are
   a. car condition, roadway condition, and speed.
   b. steering ability, centrifugal force, and ocular tracking.
   c. tread depth, controlled recovery, and the motion of energy.
4. One way to stop a skid is to
   a. look for a patch of wet leaves to slow you down.
   b. keep your foot off the pedals and steer in the direction you want the car to go.
   c. slam on the brakes.
5. If your car has good directional control, then
   a. you can decrease total stopping distance by 3 seconds.
   b. you will be able to keep the car moving in the direction you steer it.
   c. you can make sharp turns at high speed.
6. After driving through a deep puddle, it is wise to
   a. only use engine braking for a while.
   b. apply light pressure to the brake pedal.
   c. stop at the nearest service station for brake fluid.

7. A power skid occurs when you
   a. apply the brakes too hard.
   b. press the accelerator too hard.
   c. downshift too quickly.
8. A driver can turn successfully as long as there is enough
   a. friction to overcome centrifugal force.
   b. centrifugal force to overcome friction.
   c. adhesion to overcome friction.
9. Because of inertia,
   a. objects at rest move in a straight line.
   b. moving objects continue to move in a straight line.
   c. moving objects continue to move along a curved path.
10. A car's speed and weight both affect
    a. the center of gravity.
    b. friction.
    c. force of impact.

Write the word or phrase that best completes each sentence.

   kinetic energy   antilock   skidding
   centripedal   inertia   center of gravity

11. Any object in motion has _____.

12. Safety belts work against _____ to keep you from being thrown forward.

13. A higher _____ makes a car less stable and harder to control on turns and curves.

14. _____ is loss of control over the direction your car is moving because of reduced traction.

15. _____ brakes permit maximum brake pressure without a loss of steering control.

DRIVER'S LOG

In this chapter, you have learned about the effect that natural laws have on a variety of driving situations. Summarize, in a few sentences for each, the meaning of inertia, gravity, and momentum. Explain how these laws help you to anticipate and manage risk.

RESPONDING TO AN EMERGENCY

Emergencies happen even to the most experienced and careful drivers. It is important to learn how to assess and handle emergencies safely, efficiently, and calmly. When you can do this, an emergency may not turn into a disaster.

CHAPTER 14 OBJECTIVES

LESSON ONE

Brake, Engine, and Steering Failures

1. Describe what to do in case of brake failure.
2. Explain what to do in case of engine stalling or other engine failure.
3. Describe what to do in case of steering failure.

LESSON TWO

Tire Failure and Other Serious Problems

4. Explain what actions to take if your car has a blowout or flat tire.
5. Tell what to do if the accelerator pedal sticks.
6. Describe what to do if the hood flies up.
7. Explain what to do if your car catches fire.
8. Tell how to jump-start a dead battery.
9. Tell what to do in case of headlight failure.

LESSON THREE

Waiting for Help and Protecting the Scene

10. Describe what to do while waiting for help when your car breaks down.

LESSON FOUR

First-Aid Guidelines and Procedures

11. List several basic first-aid guidelines.
12. Describe procedures for controlling bleeding, treating shock, and restoring breathing.
13. List the items that should be in a first-aid kit.

LESSON ONE

Brake, Engine, and Steering Failures

You see the stop sign at the intersection ahead and step on the brake. The pedal goes all the way to the floor, but the car doesn't slow down. Two teenagers start across the street. Your mind races: *"What should I do?"*

Emergencies can occur suddenly and without warning. Brakes can fail, engines can stall, steering systems can malfunction. If you're prepared to deal with such emergencies, however, you can keep a dangerous situation from becoming a tragedy.

What Actions Can You Take When Your Brakes Fail?

All new cars have a dual-service brake system. Some cars operate with separate systems for the front and back wheels. Other cars use an "X" system, which links each front wheel with its diagonal rear wheel. Total failure of both systems at once is very unlikely, although partial or temporary brake failure does happen occasionally.

In Case of Brake Failure

When brake failure occurs, the foot brake may have no resistance. The brake pedal may sink to the floor and the brake warning light may come on. Here's what to do.

1. Rapidly pump the brake pedal. Doing so may build up pressure in the brake-fluid lines, providing some braking force. After a few pumps you'll know whether or not you've restored braking power.

2. If pumping the brakes doesn't work, use the parking brake. Either keep your thumb on the release button or hold the brake handle so that you can alternately apply and release brake pressure for a smooth stop. Applying the parking brake too abruptly may lock the rear wheels—the only ones the parking brake affects— and send the car into a spin. Use an apply-release-apply-release pattern with the parking brake to slow down the car.

3. Shift down to a lower gear. Doing so will slow the engine and the forward movement of the car.

4. If you still have little or no brake control, look for a place to steer

SAFETY TIPS

In an emergency situation, try to stay calm, think clearly, and act quickly. Learning what to do in case of car failure will help you avoid panic.

Learn how to deal with emergency vehicle failures to manage risk.
▼

Tips for New Drivers

Emergency Items

It's wise to keep emergency items in the trunk of your car. Include such items as these:

- flashlight with extra batteries
- jumper cables (for starting a dead battery)
- flares, warning triangles, or reflectors
- coolant
- windshield-washer fluid
- wiping cloth
- ice scraper, snow brush, and snow shovel
- jack with flat board for soft surfaces
- lug wrench (for changing a flat tire)

- screwdriver, pliers, duct tape, and adjustable wrench for making simple repairs
- extra fan/alternator belt
- extra fuses (if needed for your car)
- fire extinguisher
- heavy gloves
- blanket
- drinking water
- first-aid kit
- pencil and notebook (for recording emergency information)

---

against the curb. Scraping the tires against the curb can help reduce speed.

5. Other ways to slow the car after you've applied the parking brake and downshifted include steering into an open area, such as a parking lot, and shifting into lower gears as quickly as possible; steering onto an uphill road; and turning the ignition to the off position —*not* the lock position, which would lock the steering wheel.

6. If you can't avoid a collision, steer so that you sideswipe an object rather than hit it head-on. If possible, steer into bushes or scrape along a guardrail or even parked cars rather than move toward pedestrians or occupied vehicles.

Note: If your car has power brakes, engine failure or a broken drive belt may cause brake malfunction. If that's the case, your brakes will still work, but you'll have to press harder on the pedal.

Other Brake Problems

You should not apply your brakes hard for a long time, such as when traveling down a long mountain slope. You could overheat them and cause "brake fade," a kind of temporary brake failure. Pull off the road as soon as possible and give your brakes time to cool.

Drive more slowly through puddles. Driving at normal speeds through deep puddles or on flooded roadways can make your brakes wet and lead to temporary brake failure. To dry your brakes, drive slowly with your left foot gently on the brake pedal. The friction will produce heat that will dry the brakes.

Power equipment, including power brakes, adds to the total weight of a car. This extra weight, in turn, leads to reduced fuel efficiency.

How Can You Respond to Engine Failure?

Engine failure occurs more often than any other kind of car failure. Engines fail for many different reasons, such as a broken timing gear, a fuel system problem, lack of fuel, an electrical system malfunction, or problems caused by extreme heat or cold.

If Your Car's Engine Stalls

If your car's engine stalls (stops suddenly) while you are driving, check traffic around you and determine the best point to leave the roadway. Signal, then steer off the road or to the curb as quickly as possible. Keep in mind that if your engine stalls, and you have power brakes and power steering, the brakes and steering will still work but will be much harder to operate. If your car has power brakes, do not pump the brake pedal. Use firm, steady pressure instead. When you are off the road, shift to Neutral, and try to restart the engine. If the engine starts, shift into Low or Drive and continue driving. If you're driving a car with a manual transmission, shift into first gear and continue moving forward.

If the engine won't start, make sure your flashers are on, and raise the hood. Place flares or warning triangles 100 feet in front of your car and at least 100 feet behind it. Signal or wait for help.

SAFETY TIPS

To prevent your brakes from getting wet when driving through deep water, apply pressure to the brake pedal as you move slowly through the water.

Your car's engine may stall and your brakes may get wet in rainy weather.

▶

If You Flood the Engine

If you pump the accelerator over and over when trying to start your car, too much gas and not enough air goes to the engine. The result is a flooded engine that won't start. When your engine is flooded, you can often smell gas.

To start a flooded engine, press the accelerator pedal all the way to the floor and hold it there. At the same time, turn the ignition switch on and hold it on for 5 to 10 seconds. If the car starts, slowly release the accelerator. If it doesn't start, wait about 10 minutes and try again.

If the Engine Overheats

Your engine may overheat for any of various reasons: driving in slow-moving traffic during hot weather, with the air conditioner running; driving up long, steep hills; a loose or broken fan belt; a broken water pump or hose; not enough coolant or antifreeze in the cooling system; a stuck or broken thermostat; or a clogged radiator.

When engine temperature is too high, the temperature gauge or warning light on your instrument panel indicates that the engine is overheating. You may also see steam or smoke rising from under the hood.

If your engine overheats, follow these steps.

1. Turn off all accessories, especially the air conditioner.
2. If the temperature gauge continues to show hot or the warning light stays on, signal and pull off the road. Raise the hood, let the engine cool, and get professional help.

▲
Be careful not to burn yourself when you check an overheated engine.

If you can't pull off the road immediately, turn on the heater to draw heat from the engine. Doing so will not solve the problem, but it will help temporarily until you can get off the road safely.

3. If there is no steam or smoke coming from the engine, carefully open the hood (wear gloves to protect your hands). Look for such problems as a broken hose or belt. Note whether the radiator overflow tank is empty, but do not touch the radiator.

4. When the engine has cooled completely, check the fluid level in the radiator overflow tank again. If the fluid level is low, you need to add coolant. Many overflow tanks have a fill line to help you determine the proper level of fluid. Start the engine, and let it run at idle speed as you add the coolant.

If the Engine Is Wet

If you drive through water, your car's engine may get wet, start to sputter, and stall. The water may short out your car's electrical system or be drawn into the combustion chamber by way of the air filter and the carburetor.

If your engine gets wet, steer off the road and turn off the ignition. Wait a few minutes, keeping the hood closed to let the heat of the engine compartment dry out the moisture. Then try to restart the engine. If it doesn't start, the engine may need more time to dry. If it's a hot, sunny day, you may be able to speed up the process by raising the hood.

What Actions Can You Take When Your Steering Fails?

Two kinds of steering failure are possible: power-assist failure and total steering system failure. The former is far more common than the latter.

If Power Steering Fails

Power-steering failure can occur if your engine stalls or the power-assist mechanism fails. When power steering fails, your steering wheel suddenly becomes very difficult to turn.

If your car's power steering fails, grip the steering wheel firmly and turn it with more force. Check surrounding traffic, signal, and when it's safe to do so, steer off the road and stop. As soon as you possibly can, have a mechanic check your steering system.

Total Steering Failure

Sudden and total steering failure is a rare occurrence. However, if a breakdown in either the steering or suspension systems does happen, your ability to control your car will be drastically reduced.

In case of total steering failure, bring the car to a stop as quickly and safely as you can, using the parking brake, not the foot brake. Stepping on the foot brake might cause your car to pull sharply to one side. Just as when responding to brake failure, keep hold of the parking brake release button or handle to avoid locking the rear wheels and going into a spin. Downshift.

WHAT WOULD YOU DO?

As you prepare to slow your car, you find that the brakes don't catch and the car does not slow down. What do you suppose has happened? How would you handle this situation?

CHECKPOINT

1. What actions would you take if your car's brakes failed?
2. What would you do if your engine stalled while you were driving? What if the engine overheated?
3. What would you do if your car's power steering suddenly failed?

Tire Failure and Other Serious Problems

A car is a complex machine that must endure years of stop-and-go driving, rough roads, and harsh weather. No matter how well you maintain your car, there's always the possibility that a part may break or a system may malfunction.

In addition to the major car failures you read about in the previous lesson, you should be prepared to deal with a number of other serious problems.

What Actions Can You Take in Case of a Blowout or Flat Tire?

A blowout and a flat tire are similar but not the same. A blowout is an explosion in a tire while the car is in motion. The tire suddenly loses air pressure, and the car may become difficult to control.

A tire can also lose pressure gradually, through a slow leak. If you don't detect the leak in time, the tire is likely to go flat. A tire can go flat either while the car is parked or when the car is moving.

If Your Tire Loses Pressure

When a tire fails while you are driving, you may feel a strong pull to the right or left. The rear of your car may shimmy or swerve back and forth. You may even hear a thumping sound. The effect may be gradual if the tire has a slow leak, or sudden if the tire blows out.

▲ *Tire failures are fairly common. You should become familiar with emergency procedures for handling tire failure.*

If one of your tires loses pressure, follow these steps.

1. Keep a firm grip on the steering wheel with both hands.
2. Release the accelerator slowly. Don't brake—you could make the car swerve out of control.
3. Check the traffic around you. When you find a gap, signal and steer off the road. You'll have to change the tire, so move as far off the main roadway as you can. As the car slows, brake gradually and come to a stop on a flat surface.
4. Shift to Park (Reverse in a manual-shift car), and put on your emergency flashers.
5. Get out of the car and have passengers get out too.

How to Change a Tire

Changing a tire is not hard, but it does require caution to change one safely. Between 300 and 400 people are killed yearly while changing tires when the car falls off the jack and onto them or they are struck by passing vehicles.

Position your car on a flat, hard surface as far from traffic as possible. Set out flares or warning triangles at least 100 feet in front and back to alert other drivers.

Use two rocks, bricks, or pieces of wood (each at least 4 inches by 8 inches by 2 inches) to block the wheel that is diagonally across from the flat tire. Put one block in front of the wheel and another behind it. The blocks will keep the car from rolling when it is jacked up.

You'll find complete instructions for changing a tire in your owner's manual or inside the trunk of your car. Here are the basic steps.

1. After the wheel blocks are in place, remove the jack, lug wrench, and spare tire from your trunk and place them near the flat tire.
2. Assemble the jack and position it according to instructions in the owner's manual. Jack up the car until the flat tire is just in contact with the ground.
3. Remove the hubcap or wheel cover from the wheel you're changing. Use the lug wrench to loosen the lug nuts enough so that they'll move easily, but do not remove the nuts.
4. Jack the car up until the tire clears the ground.
5. Take off the lug nuts and put them inside the hubcap or in some other safe place.
6. Pull off the wheel with the flat tire. Replace it with the spare tire. Put the lug nuts back on by hand, and tighten them slightly with the wrench.
7. Carefully let the car down, and remove the jack. Tighten the lug nuts as tight as you can with the lug wrench.

When you change a tire, get as far off the roadway as you can. Then continue to check for traffic in the lane nearest you.

8. Put the flat tire, jack, wrench, and other equipment in the trunk.
9. If the spare is an undersized tire or limited-mileage tire, drive no faster than 50 mph to the nearest service station. Have the flat tire repaired or replaced right away.

What Should You Do If Your Accelerator Pedal Sticks?

As you're driving along, you decide to decrease speed. You lift your foot from the accelerator but nothing changes; the car keeps moving at the same speed. The problem is a stuck accelerator: The engine does not return to idle when you take your foot off the pedal.

A stuck accelerator pedal may be caused by a sticking linkage or accelerator spring, a broken engine mount, a crumpled floor mat, or ice or snow on the floor around the pedal. Here's what to do:

1. Apply the brakes, and shift to Neutral. The engine will race, but power will be disengaged from the wheels.
2. Check traffic and signal a lane change.
3. Choose a safe path, and steer off the road, continuing to apply the brakes.
4. When you are off the roadway, turn off the ignition and apply the parking brake.
5. Don't attempt to unstick the pedal until after you've steered off the road and come to a stop. Test the pedal before reentering traffic. If the pedal problem is mechanical, have it repaired before driving again.

ips for New Drivers

15-Minute Checkup

To keep your car in good working order, follow the suggestions in your owner's manual for periodic checkups and maintenance. In addition, if you drive 10,000 or more miles a year, do a 15-minute check of the following items every month.

- all lights for burned-out bulbs
- the battery fluid level or, if your car has a sealed battery, the green battery-charge indicator
- the engine oil level and transmission fluid level
- the brake pedal for firmness and proper operation
- the brake fluid level
- the air pressure in all tires
- the tires for uneven wear
- the cooling system
- the hoses and belts that operate the fan, compressor, and the like
- the windshield washer and wipers
- the power steering fluid level

What Should You Do If the Hood Flies Up?

Anything that blocks your forward view is a threat to your safety. If the hood of your car suddenly flies up while you're driving, you must take action to avoid a collision and get off the road.

1. Lean forward and look through the space between the dashboard and the hood. If this view is blocked or limited, roll down your side window and look around the hood. Don't lean out the window so far that you lose control of the pedals. Continue to steer in the direction you were moving.
2. Check your mirrors to see what traffic is behind you. Check the traffic to either side of you.

3. Signal to indicate the direction you want to move. Maintain your lane position while waiting for a gap in traffic. Then steer off the road.

What Actions Can You Take If Your Car Catches Fire?

Car fires don't occur often, but when they do they require prompt action to minimize risk to people and property.

If the Engine Catches Fire

Engine fires are usually fuel-fed or electrical. If a fire suddenly erupts in your engine while you're driving, you'll see and smell smoke coming from under your hood. Follow these steps:

1. Steer off the road to an open space. Turn off the ignition.
2. Get out of the car, and have all passengers get out too. Move far away from the car. Call for help.
3. Decide how serious the fire is. If it is serious—high heat and flames around the hood—don't attempt to put the fire out yourself. Stay far away from the car, and wait for the fire department.
4. If the fire is not serious and you have a fire extinguisher in the trunk, you can try to put it out yourself. *Don't use water;* it is not effective against fuel and oil fires. Wear gloves, or wrap your hands in cloth. Turn your face away from the car, and crouch down so that your head is at the level of the hood. Do not open the hood. Just pull the hood release to create a small space into which you can spray the extinguishing agent.

If There Is a Fire in the Passenger Compartment

A fire in the passenger compartment is usually caused by carelessness on the part of a passenger or the driver. A common cause of such fires is a burning cigarette or match that drops to the floor or gets blown into the backseat.

If there's a fire in the passenger compartment, you'll smell something burning, and you may see smoke. Steer off the road, and stop clear of traffic. Turn off the ignition. Get out of the car, and have all passengers get out. Use a fire extinguisher or water to put out the fire.

What Should You Do If Your Car's Battery Is Dead?

It's a freezing-cold winter night. After leaving the movie theater, you and your date rush out to your car.

Get out of the car as soon as you safely can if your car catches fire.
▼

You turn the ignition switch to start. Nothing happens—no sound, no engine turnover, nothing. Your car's battery has gone dead.

A battery may go dead if you keep your headlights on or play the radio for a long time while the engine is not running. An old battery may no longer have enough power to start a car in very cold weather.

If the battery is dead, you can't start the engine. However, you may be able to restore power to your battery by using jumper cables (or "booster cables") to connect it to a working battery in another car.

Jump-Starting Your Car

The most common way to recharge your battery is to jump-start it. To do this, you need another car with a working battery that is the same voltage as yours and a pair of jumper cables.

Before you decide to jump-start your battery, make sure the battery fluid is not frozen or the level of fluid low. If it is, do *not* attempt to jump-start your battery: It might explode.

To jump-start your car, follow these steps.

1. Position the two cars so that the cables can reach between the two batteries. Don't let the cars touch.
2. Turn off the ignition and electrical equipment in both cars. Shift both cars into Park, and put their parking brakes on.
3. Double-check to make sure both car batteries have the same voltage (usually 12 volts).
4. If either battery has cell or vent caps, remove them. Check again to make sure your dead battery is not frozen.
5. Cover each battery with a heavy cloth to protect against splashing of boiling battery fluid.
6. Attach the positive jumper cable (red, or marked P or +) to the positive terminal of the good battery. Clamp the other end of the same cable to the positive terminal of the dead battery.
7. Attach the negative jumper cable (black, or marked N or −) to the negative post of the good battery.
8. Attach the other end of the negative cable to the engine or frame of the car that has the dead battery. Make this connection as far from the battery as possible. The connection should also be far from moving engine parts, such as the fan.
9. Start the engine of the car that has the good battery. Hold down the accelerator so that the engine runs at a high idle.
10. Start the engine of the car with the dead battery and, with the cables still attached, run it for several minutes.

▲
It's a good idea to keep jumper cables in the trunk of your car.

11. With both engines still running, remove the cables in reverse order from the order in which you attached them. (Remove negative first, then positive.)

12. Replace battery caps if they've been removed, and dispose of the cloth covers in case they contain acid.

What Should You Do If Your Headlights Fail?

Headlight failure at night is dangerous because without lights, your ability to see is reduced, as is the ability of other drivers to see your car.

Rarely do both headlights fail at the same time. However, if one headlight goes out, you may not notice it until the other goes too. Headlight failure is usually the result of a burned-out low-beam headlamp.

If you're driving at night and suddenly your lights flicker or die, you have to get off the road, but without making any sudden, possibly dangerous moves. Here's what to do.

1. Slow down and continue in the same direction you were going. Be aware of the traffic around you.

2. Try switching to high beams: Headlights seldom burn out on both high and low beams at the same time. If switching to high beams gives no light, try turning on parking lights, turn indicators, and the emergency flashers. These can give you enough light to help you get off the road.

3. When you see a gap in traffic, steer off the roadway. If you have no lights at all, look for the side-lane markers on the pavement. You can also use available light from other cars on the roadway.

4. If possible, stop your car off the roadway near a lighted place, such as a lighted sign, building, or streetlight. Call for help.

WHAT WOULD YOU DO?

Suddenly your front hood opens, obstructing your vision. What steps would you take to avoid a collision?

CHECKPOINT

4. What would you do if one of your car's tires suddenly lost pressure while you were driving?

5. How would you deal with a stuck accelerator pedal while driving?

6. What would you do if your car's hood flew up while you were driving?

7. How would you respond to an engine fire? To a fire in the passenger compartment?

8. List the steps for jump-starting a dead battery.

9. What would you do if your headlights failed while you were driving at night?

Waiting for Help and Protecting the Scene

◄ Raising the hood of your car is one action you can take to let others know you need help.

In an emergency, you may need assistance even though you may be miles from a phone. You may be able to correct a minor mechanical problem yourself. You might also choose to call on passing cars and pedestrians to get the help you need.

What Should You Do at the Scene of a Car Breakdown or Other Emergency?

If your car breaks down, you may be able to remedy the problem yourself—by changing a flat tire, for example. If you can't fix the problem,

you'll need to get help.

After pulling out of traffic, you'll have to communicate your situation to passing drivers or pedestrians in a way that keeps you and other roadway users safe.

Make Others Aware of Your Problem

If you have to pull off the road at a place where there's no telephone within safe walking distance, you'll need to get the attention of pedestrians or other drivers. To do this safely—in a way that protects you as well as other drivers—raise the hood of your car, and tie a handkerchief or

If your car breaks down on a highway, your immediate goal is to get your car safely off the roadway onto the shoulder. Then set out flares or other warning devices to increase your car's visibility to other drivers.

scarf to the antenna or left door handle. You can also hold the handkerchief or scarf in place by closing a window on it. Stay in the car if you have pulled well off the roadway. Otherwise, get as far away from the road as you can. Switch on your emergency flashers to alert passing drivers to your situation.

Protect Yourself

You can wait inside your car if the weather is bad and you're far enough off the road. Keep the windows almost closed and the doors locked. Do not sit in a stopped car with windows closed, engine running, and heater on. You could be putting yourself and your passengers at risk of carbon monoxide poisoning.

It is very dangerous to lower your window or open your car door to strangers. If a stranger does stop to offer help, just ask the person to call for emergency road service.

If your car is not far enough from roadway traffic, or if you think it might be struck from behind by another vehicle, leave the car and walk to a safe place. Proceed carefully—especially at night or in bad weather, when visibility is limited.

Never stand behind or directly in front of your car. Other roadway users will have trouble seeing you, and you could be struck by an oncoming vehicle.

Make Decisions When Help Comes

Emergency road service operators can usually change a flat tire or do minor repairs on the spot. They may also have gasoline and a booster battery in case you've run out of gas or have a dead battery.

If you need to be towed to a service garage, you should know whether or not your insurance covers all or part of the towing charge. You should also find out how many miles away the service garage is and what the charge is for towing.

If your car is towed, you'll have to arrange transportation for yourself and your passengers. Passengers are not allowed to ride in a vehicle when it's being towed.

WHAT WOULD YOU DO?

Your car has broken down and you have moved it to the side of the road. What actions would you take to find assistance?

CHECKPOINT

10. What should you do while waiting for help if your car breaks down?

First-Aid Guidelines and Procedures

First aid is emergency treatment given to a person who is injured or ill, before professional medical care arrives. Learning about first-aid procedures may help you prevent further injury or even save someone's life in an emergency.

What Are Some Basic First-Aid Guidelines?

All drivers should have some knowledge of first aid. You can learn first aid by taking a course given by the American Red Cross. You can also read about first-aid procedures in a manual or book. However, to really know what you're doing, you need both training and practice in first aid.

Here are some basic first-aid guidelines for emergency situations.

◆ Quickly scan the scene and decide if you can help. If you feel confused and uncertain, don't try to give first aid. Call for help.

◆ The person with the most experience should give first aid. If there are other uninjured people nearby, quickly find out who among you has the most experience with first aid.

◆ If more than one person is injured, care for the most seriously injured person first.

◆ Keep calm and act quickly and quietly. Speak in a normal tone of voice. Try not to worry the victim.

◆ Find out if the injured person is bleeding. Try to stop any serious bleeding as quickly as possible.

◆ Check that the injured person is

The Good Samaritan Law states that no person who gives emergency care in good faith at the scene of an emergency shall be held liable for civil damages.

◀

First aid can be given to injured persons before an ambulance arrives on the scene.

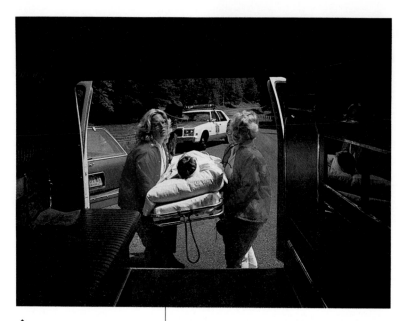

Professional medical personnel are the only ones who should move an injured person.

FYI

A rear-end car collision may cause a *whiplash* injury, in which the victim's head snaps backward, then abruptly whips forward. Such an injury can cause severe neck damage.

breathing. If the victim is not breathing, start mouth-to-mouth resuscitation. (See page 271.)

◆ *Never* move an injured person unless you must do so for his or her safety. Moving an injured person can worsen the injury. Try to keep injured persons from moving.

◆ Get trained medical help as soon as possible. However, if you are the only uninjured person at the scene, do not leave the victim in order to get help unless you have no other choice.

◆ A person may look uninjured but be unable to move. This could indicate injury to the spine. *Do not* try to move the person. Cover the victim with a blanket, and go for help.

What Are Some Specific First-Aid Procedures?

Three first-aid procedures you should be familiar with are those for controlling bleeding, treating shock, and restoring breathing.

Controlling Bleeding

Someone who is bleeding heavily, or *hemorrhaging,* can die within minutes, so it's very important to try to stop heavy bleeding immediately.

You can control heavy bleeding by applying direct pressure. Put a clean cloth—such as a folded handkerchief or piece of a shirt—directly over the wound and press down firmly. If you don't have a clean cloth, press directly on the wound with your hand. Keep pressing, without lifting your hand, until medical help arrives.

Other means of stopping heavy bleeding are to apply arterial pressure or to use a tourniquet. Do not use either of these methods unless you are fully trained to do so.

Treating Shock

Serious injury, bleeding, or burns can cause shock. When a person is in a state of shock, the blood does not circulate properly. As a result, the brain and other tissues fail to get enough oxygen. Shock can cause death if it is not treated.

A shock victim usually feels faint, weak, cold, and often nauseous. The person's skin will feel cold and clammy and may look pale—even blue. Breathing is irregular, and the pulse is weak and fast.

It is wise to treat seriously injured persons for shock even if they don't exhibit signs of shock. To treat shock, keep the victim warm, but don't overdo it. Place a blanket or coat over the victim. Try to keep the person's body temperature close to normal. Control any bleeding, and loosen any tight clothing. Do not give shock victims anything to eat or drink.

Restoring Breathing

Two or three minutes without breathing can cause permanent brain damage. Six minutes without breathing can cause death. To try to restore breathing, apply mouth-to-mouth resuscitation.

1. Place the person faceup. Then kneel down and clear the victim's mouth with your fingers.

2. Put one hand under the victim's neck. Gently tilt the head backward, pushing the chin up. Using your thumb and index finger, pinch the victim's nostrils closed.

3. Put your mouth right over the victim's mouth. Blow air into the victim's mouth until you see his or her chest rise. Remove your mouth. Let air escape from the victim's lungs while you take another breath.

4. Repeat the procedure. You should blow air into an adult's mouth at a rate of about 12 times per minute. For children, the rate should be about 20 times per minute. Continue until you are sure the victim is breathing independently or until medical help arrives.

What Items Should You Include in a First-Aid Kit for Your Car?

Always keep a first-aid kit in your car. The contents of the kit may enable you to save a life—or enable someone else to save your life.

The American Red Cross suggests that the following items be included in a first-aid kit:

◆ plastic adhesive bandages (25, in various sizes)
◆ gauze dressings (12, 4 inches square)

THE HISTORY CONNECTION

In 1881 Clara Barton founded the American Red Cross in Washington, D.C. It is a nonprofit humanitarian organization with the express purpose of preventing and easing human suffering. In 1905 the organization was renamed the American National Red Cross. It made a commitment to provide a worldwide network of emergency relief.

Throughout the 20th century the American National Red Cross has been a pioneer in the field of emergency relief and medical assistance. The organization provided assistance during World Wars I and II, contributing medical supplies, blood plasma, and able-bodied volunteers. Following World War II, the organization launched a program to provide blood to people of all races, colors, and creeds who need it.

During the past 40 years the American National Red Cross has become deeply involved in the field of public health. The organization offers many instructional programs in first aid, lifesaving, nurse's aide training, baby care, and home nursing. Many people serve in first-aid stations and mobile units along highways.

There are now more than 2 million Red Cross volunteers nationwide. In addition, more than 20 million Junior Red Cross members participate in activities geared toward helping people in their communities as well as underprivileged children in other countries.

Loretta J. Martin, Coordinator, Safety and Driver Education, Chicago Public Schools

Loretta J. Martin

Roadside emergencies can happen anytime. You can minimize their consequences if you mentally prepare for them, know how to handle common vehicle failure, and know what to do at the scene of an emergency.
• Don't drive unless you are fit.
• Wear your safety belt.
• Carry an emergency car kit.
• Carry a good first-aid kit and know how to use it.
• Protect the scene.
• Know how to get help quickly.

WHAT WOULD YOU DO?

You have been involved in a collision with another car. You are uninjured, but the other driver is bleeding. How can you help?

◆ roller gauze bandages (2 rolls, 3 inches wide)
◆ safety pins (10, in various sizes)
◆ adhesive tape (1 roll, 1-inch wide)
◆ scissors

◆ triangular bandages (5)
◆ moist towelettes (6)
◆ combine dressings (3)
◆ tweezers
◆ bottle of syrup of ipecac; bottle of activated charcoal (both for use only on advice of medical professional)
◆ change for phone calls
◆ pencil and notebook

Check the contents of your first-aid kit regularly, and replace any items as needed. Be sure to keep the kit out of children's reach.

CHECKPOINT

11. What first-aid guidelines should you follow in an emergency?
12. What are the first-aid procedures for controlling bleeding, treating shock, and restoring breathing?
13. What items should you include in a first-aid kit for your car?

CHAPTER 14 REVIEW

KEY POINTS

LESSON ONE

1. In case of brake failure, rapidly pump the brake pedal. If that doesn't work, use the parking brake. Downshift.

2. If your engine stalls while you're driving, signal and steer off the road. If your car is in motion, shift to Neutral and try to restart the engine. If the engine won't start, steer near the curb or shoulder and stop.

3. If your car's power steering fails, grip the steering wheel firmly and turn it with more force than usual. Steer off the road and stop. In case of total steering failure, use the parking brake to stop.

LESSON TWO

4. If your car has a blowout or flat tire, keep a firm grip on the steering wheel. Release the accelerator slowly, but don't brake. Steer off the road.

5. If the accelerator pedal sticks, brake and shift to Neutral. Carefully steer off the road.

6. If the hood flies up, look through the space between the dashboard and the hood or out of the driver's side window. Continue to steer in the direction you were moving until you can leave the road.

7. In case of a car fire, steer off the road to an open space. Turn off the ignition. Get out and move away from the car. Call for help.

8. To jump-start a dead battery, turn off the ignition in both cars, shift both into Park, and set their parking brakes. Attach the jumper cables properly. Start the engine of the car with the good battery, then the engine of the other car.

9. If your headlights fail, slow down and switch to high beams. If that doesn't help, turn on the parking lights, turn indicators, and flashers.

LESSON THREE

10. If your car breaks down, let other drivers know you need help. Wait inside your car.

LESSON FOUR

11. Stay calm. See if you can help. Give first aid if necessary, especially to stop bleeding or to restore breathing. Never move an injured person.

12. To control bleeding, apply direct pressure to the wound. To treat shock, keep the victim warm. To restore breathing, give mouth-to-mouth resuscitation.

13. A first-aid kit should contain different kinds of dressings and bandages, adhesive tape, scissors, tweezers, change, and a pencil and notebook.

PROJECTS

1. Borrow a car owner's manual. What special directions does the manual contain for avoiding and responding to car failures and emergencies? What preventive maintenance tips does the manual offer?

2. Interview an emergency medical technician or member of a first-aid squad. Ask what collision-related injuries occur most commonly. Also find out what kinds of first-aid treatments are given most frequently and what new methods, if any, are being used.

BUILDING CRITICAL THINKING SKILLS

Benjamin Banneker

To drivers traveling through the United States, it seems as though many major cities just grew without any plan at all. In many cases, this is true. However, our capital city, Washington, D.C., is one of the few cities in this country that was designed before it was built. This is particularly evident in the area surrounding the United States Capitol, which is located near the center of Washington. Like the spokes of a wheel, broad streets extend out from the Capitol in all directions. This roadway pattern can also be seen near Union Station, the Lincoln Memorial, and Mt. Vernon Square.

President George Washington chose Pierre L'Enfant, a French engineer, to draw up the plans for the new capital. Benjamin Banneker helped L'Enfant to work out the city's plan and to survey, or measure, the size, shape, and area of the land. Banneker was the first African American ever to be appointed to work for the government.

L'Enfant left the United States before the building of Washington, D.C. was completed, taking the plans with him. However, Benjamin Banneker stepped in and finished laying out the city from memory.

Benjamin Banneker was the son of a free woman and slave father. He was born free in 1731 on a farm in Maryland. Banneker was educated in a Quaker school where he became interested in mathematics and science. He later taught himself astronomy.

Banneker used his knowledge to make astronomical and tidal calculations in order to write a yearly almanac predicting weather conditions. He sent a copy of his almanac to Thomas Jefferson along with a letter urging the abolition of slavery. Those against slavery held Banneker up as an example of the talents and abilities of African Americans.

In addition to his work on the almanac, Banneker was also fascinated by the workings of clocks. He fashioned a clock entirely out of wood, carving each gear by hand and using a pocket watch as his only model.

What Do You Think Now?

What do you think was the most important accomplishment of Benjamin Banneker? Why?

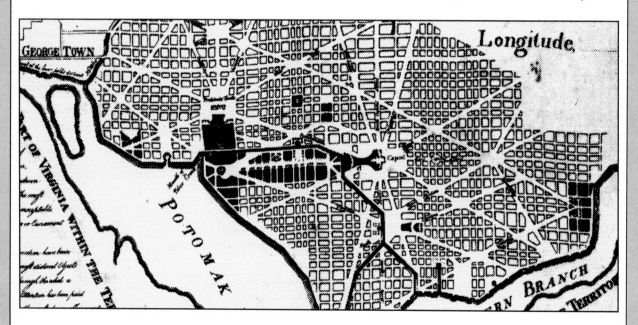

CHAPTER 14 REVIEW

CHAPTER TEST

Write the letter of the answer that best completes each sentence.

1. If your car breaks down and you pull over to the side of the road, you should
   a. phone for help or get the attention of passing drivers.
   b. stand directly in front of your car until help arrives.
   c. stand in the middle of the road and wave your arms.
2. If your steering wheel suddenly becomes very hard to turn, the problem probably is
   a. power-steering failure.
   b. engine overheating.
   c. wet brakes.
3. If one of your tires suddenly loses pressure,
   a. release the accelerator slowly.
   b. brake hard.
   c. immediately shift into Park.
4. A collision victim who looks uninjured but cannot move
   a. should try to get up and walk around.
   b. may have a spinal injury.
   c. should be moved as quickly as possible.
5. If your battery is frozen and the engine won't start,
   a. use jumper cables.
   b. do not use jumper cables.
   c. turn on the heater before using jumper cables.
6. If the hood flies up while you're driving,
   a. stop immediately.
   b. honk your horn and move right.
   c. look through the space between the hood and the dashboard.

7. If your foot brake suddenly loses power,
   a. turn the ignition to the lock position.
   b. shift into reverse.
   c. rapidly pump the brake pedal.
8. A victim who feels faint, weak, and cold
   a. needs artificial respiration.
   b. should be kept as cool as possible.
   c. may be suffering from shock.
9. To dry wet brakes,
   a. drive slowly with your left foot pressing gently on the brake pedal.
   b. stamp down on the brake pedal several times.
   c. drive in low gear.
10. To put out a minor engine fire, use
    a. a fire extinguisher.
    b. water.
    c. a heavy cloth.

Write the word or phrase that best completes each sentence.

engine flooding   hemorrhaging   first aid
cooling system   brake fade   resuscitation

11. A person who is ____ can die within minutes.

12. Applying your brakes hard for a long time may cause ____ .

13. Your engine may overheat if there is not enough coolant in the ____ .

14. ____ is emergency treatment given to a person who has been injured.

15. Pumping the accelerator repeatedly when trying to start your car can result in ____ .

DRIVER'S LOG

In this chapter, you have learned about how to deal with emergency situations caused by vehicle failures and those in which personal injury is involved. Write two paragraphs giving your ideas on the most important factors to keep in mind when confronted with an emergency.

CUMULATIVE REVIEW

This review tests your knowledge of the material in Chapters 1–14. Use the review to help you study for your state driving test. Choose the answer that best suits the question.

1. The penalties for DWI and DUI
   a. are the same in all states.
   b. differ from state to state.
   c. are set by the National Highway Safety Act.
   d. are not very severe.

2. When driving at 55 mph, your following distance should be
   a. 10 seconds
   b. 6 seconds
   c. 4 seconds
   d. 1 minute

3. When turning left from a two-way street,
   a. yield right of way to traffic behind you.
   b. yield right of way to oncoming traffic.
   c. use hand signals.
   d. shift into Reverse gear.

4. While driving, you should
   a. aim low and look down.
   b. keep your head moving.
   c. keep your windows open.
   d. keep your eyes moving.

5. Electricity is fed to the engine by the
   a. accelerator.
   b. transmission.
   c. odometer.
   d. alternator.

6. Lane-use lights are mounted
   a. on slow-moving vehicles.
   b. below warning signs.
   c. above reversible lanes.
   d. on telephone poles.

7. The best way to avoid becoming a problem drinker is to
   a. drink only on weekends.
   b. drink beer only.
   c. avoid drinking in the first place.
   d. drink at home.

8. One problem common to rural roads is the presence of
   a. busy intersections.
   b. slow-moving vehicles.
   c. HOV lanes.
   d. smog.

9. A driver can avoid skidding in rainy weather by
   a. changing speed gradually instead of abruptly.
   b. driving between 45 and 60 mph.
   c. frequently changing gears.
   d. riding the clutch.

10. Inertia, friction, and kinetic energy are
    a. difficult to manage.
    b. natural laws.
    c. different words for visibility, time, and space.
    d. culprits.

11. All cars manufactured since 1986 are required to have
    a. air bags.
    b. a third red brake light.
    c. power windows.
    d. antilock brakes.

12. To make a turnabout safely, you need
    a. 100 yards of visibility.
    b. 1,000 feet of visibility in each direction.
    c. 500 feet of visibility in each direction.
    d. at least one minute.

13. Friction between the road and a car's tires is called
    a. latex.
    b. adhesion.
    c. centrifugal force.
    d. gravity.

14. If your accelerator sticks, you should
    a. reach down and grab it.
    b. shift to Neutral and steer off the road.
    c. jump out of the car.
    d. pump the brakes.

15. Crosswalks are most frequently located at
    a. bridges.
    b. steep grades.
    c. campsites.
    d. intersections.

16. A good driver is one who has learned
    a. to eliminate risk completely.
    b. how to manage risk.
    c. to drive very fast.
    d. to read a map while driving.

17. Parking at 90-degrees to the curb is called
    a. parallel parking.
    b. illegal parking.
    c. double parking.
    d. perpendicular parking.

18. *Jaywalking* refers to the act of
    a. walking across a street without regard for traffic rules.
    b. smoking marijuana in public.
    c. obeying traffic rules.
    d. yielding the right of way to others.

19. Gravity pulls objects
    a. toward a collision.
    b. across a banked road.
    c. toward the earth's center.
    d. into kinetic energy.

20. Lanes of traffic moving in the same direction are separated by
    a. white lines.
    b. yellow lines.
    c. electronic signals.
    d. prosthetic devices.

21. When making a right turn, you should wait until there is a
    a. 2-second gap to your left.
    b. 7- to 8-second gap to your left.
    c. 9-second gap to your right.
    d. 12-second gap to your right.

22. You can reduce glare in snowy weather by wearing
    a. sun visors.
    b. sunglasses.
    c. a defroster.
    d. a hat.

23. Points at which you can safely enter or exit a limited-access highway are called
    a. intersections.
    b. HOV lanes.
    c. crosswalks.
    d. interchanges.

24. As you enter a turn or curve, you should
    a. decrease speed.
    b. increase speed.
    c. maintain an even speed.
    d. apply centrifugal force.

25. A way to restore breathing is
    a. direct pressure.
    b. mouth-to-mouth resuscitation.
    c. a tourniquet.
    d. an air bag.

26. A car with a manual shift has
    a. an automatic transmission.
    b. two brake pedals.
    c. a selector lever.
    d. a gearshift.

27. A car's rate of acceleration is
    a. lower at high speeds.
    b. higher at low speeds.
    c. perception distance.
    d. set by the Uniform Vehicle Code.

28. Truck drivers have poor visibility
    a. behind a car.
    b. in daylight.
    c. at speeds of 55 mph.
    d. to the sides.

29. Engine fires are often
    a. caused by cigarette smoking.
    b. electrical in nature.
    c. best ignored.
    d. easily extinguished by water.

30. Cyclists are endangered by
    a. careless drivers.
    b. the SIPDE process.
    c. administrative laws.
    d. ground viewing.

PLANNING FOR YOUR FUTURE

As a driver, you will make many important decisions. This unit will help you develop guidelines so that your decisions will be based on understanding your needs, intelligent planning, and informed judgment.

UNIT CONTENTS

BUYING A CAR

Purchasing a car requires mature judgment, evaluation of needs, and ability to manage expense. It is important to learn how to assess safety features, fuel efficiency, comfortability, and insurance needs to make a wise choice.

CHAPTER 15 OBJECTIVES

LESSON ONE

Determining Personal Need When Considering Buying a Car

1. List factors to consider that may determine your need to buy a car.
2. Describe what you should consider in determining the kind of car you need.

LESSON TWO

Factors That Are Involved in Selecting a Car

3. List several considerations for selecting a safe car.
4. Describe how to select a comfortable car.
5. Name several factors affecting a car's fuel efficiency.
6. List what you should know about buying a used car.

LESSON THREE

How to Obtain Financing for a New or Used Car

7. Explain what you should know about financing a car.

LESSON FOUR

Choosing and Purchasing Automobile Insurance

8. Describe the types of automobile insurance.
9. List the factors that determine the cost of insurance.

Determining Personal Need When Considering Buying a Car

If you are considering buying a car, the first question you should ask yourself is not about the car—it's about you. That question is: "Am I mature enough to accept the responsibility that goes with owning and driving a car?" To answer that question, begin by examining the reasons you are considering the purchase—including both your wants and your needs.

There are many reasons to *want* your own car.

◆ Cars make you more independent.
◆ They save you time getting from one place to another.
◆ Owning a car makes you feel more grown-up.
◆ Going places in your own car is fun.

Make your own *want list*. Why do you really want a car? Then think about another question: "Do I really *need* to own a car?"

How Can You Tell Whether You Need Your Own Car?

The following questions may help you focus on your needs.

◆ How close to your home and to each other are the places that you go to most often?
◆ How do you get to these places now?
◆ How available is public transportation?
◆ Is there a family car, and if so, how available is it to you?

Think about your answers. If you live close to the places you normally go to, if public transportation is convenient, or if the family car is available to you, you may not need to own a car at all.

If your answers to all of those questions indicate that you don't just *want* a car, you really *need* one, you still have other questions to consider.

Can you afford a car? You will need to examine all of the costs involved in buying and owning a car. In addition to the car's purchase price, you'll have to pay for fuel, oil, tune-ups, and repairs. You must also pay for insurance, licensing and registration, tolls, property taxes, and, often, parking.

How will a car affect your schedule? For students who have to earn the money to pay for buying and operating a car, the cost can be measured in hours as well as dollars. Working enough hours to pay car expenses takes away time needed for studies, sports and other extracurricular activities, and a balanced social life. Students who work in order to keep a car often wind up with lower grades than students who do not work.

Are you mature enough to manage the responsibilities of owning a car? Often, increased responsibility means increased stress. You need to determine whether you can cope with that stress. Are you mature enough to distinguish your wants from your needs? Are you able to evaluate honestly all of the costs

Automobile design and engineering have been fields in which few women have been employed. But that may be changing now. Sylvia Oneice Lowe is one of the exceptions. This gifted African-American has the position of product design engineer for the Ford Motor Company. Ms. Lowe was born in Detroit, Michigan, in 1946. She attended Wayne State University, graduating with an engineering degree, and later earned a Master's degree from Central Miami University.

(both time and money) involved in car ownership?

Can you deal in a mature way with the social pressures of driving and owning a car? Driving a car always involves risk to yourself and to others. If you're not mature enough to manage that risk responsibly, you shouldn't buy—or drive—a car, regardless of your age.

What Personal Factors Influence the Kind of Car You Need?

Be prepared when you shop for a car. Before you go, think about how your car usually will be used and what your needs are. Answering the following questions will help you to sort out what *you* should be looking for in a car.

How many passengers will you usually have? The answer may help you decide what size car you should buy.

What age are your passengers? Considering your passengers' comfort and space needs can help you decide what size car you need and whether it should be a two- or four-door model. For example, if your regular passengers include elderly people, you need to think about the ease with which they can enter or leave the car.

How many miles do you expect to drive each day, month, or year? Consider your expected mileage to help you determine how fuel-efficient your car needs to be.

Will you use the car to carry heavy loads or to tow a trailer? The heavier the load or tow, the more powerful the engine you need.

What is the cost of the car plus the cost of insurance? Expensive cars cost more to insure than less expensive ones. Insurance rates are higher, too, for sports cars than for family-type sedans.

How much will you have to spend to maintain the car? A new car usually costs much less to maintain than a used car. You need to make sure that you can afford repairs and maintenance for your car so that you can operate it safely.

CHECKPOINT

1. How can you tell whether you really need a car?
2. How should passenger comfort and maintenance costs influence the kind of car you buy?

WHAT WOULD YOU DO?

How would you explain to the driver what factors she should think about before buying a car?

Factors That Are Involved in Selecting a Car

The presence of air bags is a safety factor you should consider when buying a car. ▶

SAFETY TIPS

The color of a car affects how visibile it is to other drivers. White, fire-engine red, mint green, and yellow are high-visibility colors. Brown, gray, navy blue, and black are low-visibility colors.

You've decided that you really need to own a car. You've thought carefully about how your car will be used and what your needs are. Now you need to know what to look for in a car in order to choose one that is safe, comfortable, and fuel efficient.

There's a lot to think about when you really get down to choosing a car. However, the very first thing you should check out is the car's safety. In fact, if safety is *not* your first concern, you shouldn't be buying a car.

How Can You Select a Car That Is Safe?

You should ask a number of questions about safety before purchasing

a car. To find the answers, you may have to do a little research.

Is the car equipped with airbags? In head-on collisions, most fatalities occur when the driver hits the steering wheel and suffers serious chest injuries. Air bags help prevent this kind of injury.

What is the death rate per 10,000 registered models of the car? If the death rate of a particular model is more than 2 per 10,000 registered cars, think twice before buying the car.

How does the car hold up in a crash test? Information about the results of crash testing is available from the Insurance Institute for Highway Safety.

Does the car have antilock brakes? Cars with antilock brakes stop in a shorter distance than cars

FYI

Most single-car crashes involve drivers under the age of 21. Drivers under age 21 are also more often held responsible for multiple-car crashes.

without these brakes. Antilock brakes also allow you to steer even if you panic and brake too quickly.

What is the size of the car? Most recent studies show death rates in the smallest cars to be almost twice as high as in the largest cars.

Getting all of the information you can about your potential car's safety record could save your life!

Car models differ by as much as 800 percent in their safety records. The Insurance Institute for Highway Safety analyzes the safety records of most automobiles sold in the United States. The institute examines two kinds of data.

The death rate based on 10,000 registered cars of one manufacturer and model Vehicle death rates range from 0.5 deaths per 10,000 registered vehicles to 4 deaths per 10,000 registered vehicles. Generally, the higher the death rate, the less safe the car.

The death rate in single-vehicle crashes compared to multivehicle crashes If more than 45 percent of the deaths occurred in single-vehicle crashes, the particular car model may encourage unsafe driving.

How Can You Check a Car's Comfort Features?

You will spend a lot of time in your car, so check to be sure that it's comfortable for you. Get into the car. Does it fit you? Are the seats adjustable? Can you adjust the steering wheel height so that the top of the wheel is at or below the top of your shoulder? After adjustments, do the seat and steering wheel positions give you maximum control of the car?

Ask to take the car for a test drive. Once you're in the driver's seat, check to be sure that you can reach all accessory switches and dials easily. Be sure the seat is comfortable enough so that a long drive won't leave you with an aching back.

How Can You Determine Whether a Car Is Fuel Efficient?

Fuel consumption is an important consideration when choosing a car. An energy-efficient car can save you money and help conserve this planet s energy resources.

The Insurance Institute for Highway Safety provides free information on death rates and crash test data. You can write to the institute at 10005 N. Glebe Road, Arlington, Virginia, 22201.

You can see by the graph that small two-door cars are the least safe.

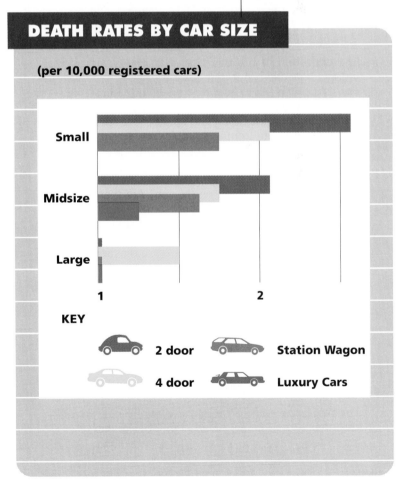

DEATH RATES BY CAR SIZE

(per 10,000 registered cars)

Small

Midsize

Large

1   2

KEY

 2 door   Station Wagon

4 door   Luxury Cars

Fuel consumption depends on a car's weight, type of engine, design, and type of transmission, among other factors.

The Weight of the Car

You cannot always judge a car's weight just by looking at the car. Find out the exact weight. The less weight an engine pulls, the more efficiently it works. This saves fuel. However, there is a trade-off to consider: The heavier the car, the safer it is.

The Type of Engine

The more cylinders in the engine, the more fuel it uses. Unless you will be going up steep hills a lot, a 4- to 6-cylinder engine probably will meet the needs of most intermediate-size cars. This size engine is also fuel efficient.

The Design of the Car

One key to fuel economy is how well the vehicle overcomes air resistance. A streamlined car has less air resistance than a car with a boxy design.

The Type of Transmission

When used correctly, a manual transmission consumes less fuel than an automatic one. A manual transmission car also is less expensive to buy. However, there are trade-offs. An automatic is easier to use and learn to drive than a manual one, and there are more models available.

The Power Train

The power train powers the wheels that move the car. The number of times that the drive shaft revolves to make the wheels turn once is known as the axle-gear ratio. The higher the axle-gear ratio, the greater the fuel consumption.

Power Equipment

Power brakes and steering add extra weight to a vehicle, which leads to

Tips for New Drivers

Used Car Checks

When purchasing a used car, check the following.

The condition of the paint New paint can indicate collision damage.

For rust Don't buy a car with rusted-out areas unless you can afford repairs.

For worn tires, including the spare Uneven wear on any tire may indicate front-end problems.

The tail pipe A light-gray color indicates proper combustion.

The radiator Remove the radiator cap. Is the coolant clean? Is there caked-on rust on the cap? Are there signs of leaks on the back of the radiator?

The transmission Pull out the transmission dipstick and sniff it. A burned smell may indicate an overheated transmission. Feel the oil on the crankcase dipstick. If it is gritty, there may be dirt in the engine.

The service stickers Service stickers tell you how often a car has been tuned up and had the oil changed.

All windows and door locks Check for ease of operation.

The engine Listen for loud or unusual noises when you start the car. Check that all gauges and warning lights go on and off when you start the engine.

The headlights, taillights, brake lights, and turn indicators

For slamming sounds or lurching as the car starts An automatic transmission should take hold promptly when in gear.

higher fuel use. When choosing a car, you need to evaluate whether ease of operation is worth extra fuel cost to you.

Extra Equipment

Features such as air-conditioning also increase fuel use.

You can choose features that use extra fuel because they are important to you for safety, comfort, or convenience. At the same time, you can also make choices that will save fuel. It's your decision.

What Should You Know About Buying a Used Car?

Many consumers decide to buy a used car, usually for economic reasons. Consider many of the same factors when buying a used car that you would when buying a new one. But there are other considerations as well.

You can buy a used car from a private owner or a used car dealer. Buying from the owner can cost less, but you will not get a *warranty*, a written guarantee that the seller will repair the car if something goes wrong within a given amount of time. Dealers, on the other hand, often offer warranties.

The *Blue Book* is a good guide to the average price paid to dealers for different makes and models of used cars. The actual price may differ from "book" price depending on the condition of the car and its mileage.

Before buying a used car, test-drive it. Shaky steering and a wobbly ride may mean misaligned front wheels or the need for wheel balan-

cing. Make several sharp turns at a low speed. Steering should not stiffen up. If the car has power steering, there should be no squeaks or other noises.

Slow down from 50 mph to 15 mph without stepping on the brakes. Then step hard on the accelerator. If there is blue exhaust smoke, the car may need an engine overhaul. Having diagnostic tests performed on the car you choose *before* you buy it may be more economical in the long run.

CHECKPOINT

3. How can information from the Insurance Institute for Highway Safety help you evaluate a car's safety?
4. Describe how test-driving a car can help you evaluate how comfortable it is.
5. How does the type of engine a car has affect its fuel efficiency?
6. What should you check when you select a used car?

ENERGY TIPS

If you are buying a new car, look carefully at the dealer's sticker. It contains information about miles per gallon of gasoline. The greater number of miles per gallon, the more fuel efficient the car.

WHAT WOULD YOU DO?

You want some of these features, but you also want fuel economy. What would you do?

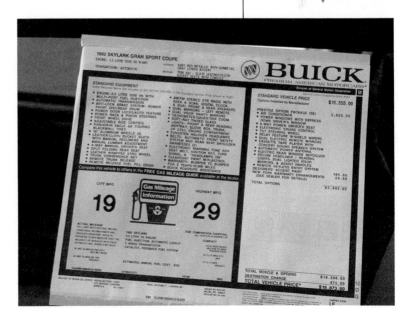

How to Obtain Financing for a New or Used Car

Once you have chosen the car you want to buy, you have to decide how to pay for it. Very few people can afford to pay cash for a new car or for a late-model used car. Most people have to take out a loan to pay for the car. How do you get a loan?

Ask about a car loan at the bank where you have a checking or savings account. ▶

What Should You Know About Financing a Car?

To finance the purchase of an automobile, you need to know where to get a car loan and the amount of the monthly payments.

Where to Get Financing

If you are a full-time high school student, you will not be able to obtain financing on your own. The lending institution will require that an adult be responsible for repayment. You may be able to get a loan if you are 18 years old and work full time. In most cases, however, a responsible adult will need to co-sign the loan.

Drivers finance their cars through banks, credit unions, finance companies, and, if buying a new car, often

---

THE MATH CONNECTION

Calculate the interest on a car loan to estimate the monthly payments. Suppose you want to buy a used car for $3,000. You've saved $1,000 and want to borrow the rest. Further suppose a bank will lend you $2,000 for 24 months (2 years) at 12 percent interest. Follow these steps to estimate the amount you'll pay in interest and what your monthly payments will be.
1. Multiply the amount of the loan by the interest. $2,000 × 0.12 = $240
2. Multiply the interest by the number of years. $240 × 2 = $480
3. Add the interest to the amount of the loan. $2,000 + $480 = $2,480
4. Divide the total by the number of months to find out how much you'll pay per month. $2,480 ÷ 24 = $103.33

Amount of Loan	Interest on Loan	Total Amount of Loan	Loan Period	Monthly Payments
$2,000	12%	$2,480	24 Mos.	$103.33

Car dealerships may offer financing at low interest rates as part of their sales promotions.

through the dealer. You should check out each possible source of financing as carefully as you've checked out the car you want to buy.

The Amount of Monthly Payments

Loan agencies lend money to make money. They make money by charging interest on the money they lend. Different sources of financing often charge different interest rates. Compare rates to get the best deal.

The amount of the loan is based on the cost of the car. The amount of time you have to pay back the loan is based on whether the car is new or used. Used car loans have to be repaid more quickly than new car loans.

You should try to pay as much as you can toward the purchase of the car—the down payment—and then borrow the rest. The lender will give you a schedule of monthly payments. The amount of these payments will depend on how much money you borrow, the interest on your loan, and whether or not your car's insurance is included in the loan.

CHECKPOINT

7. What advice would you give to someone about financing a car?

WHAT WOULD YOU DO?

The buyer can make a down payment of either $1,000 or $1,500 on a used car. Which should he choose to do? Why?

Choosing and Purchasing Automobile Insurance

Liability insurance provides coverage if you cause injury or property damage.

▶

Although most car owners buy insurance, some states only require that owners show proof of their ability to pay if they injure other people or damage their property. Some states permit an owner to put up a deposit in the form of cash, a bond, or stocks of a fixed amount.

When you buy a car, you should also purchase automobile insurance. Many different kinds of car insurance policies are available, and you should investigate each kind carefully before deciding what you will need.

What Kinds of Insurance Might You Need?

Suppose you are involved in a collision that results in property damage and serious injury. How will you pay the costs involved? Unless you're very rich, you'll need automobile insurance. That's why many states require anyone who owns a car also to have one or more kinds of automobile insurance.

Liability Insurance

Liable means "responsible." Liability insurance is proof that you will be financially responsible if you cause damage to property or injure other people. Many states require drivers to prove they have a certain amount of liability insurance before their cars can be registered.

Liability insurance protects you against claims if you are at fault in a collision. It helps you to pay for any injury or property damage caused by your actions. Liability insurance not only protects you, it also protects anyone else who has your permission to drive your car. (Check your policy first to see if there are restrictions on who can and who cannot drive your car.)

Most drivers have two kinds of liability insurance—bodily injury liability insurance and property damage liability. Both are usually sold in amounts of $10,000 to $500,000.

Bodily injury liability insurance covers you if your driving causes injury to or the death of another person or persons. It also covers legal fees, court costs, and lost wages.

Property damage liability covers you if your driving causes damage to the property of other persons. It covers damage to their car, property in their car, and damage to buildings, telephone poles, and traffic lights.

Of course, you are covered only for the amount of insurance you have purchased. If a court determines that you have caused more damage than your insurance will pay, you are held *personally* liable.

Uninsured Motorist Insurance

Although many states require that car owners have liability insurance and show proof of it before their cars can be registered, some drivers allow their policies to lapse or cancel their policies. If you are involved in a collision with such a driver, or if you are involved with a hit-and-run driver, uninsured motorist insurance protects you. Uninsured motorist insurance also protects you in states where no liability insurance is required. It pays for any bodily injury that you may suffer. Generally it does not pay for damage to your car.

Collision Insurance

Collision insurance pays for damage to your car even if you are to blame in a crash or are involved with an uninsured driver. Collision insurance also covers repairs if your car is damaged in a parking lot or in a parking space on the street.

Due to the increasing cost of repairing collision damage, very few insurance companies offer full-coverage collision insurance that pays the entire amount of any damages. Most drivers have a *deductible* policy. With this kind of policy, you agree to pay a fixed amount, such as the first $50, $100, $250, or $500 worth of damages. The insurance company pays the rest. The greater the fixed amount, or deductible, you pay, the less this insurance costs.

Banks or companies that finance car loans usually require a car owner to have collision insurance with a deductible of no more than $250. However, once the car loan is repaid, it is a good idea to raise the deductible to $500 in order to lower the cost of the insurance.

Collision insurance covers the cost of damage to a car no matter who is at fault.
▼

You are responsible for the cost of repairs up to and including the deductible amount. ▶

Comprehensive Insurance

If your car is damaged by anything other than a collision, comprehensive insurance pays the bills. For example, comprehensive insurance covers theft or damage caused by fire, explosions, natural disasters, or riots.

Medical Payment Insurance

Medical payment insurance covers medical, hospital, or funeral costs regardless of who is at fault. It pays a fixed amount if you or passengers in your car are injured or killed in a collision. It also pays if you or a member of your family is injured or killed while riding in someone else's car. Very often, medical payment insurance pays if you or a member of your family is struck as a pedestrian or a bicycle, bus, or taxicab rider. The amount paid is determined by the policy and usually ranges from $1,000 to $5,000 per person.

No-Fault Insurance

An increasing number of states have *no-fault insurance* laws. In this system, your insurance company pays your medical bills and any other costs resulting from a collision-related injury. The system is called no-fault insurance because blame is not considered before the insurance company pays your bills. In very serious accidents, the injured parties can still go to court and sue the person responsible for damages.

Towing Insurance

Towing insurance covers the costs of on-road repairs and the cost of having your car towed.

Which Factors Determine the Cost of Insurance?

You purchase car insurance by paying a premium, or a set amount, to an insurance company, usually every six months. How is this premium decided on?

Insurance companies rely on statistics to determine their rates. The statistics indicate the likelihood that persons of a certain age, sex, or marital status will be involved in a crash. They also indicate the likelihood of certain types of cars being involved in a crash. Insurance companies use the following factors to determine rates.

Your age Drivers under the age of 25 pay the highest premiums.

Your driving record Convictions, collisions, and insurance claims can increase your insurance costs.

Mileage per year The farther you drive, the more your insurance will cost.

If you drive to work Carpooling reduces the cost of insurance.

Where you live If you live in a city, your insurance costs will be greater than a person who lives in the country.

Your gender Women pay lower rates than men. Statistics show that men drive more often and farther

Insurance companies pay damages only up to a car's "book" value. This amount can be less than an owner thinks the car is worth.

◀

Most drivers receive minimum coverage at a base rate. You can see that single males pay the highest insurance premiums.

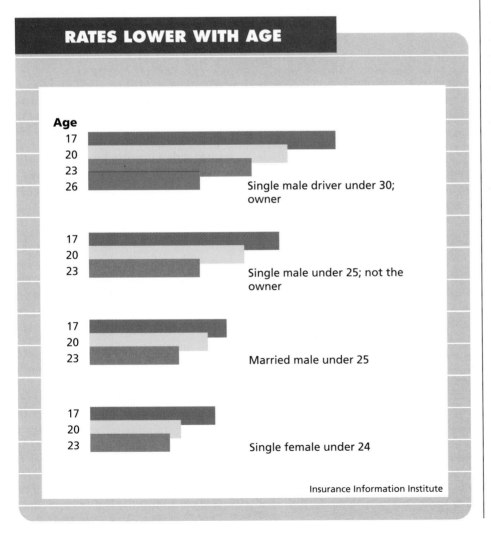

RATES LOWER WITH AGE

Age

17
20
23
26
Single male driver under 30; owner

17
20
23
Single male under 25; not the owner

17
20
23
Married male under 25

17
20
23
Single female under 24

Insurance Information Institute

Advice From the Experts

Chuck Hurley, Senior VP, Communications, Insurance Institute for Highway Safety

Chuck Hurley

ADVICE FROM THE EXPERTS

Shopping for a car? Consider car size. In relation to their numbers on the road, small cars account for about twice as many deaths as large cars. Larger is safer, but high performance vehicles should be avoided.

Air bags and lap/shoulder belts are also very important. Car buyers should take note that all belt systems aren't alike. Some provide better crash protection than others.

Even good drivers can't avoid all collisions. So, it is important to have the best available occupant-protection features.

? WHAT WOULD YOU DO?

You plan to drive in a state that does not require liability insurance. What would you do to be sure you are adequately covered?

---

and are involved in more collisions.

Your marital status Young married men pay less than men of the same age who are single. Young married men are involved in fewer collisions than single men.

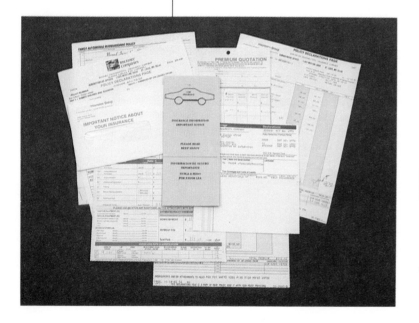

The value of your car The more expensive the car, the greater the cost of insurance.

The type of car A sports car or sports sedan costing less than a larger sedan will cost more to insure.

Many insurance companies offer discounts to students who have completed a driver education program and to students whose grade average is B or higher. Companies may also offer discounts to drivers whose cars have air bags or antilock brakes. Discounts may be given as well to car owners who garage their vehicles or install antitheft devices.

CHECKPOINT

8. How is liability insurance different from other kinds of automobile insurance?
9. How does being male or female play a role in the amount you pay for automobile insurance?

CHAPTER 15 REVIEW

KEY POINTS

LESSON ONE

1. To determine your need for a car, think about how close you are to places that you go to most often, how available public transportation is for you, how available the family car is to you, and whether you are mature enough to take on the responsibilities of owning a car.

2. Before buying a car, think about the number of passengers you will have and their age; the number of miles you expect to drive daily, monthly, and yearly; whether you'll use the car to tow a trailer or carry heavy loads; and the cost of the car plus the cost of maintenance and insurance.

LESSON TWO

3. To select a safe car, consider whether it is equipped with air bags and antilock brakes, its death rate per 10,000 models, how it holds up in crash tests, and its size.

4. To select a comfortable car, sit in the driver's seat and adjust the seat and steering wheel (where possible), making sure you can reach accessory switches and dials easily.

5. Factors that affect fuel efficiency are a car's weight, engine and transmission type, design, power train, and whether it has power equipment and other fuel-consuming accessories.

6. If you're thinking of buying a used car, find out if a warranty is available, know the *Blue Book* value of the car, test-drive the car, and assess the car's general condition and appearance.

LESSON THREE

7. You can get financing through banks, credit unions, finance companies, or the car dealer. Shop around to get the best interest rates, and know what your monthly payments will be.

LESSON FOUR

8. The basic types of insurance are liability (bodily injury and property damage), uninsured motorist, collision, comprehensive, medical payment, no-fault, and towing insurance.

9. Factors that determine insurance cost include age, driving record, mileage per year, carpooling where you live, gender, marital status, and the car's value. Insurers may offer discounts to students who have completed a driver education course and to drivers who have safety devices, keep their car in a garage, and install antitheft devices.

PROJECTS

1. Visit several car dealerships in your area. Talk to salespeople and compare prices, safety features, and repair facilities. Select a car that you might want to own. Interview a mechanic certified by the National Institute for Automotive Service Excellence (NIASE) about the car you have selected.

2. Interview a local insurance agent to find out if there are differences in rates for new drivers under the age of 25. Use what you learn to propose ways a new driver can reduce insurance costs. Share your information and ideas with your class.

CHAPTER 15 REVIEW

BUILDING MAP SKILLS

Understanding Map Symbols

Look at the symbols on a map and the legend to learn about the area you are traveling through.

You can see that there is an airport near Great Falls, Montana at D, 7, and a campground near Choteau at C, 6.

Try It Yourself

1. At what coordinates can ski areas be found?
2. How many campgrounds can you find in the Blackfeet Indian Reservation?
3. What does ⚒ stand for at A, 4?

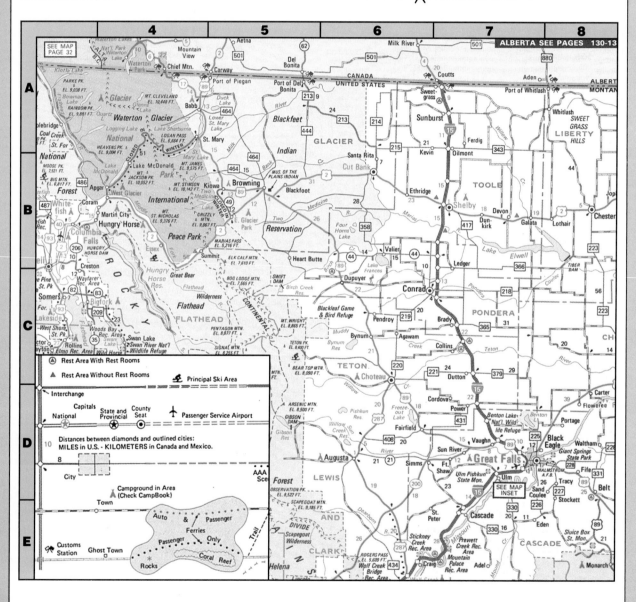

CHAPTER 15 REVIEW

CHAPTER TEST

Write the letter of the answer that best completes each sentence.

1. A driver interested in fuel efficiency would probably buy a car with
   a. 4 cylinders.
   b. 8 cylinders.
   c. 16 cylinders.
2. When buying a car, most people
   a. pay with a credit card.
   b. pay cash.
   c. take out a loan.
3. Before buying a car, consider
   a. how clean it is.
   b. how many passengers you will have.
   c. whether it is a convertible.
4. Your driving record and marital status are two factors that can affect
   a. the cost of your insurance
   b. the purchase price of a car.
   c. your concentration at the wheel.
5. Expensive cars
   a. cost more to insure than inexpensive cars.
   b. cost less to insure than inexpensive cars.
   c. are more fuel efficient than inexpensive cars.
6. The death rate in the smallest cars is
   a. lower than that in the largest cars.
   b. the same as that in the largest cars.
   c. twice as high as that in the largest cars.
7. The *Blue Book* is a guide to
   a. used car dealerships in the United States.
   b. the average price paid to dealers for various used cars.
   c. different types of car engines.

8. Liability insurance
   a. protects you against claims if you are at fault in a collision.
   b. is available to drivers over 21 years of age.
   c. protects you if you are accused of lying.
9. The purchase price of a car
   a. is one of the many expenses associated with owning a car.
   b. is the only major expense in owning a car.
   c. is generally lower than it was ten years ago.
10. Bodily injury insurance covers
    a. any damages to the body of your car.
    b. the death or injury of others while you are driving.
    c. only the driver of a vehicle.

Write the word or phrase that best completes each sentence.

deductible   comprehensive insurance
uninsured motorist insurance   warranty
financing   fuel consumption

11. A _____ is a written guarantee that the seller will repair your car if something goes wrong.

12. If your car is damaged by anything other than a collision, _____ will pay the bills.

13. There can be large differences in _____ among different car models.

14. In many cases, car dealers can offer you a _____ arrangement when you buy a new car.

15. If you are involved with a hit-and-run driver, _____ can protect you.

DRIVER'S LOG

In this chapter, you have learned some considerations to keep in mind when you are ready to buy a car. Write a paragraph in response to each of the following questions.
◆ Describe the guideposts you use to measure maturity. Which do you need to work on?
◆ What will you look for when you buy a car? What do you think your choice will say about your maturity? Why?

CHAPTER ◆ 16

CAR SYSTEMS AND MAINTENANCE

Good drivers make sure that their cars are safe to drive.
Good drivers understand their car's different systems and make
sure that these systems are properly maintained.

LESSON ONE

Checking Your Car Before and After You Start the Engine

1. List several things on your car that you can inspect before entering it.
2. List what to check after starting the engine.
3. Explain when to have your car serviced.

LESSON TWO

Becoming Familiar with the Engine and Power Train

4. Explain how a typical car engine works.
5. Tell what the power train is and what it does.
6. Describe four guidelines for maintaining the engine and power train.

LESSON THREE

Understanding and Maintaining Car Systems

7. Explain how the fuel and exhaust systems work and how to maintain them.
8. Explain how the electrical and light systems work and how to maintain them.
9. Describe how the lubricating and cooling systems work and how to maintain them.

LESSON FOUR

Suspension, Steering, Brakes, and Tires

10. Describe four systems that are important for comfort and safety.
11. Describe warning signs of possible problems with the suspension, steering, or tires.

Checking Your Car Before and After You Start the Engine

You've probably heard the old saying that an ounce of prevention is worth a pound of cure. That maxim is especially important for drivers.

Inspecting and caring for your car *before* something goes wrong can save you both money and aggravation. More important, maintaining your car can save your life.

Different car makes and models are alike in some ways, different in others. To be able to check your particular car properly, you should refer to the owner's manual. If you don't have the manual for your car, obtain a copy from a dealer or order one from the car manufacturer. Car manuals are also available in many bookstores. Keep the manual in your glove compartment so you'll have it handy when you need it.

What Can You Inspect Before Entering Your Car?

You don't need to be a mechanic to inspect your car. You can check many items quickly and easily before driving. Make these checks at least once a month and before long drives.

In addition to the guidelines below, refer to Chapter 6 for other important predriving checks and procedures.

Fluid Levels

You can inspect the different fluid levels in your car before you get into it. Check:

◆ the engine oil (when the engine is cool and not running)
◆ the level of coolant in the radiator overflow tank or radiator
◆ the transmission fluid and the fluid level in the power-steering and master-brake-cylinder reservoirs
◆ the battery fluid (if necessary for your battery)
◆ the windshield-washer fluid

Belts, Hoses, and Wires

Before you enter your car, you should inspect belts, hoses, and wires.

◆ Check the fan belt and the belts that run the power-steering and air-conditioning units. Belts may need tightening or adjustment. Replace frayed or cracked belts as soon as possible.

Before you enter your car, check under the hood for items such as the level of battery fluid.
▼

◀
Learning how to make your own checks can save you the cost and inconvenience of repairs.

◆ Check all hoses and hose connections for leaks.

◆ Look for loose, broken, or disconnected wires. Also check for cracked insulation on wires.

◆ Make sure the battery cables are tightly connected and the terminals are free from corrosion.

What Can You Check After Starting the Engine?

Once your engine is running, you should make several routine checks to ensure that your car is operating properly and safely.

Gauges and Warning Lights

You have already read about the various gauges and warning lights that provide information about your car. Check these gauges and lights regularly as you drive. They will warn you of a wide range of problems, such as low oil or fuel level,

engine overheating, and alternator malfunction.

Brakes

Your car's brake-warning light will make you aware of some—but not all—brake-system problems.

If you have to remove the radiator cap, do so *only when the radiator is cool.* If you remove the cap when the radiator is hot, boiling water could spurt out and scald you.

Having Your Car Serviced or Repaired

• To find a reliable mechanic or garage, ask friends and relatives for their recommendations. You can also call your local American Automobile Association.

• Ask the mechanic for an estimate.

• Find out for how long the mechanic will guarantee work done. Save your bill or receipt.

• Know what you're paying for. If there's something you don't understand, ask for an explanation.

• If the mechanic replaces a part, ask to see the old part.

• Warranties may cover many repairs. Know what your warranty does and does not cover.

Some mechanics use a sticker that has space for writing the dates of your oil changes. The sticker is usually placed on the door near the latch or on one of the door posts.

WHAT WOULD YOU DO?

Your sister has agreed to let you use her car while she's on vacation. What checks will you make before getting into her car? What checks will you make after starting the engine?

For this reason, always test your brakes as soon as you begin driving. When you step on the brake pedal, you should feel firm resistance, and your car should come to a smooth, straight stop. The pedal should stay well above the floor.

Specific warning signs of a brake-system malfunction are discussed later in this chapter.

Horn

Periodically check to make sure your horn works. If you're driving an unfamiliar car, always locate and try the horn *before* you begin driving. Horn position on the steering wheel varies from car to car.

Lights and Turn Signals

It's a good idea to check all exterior lights and turn signals before you begin to move. You should use your low-beam headlights even in daylight hours, especially when visibility is poor. Periodically have a friend or family member stand outside the car and tell you if your brake lights work when you press the brake pedal.

How Do You Know When Your Car Should Be Serviced?

Your owner's manual contains guidelines for servicing and maintaining your car. The guidelines vary, depending on the kind and amount of driving you do and on the manufacturer's recommendations.

Some systems and parts require more frequent attention than others. Recommended intervals for servicing may be based either on time or on miles driven. For example, your manual might recommend checking tire pressure once a month, changing the oil every few months, and having the suspension checked every 20,000 miles.

Keeping good records will help you maintain a car-care schedule. An easy way to keep track of repairs and maintenance is to keep a small notebook in your car. Each time you or a mechanic service or repair the car, jot down exactly what was done and the date. Save your receipts in an envelope in the glove compartment.

CHECKPOINT

1. What kinds of problems might you spot as you check your car before entering it?
2. What can you check after you start the engine?
3. What can help you determine when to have your car serviced?

Becoming Familiar with the Engine and Power Train

Many parts work together to produce a car's power and motion. By keeping these parts operating smoothly, you help your car run safely and fuel efficiently.

How Does the Engine Work?

Your car's engine is known as an *internal combustion engine*. It's called that because the power it produces comes from burning a mixture of fuel and air inside, rather than outside, the engine.

When you start your car's engine, you're setting off a chain of events.

1. Turning the key in the ignition causes power to be drawn from the battery to a small electric *starter motor*, commonly called the starter.

2. The starter turns the *flywheel* of the engine. When the flywheel turns, it turns the *crankshaft*.

3. A *piston* in each *cylinder* of the car is attached to the crankshaft. Most cars have four, six, or eight cylinders. The more cylinders in a car, the more power the engine has, but the more gasoline it uses.

4. In each cylinder, a *spark plug* produces a spark. This spark causes the fuel-air mixture inside the cylinder to explode. The explosion pushes down the piston, which turns the crankshaft.

5. The continuous up-and-down motion of the pistons keeps the crankshaft turning. Power sent from the crankshaft is transmitted to the wheels, making the car move. The more explosions per minute in the cylinders, the faster the engine runs.

FYI

In 1977, Janet Guthrie was the first woman to participate in the Indianapolis 500 automobile race. Mechanical problems forced her to quit after only 27 laps. However, the next year she finished the race, coming in ninth. Before becoming interested in automobile racing, Guthrie was a pilot and worked as a research and development engineer for Republic Aviation. In 1966, she gave up this job to devote herself to a career as a professional race car driver.

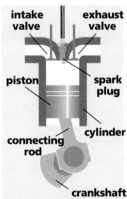

The parts of a cylinder. Most cars have four, six, or eight cylinders. The piston in each cylinder is attached to a part of the crankshaft.

Step 1. As the piston moves down, the air-fuel mixture is drawn into the cylinder through the intake valve.

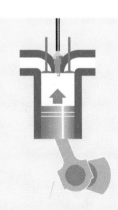

Step 2. The piston moves up and compresses the air-fuel mixture. (The intake and exhaust valves are both closed.)

Step 3. A spark explodes the compressed air-fuel mixture. This pushes down the piston, which turns the crankshaft.

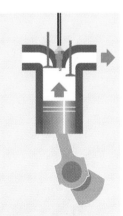

Step 4. The piston moves up and forces the burned gases out through the exhaust valve. The cycle begins again.

Power is transmitted differently to vehicles with rear-wheel drive, front-wheel drive, and four-wheel drive. ▶

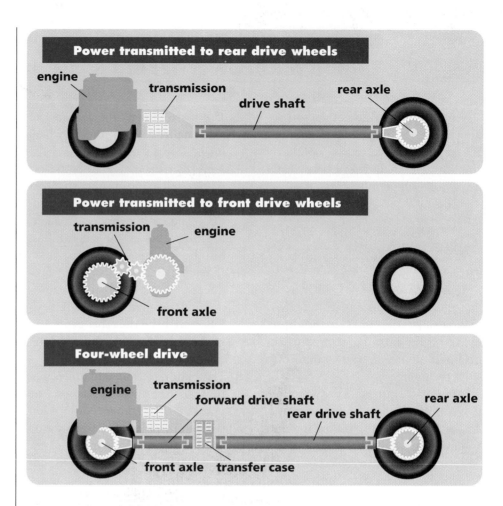

Power transmitted to rear drive wheels

engine · transmission · drive shaft · rear axle

Power transmitted to front drive wheels

transmission · engine · front axle

Four-wheel drive

engine · transmission · forward drive shaft · rear drive shaft · rear axle · front axle · transfer case

What Is the Power Train and What Does It Do?

Several parts of your car work together to transmit power from the engine to the wheels. These parts make up the *power train*.

In most cars, the power train sends power from the engine to only two of the four wheels. The wheels that receive the power are called the *drive wheels*. If the two front wheels are the drive wheels, the car has front-wheel drive. If the two rear wheels receive the power, the car has rear-wheel drive. A car has four-wheel drive if all four wheels receive power.

The transmission is part of the power train. Gears in the transmission allow it to transfer power to the drive wheels. In a car with a manual transmission, the driver uses the clutch pedal and the gearshift lever to shift gears and change the amount of power that goes to the drive wheels. In a car with automatic transmission, the clutch works automatically, so the gears are shifted automatically, too.

In a car with rear-wheel drive, the transmission is connected by a *drive shaft* to the *differential, rear axle,* and *rear wheels*. The differential allows the rear wheels to turn at different speeds when the car turns.

In a car with front-wheel drive, engine power is sent to a combination transmission and differential, and then directly to the front wheels.

How Can You Maintain the Engine and Power Train?

Cars that are well maintained perform better, are more fuel efficient, and last longer than cars that are neglected.

Here are some basic guidelines for keeping your car's engine and power train in top condition. Your owner's manual will give you additional specific recommendations.

Check and Change the Oil Regularly

Check your car's oil level at least once a month. Have the oil changed at least twice a year, or every 4,000 miles. If you drive over 10,000 miles a year or if you use your car to pull a trailer, you may have to change the oil more often.

Have Regular Tune-ups

If you drive 10,000 to 12,000 miles a year, you should take your car in for a one major and one minor tune-up during that period. In addition to the 15-minute monthly checkup you can perform yourself (see Chapter 14), a mechanic might do some or all of the following.

◆ Change the oil filter.
◆ Check the carburetor adjustment or fuel-injection system.
◆ Clean or replace the spark plugs.

◆ Check and, if necessary, replace the air and fuel filters.
◆ Check the alternator, battery, and voltage regulator.
◆ Check the ignition wires and timing or electronic ignition system.
◆ Check and, if needed, clean the battery terminals.
◆ Check the car's pollution-control devices and exhaust system.

Keep in mind that the kind of driving you do will affect how often you need to have your engine tuned. Stop-and-go city driving, for example, is much harder on a car than steady highway driving.

CHECKPOINT

4. What is an internal combustion engine and how does it work?
5. What parts make up the power train, and how do they supply power to the wheels?
6. What are some of the tasks a mechanic might do to tune up your car?

WHAT WOULD YOU DO?

The used car you've just bought is running beautifully. You'd like to keep it that way. Describe the actions you would take to maintain your car in top shape.

Today it's easy to take motor vehicles for granted. They're everywhere, and they've been around for a long time. But they are still among the most complicated machines ever invented. Every time you get behind the wheel, you take control of a network of many different systems that work together to make your car work the way it does.

How Do the Fuel and Exhaust Systems Work?

The fuel and exhaust systems in a car must operate properly to maximize engine efficiency and minimize pollution.

The Fuel System

Your car's fuel system includes the *fuel tank, fuel pump, fuel filter, carburetor,* and *air filter.* Fuel is stored in the tank. The pump forces fuel from the tank through the filter to the carburetor. There the fuel is mixed with air drawn in through the air filter. The mixture of air and fuel becomes a misty fuel vapor that then goes to the engine's cylinders, where it is ignited.

Some cars have a *fuel-injection system* instead of a carburetor. In cars with fuel-injection systems, an electronic mechanism senses fuel demand and injects the correct fuel-air mixture into the cylinders.

Using gasoline with a high octane rating may not increase your engine's power or fuel efficiency. Choose the lowest-octane gasoline you can use without causing your engine to make a pinging sound when accelerating or driving uphill. See your owner's manual for manufacturer's recommendations.

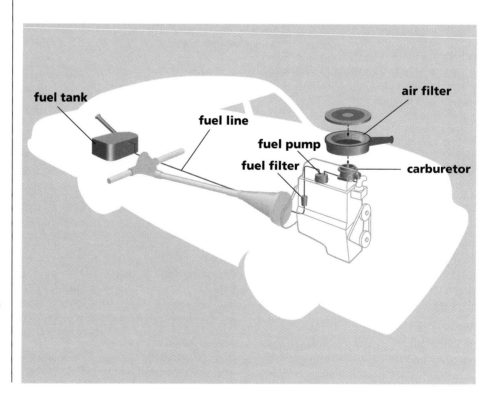

fuel tank

fuel line

air filter

fuel pump

fuel filter

carburetor

▶

The fuel system both stores fuel and delivers the correct air-fuel mixture to the engine.

THE
SCIENCE
CONNECTION

Carbon monoxide is an odorless, colorless, and tasteless gas. Small amounts of carbon monoxide can make you sleepy or nauseous or give you a headache by interfering with the ability of your red blood cells to carry oxygen. Large amounts of carbon monoxide can kill you.

Avoid driving a car that has an exhaust leak or a broken tailpipe. Such defects allow carbon monoxide and other harmful exhaust gases to be trapped beneath the car, even when the car is moving. These gases may leak up into the car's interior.

To guard against carbon monoxide poisoning, also avoid:
• running a car's engine in a closed garage.
• sitting in a parked car with the windows closed, the engine running, and the heater on.
• driving with the trunk lid up.
• driving with the rear window of a station wagon open.
• stopping so close to the car ahead that your heater or air conditioner draws in exhaust gases from the car's tailpipe.

The Exhaust System

The exhaust system serves two main purposes. First, it carries off carbon monoxide and other harmful gas by-products of combustion. Second, it muffles engine noise.

The pipes that make up the *exhaust manifold* collect unburned gases from the engine and carry them to the *muffler*. The muffler absorbs noise from the explosions in the cylinders. Exhaust gases exit through the *tailpipe*. Pollution-control devices, such as the *catalytic converter*, reduce the amount of harmful gases coming from the tailpipe.

How Can You Maintain the Fuel and Exhaust Systems?

To maintain your car's fuel system, replace the air and fuel filters as needed. You may also have to adjust the carburetor occasionally to ensure fuel efficiency.

Most cars today operate on lead-free gasoline. Using leaded gasoline will destroy the catalytic converter.

How much maintenance or repair the exhaust system requires varies with the conditions under which you drive. Short trips, for example, are harder on a car than long highway

The exhaust system carries off poisonous gases and muffles engine noise.
▼

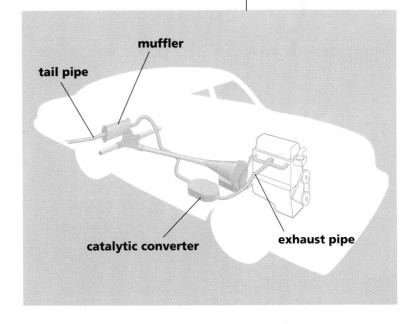

tail pipe

muffler

catalytic converter

exhaust pipe

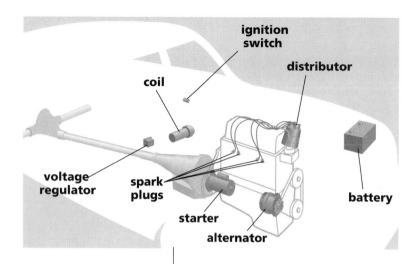

ignition
switch

distributor

coil

voltage
regulator

spark
plugs

starter

alternator

battery

▲
*The electrical system
supplies energy to start the
car and sends electrical
current to the spark plugs.*

drives. Be on the lookout for loose, rusting, or damaged parts. Always have your exhaust system thoroughly inspected as part of a tune-up.

How Do the Electrical and Light Systems Work?

The electrical and light systems help to keep your car running smoothly and safely.

*Be sure your headlights are
properly aligned to reduce
driving risk at night.* ▶

The Electrical System

The heart of your car's electrical system is the *battery*. The battery provides the power to start the engine. It also enables you to operate, for a short time, such equipment as your radio and lights when the engine isn't running.

After you turn the key in the ignition switch to start your car, the *alternator* or *generator* supplies electricity needed to keep the engine running, operate equipment, and recharge the battery. The *voltage regulator* controls the amount of electricity generated and the rate at which the battery is recharged. The *distributor* sends electric current to the individual spark plugs to ignite the fuel-air mixture in the engine cylinders.

To protect electrical circuits from overloading, your car is equipped with *fuses*, usually located in a box beneath the dashboard. These safety devices burn out in case of an electrical problem, preventing damage to the car's wiring.

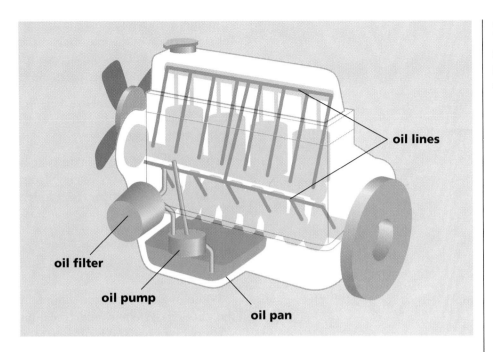

oil lines

oil filter

oil pump

oil pan

◀ The lubricating system reduces heat by coating the parts of the engine with oil.

The Light System

Your car's light system enables you to see and be seen.

Exterior lights include headlights, taillights, side-marker lights, brake lights, signal lights, parking lights, and emergency flashers. Interior lights include the dome light on the roof of the car and the various dashboard lights that provide you with information about the car or warn you of malfunctions.

How Can You Maintain the Electrical and Light Systems?

The first step in maintaining the electrical and light systems is to keep your battery in top working condition. Keep the battery terminals free of corrosion and the battery cables firmly connected. Unless you have one of the newer type "maintenance-free" batteries, check the fluid level at least once a month and add water when needed.

Be sure to have the electrical system checked as part of your car's regular tune-up. While driving, keep an eye on the alternator gauge or warning light for signs of trouble.

Keep headlights clean and properly aligned. Even a thin layer of dirt can cut light output by as much as 90 percent. Misaligned lights can reduce your ability to see the roadway and can momentarily blind oncoming drivers.

Check exterior lights at least once a week and promptly replace any burned-out bulbs.

How Do the Lubricating and Cooling Systems Work?

As the parts of your car's engine move rapidly and rub against each other, they produce friction and

Each year, electrical system failures disable more cars than the combined next two causes of vehicle breakdowns.

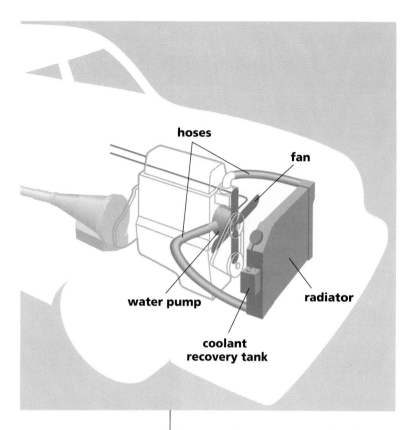

hoses

fan

water pump

coolant recovery tank

radiator

▲
The so-called water-cooled engine actually uses a coolant in its cooling system.

In addition to oil, grease is used to lubricate parts of the car, such as the steering system. Like oil, grease reduces friction and helps parts move smoothly.

The Cooling System

The purpose of the cooling system is to keep your car's engine from overheating. To do this, the cooling system circulates *coolant*—a mixture of water and antifreeze—through the engine by means of a network of pipes, channels, and connecting hoses.

Without antifreeze, the liquid in the cooling system would freeze in very cold weather and could boil over in hot weather, especially in traffic jams and on long trips. Frozen or boiling coolant does not circulate, and the engine can overheat.

The coolant is stored in the *radiator* and radiator *overflow tank*. A *water pump* pumps the coolant through the radiator and the circulating network. A fan forces air through the radiator to cool the liquid. A *thermostat* in the system works to control the flow of coolant so as to maintain the best operating temperature.

Although water-cooled engines are the most common, some cars have air-cooled engines. The cooling system for these engines circulates air rather than water to control engine heat buildup.

heat. At the same time, the fuel-air explosions in the cylinders create more heat. Small wonder then that the engine temperature may exceed 4,000° Fahrenheit.

Too much heat can destroy your car's engine. The lubricating and cooling systems are designed to keep that from happening.

The Lubricating System

Oil is the key element in your car's lubricating system. Coating engine parts with oil reduces friction, heat, and wear. Oil also helps clean internal engine surfaces and prevent rust and corrosion.

An *oil pump* moves oil from the *oil pan,* where it is stored, to all moving engine parts. The *oil filter* cleans the oil as it circulates.

How Can You Maintain the Lubricating and Cooling Systems?

Checking and changing the oil and oil filter regularly is the key to main-

You can learn to use a dipstick to check whether or not your car needs more oil.

taining your car's lubricating system. Low oil pressure allows the engine to become too hot, which may cause excessive wear of moving parts.

Keep in mind that the oil-pressure gauge or warning light does not indicate how much oil is in the engine, but it will signal a drop in oil pressure. To check the actual level of oil, use the oil dipstick. *Never* drive your car with insufficient oil: You could destroy the engine.

Driving with an overheated engine can also damage your car. If the temperature gauge or warning light indicates overheating, stop driving as soon as possible. Let the engine cool before you look for the cause of the problem.

To maintain the cooling system, use the proper coolant, and check the fluid level whenever the car is serviced. Also check the fan belt and connecting hoses. Have the cooling system completely drained, flushed, and refilled every two years.

CHECKPOINT

7. Why is it important to keep the fuel and exhaust systems of your car in good condition?
8. Explain how your car uses electricity, and name the source of electrical power in your car.
9. How do the lubricating and cooling systems work?

❓ WHAT WOULD YOU DO?

You've been stuck in bumper-to-bumper traffic for nearly an hour on a hot summer day. The temperature warning light has just come on. How would you handle this situation? What safety precautions would you take?

Suspension, Steering, Brakes and Tires

Your comfort and safety in a car depend not only on how well you drive but also on how your car handles. To protect yourself and others, make sure your car's suspension, steering, and brake systems as well as all four tires are in good operating condition.

What Car Systems Are Important for Comfort and Safety?

Suspension, steering, and brake systems work together to give you control over your car and provide a comfortable ride.

The Suspension System

The suspension system supports your car's weight, cushions the ride, and helps keep the car stable when you drive over bumps or uneven roadway surfaces.

Springs and *shock absorbers* are the main parts of the suspension system. These parts connect the car's frame to the wheels.

The springs soften the impact of bumps in the roadway. If your car had only springs, however, it would continue bouncing after hitting a bump. This bouncing would reduce the contact between the tires and the road and make it harder for you to control the car.

The shock absorbers—*shocks,* as they're commonly called—work to control bouncing. By absorbing the shocks of driving, they make the ride smoother and help you maintain steering and braking control.

The Steering System

The steering system enables you to turn the front wheels. The steering wheel is connected to the front wheels by a steering shaft and movable rods.

The front wheels are designed to remain in an upright position and move up and down over bumps, even when they are turned.

The Brake System

Brakes slow or stop a car by applying *hydraulic pressure*—pressure created by the force of a liquid—against the four wheels. Stepping on the

The suspension system cushions the car's frame against bumps in the road.
▼

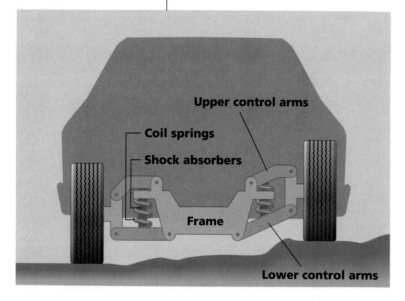

- Upper control arms
- Coil springs
- Shock absorbers
- Frame
- Lower control arms

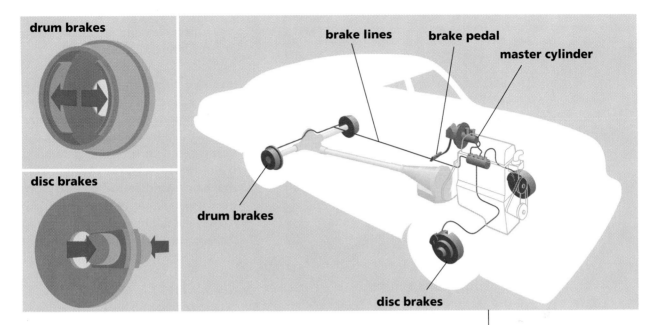

drum brakes

disc brakes

brake lines **brake pedal**

master cylinder

drum brakes

disc brakes

brake pedal forces brake fluid from the *master brake cylinder* through the brake-fluid lines to the wheel cylinders. There are two types of brakes: *drum brakes* and *disc brakes.*

Drum brakes   In a drum brake, the fluid pressure causes the *brake shoes* to push against the *brake lining.* The lining then presses against the round hollow metal drum inside the wheel. Friction slows and stops the wheel's turning motion.

Disc brakes   In a disc brake, pressure squeezes the *brake pads* against a flat metal wheel disc, producing the friction needed to stop the wheel from turning.

Many cars are equipped with disc brakes on the front wheels and drum brakes on the back wheels. Often the brakes are *power brakes,* which engage with less pressure on the brake pedal than do non-power brakes. Power brakes *do not,* however, shorten a car's stopping distance.

To minimize the risk of brake failure, brake systems are designed so that front and rear brakes are con-trolled independently. If one pair of brakes fails, the other pair will still work to stop the car.

Antilock brakes   Many newer cars are equipped with *antilock brakes,* which are designed to prevent the wheels from locking when the driver is forced to brake suddenly.

Parking brake   A parking brake is a mechanically operated brake that is separate from the hydraulic brake system. Attached by cable to the rear wheels, it is used to prevent a parked car from rolling.

The Tires

Sometimes, whether your car grips the road or skids out of control depends on the condition of the tires.

Tire inflation   Tires must be inflated properly to provide maximum traction and control. Too little tire pressure (underinflation) or too much tire pressure (overinflation) reduces traction, makes the car harder to handle, and lowers fuel efficiency.

▲
A hydraulic brake system gives all four wheels stopping power.

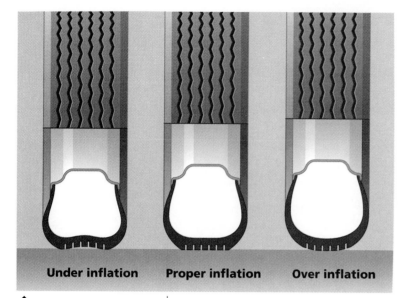

Under inflation **Proper inflation** **Over inflation**

It is important for fuel efficiency and traction that a car's tires be properly inflated.

pressure exceed the tire manufacturer's recommendation.

Tire tread The grooved outer surface of a tire is its *tread*. On wet or slippery surfaces, the amount of tread on your tires determines how much traction your car will have. Compared with tires that have good tread, overly worn tires have double the risk of skidding and are also more likely to go flat or blow out.

Tires should be replaced when the depth of tread is $\frac{1}{16}$ inch. To help you judge tread depth, you can buy a tread-depth gauge at an automotive supply store.

Tire rotation A car's front tires generally wear faster than the rear tires. To equalize tire wear, have your car's tires rotated about every 5,000 to 6,000 miles. Rotating tires means switching their position from front to rear and sometimes from one side to the other. Check your owner's manual for the recommended tire-rotation pattern.

When tires are rotated, they should also be balanced. Balancing helps to

The tire manufacturer's recommended maximum air pressure is stamped on the sidewall of each tire. On certain cars, such as those with engines mounted in the rear and station wagons, the pressure recommended for the rear tires is higher than that for the front tires. If in doubt, check with a mechanic, ask your local tire dealer, or contact the manufacturer. In no case should tire

The tire manufacturer stamps the maximum air pressure on the sidewall of the tire. ▶

ensure that weight is evenly distributed as the wheel turns. Balanced tires provide better steering control, a smoother ride, and longer tire life.

What Are Some Warning Signs of Car Problems?

Sometimes car problems appear unexpectedly. More often, though, advance warnings signal that a part or system needs attention.

Suspension and Steering Problems

Most problems affecting the suspension and steering system develop gradually as a result of wear. Watch for the following warning signs.

◆ There's too much play (free movement) in the steering wheel. With power steering, there should be virtually no play in the wheel. In a manual system, there should be no more than 2 inches of play.

◆ The steering wheel vibrates or is difficult to turn.

◆ The front end of the car wobbles or shimmies.

◆ The car bumps as you turn the wheel while driving on a smooth road.

◆ The car pulls to one side as you drive.

◆ The car bounces too much after hitting a bump.

◆ Tread wear on the front tires is uneven.

Have a mechanic check your car if any of these warning signs appear. The front end of your car may need aligning, the tires may need to be balanced, or some other problem may need correction.

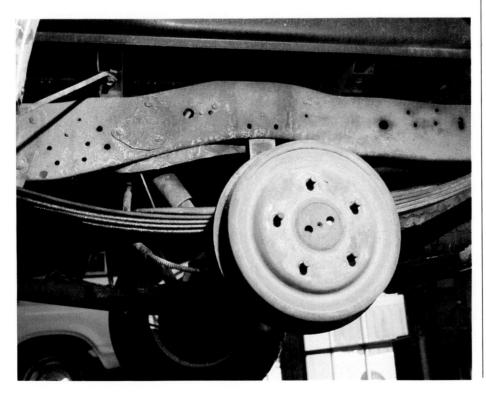

◀
Have a mechanic check the car if any warning signs of suspension or brake problems appear.

Jack Herr, Senior Service Specialist, Approved Auto Repair, AAA

Jack Herr

ADVICE FROM THE EXPERTS

If the oil pressure light comes on, do not drive your car, even if the dipstick reads full. This gauge senses oil pressure, not oil level.

Check your fluid levels at every fourth fill up. Change your oil and filter at 3,000 miles or 3 months, whichever occurs first. Most late-model engine compartment dipsticks are color-coded for easy identification.

Tire rotation, at 6,000 mile intervals, permits a quick peek at the brakes and opportunity for a tire inspection.

? WHAT WOULD YOU DO?

As you step on the brake of a used car, the car pulls to the right. What could cause this problem? Would you buy the car?

Brake Problems

See Chapter 14 for a description of brake failure. Neglecting a brake-system problem can have fatal consequences. Check with a mechanic if any warning signs appear.

Tire Problems

Inspecting your tires regularly *before* you drive will help to avoid problems on the road. Watch for the following warning signs of tire troubles:

◆ less than $\frac{1}{16}$ inch tread
◆ areas of little or no tread—"bald" spots
◆ uneven wear
◆ bulges
◆ embedded nails, glass, or metal
◆ frequent pressure loss in one particular tire, suggesting a slow leak

CHECKPOINT

10. How are the steering, suspension, brakes, and tires important to your safety?
11. What are some warning signs that indicate tire problems?

CHAPTER 16 REVIEW

KEY POINTS

1. Before entering your car, check fluid levels, belts and hoses; and connections.

2. After starting the engine, check gauges and warning lights and test your brakes and horn.

3. Service your car depending on the kind and amount of driving and on manufacturer recommendations.

LESSON TWO

4. An internal combustion engine burns a mixture of fuel and air. In each cylinder, a spark causes the mixture to explode, pushing down the piston, turning the crankshaft.

5. The power train sends engine power to the wheels through the transmission and clutch.

6. Regularly check and change the oil, have a tune-up, check the transmission fluid and change filters.

LESSON THREE

7. The fuel pump forces fuel from the tank to the carburetor to mix with air. The Vapor is ignited in the cylinders. Unburned gases from the engine exit through the tailpipe. Replace filters as needed. Have your exhaust system inspected as part of a tune-up.

8. The battery is the source of electrical power. Alternators supply electricity to run engines, operate equipment, and recharge batteries. Voltage regulators control the amount of electricity. Distributors send electricity to spark plugs. Have regular tune-ups, keep headlights clean and aligned, and replace any burned-out bulbs.

9. Lubricating and cooling systems keep heat from destroying the engine by sending oil to moving engine parts. A mixture of fluid and antifreeze cools the engine.

   Change oil and oil filters regularly. Use coolant, and check the fluid level when the car is serviced.

LESSON FOUR

10. The suspension supports a car's weight, cushions the ride, and stabilizes the car; the steering system enables the front wheels to turn; brakes stop the car; tires help it grip the road.

11. Warnings include too much play in the wheel; front-end wobble; pulling to one side.

PROJECTS

1. In an owner's manual, find the sections that deal with the car systems discussed in this chapter. What information does the manual provide that applies specifically to the particular make and model car? In what other ways does the manual help the owner maintain the car?

2. Research and report on the various types of tires, including *radial*, *bias-ply*, and *belted* tires as well as snow tires and all-weather tires. What are the advantages and limitations of each? Why are people advised not to use radial tires in combination with other types of tires on the same car?

BUILDING SCIENCE SKILLS

Graphing Braking Distances

After you apply the brakes, the distance it takes to come to a stop depends in part on the speed at which your vehicle is moving.

The formula for figuring out braking distance is

$$D = S \times \frac{1}{10}S \div 2$$

where S = speed and D = distance in feet.

Here is how you would figure braking distance at 35 mph.

$$D = 35 \times (\tfrac{1}{10} \times 35) \div 2$$

$$D = 35 \times 3.5 \div 2$$

$$D = 61.25$$

So, braking distance at 35 mph is 61.25 feet, or a little over 20 yards.

Make a graph to show how braking distance changes in relation to speed.

Try It Yourself

1. First, use the formula to figure the stopping distance for these speeds:
20 mph   30 mph   40 mph   50 mph   60 mph

2. On a sheet of graph paper, write the speeds along the bottom of the graph at regular intervals, as shown below.

3. On the left side of the graph, write distances in regular intervals, as shown below.

4. For each distance you figure, put a dot at the appropriate place on your graph.

5. Finally, draw a line from the first dot to the second, from the second to the third, and so on, beginning with the dot at the shortest braking distance.

What conclusion can you draw from your graph?

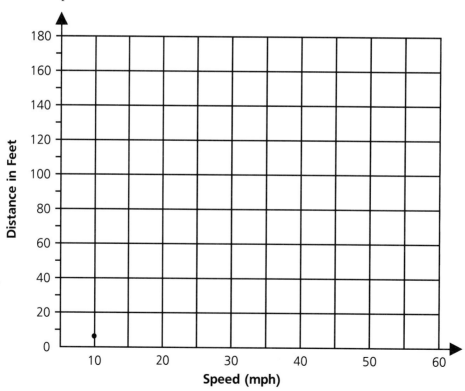

CHAPTER 16 REVIEW

CHAPTER TEST

Write the letter of the answer that best completes each sentence.

1. A fuel-injection system replaces a
   a. voltage regulator.
   b. carburetor.
   c. crankshaft.
2. You should check your engine oil
   a. while your engine is running.
   b. before your engine is running.
   c. every 12,000 miles.
3. Springs and shock absorbers are parts of a car's
   a. transmission.
   b. front-end alignment.
   c. suspension system.
4. Most cars' engines are known as
   a. a turbine engine.
   b. an external combustion engine.
   c. an internal combustion engine.
5. When you step on your brake pedal, you should feel
   a. firm resistance.
   b. no resistance.
   c. the floor.
6. Your car should have one major and one minor tune-up each year if you
   a. drive 10,000 to 12,000 miles during that period.
   b. drive less than 2,000 miles during that period.
   c. use high-octane gasoline.
7. You should rotate your car's tires to
   a. equalize tire wear.
   b. increase fuel efficiency.
   c. improve suspension.

8. Most cars today operate on
   a. lead-free gasoline.
   b. leaded gasoline.
   c. diesel fuel.
9. Many cars are equipped with
   a. a power clutch.
   b. drum brakes on the front wheels and disc brakes on the back wheels.
   c. disc brakes on the front wheels and drum brakes on the back wheels.
10. Your car's alternator
    a. controls suspension.
    b. mixes oxygen with gasoline.
    c. supplies electricity to keep the engine running.

Write the word or phrase that best completes each sentence.

    pistons   muffler   owner's manual
    hydraulic pressure   electrical system
                power train

11. The parts of your car that transmit the engine's power to the wheels make up the _____ .
12. The heart of a car's _____ is called the battery.
13. Brakes slow or stop a car by applying _____ against the four wheels.
14. Your _____ contains specific guidelines for servicing and maintaining your car.
15. The pipes that make up the exhaust manifold collect unburned gases from the engine and carry them to the _____ .

DRIVER'S LOG

In this chapter, you have learned how the systems that operate a car function and what the maintenance requirements of these systems are. Based on your observations, do most drivers pay attention to these maintenance requirements? Write a paragraph about what you would tell those who do not.

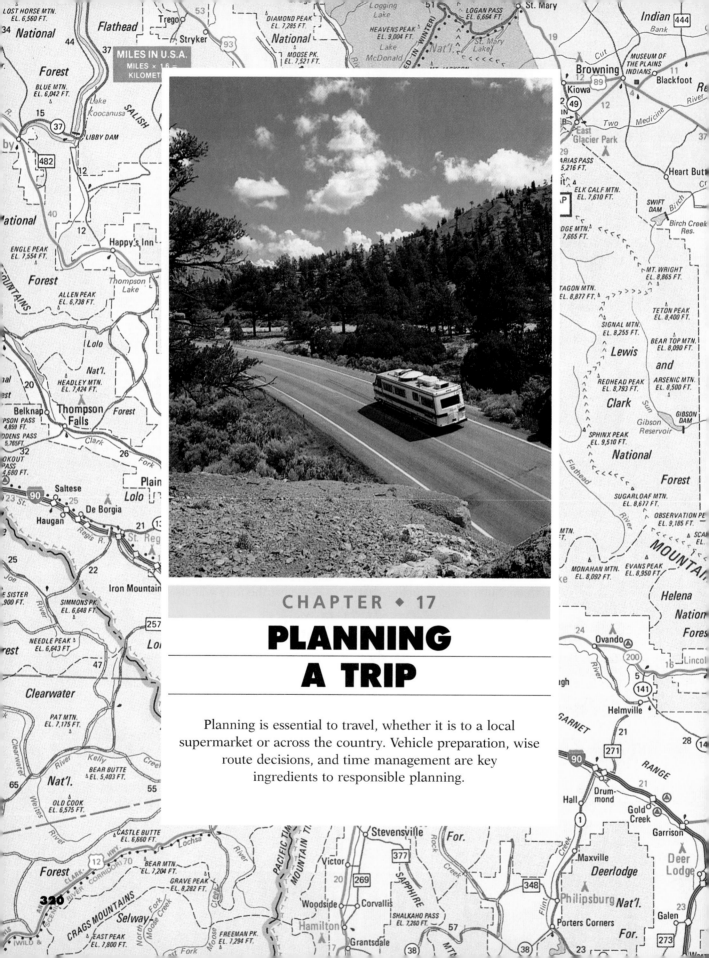

CHAPTER ◆ 17

PLANNING A TRIP

Planning is essential to travel, whether it is to a local supermarket or across the country. Vehicle preparation, wise route decisions, and time management are key ingredients to responsible planning.

CHAPTER 17 OBJECTIVES

Preparing Yourself and Your Car for a Short Trip

1. Describe how you would prepare yourself and your car for a short trip and the reasons for doing so.

Getting Ready for a Long Trip

2. Explain how you would get ready for a long trip and how you would prepare yourself and your car, as well as budget your money and plan your time.

Loading and Driving with a Trailer

3. Describe factors you should be aware of when planning to use a trailer.
4. Explain the procedures for driving a car with a trailer attached.

Driving Safely in a Recreational Vehicle

5. Explain the importance of visibility and vehicle size when driving a recreational vehicle, and describe how you can protect yourself and other motorists.

Preparing Yourself and Your Car for a Short Trip

Most traffic fatalities happen within 25 miles, or a short trip's distance, of the driver's home. Have you thought about ways to reduce your chances of being in a collision when you take a short trip away from home?

What Steps Should You Take When Planning a Short Trip?

A short trip can be a 5-mile drive to a neighborhood shopping center, a 2-mile drive to work or school, or a 45-mile trip to visit a relative who lives in another town. Even if you make the same trip every day, being prepared can help you reduce the risk of being in a collision.

Prepare Yourself

You need to make advance preparations for a trip even if you'll only be driving a short distance. Ask yourself these questions before you get into the car.

Do I know how to get where I'm going? If you are going someplace you have never been before, work out your route in advance. Make sure that you have specific directions to follow, and use a map to check them out. Know the names of the streets and roads that you have to follow. Make sure that you are able to drive on them in the direction you want to go.

Do I know another way to get there? Sometimes even the best plans just don't work out. Your planned route may be blocked for many reasons, so it's smart to have alternative plans to get where you're going by another route.

Do I have everything I need? Even though you will probably not take any luggage on a short trip, you may need some or all of the following items: identification; money; addresses; directions or a map; and a list of things to do, see, or buy.

Have I given myself enough time? Hurrying can make you nervous and careless. First figure out how long the trip should take, then add some time for the unexpected. You can anticipate some delays by listening to the radio for weather conditions and traffic reports.

Use a map to make sure you know how to get where you're going. ▼

Tips for New Drivers

Working a Self-Service Gas Pump

To operate a self-service gas pump, pull up to the pump that dispenses the kind of fuel your vehicle uses. If a sign says "Pay Cashier Before Pumping," the pumps will not operate until you pay. Otherwise, pump the amount you need, and pay when you are done.

1. Open the fuel filler door and take off the gas cap.
2. Take the pump nozzle off its cradle and place the nozzle in the fuel tank opening.
3. Turn on the pump switch. It is usually located near the pump nozzle cradle.
4. Squeeze the lever on the pump nozzle to begin pumping the fuel.
5. If you have pre-paid, the pump will shut off automatically. If not, shut the nozzle off and put it back on its cradle. Turn off the pump switch. Then put the gas cap back on and shut the fuel filler door.

Am I going at a good time? Try to avoid rush-hour traffic. There's no reason to get involved in a traffic jam if you don't absolutely have to. As you plan your route, remember that roads leading into urban areas will be busiest during the morning rush hours and roads leading out will be busiest in the evening rush hours.

Prepare Your Car

Every time you use your car, you should check to be sure that it is in proper condition to be driven. (See Chapter 6 for pre-driving checks.) You should check that:

♦ tires are properly inflated
♦ signal lights are working
♦ front and back lights are in order
♦ you have enough fuel and oil

Preparing yourself and your car for a trip does not take a lot of time. However, the time you spend in prep-aration will save you time and trouble in the long run.

CHECKPOINT

1. What are some helpful questions to ask yourself as you prepare for a short trip?

WHAT WOULD YOU DO?

You had last-minute errands and are going to be late for an appointment. What would you do next time to avoid this situation?

Getting Ready for a Long Trip

You face risk when you take a long trip, just as you do when you take a short trip. Fatigue, unfamiliarity with the area, and uncertain weather conditions are some factors that can increase driving risk on a long trip. Long trips also present you and your car with some different needs.

What Should You Do to Prepare for a Long Trip?

If you plan to take a long trip, some of the preparations you should make are similar to those you make for a short trip. Others, however, are important only when you are traveling long distances.

Prepare Yourself

Here are some questions that you should ask yourself to prepare for a long trip.

◆ **How will I get where I want to go?** You may choose the most direct route to your destination, or you may choose to drive on a more leisurely route through scenic country. Whichever you choose, plan your route carefully. Use a map and keep in mind the risks that each route may pose. The most direct route may involve expressway driving, where high speeds and large trucks present special problems. On the other hand, a scenic route may lead through congested towns or wilderness areas with no gas stations or places to stay.

ENERGY TIPS

Although a scenic route is more enjoyable, a route using limited-access roadways will be more energy efficient. You'll have fewer stops, starts, curves, and hills, and you'll be able to maintain a steady speed for longer periods of time.

Call ahead to make reservations at hotels or motels along your route and at your destination.
▶

BUDGET					
	Food	Lodging	Gas	Tolls	Parking	Recreation
Day 1	$75	$95	$18	$5	—	$20
Day 2	$120	$70	$15	—	$5	—
Day 3	$70	$80	$15	$3	—	$15

SCHEDULE					
	Depart		Average Speed	Arrive	
	Place	Time		Place	Time
Day 1	Holyoke	7:00 A.M.	40 mph	Boston	9:00 A.M.
Day 2	Boston	2:00 P.M.	45 mph	NYC	6:00 P.M.
Day 3	NYC	6:00 A.M.	45 mph	Washington, D.C.	11:00 A.M.

Plan your route before you start the trip. Don't try to read a map while you're moving on the roadway. If you need to check the map, pull into a rest area or onto the shoulder when it is safe to do so.

You may want to write to or visit an auto club or travel agency to obtain maps, route suggestions, and recommendations on places to stay.

◆ **Where will I spend the night while I am on the road?** Plan where you will spend each night, and make your reservations in advance. Ask about rates and parking facilities, and figure this information into your budget and schedule.

◆ **Have I had enough sleep the night before driving?** Be sure that you get enough rest before getting

behind the wheel. If you become tired while driving, pull over at a rest stop.

A good plan is to drive in two-hour stretches with 15-minute breaks in between. Don't try to drive more than a total of eight hours in a day. If you're traveling with a partner who also drives, share the driving task.

Budgeting Money and Planning Your Time

A long trip can be expensive. To figure out how much money you'll need, make a budget. Use the categories above, adding others if you need to. Figure your budget by the day or by the week. Your emergency supplies should include an extra set of

On most cars, the recommended tire pressures are located on either the right- or left- center posts. However, *never* exceed the maximum tire pressure stamped on the sidewalls of the tires themselves.

BEFORE THE TRIP CHECKLIST		
Emergency Supplies	**Professional Car Checkup**	**Maps and Travel Books**
extra fuses	brakes	city maps
gloves	transmission	state maps
duct tape	shocks	places of
flashlight		interest
first-aid kit		
keys		

WHAT WOULD YOU DO?

You and your family are about to take a three-week driving trip. What would you do to make this car trip-worthy?

car keys as well as replacements for or additions to supplies you normally carry in your trunk. (See Chapter 14 for a list of emergency supplies.)

Planning your travel time by making a schedule is also helpful. In making up your schedule, consider such factors as rush-hour traffic, speed limits, the kind of route you want to take, how far you want to drive at a time, and occasional stops for stretching, eating, and relaxing. Plan your driving time so that you avoid morning and early-evening rush-hour traffic.

Prepare Your Car

Your car should always be in good condition. However, before a long trip, you should have a mechanic check the following:

◆ brake shoes and pads
◆ exhaust-system leaks
◆ front-end alignment
◆ tire condition
◆ fluid levels in the engine, transmission, and battery
◆ shock absorbers
◆ belts and hoses

Pack the car carefully. Overloading can have an adverse effect on your car's handling, acceleration, and fuel efficiency.

Before you load your car, consult your owner's manual for the maximum weight load recommended per tire. Then be sure that your tires are inflated to the tire pressure recommended to carry any extra weight.

When you pack the car, follow these additional guidelines.

◆ The heaviest objects should be packed at the bottom of the trunk.
◆ If you use a car-top carrier, be sure to place only lighter objects in it.
◆ Do not put anything on the rear-window shelf that will obstruct your view of the roadway behind you or that can be thrown forward in a sudden stop. Do not hang clothing over the back-seat windows.

CHECKPOINT

2. How can making a budget and schedule help you plan a long trip? How can you prepare yourself and your car for a long trip?

Loading and Driving with a Trailer

Many drivers tow boats, campers, or other kinds of trailers behind their cars. Towing a trailer, however, can make the driving task more difficult.

What Do You Need to Know About Trailers?

Knowing some of the special features and needs of trailers can help you to minimize the risk when driving with one attached to your car.

Weight of the Trailer and Its Load

Many vehicles are limited in the amount of weight they can pull in a trailer. The weight of the car and the weight of the trailer must be carefully considered. Know the weight of the trailer you're planning to haul and the weight of its load, and check that your car has the power to haul it. Look in your owner's manual to be sure that you will not exceed the recommended factory load limits.

Necessary Equipment

If you intend to haul a trailer frequently, your car may need additional equipment, such as a heavy-duty suspension, a large-capacity radiator, and heavy-duty shock absorbers. For any size trailer, you will need to add mirrors on the car to increase visibility. You also need extra emergency equipment for heavier trailers. Extra equipment includes a hydraulic jack, blocks for holding on grades, and tow ropes.

To tow a trailer, the car needs a hitch and safety chains. For ordinary loads, use a hitch that is welded

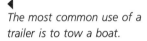

The poorest trailer hitch is a bumper attachment unit. Do not use this kind of hitch for anything except the very lightest loads.

◀

The most common use of a trailer is to tow a boat.

Preparing Your Car to Tow a Trailer

The increased load that a trailer puts on your car means that you will need to check your oil and transmission fluid more often than usual. You will also need to replace air, oil, and fuel filters sooner than you ordinarily would. In addition, you may need to increase the air pressure in your tires.

Packing a Trailer

The rear end of your car will have to support 10 to 15 percent of the trailer load. Therefore, the car itself should carry 10 to 15 percent less than the maximum weight recommended by the owner's manual. Too much weight in the back of the car will cause its front to rise and will affect steering, braking, and the aim of the headlights.

When you pack the trailer, follow manufacturer's guidelines. Load the heaviest items at the bottom, over the trailer wheels. About 60 percent of the weight should be packed in the front half of the trailer, and the total weight should be about equal from

▲
Be sure to use safety chains when you hitch a trailer to your car.

or bolted to the frame of the car. You can buy such a hitch from auto supply outlets or through a car dealership. For heavier loads, there are special hitches for load equalizing. When your hitch is installed, make sure that also installed is an electrical outlet for the trailer's taillights, stoplights, and turn signals. More information about installing hitches can be found in the trailer's manual.

THE SOCIAL STUDIES CONNECTION

To drive in many foreign countries, all you need is your valid driver's license and a tourist visa for the country you'll be visiting. However, an international driving permit is accepted nearly everywhere. An international driving permit is especially useful if you do not speak the language of the country you'll be driving in.

You can request an application for an international driving permit from your local American Automobile Association (AAA) in writing, or go there in person. The AAA is the only authorized organization in the United States that can issue such a permit.

To obtain an international driving permit, you need to fill out an application form, have a passport-size photograph taken, pay the appropriate fee, and show proof that you have a valid driver's license from your state.

◀
Pack a trailer so that 60 percent of the load is in the front half.

side to side. Be sure to pack all items tightly or tie them so that they cannot shift during driving maneuvers.

After you have loaded the trailer, check what you have done. The bottoms of both the car and the trailer should be nearly parallel to the ground. The back springs of the car should not be extended so that its front end rises. On the road stop frequently at rest stops to make sure that the load and the hitch are still secure.

How Do You Drive a Car with a Trailer Attached?

No matter how skillful you are behind the wheel of a car, towing a trailer requires new driving skills and plenty of practice.

Starting

Your car's maneuverability and acceleration are limited when you're towing a trailer. Check traffic carefully and signal before moving. Allow a very large gap before entering traffic. Start slowly, and check other traffic movement in the rearview and side mirrors frequently.

Backing

Backing is a difficult maneuver when you're towing a trailer. Before you begin, get out of your car and check behind the trailer to be sure that the way is clear. Try to have someone guide you from outside the car.

If you are pulling a trailer, you will need twice the distance to merge into traffic, to pass another vehicle, or to stop.

Practice backing with a trailer before you actually need to do it.
▼

Turn wheel this way to make trailer go right.

Turn wheel this way to make trailer go left.

The wheel may be civilization's most important technological development. The wheel is believed to have been invented in about 3500 B.C. Its invention is credited to the Sumerians, a civilization that developed in the Tigris-Euphrates Valley in what is now known as Iraq.

It is easier to turn while backing up if the trailer turns to the left side of your car. This way, you can see the trailer over your left shoulder.

Follow these guidelines to back with a trailer.

♦ Back slowly.
♦ To go left, turn the steering wheel to the *right* and then straighten it.
♦ To go right, turn the steering wheel to the *left* and then straighten the wheel.
♦ Don't turn the steering wheel too much or hold it in the turned position too long. Doing so can cause the trailer to jackknife.

Making a Right Turn

As you approach an intersection where you want to turn right, follow these steps.
1. Check traffic and signal for the right turn in advance of the intersection.
2. Take a position farther from the curb than you would if you didn't have a trailer attached.
3. Steer the car straight ahead until the front wheels are well beyond the curb line.

4. Turn the steering wheel sharply right.
5. Complete the turn by straightening the steering wheel.

Making a Left Turn

To turn left, follow these steps.
1. Check traffic and signal early.
2. Proceed farther into the intersection than usual, to allow for the trailer.
3. Swing wide enough so that the trailer will not cut the corner.
4. Complete the turn and move into traffic.

Overtaking and Passing

When you plan to overtake and pass another vehicle, allow much more time and space because of the length and weight of the trailer.
1. Be sure that there is plenty of clear distance ahead.
2. Check blind spots to the left and right before starting.
3. After passing, be sure you can see the overtaken vehicle in the rearview or side-view mirrors before signaling and moving gradually back into the right lane.

Don't swerve suddenly. Doing so may cause the trailer to tilt, sway, or even go out of control.

Being Overtaken

When you are being passed by a light vehicle, observe the same rules that you do in a car. (See Chapter 8.) However, if a heavy vehicle is passing you, the air that it displaces will tend to push the trailer to the side. Be ready to adjust your steering. If you notice traffic piling up behind you,

Changing a Trailer Flat

Changing a tire on a trailer is different from changing a tire on a car. A typical trailer only has two tires, although some have four. When you jack up a two-tire trailer to remove one tire, the trailer balances on the other tire and the hitch. The trailer may fall off the jack. To manage this risk, put a block between the frame of the trailer and the ground to stabilize the trailer.

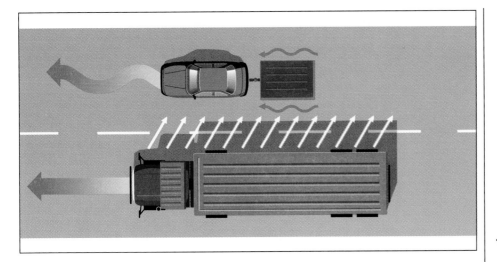

The draft from large vehicles can make a trailer move from side to side. Be ◀ ready to adjust steering.

try to find a place to stop and pull off the roadway. Be courteous and help other drivers to pass you.

Slowing and Stopping

If your trailer does not have brakes, the brakes on your car control all slowing and stopping. If the trailer does have brakes, then your car's brakes control the trailer's brakes. Be sure to practice braking before entering traffic.

The additional weight and length of the trailer means that you will need more time and space to stop. When you do enter traffic, allow a greater following distance than you ordinarily would.

If you have never driven with a trailer before, practice in an empty lot or on a lightly traveled roadway until you are sure you have the skills necessary to handle the extra load. Don't just get in your car and start driving on a high-speed roadway!

Before driving with a trailer, check your insurance to be sure that you are covered for towing a trailer. Also check the laws about trailers in states that you will be traveling through. Be

aware that in some states, passengers may not ride in a trailer while it is in motion. If you will be driving with passengers in the trailer, have safety belts or harnesses installed, and be sure your passengers use them.

CHECKPOINT

3. Why is it important to pack a trailer carefully?
4. Describe some of the ways in which driving with a trailer is different from driving without one.

WHAT WOULD YOU DO?

You want to make a left turn. What would you do?

Driving Safely in a Recreational Vehicle

A recreational vehicle, or RV, is not just a big toy. Recreational vehicles are heavier, longer, more powerful, and potentially more dangerous than most cars. Vans, caps on pickup trucks, and large motor homes are among the types of RVs.

How Do You Drive Recreational Vehicles?

Before you drive any recreational vehicle, you need to know its special features and requirements.

Visibility

Drivers of RVs can see farther ahead than drivers of cars because they are sitting higher. This gives RV drivers an advantage in planning driving strategy.

Although the ability to see ahead is improved when driving a recreational vehicle, visibility to the rear can be a problem because RVs are wider than ordinary cars. To overcome this problem, adjust the large mirrors on the sides of the vehicle to be sure that you have maximum visibility in all directions.

Vehicle Size

Recreational vehicles are wider and higher than cars. This greater width and height, and the greater weight of RVs, pose special problems that you must learn to deal with in order to manage risk.

SAFETY TIPS

If you're driving an RV or have a trailer attached to your car, keep to the right on a left curve, in order to keep the vehicle from crossing the center line. Reduce speed for better vehicle control.

Because you sit higher in an RV, you can see farther ahead than you do in a car.
▶

CLEARANCE 16'-6"

◀
*Look for signs on
underpasses that tell you
what the maximum
clearance is.*

Be alert for wind. Recreational vehicles tend to sway in heavy winds because of their greater height and their higher center of gravity. Slow down or stop, if possible, if the wind is strong and you are having trouble controlling the vehicle.

Know the height of your vehicle. Remember, you are driving a vehicle that is much higher than a car. Be alert to anything above the roadway, including tree branches and overhanging wires. Look for signs that indicate height restrictions for tunnels or underpasses. Do not attempt to maneuver the vehicle through a too low tunnel or underpass. Instead, if traffic is light and it is legal, make a turnabout. If you are traveling on an expressway, signal, and move well off the roadway. Wait for a police officer to assist you off the expressway.

Know the weight of the fully- loaded vehicle. Many bridges are posted with signs that show the maximum allowable tonnage per vehicle. You increase risk enormously if you try to cross a bridge when your vehicle is over the weight limit.

Protecting Other Motorists

Adjust your driving to take into account that you are driving a larger and wider vehicle than most of the others on the road. Maintain a greater margin of space around the vehicle. Keep in mind that you may be blocking the visibility of other drivers. Take this into consideration when you spot potentially threatening conditions ahead that cars behind you may not see.

Increase your following distance to give yourself more time to maneuver and stop. Manage the risk to yourself

More than half of all deaths of passenger vehicle occupants occur on Friday, Saturday, and Sunday. Keep this in mind when planning recreational trips.

On roads curving to the right, steer farther from the edge of the pavement than usual. Otherwise the wheels of your RV or trailer may drop to the shoulder, causing a dangerous sway or tire damage.

Deborah Ranson, Director,
National Travel, AAA

Deborah Ranson, Director

Allow sufficient time to get to your destination to avoid feeling rushed and making last minute decisions. Keep a sufficient amount of fuel in your vehicle—you may not know how long it is to the next service station. Plan your stops so that you don't find yourself in an area where suitable accommodations cannot be found. Select a map that offers the proper level of detail to ensure that you can find your way safely. Check the map for toll roads to make certain you have enough cash to get to your destination.

WHAT WOULD YOU DO?

Before pulling out, what would you do to check the vehicle?

and to others by staying alert and allowing extra time and space to accomplish driving maneuvers.

Protecting Yourself

Driving long distances is always strenuous and requires frequent rest stops and careful planning. Because of a recreational vehicle's size and difficulty in maneuvering, you will get tired even more quickly than when you are driving a car. Manage risk to yourself and your passengers by planning to drive shorter distances and resting more often than you would if you were driving a car. If possible, share driving duties.

As with a trailer, check your insurance to be sure that you are covered for driving a recreational vehicle. Also check the laws about RVs in all of the states that you will be driving through. Install safety belts in the living quarters of the RV, and insist that passengers who ride there use the belts.

CHECKPOINT

5. How do the size and weight of a recreational vehicle make driving it more difficult than driving an ordinary car?

CHAPTER 17 REVIEW

KEY POINTS

LESSON ONE

1. To prepare yourself for a short trip, have good directions or a map, know an alternate route, take all the items you need, allow extra time, and avoid rush-hour traffic. To prepare your car, be sure that tires are properly inflated, signal lights are working, front and back lights are in order, and that you have enough gas and oil. You need to prepare for a short trip in order to reduce the risk of a collision.

LESSON TWO

2. Prepare yourself for a long trip by planning your route, making a budget and schedule, making reservations, and being sure you get enough rest.

Prepare your car by having it checked by a mechanic and making sure you have adequate emergency equipment. Pack the car carefully.

LESSON THREE

3. When planning to use a trailer, consider the weight of the trailer and its load and whether your car has the power to haul it. Be sure you have the proper hitch and any additional necessary equip-ment. Check the engine and transmission more often than usual. Pack the trailer so that 60 percent of the load is in the front half and the heaviest items are on the bottom, making sure the load is secure. Do not load your car to its maximum capacity.

4. To start a car with a trailer attached, check traffic, signal, allow a very large gap when entering traffic, and start slowly. To back with a trailer, move slowly and turn the wheel left when going right and right when going left. To turn, signal early, position the car beyond the curb line, and turn the steering wheel so that the trailer does not cut the corner. Allow extra time and space to pass, to be passed, and to slow and stop.

LESSON FOUR

5. Although RV drivers can see farther ahead than car drivers, they must compensate for the RV's width by using larger mirrors. The size of the RV may cause problems in winds, under overpasses, and on bridges. Protect yourself by resting often, driving shorter distances, and making sure you have proper insurance. Protect other motorists by increasing your following distance and allowing an extra margin of space.

PROJECTS

1. Choose four neighboring states through which you might drive to take a trip. Find out what their laws are about trailers and recreational vehicles. Compare other state laws with the laws in your own state. Prepare a report on their differences and similarities.

2. Find out where your ancestors lived or where they entered this country. Plan a trip to that place. Plot out your route, and make a budget and schedule. Visit an auto club or travel agency for advice. Mark your route on a map for display and report on your travel plans.

CHAPTER 17 REVIEW

BUILDING MAP SKILLS

Reading City Maps

Driving in a new city is often very confusing. Sometimes, merely figuring out how to get in and out of a city is puzzling.

Most maps have insets that show major cities in larger scale. Below is an inset map of Wichita, Kansas.

Suppose you are coming into Wichita from the north, on Interstate 135. To get to the Court House, you would leave Route 96 at the interchange for Central Avenue. Then you would head west to the intersection of Central Avenue and Broadway. To get from the Court House to Watson Park, you would drive about 3 miles south on Broadway.

Try It Yourself

1. Locate Wichita State University on the map. How would you get from there to Friends University?

2. Suppose you are at the airport. How would you drive to Planeview Park?

3. How would you get from the corner of 25th Street and Amidon Avenue to the Wichita Art Association?

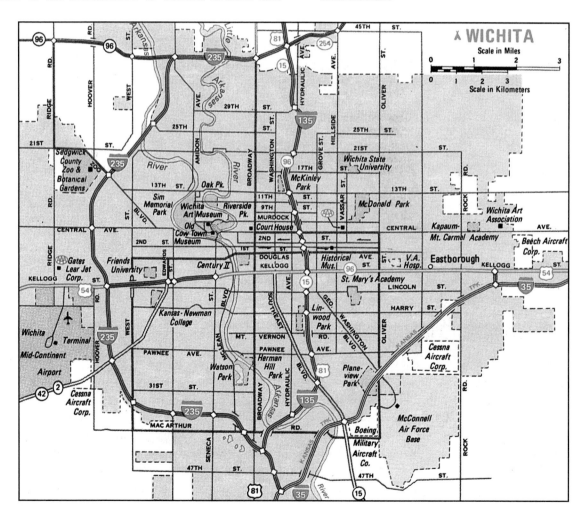

CHAPTER 17 REVIEW

CHAPTER TEST

Choose the letter of the answer that best completes each sentence.

1. When packing a trailer, 60 percent of the load should be
   a. over the wheels.
   b. in the front half of the trailer.
   c. at the bottom of the trailer.

2. You should not drive more than a total of
   a. eight hours a day.
   b. five hours a day.
   c. twelve hours a day.

3. Most traffic fatalities occur
   a. within 50 miles of the driver's home.
   b. within 25 miles of the driver's home.
   c. when a car is changing lanes.

4. If you are going someplace you have never gone before, you should
   a. use a road map while you are driving.
   b. stop periodically to ask directions.
   c. plan your route ahead of time.

5. If you haul a trailer frequently, you may need
   a. a hydraulic jack.
   b. a car-top carrier.
   c. a boat.

6. You can anticipate some delays by
   a. using a map.
   b. having an alternate route.
   c. listening to the radio for traffic and weather reports.

7. Before starting on a long trip, you should
   a. choose the quickest route.
   b. choose the most leisurely route.
   c. keep in mind the risks that each route may have.

8. You can make a schedule to
   a. know when to exceed the speed limit.
   b. plan your travel time.
   c. keep track of how much money you spend on a trip.

9. When backing a trailer
   a. turn right to go left.
   b. turn left to go left.
   c. look over your right shoulder.

10. Drivers of RVs can see farther ahead because they
    a. are sitting higher than in a car.
    b. have an advantage in planning driving strategy.
    c. use extra large mirrors.

Write the word or phrase that best completes each sentence.

overloading   following distance
restrictions   trailer hitch
shock absorbers   urban areas

11. Roads leading into ____ are busiest during the morning rush hour.

12. ____ can have an adverse effect on your car's acceleration.

13. Have a mechanic check for worn ____ before a long trip.

14. Use a ____ that is welded or bolted to the frame of your car.

15. When you drive an RV, you should increase your ____ .

DRIVER'S LOG

In this chapter, you have learned how to plan long and short trips and how to safely drive recreational vehicles and tow trailers. Make a personal checklist to remind you of considerations that you would take into account when planning a cross-country trip in a recreational vehicle.

GETTING READY: YOUR STATE DRIVING TEST

You have learned a great deal about driving that will help you with your state's driving test. It is important that you know how to prepare yourself and your car for the test. Understanding how to prepare will help you to succeed.

CHAPTER 18 OBJECTIVES

LESSON ONE

Getting Ready for the Knowledge Test

1. Name four ways in which you can prepare yourself for the knowledge test, and describe how you would go about implementing each.

LESSON TWO

Getting Ready for the In-Vehicle Test

2. List three preparations you can make for the in-vehicle test, and explain how to carry out each of the preparations.

LESSON THREE

Getting the Vehicle Ready for the Test

3. Name two ways in which you can prepare your car for the in-vehicle test, and list the actions you should take before and on the day of the test.

LESSON FOUR

Taking the Final Test: The In-Vehicle Test

4. Name at least four guidelines to keep in mind when taking the in-vehicle test, and describe in detail what each guideline entails.

Getting Ready for the Knowledge Test

FYI

The first drivers' licenses in the United States were issued by the Board of Examiners of Operators of Automobiles in Chicago, Illinois on July 6, 1899.

To qualify for a driver's license, you have to show that you know the traffic laws in your state and that you have basic control of a motor vehicle. In addition to a vision test, you must pass a knowledge or written test and a driving performance test. Application and testing procedures for obtaining a driver's license vary from state to state. To find out what the requirements are where you live, check your state driver's manual or ask your driver education instructor.

In a number of states, your driver education teacher will administer the in-vehicle performance test, or road test, after you have passed a knowledge test. In some states your teacher will arrange for an examiner to come to your school to give the test. In both of these cases, you will take your in-vehicle performance test in the car you've been using during the driver education course. In other states, you must make your own arrangements with the department of motor vehicles to take all the necessary tests.

How Can You Prepare for the Knowledge Test?

Getting ready to take the knowledge test for your driver's license is not much different from preparing for a test in school. Study the material in advance, be well rested when you take the test, and think carefully before answering the questions.

Study Wisely

Your state driver's manual contains the information that you will need in order to study for the knowledge test. Follow these guidelines for studying the manual.

◆ Read one section at a time. Use a marker to highlight important information you think may be on the test, or keep a notebook in which you write this information.

◆ Reread the section and summarize it for yourself. Write your summary in your notebook.

◆ Study with someone else who is going to take the test, or ask a friend or family member to quiz you on information from the manual.

◆ Take the sample test, if there is one in your state's manual. If there's anything in the manual that you don't understand, ask your driver education instructor to explain it to you.

◆ Review the chapter and unit tests in this book. Look up the answers if you don't remember them.

Budget your study time. Don't wait until the last minute and then try to cram for the test. Figure out how much time you have to study. Then decide how much time you'll devote to studying each day or week, perhaps leaving additional study time just before you take the test.

Keep in mind that the real purpose of studying the driver's manual is not just to pass the test. Your true goal is to learn driving rules and safe practices so that you can be a responsible driver.

THE SCIENCE CONNECTION

In the late 1800s Hermann Ebbinghaus conducted the first experiments to find out how human memory works. He found that the mind rapidly forgets information it has learned recently unless the learning is repeated frequently. His studies showed that each relearning takes much less time than the initial learning and slows the process of forgetting.

Get Yourself Ready Physically

Get a good night's sleep before the test. No matter how much you have learned, you'll never pass the test if you're too sleepy to think clearly.

Don't skip meals before taking the test. Eating right will keep your energy level high and help you focus your thoughts.

Bring the Necessary Papers

If you have to go to the department of motor vehicles office to take your test, you will have to bring several documents with you. You'll need proof of age and identity. The best proof of both is your birth certificate.

Some states require that you bring proof of having satisfactorily completed a course in driver education if you are under age 18 or 19. In most cases, a parent or some other adult who has a driver's license will have to accompany you.

Check the driver's manual or call the department of motor vehicles beforehand to find out the specific documents your state requires. People who work for a state's department of motor vehicles usually allow no exceptions to the rules. If the manual says to bring your Social Security card with you, then be sure to do so. Failure to bring necessary documents may result in your not being able to take the test.

Stay Calm

As you prepare for the knowledge test and on the day that you actually take it, stay calm.

Read each question carefully, and take time to think before selecting your answer. If you get stuck on a question, skip it and return to it later.

Don't let a tough question throw off your concentration. Just relax and keep going.

CHECKPOINT

1. How can you plan to study for the knowledge test?

WHAT WOULD YOU DO?

A friend tells you to skim through the manual right before the knowledge test, and cross your fingers. Is this good advice? Why or why not?

Getting Ready for the In-Vehicle Test

While most states still give road tests in actual traffic, some states do all their testing on closed courses. These tests stress parallel parking, turns, and turnabouts.

Passing the knowledge test is an important step toward obtaining your driver's license. The next step is demonstrating your driving ability during an in-vehicle test (sometimes called a road test).

How Can You Prepare for the In-Vehicle Test?

To pass the in-vehicle or road test, you need to show the examiner that you have a working knowledge of the rules of the road and that you have mastered basic driving skills. As with most tests, the key to success is advance preparation.

Know What You're Doing

Practice, practice, practice—that's the best advice for preparing for the in-vehicle test. The more hours you spend behind the wheel, the more skilled and confident you will become as a driver.

When you practice driving, ask the person you're with to point out any areas in which you might need improvement. Spend extra time perfecting maneuvers you may find difficult, such as parallel parking or shifting a manual transmission smoothly. Determine if there are maneuvers, such as three-point turns, that are always covered in your locality. Practice these maneuvers as well.

Be alert for road signs as you practice. Be sure you understand what each sign means and what procedures you should follow at each. Review your driver's manual if you're uncertain about any sign or traffic rule.

Remember, too, that driving is more than just a series of physical movements. Becoming a good driver means exhibiting sound judgment and decision-making skills. In other words, knowing how to make a left turn is important, but knowing when it's safe to make the turn is even more important.

If possible, practice driving in the same vehicle in which you will take your test. Ideally, this should also be the vehicle you'll be driving *after* you get your license. At the very least, your practice vehicle should be similar to the one you'll be using. If, for example, you'll be using a stick shift on the day of the test, be sure to practice in a stick shift vehicle.

Tips for New Drivers

Practicing for the In-Vehicle Test

When practicing your driving, remember to practice all the skills you may need to demonstrate, such as:

- parallel parking
- starting and stopping smoothly
- shifting gears
- backing up safely
- turning
- passing
- following at a safe distance
- signaling
- turnabouts

Practice the maneuvers you find especially difficult, such as backing or three-point turns.

Be Alert and Ready

Many of the same suggestions made earlier about preparing yourself for the knowledge test apply for the in-vehicle test. To be at your best, get a solid night's sleep before the day of the test, and don't skip meals before the test.

Bring What You Need

For the in-vehicle test, you will need certain documents. Your state may require you to present your valid driver's permit as well as proof of vehicle registration and adequate insurance for the vehicle you're driving. You may also need proof that the vehicle has been properly inspected and has passed an emissions test. Check your state driver's manual to learn what documents your state requires.

Also take along enough money or a check to pay the licensing fees, and any other items you may need, such as a seat or back cushion and your prescription glasses or sunglasses, if you need to wear them when you drive.

CHECKPOINT

2. Why is it important to practice in the same vehicle you'll be using to take the test?

?

WHAT WOULD YOU DO?

Your in-vehicle test is exactly one week away. What will you do between now and then to prepare for the test?

Getting the Vehicle Ready for the Test

If you're not going to take your in-vehicle test in the school's driver training car, you will have to provide the vehicle. Be sure the one you use is as ready for the test as you are.

How Can You Get the Test Vehicle Ready?

The vehicle you drive for your test should be in top condition. The vehicle should be cleaned inside and out. All windows should be in good condition, and the door handles should work properly. In addition, the vehicle should be in good mechanical condition. The last thing you need on the day of your test is a mechanical or other problem.

Choose Your Car Wisely

If you have a choice of which vehicle you'll use for your test, choose one that is in good all-around condition and that you feel comfortable driving.

Remember that you may have to show proof that the vehicle is registered and insured and that it has been properly inspected and has passed an emissions test. Do *not* bring a vehicle to the test that:

- you have seldom or never driven
- frequently stalls
- restricts your ability to see
- doesn't have safety belts
- has muffler problems
- you have difficulty getting into or out of

Check Out the Vehicle in Advance

Before the day of the test, make basic predriving checks on:

- defroster/defogger
- brakes

Be sure that your mirrors are clean and that you adjust them properly.

▶

Tips for New Drivers

Choosing a Vehicle for the Test

Suppose you have practiced in and are equally comfortable driving two cars, both of which are in good mechanical condition. Which car should you choose to use for your in-vehicle test? Here are some tips that may make your decision easier.

• Choose a car with an automatic transmission over one with a manual transmission. Nervousness can make you have trouble coordinating the clutch, the gearshift, and the accelerator.
• Choose a smaller car over a larger car. Smaller cars are generally easier to maneuver than larger cars.
• Choose a conservative, family-type car over a sports car or "souped-up" vehicle. Make a good first impression on the examiner.

◆ clutch and gas pedals
◆ lights
◆ horn
◆ fluid levels
◆ tire pressure
◆ windshield wipers and washer fluid

By checking out the test vehicle in advance, you can make sure that whatever is not in good working order will be fixed in time for the test. Be sure you know where all the controls are and how to operate them.

On the day of the test:

◆ clean the interior of the vehicle
◆ clean the windows
◆ adjust and clean the mirrors
◆ clean the lights
◆ verify that you have enough fuel

Remove any obstructions from inside the car, such as packages or hanging ornaments. Be sure your vehicle's safety belts are working properly.

To review other suggestions for ad-vance preparation of your vehicle, see Chapter 6 and Chapter 16.

CHECKPOINT

3. Why is it important to check out your vehicle in advance of taking the test?

WHAT WOULD YOU DO?

Which car would you choose for your test next week? Explain your choice.

LESSON FOUR

Taking the Final Test:
The In-Vehicle Test

The big day has finally arrived: You're taking the in-vehicle test for your driver's license. You've practiced driving for many hours, but you feel nervous just the same. You want to pass the test on your first try.

What Should You Do Once You're Sitting Behind the Wheel?

The examiner who rides with you on your test will evaluate your skill at handling the car as well as your ability to drive safely and responsibly. In most states you will fail the test automatically if you violate a traffic law or commit a dangerous act.

Make All Necessary Adjustments First

Before you start the engine, recheck the adjustments to see if any are needed.

◆ Make sure your seat is adjusted so that you have a clear view of the road and can reach the accelerator and brake pedals comfortably. If you use a seat or back cushion, put it in place.
◆ Make sure your head restraint is correctly adjusted.
◆ Make sure the rearview and side-view mirrors are positioned for maximum visibility.
◆ Make certain that no objects inside the car are blocking your view.
◆ Fasten your safety belt.

Follow these procedures after you've started the engine.

◆ If necessary, turn on window defrosters and windshield wipers.
◆ Turn on the low-beam headlights.
◆ If the radio is on, turn it off.
◆ Check your mirrors and blind spots before starting to drive.

Concentrate on What You're Doing

Follow these guidelines for keeping your mind on your driving during the in-vehicle test.

Listen carefully to any instructions. Follow the examiner's instructions exactly. If you don't understand

SAFETY TIPS

If your car has automatic shoulder belts, be sure you also fasten your lap belt for maximum protection.

Concentrate on your driving and the examiner's intructions during the in-vehicle test.

▼

something the examiner says, ask for clarification.

Don't chat with the examiner. During the test, the examiner may hardly speak to you. Don't let it bother you if your examiner is the silent type. This may just be his or her personality. On the other hand, if your examiner is talkative and asks you a lot of questions, don't let that distract you from concentrating on driving.

Don't worry about what the examiner is writing. During the test, expect the examiner to be writing and making notes on a form. Don't assume the examiner is being critical. Many categories have to be tested and noted. The examiner may be writing favorable comments too.

Don't let a mistake throw you. If you make a mistake, maintain your concentration. Don't let a minor error rattle you so much that you make a worse mistake. If you're going through a complicated maneuver, move the car slowly, paying special attention to the gear you're in, the direction your wheels are turned, and the obstacles and traffic around you.

Stay Calm

Because this is an important test and you care about the results, you are going to be nervous. This is natural. But you can do some things to minimize your nervousness and help you concentrate on your driving.

Be well prepared. If you have practiced a great deal, you should be prepared for the in-vehicle test. Thorough preparation is the best defense against making mistakes during the test.

Don't Rush Yourself

Once you get your license, you may have the urge to drive under more challenging circumstances than those you encountered in the in-vehicle test.

Regardless of how well you have done in your driver education course, you still have a lot to learn. It takes about five years for a new driver to gain the experience necessary to make quality judgments and decisions.

You can still drive responsibly, however. Resist the urge to drive beyond your capabilities. For the next several months, you should continue to practice driving with a licensed adult in the car. Practice under low-stress conditions until you have enough experience to tackle more difficult driving situations. Remember that when you're behind the wheel, you have assumed responsibility for yourself and for others. Take that responsibility seriously: Lives depend on it.

Admit that you're nervous. It's helpful to admit that you're nervous in a situation that is making you tense. Even though you've prepared thoroughly, be aware of how you feel, and don't be afraid to tell your examiner. Don't be disappointed, however, if the examiner does not reassure you.

Have a positive attitude. Remember that you are well prepared. Be confident that you are going to do your best.

Bring support. The licensed driver who drives you to the test should be positive, optimistic, supportive, and calm. However, do not expect that the person will be allowed to accompany you while you are taking the in-vehicle test.

Breathe deeply. Pay attention to the way you're breathing. When you

Don't rev the engine when you are stopped at a stop sign or red light or while you are stopped in traffic. Revving the engine wastes fuel and can annoy the examiner.

Judy L. Alton, Sergeant, Texas Department of Public Safety

Judy L. Alton

When you take the in-vehicle test, try to relax. Imagine that the examiner is your best friend. In Texas we grade on four categories: control, observation, position, and signaling. Controlling the vehicle is knowing how to handle it. Observation is making sure you look at all times—turn your head so the examiner can tell when you are looking. Position has to do with always maintaining the proper lane position. You should signal to make a turn or lane change and also with your horn if you need to give a warning.

WHAT WOULD YOU DO?

The examiner is ready for you to begin the in-vehicle test. What actions would you take before starting the engine?

are anxious, you tend to hold your breath. Deep breathing keeps the oxygen moving through your system and helps you stay calm.

Exercise Good Judgment

Show the examiner that you are a mature, responsible person. Always be courteous, both to the examiner and to the pedestrians and other drivers you may meet on the roadway. Above all, don't smoke while you are taking the in-vehicle test.

Demonstrate the skills you learned in your driver education course. Allow yourself plenty of time to pull out into traffic. Search the path ahead for any object or condition that could raise the level of risk. Follow other cars at a proper distance. Be alert for traffic control devices, and remember to signal your intentions.

CHECKPOINT

4. How can you concentrate and stay calm during the in-vehicle test?

CHAPTER 18 REVIEW

KEY POINTS

LESSON ONE

1. To prepare for the knowledge test, study your state driver's manual thoroughly. Read one section at a time and summarize it, study with a friend, and take any sample tests. Go for the test well rested, and take with you any documents you may need such as a birth certificate, social security card, learner's permit, vehicle registration, and proof of inspection and insurance coverage. When you take the test, stay calm, read each question carefully, and take time to think before selecting your answer.

LESSON TWO

2. To prepare for the in-vehicle test, practice driving as much as you can, preferably in the same vehicle that you will take your test in. Be alert and ready by getting a good night's sleep before the day of the test and not skipping meals. Bring what you need, including correct documentation, money or a check, and other necessary items such as sunglasses and cushions.

LESSON THREE

3. Be sure the vehicle you choose for the test is in top condition. Make predriving checks in advance before the day of the in-vehicle test by checking the brakes, fluid levels, pedals, lights, horn, tires, defoggers and windshield wipers. On the day of the test, make sure that your vehicle's windows, mirrors, lights and interior are clean.

LESSON FOUR

4. When taking the in-vehicle test, first make all necessary adjustments before you start to drive: seat, head restraint, mirrors, and safety belt. Stay calm. Be prepared, admit you're nervous, be positive, bring support, and breathe deeply. Concentrate on what you are doing while you are driving. Listen carefully to the examiner, don't chat with him or her, and try not to worry.

PROJECTS

1. Interview two or three people who have acquired their driver's licenses within the past year. Find out the maneuvers they were required to make for the in-vehicle test. Ask what was easiest and hardest about the test. Discuss your findings with your class.

2. Write five questions that you think may be on your state's knowledge test. Exchange questions with a partner in your class. Try to answer your partner's questions. Check your answers and your partner's answers in your state driver's manual.

BUILDING CRITICAL THINKING SKILLS

The High Cost of Fuel

Oil, the precious resource that is the source of the gasoline that powers our automobiles, has been the cause of a confusing mixture of benefits and drawbacks to the Inuits and Eskimos of Alaska. In the 1800s, these native peoples witnessed the exploration of their homeland by navigators searching for a quick Arctic sea route from the "New World" to the wealth of Asia. This sea route, the Northwest Passage, was finally traveled in 1903 by the Norwegian explorer Roald Amundsen.

Today, the Inuit are affected by another exploration—the search for oil in the waters of the Northwest Passage. With the discovery of oil at Prudhoe Bay on Alaska's north coast, human-made oil-drilling islands have been built amidst the 18,000 islands of the 4,000 mile long Northwest Passage.

The trans-Alaska pipeline carries the oil from Prudhoe Bay to ports in Southern Alaska where it is transferred to huge icebreaking tankers that carry the oil to refineries outside of Alaska.

For many of the Inuit, the frozen-over sea is like the land. Driving a ship through it is like driving a bulldozer across a farmer's field. The tankers also pose a danger to the environment such as that caused when the *Exxon Valdez* struck a reef and poured 10.9 million gallons of crude oil into Prince William Sound. The oil destroyed much of the wildlife that lived in these waters and was absorbed in the gravel beaches along the rocky shoreline.

The threat to the environment and to their way of life are somewhat balanced by the increased income and other material gains that oil has brought to the Native American of Alaska. In the Alaskan Native Claims Settlement Act of 1971, the U.S. government gave Alaskans with at least one Native-American grandparent a share in the oil-rich lands.

The Inuit are in the forefront of a movement that while recognizing the need for oil and its economic benefit, also recognizes the need to protect the environment against pollution. The threat of pollution has been an important topic in the five Inuit Circumpolar Conferences held since 1977 to discuss the future of Arctic peoples.

What Do You Think Now?

How can the need for oil and the economic advantages it brings be balanced by the need to protect and preserve the environment?

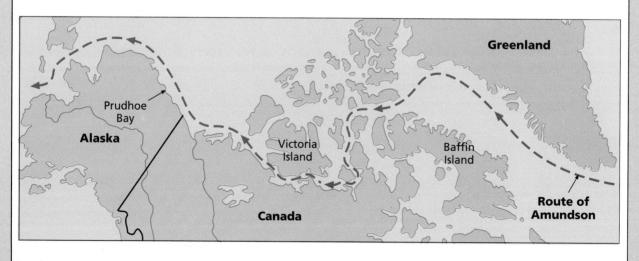

CHAPTER 18 REVIEW

CHAPTER TEST

Write the letter of the answer that best completes each sentence.

1. If you are not going to take your test in the school's driver education car
   a. the driving instructor will provide a car.
   b. you will have to pay more for your license.
   c. it will be up to you to provide the vehicle.
2. To qualify for a driver's license, you have to show that you
   a. have a savings account.
   b. have driven at least 300 miles.
   c. know and understand traffic laws and can safely operate a car.
3. If possible, practice driving in
   a. many different vehicles.
   b. the same vehicle that you will take your test in.
   c. a rental car.
4. One way to stay calm during the in-vehicle test is to
   a. rev the engine.
   b. breathe deeply.
   c. take the sample test.
5. When taking your in-vehicle test, it is
   a. okay to tell the examiner that you are nervous.
   b. a good idea to chat with the examiner.
   c. helpful to bring audio cassettes.
6. Your goal in studying for the test is to
   a. learn the rules of the road so that you can be a responsible driver.
   b. pass your driving test.
   c. answer all the questions correctly.
7. You should check your car's fluid levels
   a. before the day of your in-vehicle test.

   b. in the presence of the examiner.
   c. during the knowledge test.
8. Three ways to prepare for your knowledge test are to
   a. eat right, sleep well, and study.
   b. study, bring documents, and exercise.
   c. eat right, read, and check the brakes.
9. If you violate a traffic law while taking your in-vehicle test, you
   a. will automatically fail the test in most states.
   b. can usually still pass the test.
   c. will be banned from driving for one year.
10. Your best proof of age is your
    a. parent's sworn testimony.
    b. birth certificate.
    c. driver's permit.

Write the word or phrase that best completes each sentence.

   documents   anxious   clarification
   emissions inspection   responsible   license

11. Being a _____ driver means exhibiting sound judgment and decision-making skills.

12. You may need proof that the vehicle you bring for the test has passed a(n) _____ .

13. If you don't understand something the examiner says, ask for _____ .

14. When you are _____ , you tend to hold your breath.

15. Take with you to the test all the _____ that you will need.

DRIVER'S LOG

In this chapter, you have learned how to prepare yourself and your vehicle for the state driving test. Do you think you will have more difficulty with the in-vehicle or the knowledge? Write two para-graphs in which you analyze the reasons for the difficulty, and explain what you will do to remedy the situation.

This review tests your knowledge of the material in Chapters 1–18. Use the review to help you study for your state driving test. Choose the answer that best suits the question.

1. To stop heavy bleeding, use
   a. an air bag.
   b. shock.
   c. adhesion.
   d. direct pressure.

2. This sign ▽ requires that you
   a. watch for falling rocks.
   b. come to a complete stop.
   c. yield to traffic in the cross street.
   d. slow down and proceed with caution.

3. At a flashing red traffic signal, you must
   a. slow down.
   b. yield to an emergency vehicle.
   c. come to a full stop.
   d. reverse direction.

4. A car's weight, body design, and engine type all contribute to
   a. the driver's popularity.
   b. oil consumption.
   c. fuel efficiency.
   d. night vision.

5. Plan your time on a trip by
   a. making a budget.
   b. making a schedule.
   c. taking a scenic route.
   d. wearing a watch.

6. Every time you drive your car, check
   a. brake linings.
   b. fluid levels.
   c. shock absorbers.
   d. front end alignment.

7. At a four-way stop, yield to
   a. vehicles coming from the right.
   b. vehicles behind you.
   c. trucks coming from the left.
   d. oncoming cars.

8. To prove your identity at the department of motor vehicles, you can take
   a. a phone bill.
   b. your parent's tax return.
   c. a birth certificate.
   d. a report card.

9. Coolant is stored in the
   a. glove compartment.
   b. power train.
   c. radiator.
   d. steering column.

10. Car financing can be obtained through
   a. a bank.
   b. your school.
   c. an insurance company.
   d. the federal government.

11. A joystick driving system can
   a. help authorities to control traffic flow.
   b. decrease risk.
   c. help a person compensate for a physical disability.
   d. help people learn to drive.

12. Tires should be rotated every
   a. 50 miles.
   b. 500 to 600 miles.
   c. 5,000 to 6,000 miles.
   d. two years.

13. You should pack a trailer so that
   a. 25 percent of the load is in the front half.
   b. 60 of the load is in the front half.
   c. the load is evenly distributed.
   d. your car's rear bumper touches the ground.

14. Narcotics
   a. stimulate the central nervous system.
   b. are safe and easy to use.
   c. are often used by truck drivers.
   d. can cause death.

15. One problem common to urban driving is
 a. busy intersections.
 b. large animals on the road.
 c. high altitudes.
 d. interchanges.

16. Driving through deep puddles can lead to
 a. brake failure.
 b. front end alignment.
 c. engine lock.
 d. clutch fade.

17. You are responsible for providing a vehicle for the
 a. in-vehicle test.
 b. knowledge test.
 c. Smith System.
 d. visual acuity test.

18. A factor in the cost of car insurance is
 a. ethnic background.
 b. your age.
 c. your parents' driving records.
 d. number of school years completed.

19. The night before your knowledge test,
 a. stay awake and study.
 b. get plenty of rest.
 c. take a stimulant.
 d. go out with your friends and relax.

20. Driving faster than the posted speed limit is
 a. sometimes necessary.
 b. legal on country roads.
 c. always illegal.
 d. legal but irresponsible.

21. You can increase visibility in dense fog by using
 a. your dome light.
 b. brake lights.
 c. low-beam headlights.
 d. high-beam headlights.

22. If you are stuck on the side of the road,
 a. raise the hood of your car.
 b. stand in the middle of the road.
 c. hitchhike home.
 d. stand on top of your car.

23. The catalytic converter
 a. is a pollution-control device.
 b. is an optional feature.
 c. is attached to the battery.
 d. converts miles to kilometers.

24. Do not buy a car if its death rate is
 a. less than 1 per 10,000 vehicles.
 b. more than 2 per 10,000 vehicles.
 c. less than 2 per 10,000 vehicles.
 d. more than 1 in 100,000.

25. To relax during the in-vehicle test,
 a. chat with the examiner.
 b. admit that you are nervous.
 c. hold your breath.
 d. wear loose clothing.

26. The odometer tells you
 a. the speed of the car.
 b. how far you have driven.
 c. the engine temperature.
 d. how much fuel is in the tank.

27. One step of the Smith System is
 a. the SIPDE process.
 b. risk.
 c. angle parking.
 d. keep your eyes moving.

28. To start a car, insert a key in the
 a. steering wheel.
 b. dashboard.
 c. ignition switch.
 d. carburetor.

29. Traction is poorest at about
 a. 32 degrees Fahrenheit.
 b. 112 degrees Fahrenheit.
 c. 0 degrees Fahrenheit.
 d. the equator.

30. The air filter is part of the
 a. cooling system.
 b. exhaust system.
 c. protection system.
 d. fuel system.

GLOSSARY

acceleration An increase of speed.

accelerator The gas pedal; it controls speed.

adhesion Sticking together; in automotive terms, traction.

administrative laws Laws that regulate driver licensing, vehicle registration, financial responsibility of drivers and vehicle owners, and minimum equipment and car standards for vehicles.

air bag A safety bag that fills with air automatically upon impact in a collision.

alternator A generator that produces the electricity needed to run a car and its electrical devices.

angle parking Parking so that cars are arranged at a 30- to 90-degree angle with a curb or other boundary.

antifreeze A substance with a low freezing point, usually added to the liquid in a vehicle's radiator to prevent freezing.

antilock brakes A braking system that is designed to keep a car's wheels from locking when the driver brakes abruptly.

antitheft device Any device used to protect a vehicle from being stolen or entered.

area of central vision That area of vision directly ahead of a person.

atmospheric conditions Weather and light conditions; these have an effect on visibility.

automatic transmission A system that transmits power to the drive wheels; gears are changed automatically in a car with this type of transmission.

automobile insurance Motor vehicle insurance; types include liability, no-fault, comprehensive, collision, medical payment, uninsured driver, and towing.

axle The shaft or rod connecting two opposite wheels on which the wheels revolve.

banked curve A curve that is sloped up from the inside edge.

basic speed rule A law that specifies that drivers must always drive at a speed that is reasonable and proper for existing road, traffic, weather, and light conditions.

battery A unit that stores an electrical charge and furnishes current.

beltway A highway that passes around an urban area.

blind spot An area outside a vehicle that is not visible to the driver in the rear- or side-view mirrors.

blood-alcohol concentration (BAC) The percent of alcohol in the blood.

blowout A sudden loss of air pressure in a tire.

blowout skid A skid occurring as a result of a blowout.

blue book A guide to the average price paid to dealers for different makes and models of used cars.

brake fade A temporary brake failure resulting from brakes being overheated after being applied hard for too long.

brake pedal A pedal that enables a driver to slow or stop a vehicle.

brake system The system that includes disc and drum brakes and enables a vehicle to slow down and stop by means of hydraulic pressure.

braking distance The distance a car covers from the time the driver applies the brakes until the car stops.

braking skid A skid caused when the brakes are applied so hard that one or more wheels lock.

carbon monoxide A colorless, odorless, highly poisonous gas; a by-product of burning fuel.

carburetor The part of an engine that combines fuel with air so the mixture will burn properly.

catalytic converter An antipollution device, part of the exhaust system, that reduces harmful emissions.

center of gravity The point around which all the weight of an object is evenly distributed.

centrifugal force The force that tends to push a moving object out of a curve and into a straight path.

choke The valve that cuts off air from the carburetor; in many cars the choke functions automatically.

clutch A device that engages and disengages the engine and is connected to the drive shaft; the pedal by which the device is operated.

collision A crash; when one object hits another with sudden force.

color blindness The inability to distinguish between certain colors.

controlled-access highway See **limited-access highway.**

coolant A liquid added to a motor vehicle's radiator to reduce heat.

cooling system The system that keeps the engine cool by forcing air over metal cooling vanes that surround the cylinders; it includes the radiator, overflow tank, water pump, and thermostat.

cornering skid A skid on a turn or curve.

crankshaft The shaft that is turned as the pistons move up and down in the cylinders of the engine.

crosswalk A path marked off for use by pedestrians when crossing a roadway.

crowned road A road that is higher in the center than at either edge.

cruise control A car feature that allows a driver to maintain a desired speed without manually pressing the accelerator; intended for highway driving.

cylinders The parts of the engine that house the pistons; most cars have four, six, or eight cylinders.

decelerate To slow down.

deceleration lane An expressway lane used for slowing down before an exit.

defogger See **defroster.**

defroster A heating unit that clears moisture from the inside of the front and/or rear windows and ice from the outside surfaces.

depth perception Vision that gives objects their three-dimensional appearance and that enables a person to judge the relative distance between two objects.

differential An arrangement of gears that allows each drive wheel to turn at a different speed when going around a curve.

directional control The ability of a motor vehicle to hold to a straight line.

directional or turn signal A device that allows drivers to communicate their intentions to move right or left by means of blinking lights; or an arm or hand signal.

distributor The engine switch that sends electric current to each spark plug in proper order and at the proper time.

downshift To shift to a lower gear from a higher one.

Drive The most frequently used forward gear in a vehicle with an automatic transmission.

drive train See **power train.**

drive wheels The wheels that move a vehicle.

driving under the influence (DUI) See **driving while intoxicated.**

driving while intoxicated (DWI) An offense with which drivers may be charged if their blood alcohol concentration is above a certain percent.

electrical system A system that carries electricity throughout the car and consists of the battery, the alternator or generator, the voltage regulator, and wires.

emergency brake The parking brake.

emergency flashers A signaling device that makes all four turn signals flash at once; used to warn other drivers that a vehicle has stopped or is moving slowly.

engine See **internal combustion engine.**

exhaust manifold A collecting system for unburned gases as they exit from the cylinders.

exhaust system The system that gets rid of waste gases and vapors from the engine and reduces the noise of the explosions within the engine cylinders.

expressway A divided highway with limited access that has more than one lane for traffic moving in the same direction; designed for high-speed travel.

fatigue Temporary physical or mental exhaustion; usually indicates the need for rest or sleep.

field of vision The area ahead and to the left and right that can be seen when looking straight ahead.

first aid   Emergency treatment given to an injured or ill person before professional medical personnel arrive.

fixed speed limit   A posted speed limit that cannot legally be exceeded.

flywheel   The part of the engine that is turned by the starter and, as a result, turns the crankshaft.

following distance   The time-and-space gap between vehicles traveling in the same lane of traffic.

force of impact   The force with which a moving vehicle hits another object.

freeway   An expressway; a highway that is not a toll road.

friction   Resistance to motion between two objects when they touch.

friction point   The point at which the clutch pedal and other parts of the power train begin to work together as the driver releases the clutch pedal.

fuel system   A system that consists of the fuel tank, fuel pump, carburetor, fuel filter, and air filter. Some cars have a fuel-injection system instead of a carburetor.

fuses   Safety devices, usually located beneath the dashboard, that protect a car's electrical circuits from overloading.

gas pedal   See **accelerator.**

gear   Toothed wheels that mesh with each other to transmit motion or change a vehicle's speed or direction.

gear selector lever   The lever on a car with automatic transmission that allows the driver to select a gear.

gearshift   The lever in a car with a manual transmission that permits gears to be changed.

gravity   The invisible force that pulls all objects on the earth toward its center.

ground viewing   Scanning beneath parked vehicles and other objects for signs of movement.

guide sign   See **informational signs.**

hand brake   The parking brake.

hand-over-hand steering   A steering method in which the driver's hands cross when turning.

hazard flashers   See **emergency flashers.**

head restraint   A safety device attached to the back of the seat that is designed to prevent injury to the head and neck.

hemorrhage   Heavy bleeding.

High Occupancy Vehicle (HOV) lane   A lane reserved for use by vehicles carrying two or more passengers.

highway   A main public roadway, especially one that runs between cities.

highway hypnosis   A drowsy state that may occur during long hours of highway driving.

highway transportation system (HTS)   A system made up of roadways, motor vehicles, and people.

hitch   A device attached to the back of a car to haul a trailer.

hydraulic pressure   The pressure created by a liquid being forced through an opening or tube.

hydroplane   To skim on top of a film of water.

idle   To operate the engine without engaging the gears.

ignition   A system that provides the spark that causes the fuel-air mixture in the engine to burn.

implied consent law   A law stating that any licensed driver charged with driving under the influence or while intoxicated cannot legally refuse to be tested for blood-alcohol concentration.

inertia   The tendency of an object in motion to stay in motion and for an object at rest to stay at rest.

informational signs   Signs, including route markers and destination, mileage, recreational area, and roadside service signs, used to guide and direct drivers.

inhibitions   Personality elements that stop a person from behaving without regard for possible consequences.

interchange   A point at which a driver can enter or exit an expressway or connect with a highway going in another direction.

internal combustion engine   The part of a car that produces its power by exploding an air-fuel mixture within its cylinders.

international sign A road sign with symbols, used internationally.

intersection The place where two or more roadways cross.

in-vehicle test A performance test that evaluates a driver's ability to perform basic maneuvers; sometimes called a road test.

IPDE process See **SIPDE process.**

jaywalking The pedestrian practice of crossing a roadway without regard for traffic rules or signals.

jump-starting Attaching a car's dead battery by cables to a charged battery to start the car.

kinetic energy The energy of motion.

knowledge test A test on rules of the road and traffic signs, signals, and markings; sometimes called a written test.

lane-use lights Electronic signals mounted above reversible lanes that indicate which lanes can or cannot be used.

limited-access highway A highway that has fixed points of entry and exit.

lubricating system A system that reduces heat by coating the engine parts with oil, consisting of the oil pump, oil pan, and oil filter.

manual shift A hand-operated gearshift.

margin of space The amount of space that should be allowed in front of, behind, and to both sides of a vehicle, giving it room to maneuver in threatening situations.

momentum The product of weight and speed.

mouth-to-mouth resuscitation A method of restoring breathing to a victim.

muffler A device in the exhaust system that reduces engine noise.

multiple-lane highway A highway that has more than one lane for traffic moving in each direction.

Neutral A gear position in which the gears are not engaged and cannot transmit power.

night blindness The inability to see well at night.

odometer A device that measures distance traveled by a vehicle; its gauge.

Overdrive The highest forward gear in many newer vehicles with automatic transmissions; it allows the vehicle to travel more efficiently at higher speeds. In a car with a manual transmission, the fourth and fifth gears are sometimes identified as overdrive gears.

overdriving one's headlights Driving so fast at night that the driver is unable to stop within the range of the headlights.

parallel parking Parking parallel and close to the edge of the road.

parking brake The brake that holds the rear wheels; it is used to keep a parked car from moving.

parkway A broad highway that may be limited to noncommercial vehicles.

passive safety devices Devices, such as air bags or head restraints, that function without the user having to operate them.

pedestrian A person traveling on foot.

peer pressure The influence of friends and contemporaries on one's beliefs, values, and behavior.

perception distance The distance a vehicle covers during the time in which its driver identifies a need to stop.

peripheral vision The area of vision to the left and right of central vision.

perpendicular parking Parking so that a car forms a 90-degree angle with a curb or line.

physical disability A long-term or permanent physical condition that may limit or challenge a person's movement.

piston A cylinder enclosed in another cylinder within the engine; its up-and-down movement turns the crankshaft.

point system A system used to keep track of traffic violations by individual drivers.

power brakes Brakes that make it easier to slow or stop without an increase of foot pressure on the brake pedal.

power skid A skid caused when the gas pedal is pressed too hard and suddenly.

power train The parts of a motor vehicle that transmit power from the engine to the wheels; the engine, transmission, and clutch.

prosthetic device A device, such as an artificial limb, that enables a person to compensate for a physical disability.

push-pull steering A steering method in which the driver's hands do not cross even when changing lanes or turning.

radiator A cooling device that air-cools liquid pumped from the engine.

rate of acceleration The time it takes to speed up from a stop or from one speed to a higher one.

rate of deceleration The time it takes to slow down from one speed to a lower one or to a stop.

reaction distance The distance a car covers between the time a driver identifies a situation that requires braking and the moment that the brakes are applied.

recreational vehicle A large vehicle, such as a motor home, used mainly for pleasure.

regulatory sign A sign that controls the flow of traffic.

Reverse The gear used to back a vehicle.

reversible lanes Lanes on which the direction of traffic changes at certain times of day.

right of way The right of one roadway user to cross in front of another; right of way must be yielded to others in many situations.

risk The chance of injury to oneself or others and of damage to vehicles and property.

road test See **in-vehicle test.**

safety belt A restraining belt designed to protect the driver and riders; seat belt.

shared left-turn lane A lane that drivers moving in either direction use to make a left turn.

shift To change gears by means of a mechanism; the mechanism itself.

shock A physical disorder often accompanying serious injury; characterized by faintness, weakness, feeling cold, and nausea.

shock absorbers Devices that cushion a car's frame against the impact of bumps in the road.

shoulder The strip of land along the edge of a roadway, sometimes referred to as a berm.

SIPDE process A five-step driving strategy (search, identify, predict, decide, execute) that enables drivers to process information in an organized way.

skid A driver's loss of control over the direction in which the car is moving.

Smith System A set of five principles that help drivers operate safely and defensively.

space margin See **margin of space.**

spark plug A device in an engine's cylinder that ignites the fuel-air mixture by means of an electric spark.

speedometer A device that measures the speed of a vehicle in miles per hour or kilometers per hour; its gauge.

steering wheel The wheel that enables a driver to turn a vehicle's front wheels.

suspension system The system, including shock absorbers, that protects the body of a vehicle from road shocks.

tailgate To drive behind another vehicle too closely.

three-point turn A turnabout made by turning left, backing to the right, then moving forward.

threshold braking A braking technique in which the driver firmly presses the brake pedal to a point just before the wheels lock.

total stopping distance The distance covered by a vehicle from the perception distance, to the moment that the vehicle comes to a stop.

tracking Steering; keeping a vehicle steadily and smoothly on a desired course.

traction The friction between a vehicle's tires and the road surface.

traffic control signals Electronic signals, such as colored lights, used to keep traffic moving in an orderly manner.

transmission The gears and related parts that carry power from the engine to the driving axle.

tread   The outer surface of a tire, with its pattern of grooves and ridges.

turnabout   Any turning maneuver by which a driver moves a vehicle to face in the opposite direction.

turn signal   See **directional signal.**

two-point turn   A turnabout made by first backing or heading into a driveway or alley and then heading or backing into the street.

U-turn   A turnabout carried out by making a U-shaped left turn.

visibility   The distance and area a driver can see and the ability of a vehicle or pedestrian to be seen.

visual acuity   Clarity of eyesight.

warning lights and gauges   Dashboard lights and gauges that provide information to the driver about the car; includes oil pressure, alternator, and fuel gauges, and brake, safety belt, and temperature warning lights.

warning signs   Signs that alert drivers to potential dangers or conditions ahead; includes construction and maintenance signs.

warranty   A written guarantee that a car dealer will repair a car, within a certain amount of time, at no charge to the customer.

written test   See **knowledge test.**

yield   To let another road user go first or have the right of way.

INDEX

Acceleration, 127–128, 239, 247
  evasive, 247
  rate of, 127–128
  and speed, 127–129
Accelerator, 101, 119–120, 263
  sticking, 263
Accident reports, 91
Accidents, *see Collisions*
Administrative laws, 82–83
  certificate of title, 83
  driver's license, 82
  financial responsibility, insurance, 83
  point system, 83
  vehicle registration, 83
  violations, 83
Aging and driving, 33
Air bags, 105, 284
Air conditioner, 98
Air filter, 306
Air vents, 98
Alateen, 40, 41
Alcohol, 40–46
  and blood alcohol concentration (BAC), 46
  and driving, 42–43
  driving under the influence (DUI), 45, 46
  driving while intoxicated (DWI), 45, 46
  and fatalities, 42
  and fatigue, 30
  implied consent, 46
  mental effects, 45
  myths and facts, 42–43
  penalties for intoxication, 45–46
  physical effects, 44–45
  and problem drinking, 40–41
Alcoholics Anonymous (AA), 40, 41
Alternator, 308
  gauge or warning light, 107–108
Amber traffic signal, *see Yellow signal*
American Automobile Association (AAA), 328
American Red Cross, 269, 271
Angle parking, 169–170, 171
  entering a space, 169–170
  exiting a space, 171

Animals, 51, 189, 190, 218–220
  avoiding collisions with, 218–220
  in the car, 51
  on the roadway, 189, 190, 218–220
Antifreeze, 310
Antipollution devices, *see Pollution-control devices*
Antitheft devices, 106
Arm signals, 142, 163, 205
Automatic transmission, 118–121, 144, 145
  driving uphill, 120, 143–144, 145
  driving downhill, 144, 145
  gear selector lever, 99–100
  moving a car with, 119–120
  starting a car with, 118–119
  stopping a car with, 120
Automobile insurance, 83, 290–294
  buying, 290
  collision, 291
  comprehensive, 292
  deductible, 291
  discounts, 294
  factors determining cost, 292–294
  liability, 83, 290–291
  medical payment, 292
  no-fault, 292
  towing, 292
  uninsured motorist, 291

Backing, 133–134, 165–166, 329–330
  a trailer, 329–330
  steering, 133–134
Backup lights, 108–109
Banked curves, 243
Banked roads, 243
Banneker, Benjamin, 274
Bar graph, using, 78
Barton, Clara, 271
Basic speed laws, 89
Battery, 111, 264–265, 308–309
  checking, 111, 300, 301, 305, 309
  dead, 264–265
  recharging, 265–266
Belts, 300
Bicycles, 221–223
  sharing the roadway with, 221–223
Blind spot, 103
Bleeding, controlling, 270
Blood-alcohol concentration (BAC), 46

Blowout, 245, 261
Blue Book, 287
Brake system, 247, 256, 312–313
  warnings, 108, 256–257, 315
Brake(s), 121, 247–248, 256–257, 301–302, 312–313
  antilock, 121, 247, 313
  disc, 313
  drum, 313
  emergency, 101
  failure, 256–257
  hand, 101
  hydraulic, 312
  parking, 100, 101
  pedal, 101
  power, 101, 313
Braking, 120–121, 236, 239, 247
  and deceleration, 127–128
  factors affecting, 236–237, 239, 241
  graphing distances, 318
  skid, 245
  threshold, 121
  to a stop, 121, 126
Breathing, restoring, 271
Buses, 86, 225
  school, 86, 225
  sharing the roadway with, 225
Buying a car, 282–294
  automobile insurance, 290–294
  comfort, 285
  financing, 288–289
  fuel efficiency, 285–287
  personal need, 282–283
  safety, 284–285
  selecting, 284–287
  used, 287
  warranty, 287

Carbon monoxide, 31, 32, 268, 307
Carburetor, 306
Catalytic converter, 307
Center of gravity, 240
Centrifugal force, 242
  and steering on curves, 242–243
Certificate of registration, *see Vehicle registration*
Certificate of title, 83
Changing lanes, 103, 146–147, 195–196
Changing a tire, 262–263
Checks, 110–112, 300–302, 344–345

PHOTO CREDITS, COVER

Background, © Ron Kimball; Insets, (tl) © Michael Stuckey/Comstock, (bl) © 1990 Lightscapes/The Stock Market, (r) KS Studios Inc., truck courtesy Byers Chevrolet, Columbus, OH.

PHOTO CREDITS

1: George Disario/The Stock Market; 2-3: Cindy Lewis; 3 (inset): David Sutherland/Tony Stone Worldwide; 4: Jeff Hunter/The Image Bank; 4 (inset): Mitchell Funk/The Image Bank; 8: Gary Sommer/Photo Researchers; 9 (b): W. Cody/Westlight; 17: Bob LeBlanc; 18 (b): George E. Jones/Photo Researchers; 22: Gary Gay/The Image Bank; 22 (inset): Joe DiMaggio/The Stock Market; 23 (tl): Bob LeBlanc; 23 (bl): Alex Von Koschembahr/Photo Researchers; 23 (br): Robert Capece/Monkmeyer; 26: E.B. Grunzweig/Photo Researchers; 27, 29: Bob LeBlanc; 32: Robert Capece/ Monkmeyer; 34 (b): Michal Heron; 36: The Bettmann Archive; 38: Larry Mulvehill/Photo Researchers; 38 (inset): Weinberg/Clark/The Image Bank; 39 (tl): Michal Heron; 39 (tr): Blaine Harrington/The Stock Market; 39 (br), 41: Bob LeBlanc; 44: Hank deLespinasse/The Image Bank; 49: Bob LeBlanc; 50: Michal Heron; 51: Bob LeBlanc; 52 (b): Michal Heron; 58-59: Cindy Lewis; 59 (inset): Eric Perry/Third Coast Stock Source; 60: Joe Devenney/The Image Bank; 60 (inset): G. Faint/The Image Bank; 61 (tl): Michal Heron; 61 (tr): Andy Caulfield/The Image Bank; 61 (bl): Al Satterwhite/The Image Bank; 64 (l): Day Williams/Photo Researchers; 66 (t): Michal Heron; 66 (b): Ben Simmons/The Stock Market; 69: Patti McConville/The Image Bank; 76 (b): Michal Heron; 80: Ken Biggs/Photo Researchers; 80 (inset): Dingo/Photo Researchers; 83: Michal Heron; 88: Don & Pat Valenti/Tony Stone Worldwide; 89, 92 (b): Michal Heron; 96: George Haling/Photo Researchers; 96 (inset): D.W. Production/The Image Bank; 97 (tr): David Perry Lawrence/The Image Bank; 97 (br): Bob LeBlanc; 101, 104, 106: Michal Heron; 109: Jeff Spielman/The Image Bank; 110, 112 (b): Bob LeBlanc; 116: Fokuhara/Westlight; 116 (inset): Eric Perry/Third Coast Stock Source; 117 (tr): Roy Morsch/The Stock Market; 117 (bl), 121, 124: Michal Heron; 129 (t): Sonja Bullaty/The Image Bank; 134 (b): Bob LeBlanc; 138: Pete Saloutos/Tony Stone Worldwide; 138 (inset): Peter Vadnai/The Stock Market; 139 (tl): Michal Heron; 139 (tr): Walter Bibikou/The Image Bank; 140: Michal Heron; 143 (l): Ken Straiton/The Stock Market; 143 (r): Michael Amberger/The Stock Market; 144: Santi Visalli/The Image Bank; 145, 150 (b): Michal Heron; 156-157: Cindy Lewis; 157 (inset): Doug Wilson/Westlight; 158: John Henry Sullivan Jr./Photo Researchers; 158 (inset): Walter Hodges/Westlight; 159 (bl, br), 164, 168: Michal Heron; 174: Ken Cooper/The Image Bank; 178: Richard Steedman/ The Stock Market; 178 (inset): Guy Gillette/Photo Researchers; 179 (tr): Geoffrey Cilfford/Woodfin Camp; 179 (bl): Michal Heron; 180: Bob LeBlanc; 183: Michal Heron; 184: Michael Quackenbush/The Image Bank; 185, 187, 188, 190: Michal Heron; 191 (b): Tim Bieber/The Image Bank; 200: Steve Niedorf/The Image Bank; 200 (inset): Ken Biggs/Photo Researchers; 201 (all): Michal Heron; 203: Sepp Seitz/Woodfin Camp; 204: Michal Heron; 205 (t): Tony Stone Worldwide; 205 (b): Michal Heron; 208: Dan Miller/Woodfin Camp: 210 (b): Michal Heron: 214: Jean Miele/The Stock Market; 214 (inset): Alan Becker/The Image Bank; 215 (tl, br), 216, 217, 218: Michal Heron; 219: Daniel Bosler/Tony Stone Worldwide; 223, 228 (t), 229: Michal Heron; 234: Chris Jones/The Stock Market; 234 (inset): Ross M. Horowitz/The Image Bank; 235 (tr, bl), 238, 240 (b), 243: Michal Heron; 246 (t): Tony Stone Worldwide; 254: Al Assid/The Stock Market; 254 (inset): Mark E. Gibson/The Stock Market; 255 (tl): Michael P. Gadomski/Photo Researchers; 255 (tr): Superstock; 256, 258, 260, 264, 265, 266, 267, 270: Michal Heron; 274: Library of Congress; 278-279: Cindy Lewis; 279 (inset): Ron Lowery/Tony Stone Worldwide; 280: H.P. Merten/The Stock Market; 280 (inset): Gabe Palmer/The Stock Market; 281 (tl, tr, bl), 283: Michal Heron; 284: Benelux Press/Photo Researchers; 287, 288, 289, 290, 292, 294 (b): Michal Heron; 298: Brenda L. Lewison/The Stock Market; 298 (inset): Gregory Heisler/The Image Bank; 299 (br): Michal Heron; 305: Helen Breen; 311 (t): Bob LeBlanc; 311 (b): Pete Seaward/Tony Stone Worldwide; 316 (b): Michal Heron; 320 (inset): Sobel/Klonsky/The Image Bank; 321 (tl): Helen Breen; 322: Bob LeBlanc; 323: Michal Heron; 324: Bob LeBlanc; 327: Michal Heron; 329: Warren J. Donaldson; 331, 333: Michal Heron; 334 (b): Gary Cralle/The Image Bank; 338: Michal Heron; 338 (inset), 339 (tr, bl, br), 341, 343, 344: Bob LeBlanc; 345: Michal Heron; 346, 348 (b): Bob LeBlanc.

All remaining photographs are courtesy of AAA.

ILLUSTRATION CREDITS

Andy Christie: 63, 65, 67-69, 72, 74, 75, 84-86, 99, 100, 103, 105, 107, 108, 118, 119, 122, 123, 125, 126, 128, 130-133, 149, 160-171, 173, 195, 221, 224; Jared Schneidman Design Inc: 78, 114, 182, 187, 189, 193, 198, 242, 243, 247, 248, 285, 293, 303, 304, 306-310, 312-314, 329, 331, 350.
Maps, courtesy of American Automobile Association: 20, 94, 136, 176, 212, 252, 296, 336.